DANIEL
A Commentary in the Wesleyan Tradition

*New Beacon Bible Commentary

DANIEL
A Commentary in the Wesleyan Tradition

JIM EDLIN

BEACON HILL PRESS
OF KANSAS CITY

Copyright 2009
by Jim Edlin and Beacon Hill Press of Kansas City

ISBN 978-0-8341-2398-4

Printed in the United States of America

Library of Congress Cataloging-in-Publication Data

Edlin, Jim, 1950-
  Daniel / Jim Edlin.
    p. cm. — (New Beacon Bible commentary)
    Includes bibliographical references (p.).
    ISBN 978-0-8341-2398-4 (pbk.)
  1. Bible. O.T. Daniel—Commentaries. I. Title.

  BS1555.53.E34 2009
  224'.5077—dc22

2008049714

10 9 8 7 6 5 4 3 2 1

COMMENTARY EDITORS

General Editors

Alex Varughese
  Ph.D., Drew University
  Professor of Biblical Literature
  Mount Vernon Nazarene University
  Mount Vernon, Ohio

George Lyons
  Ph.D., Emory University
  Professor of New Testament
  Northwest Nazarene University
  Nampa, Idaho

Roger Hahn
  Ph.D., Duke University
  Dean of the Faculty
  Professor of New Testament
  Nazarene Theological Seminary
  Kansas City, Missouri

Section Editors

Joseph Coleson
  Ph.D., Brandeis University
  Professor of Old Testament
  Nazarene Theological Seminary
  Kansas City, Missouri

Kent Brower
  Ph.D., The University of Manchester
  Vice Principal
  Senior Lecturer in Biblical Studies
  Nazarene Theological College
  Manchester, England

Robert Branson
  Ph.D., Boston University
  Professor of Biblical Literature
  Olivet Nazarene University
  Bourbonnais, Illinois

George Lyons
  Ph.D., Emory University
  Professor of New Testament
  Northwest Nazarene University
  Nampa, Idaho

Alex Varughese
  Ph.D., Drew University
  Professor of Biblical Literature
  Mount Vernon Nazarene University
  Mount Vernon, Ohio

Jeanne Serrão
  Ph.D., Claremont Graduate University
  Dean of the School of Theology and
    Philosophy
  Professor of Biblical Literature
  Mount Vernon Nazarene University
  Mount Vernon, Ohio

Jim Edlin
  Ph.D., Southern Baptist Theological
    Seminary
  Professor of Biblical Literature and
    Languages
  Chair of the Division of Religion and
    Philosophy
  MidAmerica Nazarene University
  Olathe, Kansas

CONTENTS

General Editors' Preface   9

Acknowledgments   11

Abbreviations   13

Bibliography   15

INTRODUCTION   19

   A. Interest in Daniel   20

   B. Special Literary Features   21

   C. Authorship   23

   D. Date of Writing   24

   E. Daniel the Statesman Prophet   27

   F. Original Audience   29

   G. Structure of the Book   31

   H. Greek Versions of Daniel   32

   I. Hermeneutical Issues   33

   J. Approach of This Commentary   36

   K. Theology of the Book   37
      1. Absolute Sovereignty of God, Not Dualism   38
      2. Responsible Free Will of Humans, Not Fatalism   38
      3. Hopeful Optimism for God's People, Not Pessimism   40

COMMENTARY   43

  I. Stories from a Foreign Land (1:1—6:28)   43

   A. Food Defilement: The First Test of Faithfulness (1:1-21)   44
      1. The Setting (1:1-7)   50
      2. The Test (1:8-14)   55
      3. The Outcome (1:15-21)   58

   B. Dream of a Statue: The First Test of Wisdom (2:1-49)   63
      1. Scene 1: The King and His Wise Men (2:1-13)   71
      2. Scene 2: Daniel, Arioch, and the King (2:14-16)   74
      3. Scene 3: Daniel Before God (2:17-23)   75
      4. Scene 4: Daniel, Arioch, and the King (2:24-25)   77
      5. Scene 5: The King and His Wise Man (2:26-49)   78

   C. Fiery Furnace: The Second Test of Faithfulness (3:1-30)   87
      1. The Setting (3:1-7)   91
      2. The Test (3:8-23)   94
      3. The Outcome (3:24-30)   99

   D. Dream of a Tree: The Second Test of Wisdom (4:1-37)   105
      1. Opening Confession (4:1-3)   111

       2. The Disturbing Dream (4:4-18)   112

       3. Interpretation of the Dream (4:19-27)   116

       4. Fulfillment of the Dream (4:28-33)   119

       5. Closing Confession (4:34-37)   120

   E. Writing on the Wall: The Third Test of Wisdom (5:1-31)   127

       1. The King's Crisis (5:1-9)   132

       2. The King's Hope (5:10-16)   134

       3. God's Message for the King (5:17-28)   137

       4. God's Fulfillment of the Message (5:29-31)   141

   F. Lions' Pit: The Third Test of Faithfulness (6:1-28)   146

       1. The Conspiracy (6:1-9)   152

       2. The Offense (6:10-15)   155

       3. The Execution (6:16-18)   157

       4. The Deliverance (6:19-23)   158

       5. The Conclusion (6:24-28)   160

II. Visions from a Foreign Land (7:1—12:13)   167

   A. Vision of Four Beasts (7:1-28)   168

       1. Introduction (7:1)   172

       2. Report of the Images (7:2-14)   172

       3. Interpretation of the Images (7:15-27)   180

       4. Conclusion (7:28)   187

   B. Vision of Two Beasts (8:1-27)   192

       1. Introduction (8:1)   197

       2. Report of the Images (8:2-14)   198

       3. Interpretation of the Images (8:15-26)   204

       4. Conclusion (8:27)   210

   C. Vision of Seventy Sevens (9:1-27)   214

       1. Insight from Jeremiah (9:1-2)   219

       2. Prayer of Confession (9:3-19)   220

       3. Arrival of a Heavenly Messenger (9:20-23) 226

       4. Message from Heaven (9:24-27)   227

   D. Vision of a Great War (10:1—12:13)   240

       1. Vision Setting (10:1—11:1)   240

          a. Circumstances of Daniel (10:1-4)   243

          b. Arrival of a Heavenly Being (10:5-9)   245

          c. Dialogue with the Heavenly Being (10:10—11:1) 246

       2. Vision Message (11:2—12:4)   252

          a. Overview of the Persian Empire (11:2) 259

          b. Rise and Fall of a Mighty King (11:3-4) 260

          c. Conflicts Between Kings of the South and North (11:5-20) 260

          d. Reign of a Contemptible Person (11:21—12:4) 262

       3. Final Clarifications (12:5-13)   280

          a. First Question (12:5-7)   281

          b. Second Question (12:8-10)   283

          c. Final Recap (12:11-13)   284

GENERAL EDITORS' PREFACE

The purpose of the New Beacon Bible Commentary is to make available to pastors and students in the twenty-first century a biblical commentary that reflects the best scholarship in the Wesleyan theological tradition. The commentary project aims to make this scholarship accessible to a wider audience to assist them in their understanding and proclamation of Scripture as God's Word.

Writers of the volumes in this series not only are scholars within the Wesleyan theological tradition and experts in their field but also have special interest in the books assigned to them. Their task is to communicate clearly the critical consensus and the full range of other credible voices who have commented on the Scriptures. Though scholarship and scholarly contribution to the understanding of the Scriptures are key concerns of this series, it is not intended as an academic dialogue within the scholarly community. Commentators of this series constantly aim to demonstrate in their work the significance of the Bible as the church's book and the contemporary relevance and application of the biblical message. The project's overall goal is to make available to the church and for her service the fruits of the labors of scholars who are committed to their Christian faith.

The *New International Version* (NIV) is the reference version of the Bible used in this series; however, the focus of exegetical study and comments is the biblical text in its original language. When the commentary uses the NIV, it is printed in bold. The text printed in bold italics is the translation of the author. Commentators also refer to other translations where the text may be difficult or ambiguous.

The structure and organization of the commentaries in this series seeks to facilitate the study of the biblical text in a systematic and methodical way. Study of each biblical book begins with an ***Introduction*** section that gives an overview of authorship, date, provenance, audience, occasion, purpose, sociological/cultural issues, textual history, literary features, hermeneutical issues, and theological themes necessary to understand the book. This section also includes a brief outline of the book and a list of general works and standard commentaries.

The commentary section for each biblical book follows the outline of the book presented in the introduction. In some volumes, readers will find section ***overviews*** of large portions of scripture with general comments on their overall literary structure and other literary features. A consistent feature of the commentary is the paragraph-by-paragraph study of biblical texts. This section has three parts: ***Behind the Text***, ***In the Text***, and ***From the Text***.

The goal of the ***Behind the Text*** section is to provide the reader with all the relevant information necessary to understand the text. This includes specific historical situations reflected in the text, the literary context of the text, sociological and cultural issues, and literary features of the text.

In the Text explores what the text says, following its verse-by-verse structure. This section includes a discussion of grammatical details, word studies, and the connectedness of the text to other biblical books/passages or other parts of the book being studied (the canonical relationship). This section provides transliterations of key words in Hebrew and Greek and their literal meanings. The goal here is to explain what the author would have meant and/or what the audience would have understood as the meaning of the text. This is the largest section of the commentary.

The *From the Text* section examines the text in relation to the following areas: theological significance, intertextuality, the history of interpretation, use of the Old Testament scriptures in the New Testament, interpretation in later church history, actualization, and application.

The commentary provides *sidebars* on topics of interest that are important but not necessarily part of an explanation of the biblical text. These topics are informational items and may cover archaeological, historical, literary, cultural, and theological matters that have relevance to the biblical text. Occasionally, longer detailed discussions of special topics are included as *excurses.*

We offer this series with our hope and prayer that readers will find it a valuable resource for their understanding of God's Word and an indispensable tool for their critical engagement with the biblical texts.

Roger Hahn, Centennial Initiative General Editor

Alex Varughese, General Editor (Old Testament)

George Lyons, General Editor (New Testament)

ACKNOWLEDGMENTS

Daniel is one of those books that both attracts and repulses. Its simple stories draw readers, even at an early age, to worlds and messages that are easy to grasp and apply in the life of faith. Its visions, however, are another matter. Their cryptic images confuse readers and leave them perplexed as to what should be done with this material. Many assume the visions are simply stuff for prognosticators who hold keys to unlocking their mysteries. So the average reader of Scripture might linger over the stories but read quickly past the visions, if he or she reads them at all.

I confess this to have been my own approach to Daniel for years. As a child my record player scratched out a song about Shadrach, Meshach, and Abednego in the fiery furnace and my Sunday School teachers challenged me with the resolve of Daniel in a lions' den. In later years I read about or heard the bewildering predictions of future events based upon scriptures that drew heavily from Daniel. In some of these projections, I was told that Daniel spoke directly about people and events current in my world. Such scenarios made sense at times, and yet they did not. Eventually I came to realize that many interpretations of Daniel read as much into the text as out of it. Thus I retreated to the stories and left the visions alone. This seemed to be enough of Daniel for me.

Several years ago I was drawn back into Daniel by writing assignments on Daniel for adult Sunday School materials in the WordAction series and an introductory textbook titled *Discovering the Old Testament*. I became fascinated with the literary artistry of the book and began an exploration into the world of Daniel that has eventuated into this commentary. I have discovered, at least in part, why the stories are so captivating to readers. They are masterful compositions that skillfully employ creative literary techniques in order to convey profound messages. These stories invite us to imagine ourselves standing alongside Daniel and living the life of unwavering faith.

More than that, I have come to a deep appreciation for the visions of the book. They also exhibit exceptional literary qualities that enable them to communicate significant messages. Their bedazzling special effects create a world of fantasy that permits participation in high drama without the risk of direct consequences. This kind of foray into a surreal world is not unlike the experience of modern video gaming. Though ambiguities in the text still produce frustration, the value of the theology in these visions far outweighs this inconvenience. These visions, I have discovered, speak more about present realities than past or future. They reveal a drama of two realms running parallel in the universe: the kingdoms of this world and the kingdom of God. I have become increasingly encouraged to discover through these visions that the kingdom of God is never absent from this world. It always overcomes and outlasts every dominion of earth, and someday will do so completely.

Many people have converged in my life to provide encouragement for this project. I am grateful to the leadership of Beacon Hill Press for undertaking this project and offering me an opportunity to contribute. My friend and colleague from Mount Vernon Nazarene University, Alex Varughese, has carefully read the manuscript and provided significant feedback that has only improved the final product. Students of MidAmerica Nazarene University engaged with me in the study of Daniel and apocalyptic literature, while the university graciously provided a sabbatical so that I might work on this book.

The loving support of family inspires me more than they know. I am very grateful for my wife, Jo; our two daughters, Julie and Janelle, and their spouses, Eric and Matt; our son, Jon, and his wife, Mindy; and our grandchildren Jacob, Daniel, and Addison. My parents, Glen and Ida Edlin, as well as my in-laws, Lawrence and Hazel Goodman, have invested heavily in my life as well.

Finally, I must reserve my deepest gratitude for "the Ancient of Days" who sits enthroned over all of life. This project has been a profound spiritual journey as well as an academic one. Without the gracious sovereign hand of God in my life, no words of any value could be written. To him be all honor and glory forever and ever, for "his dominion is an everlasting dominion that will not pass away, and his kingdom is one that will never be destroyed" (Dan 7:14).

James Oliver (Jim) Edlin

ABBREVIATIONS

With a few exceptions, these abbreviations follow those in *The SBL Handbook of Style* (Alexander 1999).

General

A.D.	anno Domini (precedes date) (equivalent to C.E.)
B.C.	before Christ (follows date) (equivalent to B.C.E.)
B.C.E.	before the Common Era
BDB	*Hebrew and English Lexicon of the Old Testament*
BHS	*Biblia Hebraica Stuttgartensia*
C.E.	Common Era
cf.	compare
ch	chapter
chs	chapters
e.g.	*exempli gratia*, for example
esp.	especially
etc.	*et cetera*, and the rest
f(f).	and the following one(s)
i.e.	*id est*, that is
lit.	literally
LXX	Septuagint
MS	manuscript
MSS	manuscripts
MT	Masoretic Text (of the OT)
n.	note
n.d.	no date
n.p.	no place; no publisher; no page
nn.	notes
NT	New Testament
OT	Old Testament
s.v.	*sub verbo*, under the word
v	verse
vv	verses

Modern English Versions

ESV	English Standard Version
JPS	Hebrew-English Tanakh
KJV	King James Version
NIV	New International Version
NLT	New Living Translation
NRSV	New Revised Standard Version
REB	Revised English Bible
RSV	Revised Standard Version
TNIV	Today's New International Version

Print Conventions for Translations

Bold font	NIV (bold without quotation marks in the text under study; elsewhere in the regular font, with quotation marks and no further identification)
Bold italic font	Author's translation (without quotation marks)

Behind the Text: Literary or historical background information average readers might not know from reading the biblical text alone

In the Text: Comments on the biblical text, words, phrases, grammar, and so forth

From the Text: The use of the text by later interpreters, contemporary relevance, theological and ethical implications of the text, with particular emphasis on Wesleyan concerns

Apocrypha
Sg Three — Song of the Three Young Men

Josephus
Ag. Ap. — *Against Apion*
Ant. — *Jewish Antiquities*

Greek Transliteration

Greek	Letter	English
α	alpha	a
β	bēta	b
γ	gamma	g
γ	gamma nasal	n (before γ, κ, ξ, χ)
δ	delta	d
ε	epsilon	e
ζ	zēta	z
η	ēta	ē
θ	thēta	th
ι	iōta	i
κ	kappa	k
λ	lambda	l
μ	my	m
ν	ny	n
ξ	xi	x
ο	omicron	o
π	pi	p
ρ	rhō	r
ρ	initial rhō	rh
σ/ς	sigma	s
τ	tau	t
υ	upsilon	y
υ	upsilon	u (in diphthongs: au, eu, ēu, ou, ui)
φ	phi	ph
χ	chi	ch
ψ	psi	ps
ω	ōmega	ō
ʽ	rough breathing	h (before initial vowels or diphthongs)

Hebrew Consonant Transliteration

Hebrew/Aramaic	Letter	English
א	alef	ʼ
ב	bet	b
ג	gimel	g
ד	dalet	d
ה	he	h
ו	vav	v or w
ז	zayin	z
ח	khet	ḥ
ט	tet	ṭ
י	yod	y
כ/ך	kaf	k
ל	lamed	l
מ/ם	mem	m
נ/ן	nun	n
ס	samek	s
ע	ayin	ʽ
פ/ף	pe	p
צ/ץ	tsade	ṣ
ק	qof	q
ר	resh	r
שׂ	sin	ś
שׁ	shin	š
ת	tav	t

BIBLIOGRAPHY

Commentaries

Anderson, Robert A. 1984. *Signs and Wonders: A Commentary on the Book of Daniel*. International Theological Commentary. Grand Rapids: Eerdmans.

Archer, Gleason L., Jr. 1985. "Daniel." *The Expositor's Bible Commentary*. Volume 7. Grand Rapids: Eerdmans.

Baldwin, Joyce G. 1978. *Daniel*. Tyndale Old Testament Commentaries. Downers Grove, Ill.: InterVarsity Press.

Behrmann, G. 1894. *Das Buch Daniel*. Gottingen: Vandenhoeck.

Bevan, A. A. 1892. *A Short Commentary on the Book of Daniel*. Cambridge: Cambridge University Press.

Calvin, John. 1948. *Commentaries on the Book of the Prophet Daniel*. Reprint, Grand Rapids: Eerdmans.

Charles, Robert H. 1929. *A Critical and Exegetical Commentary on the Book of Daniel*. Oxford: Clarendon Press.

Collins, John J. 1984. *Daniel: With an Introduction to Apocalyptic Literature*. Forms of Old Testament Literature. Grand Rapids: Eerdmans.

_____. 1993. *Daniel: A Commentary on the Book of Daniel*. Hermenia. Minneapolis: Fortress Press.

Davies, Philip R. 1985. *Daniel*. Old Testament Guides. Edited by R. N. Whybray. Sheffield: JSOT Press.

Doukhan, Jacques B. 1989. *Daniel: The Vision of the End*. Revised Edition. Berrien Springs, Mich.: Andrews University Press.

_____. 2000. *Secrets of Daniel: Wisdom and Dreams of a Jewish Prince in Exile*. Hagerstown, Md.: Review and Herald Publishing.

Driver, S. R. 1900. *The Book of Daniel: With Introduction and Notes*. The Cambridge Bible for Schools and Colleges. Cambridge: University Press.

Duguid, Iain M. 2008. *Daniel*. Reformed Expository Commentary. Phillipsburg, N.J.: P and R Publishing.

Fewell, Danna Nolan. 1991. *Circle of Sovereignty: Plotting Politics in the Book of Daniel*. Nashville: Abingdon.

Gangel, Kenneth O. 2002. *Daniel*. Holman Old Testament Commentary. Volume 18. Nashville: Broadman and Holman Publishers.

Goldingay, John E. 1989. *Daniel*. Word Biblical Commentary. Volume 30. Dallas: Word.

Gowan, Donald E. 2001. *Daniel*. Abingdon Old Testament Commentaries. Nashville: Abingdon Press.

Hammer, Raymond. 1976. *The Book of Daniel*. Cambridge Bible Commentary on the English Bible. Cambridge: Cambridge University Press.

Hartman, Louis F., and Alexander A. Di Lella. 1978. *The Book of Daniel*. Anchor Bible Commentary. Volume 23. Garden City, N.Y.: Doubleday.

Heaton, Eric W. 1956. *The Book of Daniel*. Torch Bible Commentary. London: SCM Press.

Huey, F. B., Jr. 1984. *Ezekiel, Daniel*. Layman's Bible Book Commentary. Volume 12. Nashville: Broadman and Holman Publishers.

Jeffrey, Arthur. 1956. "The Book of Daniel." *The Interpreter's Bible*. Volume 6. Nashville: Abingdon Press.

Jerome. 1958. *Jerome's Commentary on Daniel*. Translated by Gleason L. Archer, Jr. Grand Rapids: Baker Book House.

Keil, C. F. 1973. "Biblical Commentary on the Book of Daniel," in *Commentary on the Old Testament* by C. F. Keil and F. Delitzsch. Translated by M. G. Easton. Reprint, Grand Rapids: Eerdmans.

Koch, Klaus. 2005. *Daniel: Kapitell 1,1-4,34*. Biblischer Kommentar Altes Testament 22.1. Neukirchen-Vluyn: Neukirchener.

Lacocque, Andre. 1979. *The Book of Daniel*. Atlanta: John Knox Press.

Longman, Tremper, III. 1999. *Daniel*. NIV Application Commentary. Grand Rapids: Zondervan.

Lucas, Ernest. 2002. *Daniel*. Apollos Old Testament Commentary. Volume 20. Downers Grove, Ill.: InterVarsity Press.

Miller, Stephen R. 1994. *Daniel*. The New American Commentary. Nashville: Broadman and Holman Publishers.

Montgomery, James A. 1927. *A Critical and Exegetical Commentary on the Book of Daniel.* International Critical Commentary. Edinburgh: T & T Clark.

Owens, J. J. 1971. "Daniel." Broadman Bible Commentary. Volume 6. Nashville: Broadman Press.

Porteus, Norman W. 1965. *Daniel.* Old Testament Library. Philadelphia: Westminster Press.

Reddit, Paul L. 1999. *Daniel: Based on the New Revised Standard Version.* New Century Bible Commentary. Sheffield: Sheffield Academic Press.

Russell, D. S. 1981. *Daniel.* Daily Study Bible: Old Testament. Philadelphia: Westminster Press.

Seow, C. L. 2003. *Daniel.* Westminster Bible Companion. Philadelphia: Westminster John Knox Press.

Slotki, J. J. 1978. *Daniel-Ezra-Nehemiah.* London: Soncino Press.

Smith-Christopher, Daniel L. 1996. "Daniel." *The New Interpreter's Bible.* Volume 7. Nashville: Abingdon Press.

Stevenson, Kenneth, and Michael Glerup, eds. 2008. *Ezekiel, Daniel.* Old Testament. Volume 13. The Ancient Christian Commentary on Scripture. Downers Grove, Ill.: InterVarsity Press.

Swim, Roy E. 1966. "The Book of Daniel." *Beacon Bible Commentary.* Volume 4. Kansas City: Beacon Hill Press of Kansas City.

Towner, W. Sibley. 1984. *Daniel. Interpretation: A Bible Commentary for Teaching and Preaching.* Atlanta: John Knox Press.

Wallace, Ronald S. 1984. *The Message of Daniel.* The Bible Speaks Today. Downers Grove, Ill.: InterVarsity Press.

Walton, John H., Victor H. Matthews, and Mark W. Chavalas. 2000. *The IVP Bible Background Commentary: Old Testament.* Downers Grove, Ill.: InterVarsity Press.

Walvoord, John F. 1971. *Daniel: The Key to Prophetic Revelation.* Chicago: Moody Press.

Wesley, John. 1990. *John Wesley's Commentary on the Bible.* Edited by G. Roger Schoenhals. Grand Rapids: Francis Asbury Press.

Whitcomb, J. C., Jr. 1985. *Daniel.* Chicago: Moody Press.

Wood, Leon. 1973. *A Commentary on Daniel.* Grand Rapids: Zondervan.

Young, E. J. 1949. *The Prophecy of Daniel.* Grand Rapids: Eerdmans.

Zockler, Otto. 1960. "The Book of the Prophet Daniel," in *Lange's Commentary on the Holy Scriptures*, Volume 13. Translated by Philip Schaff. Reprint, Grand Rapids: Zondervan.

Other Sources

Beale, G. K. 1984. *The Use of Daniel in Jewish Apocalyptic Literature and in the Revelation of St. John.* Lanham, Md.: University Press of America.

Bury, J. B., S. A. Cook, and F. E. Adcock, eds. 1969. *The Cambridge Ancient History. Volume IV. The Persian Empire and the West.* Cambridge: University Press.

Carey, Greg. 2005. *Ultimate Things: An Introduction to Jewish and Christian Apocalyptic Literature.* St. Louis: Chalice Press.

Charles, Robert H. 1969. *Apocrypha and Pseudepigrapha of the Old Testament in English: With Introduction and Critical and Explanatory Notes in Several Books.* 2 Volumes. Oxford: Clarendon Press.

Charlesworth, James H. 1983-85. *The Old Testament Pseudepigrapha.* 2 Volumes. New York: Doubleday.

Collins, John J., ed. 1979. *Apocalypse: The Morphology of a Genre.* Semeia 14. Atlanta: Society of Biblical Literature.

_____. 1984. *The Apocalyptic Imagination: An Introduction to the Jewish Matrix of Christianity.* New York: Crossroads.

_____, ed. 1999. *The Encyclopedia of Apocalypticism: Volume 1, The Origins of Apocalypticism in Judaism and Christianity.* New York: Continuum.

Cook, J. M. 1983. *The Persian Empire.* New York: Schocken.

Cook, Stephen L. 1995. *Prophecy and Apocalypticism: The Postexilic Social Setting.* Minneapolis: Fortress Press.

_____. 2003. *The Apocalyptic Literature.* Interpreting Biblical Texts. Nashville: Abingdon Press.

Cook, S. A., F. E. Adcock, and M. P. Charlesworth, eds. 1954. *The Cambridge Ancient History. Volume VII. The Hellenistic Monarchies and the Rise of Rome.* Cambridge: University Press.

Gammie, J. G. 1983. *Daniel.* Knox Preaching Guides. Atlanta: John Knox Press.

Grayson, A. K. 2000. *Assyrian and Babylonian Chronicles.* Winona Lake, Ind.: Eisenbrauns.

Hanson, Paul D. 1979. *The Dawn of Apocalyptic: The Historical and Sociological Roots of Jewish Apocalyptic Eschatology.* Revised Edition. Philadelphia: Fortress Press.

_____. 1985. "Apocalyptic Literature," in *The Hebrew Bible and Its Modern Interpreters*. Edited by Douglas A. Knight and Gene M. Tucker. Philadelphia: Fortress Press.

Hellholm, David, ed. 1983. *Apocalypticism in the Mediterranean World and the Near East: Proceedings of the International Colloquium of Apocalypticism. Uppsala, August 12-17, 1979*. Tubingen: Mohr-Siebeck.

Meadowcroft, T. J. 1995. *Aramaic Daniel and Greek Daniel: A Literary Comparison*. Journal for the Study of the Old Testament Supplement Series 198. Sheffield: Sheffield Academic Press.

Moltmann, Jurgen. 1967. *Theology of Hope*. Translated by J. W. Leitch. New York: Harper and Row.

Morris, Leon. 1972. *Apocalyptic*. Grand Rapids: Eerdmans.

Mowinckel, Sigmund. 1954. *He That Cometh*. Translated by G. W. Anderson. New York: Abingdon Press.

Murphy, Fredrick J. 1996. "Introduction to Apocalyptic Literature," in *The New Interpreter's Bible*. Volume 7. Nashville: Abingdon Press.

Oswalt, John N. 1999. "Recent Studies in Old Testament Apocalyptic," in *The Face of Old Testament Studies: A Survey of Contemporary Approaches*. Edited by David W. Baker and Bill T. Arnold. Grand Rapids: Baker.

Pritchard, James B. 1969. *Ancient Near Eastern Texts Relating to the Old Testament*. 3rd Edition. Princeton, N.J.: Princeton University Press.

Reddish, Mitchell G., ed. 1990. *Apocalyptic Literature: A Reader*. Nashville: Abingdon Press.

Rowland, Christopher. 1982. *The Open Heaven: A Study of Apocalyptic in Judaism and Early Christianity*. New York: Crossroad.

Rowley, H. H. 1944. *The Relevance of Apocalyptic: A Study of Jewish and Christian Apocalypses from Daniel to Revelation*. London: Lutterworth Press.

Russell, D. S. 1964. *The Method and Message of Jewish Apocalyptic*. Old Testament Library. Philadelphia: Westminster Press.

_____. 1992. *Divine Disclosure: An Introduction to Jewish Apocalyptic*. Philadelphia: Fortress Press.

Sandy, D. Brent. 2002. *Plowshares and Pruning Hooks: Rethinking the Language of Biblical Prophecy and Apocalyptic*. Downers Grove, Ill.: InterVarsity Press.

Shea, William H. 2005. *Daniel: A Reader's Guide*. Nampa, Idaho: Pacific Press Publishing Association.

Stefanovic, Zdravko. 1992. *The Aramaic of Daniel in Light of Old Aramaic*. JSOT Supplement Series 129. Sheffield: JSOT Press.

Whitcomb, John C., Jr. 1959. *Darius the Mede: A Study in Historical Identification*. Grand Rapids: Eerdmans.

Wiseman, D. J., T. C. Mitchell, R. Joyce, W. J. Marin, and K. A. Kitchen. 1965. *Notes on Some Problems in the Book of Daniel*. London: Tyndale.

Wiseman, D. J. 1985. *Nebuchadrezzar and Babylon*. Oxford: Oxford University Press.

Woude, A. S. van der, ed. 1993. *The Book of Daniel in the Light of New Findings*. Leuven: University Press.

Yamauchi, Edwin M. 1996. *Persia and the Bible*. Grand Rapids: Baker.

INTRODUCTION

The Book of Daniel speaks a fresh message to each new generation. For over two millennia it has done so. The book invites its readers to live within a larger story than their own. It gives them a glimpse of the broad sweep of human history and the cosmic proportions of God's intentions. In light of certainties about the final outcome of this world, this book challenges believers to risk radical faith in God within the context of a hostile world.

This message has been especially relevant to those individuals and communities who have become disillusioned by present realities. Where political and social systems disappoint, Daniel provides hope. In contexts of oppressive, even anti-God, governments, Daniel infuses courage. When the strong undertow of secular values confuses, Daniel calls for clear choices. As the siren song of cultural compromise lures, Daniel gives reason for restraint. Century after century, the pages of Daniel have infused the faithful with fortitude.

A. Interest in Daniel

While the central message of Daniel continues to nurture faith for everyday living, much attention to the book has been motivated by another factor. Daniel has tended to generate interest over the centuries because of its apparent focus on the final days of human history. As a survey of interpretation reveals, groups within each new generation tended to associate their contemporary setting with the end of time (see Goldingay 1989, xxi-xxxviii). By one means or another, people felt they could identify with the characters and images presented in the book at this point. Such a sense has been true among Jewish as well as Christian communities, from earliest days to the present.

The Jewish community responsible for the Dead Sea Scrolls around Qumran, for example, applied Daniel's prophecies to their particular setting. Fragments from at least eight manuscripts of the book and several other documents attest to the importance of Daniel within this community. Living just before and into the Christian era, this group developed key features of their self-understanding in reference to Daniel. They anticipated the fulfillment of Daniel's prophecies within their lifetime, which include the coming of a messiah and the overthrow of Roman authority (see Collins 1993, 72-79).

Early Christians valued Daniel for similar reasons, but also for others. Jesus undoubtedly led the way in turning attention to the book. His teachings on the last days in Matt 24 display considerable reliance upon the images and vocabulary of Daniel. His constant reference to himself as "the Son of Man" in Mark 2:10, 8:38, and elsewhere evoked Dan 7:13-14 and provided interpretation for his identity as God's Messiah. That the Gospel writers selected this material to include in their books indicates the importance of Daniel among those early communities that they represented.

Other NT writers refer to Daniel as well. The visions of Dan 7—12 clearly shaped Paul's expositions on resurrection and the return of Christ in 1 Thess 4—5, 2 Thess 2, and 1 Cor 15. Luke and the writer to the Hebrews betray similar influences to a lesser degree. The most pervasive impact of Daniel on the NT, however, is in Revelation. John's visions of Christ and of the heavenly realms throughout this book, including the beast and his activities, repeatedly reflect the language of Daniel. (See Collins 1993, 90-112, for an excellent article by Adela Yarbro Collins, "The Influence of Daniel on the New Testament.")

From the NT era to the present, Christians have continued to turn to Daniel in order to gain perspective upon the world in which they live (see collection of comments on Daniel by earlier Christians in Stevenson and Glerup 2008). The third-century work of Hippolytus on Daniel was the first extended Christian commentary on a book of the OT. Among those who have mined the contents of Daniel in the past stand Origen, Chrysostom, Jerome, Luther, and Calvin. At every turn Daniel offered hope as well as explanation for faithful living in troubled times.

B. Special Literary Features

Daniel stands out among the OT prophetic books because of its relationship to apocalypticism. This is a particular worldview reflected in a kind of literature that gained popularity between 300 B.C. and A.D. 200 among certain Jewish and Christian circles. Though scholars debate some works, apocalyptic elements are generally recognized within Jewish writings such as *1 Enoch, Jubilees, Apocalypse of Abraham, 2 Baruch*, and *4 Ezra*. Among Christian sources there exists *Shepherd of Hermas, Apocalypse of Peter, Ascension of Isaiah*, and *Apocalypse of Paul*. In several instances Christians reworked older Jewish apocalyptic writings for their purposes.

Within the OT this sort of writing is reflected in portions of Isaiah, Joel, Ezekiel, and Zechariah, in addition to Daniel. The book of Revelation stands as the prime representative of apocalyptic literature within the NT.

This family of texts exhibits considerable diversity in form and content. Yet enough commonality can be observed to identify a category of literature that scholars label apocalyptic. The term comes from the Greek word *apocalypsis*, which means "revelation" or "unveiling." It suggests a disclosure of divine mysteries. This word occurs in the opening sentence of Revelation as an indicator of the nature of the material in that book.

A generally accepted definition of the genre identifies an apocalypse as "a genre of revelatory literature with a narrative framework, in which a revelation is mediated by an otherworldly being to a human recipient, disclosing a transcendent reality which is both temporal, insofar as it envisages eschatological salvation, and spatial insofar as it involves another, supernatural world" (Collins 1979, 9). Two subcategories within this genre have been distinguished: those that contain an otherworldly journey and those that do not (Collins 1984, 6-24).

As this definition indicates, the focus of apocalyptic literature is upon "disclosing a transcendent reality." It intends to unveil God's plans for the future, in particular the end of the world. Temporal, spatial, and moral dualisms characterize the apocalyptic worldview. The present evil world will give way to a world where the righteousness of God is fully manifested. This message is typically conveyed through an "otherworldly being to a human recipient" using fantastic images and figurative language.

A summary of typical features found in this literature includes: (1) symbolic language and surreal images, (2) heavenly visions guided by angels, (3) strong distinction between the present evil age and the future good age, (4) prediction of a climactic intervention of God in human history, (5) authorship falsely ascribed to a famous person of faith, and (6) history written as if it were prophecy. These are the most frequently occurring elements in the literature. Yet not all apocalyptic writings contain every one of these characteristics.

The effect of apocalyptic literature is to allow persons to gain perspective on their world by glimpsing realities of the heavenly realms. Readers can contemplate their place in the unfolding drama of history. They can see their struggles with evil in the context of a much larger story. Hope arises out of the realization that God and his goodness will triumph in the end.

Many features in apocalyptic literature can be found in other prophetic books of ancient Israel as well. Symbolic language, reports of visions, interest in end times, and God's ultimate triumph over evil are all characteristic of prophetic methods and concerns. Yet the manner in which apocalyptic deals with these typically differs from the prophets. In general, prophetic literature tends to look for God's salvation within history, while apocalyptic literature sees it coming to fulfillment at the end of time.

This connection with prophetic literature indicates that apocalypticism was in some sense a development or extension of the prophetic movement in Israel. Images and concepts used in apocalyptic literature are deeply rooted in Israel's prophetic tradition. Apocalyptic writings also betray connections to Israel's wisdom tradition and non-Israelite sources. Influences from Babylonian, Persian, Egyptian, and Greek thought can be detected in apocalyptic writings.

Daniel clearly stands within the tradition of Jewish apocalypticism. The dream in ch 2 and the visions of chs 7 to 12 in particular employ techniques and ideas commonly used by apocalyptic writers. Otherworldly beings guide Daniel through a vision of heavenly realms revealing things that are in the future. Daniel sees history unfolding in periods and relates some very specific events involved in that history. He makes reference to cosmic battles, resurrection, and eschatological judgment. All these features regularly occur in the literature of the apocalypses.

Scholars agree, however, that though Daniel shares many characteristics of apocalyptic books, it does not follow all the formal elements of apocalyptic genre. Daniel tends to deviate from the standards of apocalyptic writings and incorporates elements that are not found in other apocalypses. In general, Daniel exhibits less extravagant and fantastic imagery than other apocalyptic works and envisions salvation more within the realm of human history than beyond it. Daniel appears to have played a transitional role in the movement from prophetic to apocalyptic literature in ancient Judaism. Some scholars have designated the apocalyptic sections of Isaiah, Zechariah, and Ezekiel as "proto-apocalyptic" based upon their character. Daniel reflects developments beyond these books and yet does not possess features found in later apocalyptic works.

C. Authorship

The apocalyptic character of Daniel suggests the possibility that the book is pseudonymous. That is to say, a person other than Daniel wrote the book posing as the famous visionary prophet. Such a practice was widely employed in the Hellenistic world and most apocalypses were written in this manner. Both Jewish and Christian apocalyptic writers regularly ascribed their works to ancient heroes of the faith, such as Enoch, Abraham, Moses, Baruch, Ezra, or Paul. As a result, most prophecies in the book were not actual predictions. They were historical recollections. The prophecies seem very accurate because they are actually given after the fact. Usually toward the end of these pseudoprophecies, which brought readers up to the contemporary situation of the author, some predictions about the immediate future were made.

The purpose of this technique was to give credibility to the work. The point was not so much to deceive as to enhance the theological message of the book. By using a pseudonym, authors apparently sought to identify with and affirm the ancient author. They were part of a venerable tradition of faith.

Not all scholars agree that Daniel was pseudonymous, however. Many believe that the book is unique among the apocalypses and that the hero of the book authored its words. There is very little evidence that ancient interpreters, either Jewish or Christian, understood Daniel as pseudonymous. The comments from the Qumran community, the rabbis, and even other apocalyptic writers suggest that they thought Daniel was the real author. NT writers, Josephus, Jerome, and other Christians indicate the same. Jesus' statement in Matt 24:15 seems to indicate that he viewed Daniel as either the author of the book or at least the originator of the prophetic words in it. In that passage he refers to "the abomination that causes desolation" that was "spoken of through the prophet Daniel."

For the modern mind the logic of a pseudonymous work is hard to follow. Credibility of a work appears to be undermined by false authorship. The visions in the book clearly suggest that Daniel actually saw them at very specific times in the sixth century B.C. If Daniel did not really see these visions and record true prophecies about the future, then the validity of the book's central message about God's sovereignty seems lessened. This in turn appears to diminish the desired effect of the book, which is to induce faith in the God of all history.

A person's position on this issue does not necessarily brand him or her as liberal or conservative. Though some who view the book as pseudonymous might deny the possibility of genuine predictive prophecy, others do not. Some scholars who hold a high view of biblical inspiration believe Daniel was pseudonymous (for example, Goldingay 1989, xxxix). They understand pseudonymity simply as another means by which God communicated his message to an ancient audience.

The effect of accepting Daniel as pseudonymous is to diminish the element of predictive prophecy in the book. It is not totally eliminated, though, since some predictions are made beyond the author's time. The idea of detailed prediction of events in the future, however, is lessened. This brings Daniel more in line with the other prophets of Israel who preferred to speak of the future in more general terms. In addition the sense of God's sovereignty over human history is still preserved in a pseudonymous writing. The rehearsal of events in the pseudoprophecies tends to underscore God's control of this world.

D. Date of Writing

If Daniel is pseudonymous, then the date of writing must come after the lifetime of the prophet. The predominant view current among many biblical scholars is that Daniel was written in the second century B.C. during the time of the Maccabean Revolt. The precise date for composition is usually given around 167-164 B.C.

According to this theory, the book is the result of growing tradition that takes its final form in the second century. Exactly how and when the various layers were added is a matter of scholarly debate. But the essential outline is that earlier stories about Daniel in chapters 1—6 were eventually joined to the visions of chapters 7—12 (Collins 1993, 24-38).

A non-Christian philosopher named Porphyry (A.D. 233-304) first proposed the essential elements of this theory in the third century A.D. His arguments are known because Jerome (A.D. 331-420) systematically responded to them in his commentary on Daniel. During the seventeenth and eighteenth centuries biblical scholars began to reassert this view. It gained wide acceptance throughout the succeeding centuries among academics, but not generally among conservative scholars or the laity of the church.

An alternative theory for composition of the book is the sixth century B.C. A time toward the end of Daniel's life, or shortly thereafter, is suggested around 530 B.C. (Miller 1994, 23). This theory views the material as being compiled by Daniel or a disciple of his. In either case both the stories and the visions are understood as authentic compositions deriving from Daniel in the sixth century B.C. and are not pseudonymous.

The debate between these two theories involves a variety of issues. Some of the most important are the following.

(1) At the heart of the discussion is the fact that the book focuses upon the Jewish persecution under Antiochus IV Epiphanes between 167 and 164 B.C., which provoked the Maccabean Revolt in Judah. With increasing detail, the events of the book move toward this climactic point in ch 11. As the commentary will show, the correspondence between this prophecy and the events surrounding the Maccabean Revolt is remarkable.

Jewish apocalyptic works often reveal their date of composition in this way. They bring the reader up to the contemporary setting before predicting a final divine rescue. If Daniel is pseudonymous and follows the regular conventions of apocalyptic literature, then a second-century date is a logical conclusion. Scholars who view Daniel this way recognize that some material in the book originated in the sixth-century setting. But they hold that these portions were passed down within the community of faith to a second-century author who finally brought the book together.

These scholars also observe that the message of Daniel seems to be particularly appropriate for people living during the Seleucid persecution and concomitant Maccabean Revolt. The challenge to remain firm in the face of foreign oppression is exactly what Jews living through this crisis needed to hear. Being reminded of God's sovereign reign over human history would likely encourage steadfastness during the Maccabean resistance to the Seleucids.

Other scholars also recognize that much of the material relates to the second-century persecution of Judaism but hold to a sixth-century date for composition. They argue that Daniel as a whole is speaking to Jews of the sixth century first. The messages of Daniel, these scholars note, resonate with those struggling to rebuild Judah in the midst of a hostile environment and disappointing progress following the exile. Those living under Persian dominance needed to hear the encouraging words of Daniel also.

These scholars point out that though Daniel reflects many features of classic apocalyptic literature, it does not follow all of them rigidly. In particular, its visions are less surreal and salvation comes within history, which is more like the apocalyptic sections of Isaiah, Ezekiel, and Zechariah. The book, therefore, could be exceptional in other ways. As such, these scholars suggest, it may not be pseudonymous and its visions may well be genuine predictions of things to come.

Thus scholars of both camps recognize that Daniel reveals connections to both sixth- and second-century settings. If the book follows conventions of classic apocalyptic genres closely, then it was likely finally composed in the second century B.C. However, if it stands as a unique product among the apocalypses, then it could be primarily a sixth-century composition.

(2) Another area of discussion centers on certain historical references to the Babylonian and Persian periods. To some scholars these notations appear to be confused. The most problematic are Nebuchadnezzar's invasion of Jerusalem in the third year of Jehoiakim (1:1) and the identification of Darius the Mede as the conqueror of Babylon (5:31). These and other apparent historical incongruities will be discussed more fully in the commentary. Their accumulation suggests that the author was not fully informed about the sixth century or simply

not interested in such details. If the material were composed in the second century, such confusion and lack of interest might be more understandable.

Some commentators view these historical notations simply as literary devices. All references to the reigns of kings, for example, fall within the first three years. This may be a way of indicating that the events of the stories or visions occurred toward the beginning of the reign of these kings, which in each case were significant junctures in Jewish history (Goldingay 1989, 14-15). The intent may not have been to locate the material within a particular year but only in reference to a general time frame.

Scholars note, though, that at times Daniel displays a remarkable knowledge of Babylonian and Persian culture. Some information could only be expected from a writer in the sixth century and not later. A person writing much later than the sixth century would not likely have known that Nebuchadnezzar, for example, was the primary builder of Babylon and Belshazzar the ruler of that city when it fell. This kind of information, however, may only indicate that these portions of the book come from the sixth century and not necessarily the entire composition.

Those who argue for the historical reliability of Daniel point out that the kind of confusion posited does not seem likely. In light of widespread familiarity of histories by Herodotus and Xenophon it seems incredible, for example, that the author might not know Cyrus conquered Babylon. Some other explanation for reference to Darius the Mede must be sought, then. Thus, historical references that appear confused may not be, they argue. Additional information can substantiate, or at least allow for, the accuracy of the text as it stands, according to these scholars (see Baldwin 1978, 19-29, and Archer 1985, 12-26).

(3) The languages of the original text of Daniel have sometimes entered the discussion on dating the book. Aramaic is the language of 2:4—7:28, whereas the rest of the book is in Hebrew. Scholars offer various theories to explain this feature (see *Behind the Text* for ch 2). In general, however, this feature provides mixed evidence for dating. The use of Hebrew and Aramaic can be analyzed to support either the sixth- or second-century dates. Some scholars have determined that they reflect vocabulary and forms that are later than sixth century (Collins 1993, 12-23). Others have argued that they have more in common with the sixth century than the second (Wiseman and others 1965, 34-50).

Foreign loan words in the text of Daniel also provide mixed results. The presence of Akkadian and Greek words might be expected in both Persian and Hellenistic periods. The Persian loan words, however, do push the argument in favor of an early date. Translators of the Septuagint did not understand the meaning of many of these terms. Since this Greek translation of Daniel was made in the middle or late second century B.C., this fact might suggest a sixth-century date for composition, but only for those sections in which the Persian words occur. It does not follow that the entire composition must be early.

(4) A final area of discussion develops around Daniel's relationship to other canonical and Jewish religious writings. The location of Daniel in the Hebrew canon raises some questions. It is placed among the Writings rather than the Prophets. This location could indicate that Daniel was not available to be included among the Prophets at the time those books became recognized as a body of authoritative scriptures. Though some scholars date this development prior to the second century B.C., the process of canonization continued on into the first century A.D. The location of Daniel among the Writings might only indicate its association with other postexilic writings and wisdom books as well as its differences from the classic prophetic books.

According to some scholars, the omission of Daniel in the early second-century B.C. work of *Sirach* points toward a late date. *Sirach* specifically references Isaiah, Jeremiah, Ezekiel, and the Twelve but not Daniel. Yet, these references are to persons and not books. *Sirach* does not mention other notables such as Ezra and Esther either.

Scholars note that the impact of the book of Daniel upon other early apocalyptic works and the Qumran community was significant. Some texts related to Daniel at Qumran come from the late second century. Such reverence for a text at this date seems surprising if Daniel were a second-century composition. A similar statement could be made about the allusions to Daniel found in some of the early apocalyptic writings. If Daniel comes from the sixth century, its popularity at Qumran and among the apocalypses might make more sense. But this does not rule out the possibility that Daniel could have enjoyed widespread appeal relatively soon after composition, as the NT books did.

This summary of the debate illustrates that the evidence is not overwhelming in either direction. Valid points can be made for each theory. Therefore a person may choose either position and maintain academic integrity. A decision on this matter does not necessarily indicate that one is either conservative or liberal. Divine inspiration of Daniel may be affirmed or denied in either case.

E. Daniel the Statesman Prophet

Regardless of a person's position on authorship, the hero of the book is clearly a man named Daniel. He is described as an interpreter of dreams, a visionary, and an example of godly living. The book, however, is not about Daniel so much as it is about God. The dreams, visions, and stories from the life of Daniel and his friends serve primarily to reveal God and his purposes.

Traditionally Daniel is called a prophet even though the book never actually calls him such. He does not speak about a call to prophetic ministry or regularly employ the typical speech genres of prophets. Yet, he does deliver invectives against kings (5:22-24), calls for repentance (4:27), and receives visions from God like other prophets (chs 7—12). The book clearly shares a prophetic worldview and constantly alludes to other prophetic books. The prayer in ch 9 particularly reflects typical prophetic language and thought. Thus both rabbis and Christian writers consistently refer to him as a prophet. Jesus himself labeled Daniel a prophet in Matt 24:15, and the Christian canons locate Daniel among the prophetic books.

Based on the portrait of Daniel given in the book, he was a younger contemporary of the OT prophets Habakkuk, Jeremiah, and Ezekiel. He was likely born sometime around 620 B.C. during the period of national and religious revival under Josiah. While Daniel was still a young man, Josiah was killed in 609 B.C. and dreams of a new Israel were dashed. After a brief imposition of Egyptian dominance, Babylonians seized control of the region of Judah in 605 B.C. At that time Daniel was taken to Babylon along with other promising youth from prominent families in Jerusalem. Josephus suggested that Daniel and his three friends were all related to Zedekiah (*Ant.* 10.10 §1). Whether or not this is true, he was certainly from a privileged family, based on Dan 1:4.

In Babylon Daniel received advanced training that would enable him to assist in administering the expanding Babylonian Empire. His gifts of wisdom and interpreting dreams earned him status among his peers. He rose rapidly in the ranks of state leadership. Throughout his career he held various positions, including ruler over the province of Babylon (2:48), head of the wise men of Babylon (2:48), third highest ruler in the Babylonian Empire (5:29), and one of the top three administrators in the Persian Empire (6:2).

Political fortunes in the Middle East changed dramatically during Daniel's lifetime. Empires rose and fell across the Fertile Crescent. The one hundred-year-old Assyrian Empire was already unraveling at his birth. Nineveh fell in 612 B.C. while Daniel was a young boy. The Babylonians brought about its demise and established their own empire from Egypt to Elam. One of the ancient world's most famous kings, Nebuchadnezzar, led the Babylonians to the height of their power and influence. He precipitated a defining moment in Israel's national history by destroying Jerusalem and its temple in 587 B.C. Within fifty years, however, Babylon gave way to Persia. In 539 B.C. Cyrus the Great conquered the city and began returning Jews and other refugees to their homelands.

Daniel was witness to these unsettling times. The last date given in the book is "the third year of Cyrus king of Persia," which was about 535 B.C.

(10:1). If Daniel died soon after this, he would have lived over eighty years, an exceptionally long life for that time.

Daniel in Ezekiel

Scholars debate whether or not Daniel is mentioned in the book of Ezekiel. Three verses mention a person named Daniel. Ezekiel 14:14 and 20 include a person named Daniel in a list of three legendary righteous men along with Noah and Job. Ezekiel also refers to a person named Daniel in 28:3 when he asked the rhetorical question, "Are you wiser than Daniel?" Since Noah and Job are very ancient personalities, reference to a contemporary sixth-century Daniel seems out of place. Also it would be unusual for a Jewish prophet to attain such status among his peers during his lifetime.

Some scholars suggest that Ezekiel is thinking of either a person unknown to moderns or an extrabiblical person in the Ugaritic story of Aqhat. In the Ugaritic legend Daniel is a king and father of Aqhat. The drawback to this theory is that neither righteousness nor wisdom is central to the character of this Daniel.

F. Original Audience

How one views the authorship of Daniel will affect one's understanding of the original audience. The circumstances of the late sixth century B.C. were different from those of the second. Over three hundred years separate the dates of 535 B.C. and 165 B.C. Yet a number of similarities can be observed between these eras. The complications of living as faithful servants of God during periods of foreign domination are common to both. The details may differ, but the struggle was similar. In either time the message of Daniel spoke a profound word of hope.

An audience in the late sixth century B.C. would be working through a time of significant transition. The Persians established a vast empire across the Middle East during this time under the leadership of Cyrus the Great (550-530 B.C.), Cambyses II (530-522 B.C.), and Darius the Great (522-486 B.C.). Darius brought the empire to its greatest heights and organization. He pushed the boundaries westward into modern Turkey and eastward to the Indus River. This was the most extensive empire the world had seen up to that time.

With the fall of Babylon to the Persians in 539 B.C. the despairing years of Israel's exile came to a close. A more benevolent Persian rule took the place of Babylonian tyranny. Those that had been displaced under the previous regime were invited to return to their homelands. Though many remained behind in the familiar environments of Babylonia, Egypt, and elsewhere, a significant number of Israelites made the journey to Jerusalem and the surrounding region.

Cyrus Cylinder

The Cyrus Cylinder preserves the policy of Cyrus in 539 B.C., which allowed people who had been exiled by the Babylonians to return to their homelands and rebuild their temples. It is written in the Aramaic language using cuneiform script. Part of the text reads: "As far as Ashur and Susa, Agade, Eshnunna, the towns of Zamban Me-Turnu, Der, as well as the sanctuaries of which have been ruins for a long time, the images which used to live therein and established for them permanent sanctuaries. I [also] gather all their (former) inhabitants and returned [to them] their habitations" (Pritchard 1969, 316).

According to Ezra 1, Sheshbazzar led an early group from the Babylonian area around 538 B.C. The first groups of returnees rebuilt the altar at Jerusalem and laid the foundation for the temple. Harsh economic realities and opposition from neighboring peoples halted further work on the temple for over fifteen years, though. In 520 B.C. the temple was finally completed and dedicated. Its modest design and furnishing betrayed the disillusionment of the era. The hopeful vision the prophets had projected for Judah's return to her land did not transpire. Its people struggled with a poor economy, hostile neighbors, dissension within the community, and obligations to foreign rule. Judah was but a small entity located in a corner of a vast Persian Empire, an insignificant player in the scheme of world history.

To such an audience the stories and visions of Daniel could inspire new hope for the future and provide perspective and guidance for the present. The words of Jeremiah and other prophets are given further clarification. Complete fulfillment of God's promises remains in the future, some of it at the end of time when the rising and falling of nations has ceased. Meanwhile the faithful can prosper and the kingdom of God can break into a world under foreign rule. The might of Persia is no match for the providence of God at work among his people.

A similar message would be conveyed to an audience in the second century B.C. as well, although the specific characters and circumstances would have changed. In 165 B.C. Seleucid authorities replaced Babylonian and Persian counterparts. The struggles of the faithful included corruption in the high priesthood as well as a direct threat to survival in the persecution of Antiochus IV.

When the Seleucids successfully wrested Judah away from the Ptolemies in 198 B.C., they ushered in a period of unprecedented turmoil. Pressure to adopt the ways of the Greek culture increased while priests fought over control of the temple. In 167 B.C., Antiochus IV suppressed the practices of Judaism, pillaged the Jerusalem temple and rededicated it to Zeus, and martyred those who did not comply with his commands. According to 2 Macc 6:5-6, "The altar was covered with abominable offerings that were forbidden by the laws. People could neither keep the Sabbath, nor observe the festivals of their ancestors, nor so much as confess themselves to be Jews." Such events provoked a full-scale revolt, a daring guerrilla war led by Judas Maccabeus and his family of Hasmonean descendants. The odds in favor of the Seleucids were overwhelming.

In the midst of these circumstances, the book of Daniel could infuse courage into Jewish resistance. Daniel's refusal to compromise his religious convictions, his survey of the coming and going of nations, and his predictions of God's final victory would provide needed perspective and encouragement for the Maccabean rebels.

G. Structure of Book

The book of Daniel is a literary unity. Numerous creative structuring devices have been employed to bring about a sense of cohesion among the various components of the text. Whether one views Daniel as the product of a growing tradition or a singular composition, it now stands as a well-designed unit of material.

Balance is first achieved through literary genres and historical sequencing. Chapters 1 to 6 contain stories, while chs 7 to 12 consist of visions. Both sections progress historically, from the earliest date to the latest. Common themes thread through each chapter and bind both parts of the book together.

The first six chapters consist of two kinds of stories that have been arranged in a manner that heightens their impact. Three stories are tests of faithfulness and three are tests of wisdom. These two types of stories are presented alternately. Chapter 1 is a test of faithfulness story followed by a test of wisdom story in ch 2. Chapters 3 and 4 are a similar couplet. The final two chapters reverse the order of presentation. Chapter 5 is a test of wisdom story while ch 6 is a test of faithfulness.

The final six chapters of Daniel are vision reports. They are arranged in chronological order and provide increasing detail of future events. The overview of the rise and fall of kingdoms in ch 7 is filled out in subsequent chapters. The final three visions grow progressively longer with the last one in chs 10 to 12 extending more than three times beyond the others.

A simple outline of the materials unfolds as follows:

I. Stories for Those Living in a Foreign Land (chs 1—6)
   A. Food Defilement: The First Test of Faithfulness (ch 1)
   B. Dream of a Statue: The First Test of Wisdom (ch 2)
   C. Fiery Furnace: The Second Test of Faithfulness (ch 3)
   D. Dream of a Tree: The Second Test of Wisdom (ch 4)
   E. Writing on the Wall: The Third Test of Wisdom (ch 5)
   F. Lions' Pit: The Third Test of Faithfulness (ch 6)
II. Vision for Those Living in a Foreign Land (chs 7—12)

A. Vision of Four Beasts (ch 7)
B. Vision of Two Beasts (ch 8)
C. Vision of Seventy Sevens (ch 9)
D. Vision of a Great War (chs 10—12)

A unique and puzzling feature of the book is an Aramaic section of material in 2:4—7:28. Its chiastic structure creates a tight bond for the unit. Chapters 2 and 7 parallel one another, as do chs 3 and 6. Then chs 4 and 5 stand as a pair and form the fulcrum of the section. The effect of this section is to bind the stories and visions together. By arranging things so, the author has suggested that both sections of the book must be understood in light of the other.

H. Greek Versions of Daniel

The Greek versions of Daniel vary considerably from the Hebrew/Aramaic version preserved by the Masoretic tradition. The most pronounced difference is three additions found in the Greek texts. These are included along with the book of Daniel in the Roman Catholic and Orthodox canons of Scripture. The Anglican Church includes them in a separate section known as the Apocrypha or deuterocanonical books. They are titled: (1) The Prayer of Azariah and the Song of the Three Young Men, (2) Susanna, and (3) Bel and the Dragon.

The Prayer of Azariah and the Song of the Three Young Men supplies additional details to the story about the fiery furnace ordeal in Dan 3. The material is 68 verses long and fits between Dan 3:24 and 25 of the Hebrew/Aramaic text. It relates a prayer and a song spoken by the three friends of Daniel while they were in the furnace. It begins with a prayerful lament by Azariah, also known as Abednego. He confesses the sin of the nation and requests God's deliverance. Following this the three men sing a song that invites all creation to praise God. It ends with a declaration of praise for deliverance by the three.

Susanna is the story of a virtuous woman wrongly accused of adultery. Daniel brings about her rescue by seeing through the plot of her accusers and getting them to reveal their wickedness. Daniel's superior wisdom is highlighted one more time. The story was placed before the rest of the book of Daniel in ancient Greek manuscripts but as ch 13 in the Vulgate and modern Roman Catholic Bibles.

Bel and the Dragon is located at the end of the book. It tells the story of Daniel's confrontation with idol worship. By clever means he proves both Bel and a dragon (or serpent) were not truly divine. This angered some officials who had him thrown into a den of lions. As in Daniel ch 6, he is miraculously delivered from being eaten.

Each of these appears to be a later addition to the more original Hebrew/Aramaic text, though this has been debated. The material was not acknowledged as part of the canon by Judaism and thus by most Protestant churches.

Other differences between the Greek and Hebrew/Aramaic versions occur throughout the book. The most significant variations are located in chs 3 to 6. Of the several Greek versions, the Old Greek (Septuagint) adds and omits material more freely than the others. Perhaps this is why Theodotian, which follows the MT closely, replaced the Old Greek in Christian usage by the time of Jerome. The differences between the Old Greek and the MT are difficult to assess. While the Masoretic tradition has been customarily taken as more original, some scholars argue for the priority of the Greek or suggest that both versions depend on a more original text no longer extant. In any case, the points at which the Old Greek diverges from the MT significantly reshape the stories of the book, particularly in chs 4 and 5. (For further discussion, see Hartman and Di Lella 1978, 76-84, and Meadowcroft 1995, 278-80.)

I. Hermeneutical Issues

As with all literature, interpretation depends upon how one understands the nature of the material. In the book of Daniel two basic views prevail. One point of view takes the material to be fictional literature created for a particular second-century B.C. context. The other sees it as an account of actual experiences emerging from a sixth-century B.C. setting. The first emphasizes the imaginary character of the text while the latter holds to a more historical quality. Both acknowledge the literary creativity of both the stories and the visions.

Proponents of the first view believe the book draws upon earlier legends and creatively adds material in order to speak a message to a later audience. The narrative projects itself as coming from the sixth century B.C. in order to provide perspective on a crisis of faith in the second century B.C. Historical precision is not of paramount interest in this scenario, so the interpreter should not be overly concerned about such matters. The author did not intend to write history and was confused about such details at times. Prophetic prediction is not of major significance either. Though the book purports to project future events, most of the prophecies are best understood as rehearsal of the past. Only prediction of the ultimate victory of God and his people remains in the future.

The second basic approach to the book takes the historical and prophetic references more literally. Its adherents believe the material records accurate history and makes genuine predictions about future events, some of which have already come to fulfillment and others that have not. The book is seen as a product of the sixth century B.C. designed to communicate with an audience of that time period regarding things present and things to come.

Within the framework of this second basic approach, various tracks of interpretation have been taken. Some press the predictive element to include a kind of blueprint for future events. They see a map for end-time events laid out quite precisely. Others are more restrained in identifying the meaning of the symbolism. They take the images to convey more general truths about God and his purposes without intending to specify every detail of the future. Between these two poles are a variety of positions on how to deal with different passages in the book.

Whichever approach interpreters take to Daniel, they must keep in mind that within Jewish and Christian traditions the book has been set apart as sacred scripture. Thus it has been viewed as authoritative for the faith and practice of these communities. The book speaks about God's purposes for this world through stories dominated by dramatic narration and visions reflecting apocalyptic styled writings. Each of the elements in this description of the book bears upon its interpretation. To clarify, the book needs to be understood as scripture, as a literary work, as a theological document, and as historically connected material.

As scripture the book of Daniel must be read in its canonical context. It was first of all part of the Hebrew Scriptures. In this context Daniel is located among the Writings, which contain wisdom and postexilic works to which Daniel shares many connections. Interrelationships between Daniel and these kinds of books in the Hebrew canon should provide perspective for interpretation. Daniel also relies on themes, motifs, type-scenes, and other elements of other books in the Hebrew Scriptures. These connections should inform the interpreter as well.

The book also functions as a part of the Christian canon. In this setting it is located among the prophetic books. Its connections with these books supply additional insight into the motifs, themes, and designs of Daniel. In addition, as Christian scripture Daniel needs to be read in reference to the NT and Christian tradition. The ways in which both NT writers and Christian interpreters have understood and reapplied the message of the book should guide modern interpreters. The interpretations of the NT writers must bear added weight since they are not simply another opinion but inspired scripture.

At times the NT's use of Daniel may indicate fulfillment of specific predictions about Jesus as well as confirm projections about future events still to come. On other occasions, though, Daniel's images may only provide patterns of human and divine activities. In these cases Daniel did not predict messianic or end-time things so much as provide images that can be employed to describe and explain them. Many of the prophecies that find fulfillment within a second-century B.C. context can be reapplied to later events. As with other prophetic books, Daniel does not always clearly distinguish layers of time in the future. At these points it may be viewing events together that are actually eras apart.

By its very nature Scripture is designed to instruct. First of all it teaches about God and then about how humans can live in relationship to him. While one must be cautious in making Daniel's behavior normative for modern believers, this is a legitimate use of the text. Scripture intends to offer practical guidance for living as well as theological foundations for it. Daniel and his friends are models of faithfulness. As the interpreter bridges the gap between centuries, however, the dynamics of corresponding contexts need to be analyzed carefully.

As a literary work, the book of Daniel should be analyzed for the kinds of signals its author sends the readers in order to convey meaning. The author of the book, whoever that may be, surely intended to communicate certain things through the content and forms employed in its writing. The narratives in the first part of the book are well developed in the art of storytelling. Interpreters need to ponder the techniques of character and plot development as well as setting references. Wordplay, structuring devices, type-scenes, images, and a host of other literary devices must be examined for their affects upon the message of the material. The interpreter should remember to listen through ears of a Jewish audience. Though the plots are well known to ancient audiences, they enjoyed listening to them unfold. Their endings are happy endings to the Jewish community.

The apocalyptic styled visions present a specialized challenge for the modern interpreter. The highly imaginative and symbolic nature of the material needs to be kept in mind at all times. Figurative language cannot be taken literally, nor can every detail find a specific analogy to reality. Part of the power of an apocalypse is its mystery. Its symbols are not meant to be fully transparent. If every number and image is explained, something is lost. Therefore, most numbers are best understood symbolically. No calculation of any of the numbers in Daniel completely satisfies specific historical referents anyway. The same is true regarding images representing earthly kingdoms. Correspondence between these images and historical entities never fully match.

Interpreters can read Daniel fruitfully in relationship to the family of ancient apocalyptic texts to which it belongs. Parallels from Jewish and Christian apocalypses are instructive. Yet they are not wholly determinative. The images and motifs prevalent in this kind of material could as easily be dependent upon Daniel as reflective of a common style or worldview. The interpreter should keep in mind that Daniel is unique in many ways and does not display all the characteristics found in these other works.

As a theological work Daniel can be examined for what it has to say about God. The text is first and foremost a revelation of God. Therefore, this must be the central focus for interpreters of Scripture. The primary intent of Daniel, as well as all of Christian Scripture, is to communicate something about God and his dealings with creation. At each juncture in the text the main question of the interpreter must be, "What is being said about God?"

As a historically connected document, the material should be read with reference to the particular contexts presented in the text. The author of the book provided specific historical settings for both the stories and visions of the book. Whether or not the interpreter judges these to be accurate, they must be taken into account. The stories narrate remarkable interventions of God within Babylonian and Persian settings of Israel's ancient history. The visions set unusual visual experiences of the main character within these same contexts. This is the first setting within which one should read the text.

To say that the material is historically connected does not necessarily affirm its historicity. As noted above, the incredible and incongruous elements of the book suggest to many scholars that its stories and visions are primarily fictional. They hold that the stories are traditional tales retold and elaborated over the years and that the visions are essentially pseudoprophecy. Many other scholars, however, believe that the book presents authentic history in the stories and genuine prophecy in the visions. One's position on this issue affects interpretation, particularly the step of contemporary application. While the essential message put forth in the text does not change, the impact of it will. Actions that have actually taken place generally carry greater weight than those that are only imagined. While both fiction and nonfiction communicate truth, the truths conveyed through real events are usually more convincing and compelling than those emerging from one's imagination. On the other hand, those who view the book as an imaginative creation are relieved of the need to account for incongruities and fantastic elements in the text. They are free to examine the material for the meanings it intends to convey or that it evokes.

How one views the provenance of the book will affect interpretation as well. As interpreters attempt to clarify meaning in relationship to an original audience, one's position at this point will influence the meaning of certain images, allusions, and even words. Of primary issue at this point is the nature of prophetic prediction. A sixth-century dating tends to heighten this element while the second-century dating diminishes it.

J. Approach of This Commentary

Two features of commentaries on Daniel tend to distract from the full impact of the book's message. On the one hand is the undue interest in mapping out end-time events. This approach leads to highly speculative and sometimes bizarre conclusions. Proponents of this method are drawn into discussions that were not likely the kind intended by the material. The very nature of apocalypses suggests this is a misguided approach to the book. The imagery in such material is impressionistic, not precise. It intends to evoke general concepts rather than to detail particulars. To take the images of Daniel as specific markers on a timetable for the end of human history misunderstands their symbolic functions. (See Longman 1999, 176-79, and Sandy 2002, 103-28, for further discussion.)

The other distraction is the debate over the date of composition. While a position on the issue bears on some aspects of interpretation, it is not determinative for most of the book's message. Questions about original author and audience and compositional development are not overly significant for hearing the theological propositions of Daniel. Constant concern for historical-critical matters tends to hinder commentators from focusing upon the text. Interpreters will gain much more from the book if they can set aside these issues and simply enter the world of the text as it has been given to them. The primary themes of the book resonate with audiences in all ages and communicate truths that do not depend on specific setting of the original audience.

Both of these issues are legitimate concerns. How the world might end and when this book was written are important questions to explore. However, they should not be allowed to obscure the first purpose of a biblical text, which is to reveal God. Therefore, this commentary will attempt to focus upon the theological messages found in Daniel. What the text has to say about God, people, and the interface between them will be of paramount interest. The commentary will explore these dimensions by examining the world of the text as it stands. It will employ literary and grammatical analysis in order to elucidate the text. Background information on historical references within the text will also aid in this task. Debates over details of future events and the date of composition will be acknowledged but not engaged. On such matters, the commentary will note various positions and guide the reader toward other sources where the discussion is more extended.

K. Theology of the Book

The book of Daniel is an intense study of the sovereignty of God and its implications for believers. The primary theological message of the book is clear. God overrules the rulers of this world. Therefore God's people can risk faithful living because ultimate victory is assured.

The theological highlights of the book can be discussed in reference to three worldviews it discredits: dualism, fatalism, and pessimism. While each of these was prevalent in the ancient world, they have persisted throughout human history into the present. This accounts in part for the continued value of the book. It proclaims (1) absolute sovereignty of God, not dualism, (2) responsible free will of humans, not fatalism, and (3) hopeful optimism for God's people, not pessimism.

1. Absolute Sovereignty of God, Not Dualism

Daniel proclaims that there is no dualism in the cosmic realms. The God of Daniel has no equal. His God is "the God of gods and the Lord of kings" (2:47). He is "the Most High God" (3:26; 4:2; 5:18, 21) or simply "the Most High" (4:17, 24, 25, 32, 34; 7:18, 22, 25, 27). He is also known as "the King of heaven" (4:37), "the Lord of heaven" (5:23), and "the God of heaven" (2:18, 19, 37, 44). In short, all of heaven and earth, every nation and king, all wisdom and knowledge, the whole of human history and the affairs of his people come under the control of God, according to the book of Daniel.

The dominion of God includes every entity known to humans. God can do "as he pleases with the powers of heaven and the peoples of the earth" (4:35). In contrast to the kingdoms of this world that constantly come and go, "his kingdom is an eternal kingdom; his dominion endures from generation to generation" (4:3). It "will not be destroyed" and "will never end" (6:26). He holds the unchallenged authority to give "one like a son of man" who comes riding on the clouds of heaven "authority, glory and sovereign power" to establish a kingdom that is "an everlasting kingdom that will not pass away" and "will never be destroyed" (7:13-14). The kingdom of God always remains. There is never a time when God's kingdom does not exist in heaven or on earth.

Thus God possesses absolute authority over all that takes place on earth, both in the present as well as in the future. The Ancient of Days calls all of human authorities to account before his throne and judges them (7:9-13). "He sets up kings and deposes them" (2:21). So human history and the wisdom to understand it and deal with it rests in God's hands. God is "the revealer of mysteries" about this world (2:47) for "he knows what lies in darkness" (2:22). He sends visions and angels to show "what will take place in the future" (2:45; 10:14). With details that only God could know, his agents reveal exactly how human history will unfold at specific times. God stands sovereign over this entire world and orchestrates all its affairs.

2. Responsible Free Will of Humans, Not Fatalism

Though Daniel proclaims God's absolute sovereignty, it does not affirm fatalism. Human destinies are not predetermined. While God may know how human history will unfold, this does not mean events are foreordained. Choices people make determine the course of the human events.

God knows that the human experience will be filled with conflict and suffering. According to the book of Daniel, earthly kingdoms are like horrific beasts that rise "up out of the sea" of chaos and perpetrate destruction (7:3-8). One king, then another, and still another "will arise" to invade and conquer (8:3-12; 11:2-45). Each will inflict his own brand of suffering upon this world and especially God's people. God is not the author of this confusion, though.

Human will, not divine will, produces a violent world according to Daniel. People seeking self-sovereignty perpetuate chaos. Earthly kings set themselves "against the Lord of heaven" (5:23; 8:11) and build monuments for their glory (3:1-6; 4:31). They "exalt and magnify" themselves (11:36) rather than "honor the God who holds in his hand" their lives (5:23; 11:36-39). Arrogant humans are the reason for a world at war with itself.

God holds these ungodly authorities accountable for their actions. "At the appointed time" the reigns of evil kingdoms and tyrants end. God determines when "the time of wrath is completed" (8:23; 11:27, 35, 36; 12:7). He humbles unbelieving kings like Nebuchadnezzar, Belshazzar, and Antiochus for their arrogant disregard of his authority. He also restores when one is willing to "acknowledge that Heaven rules" (4:26). In the end all earthly powers appear before God's throne, hear the record of their deeds, and receive appropriate judgment. One is "slain and its body destroyed" while others are "stripped of their authority" (7:11-12).

According to Daniel, God's people can expect to suffer in such a world. Earthly authorities force them to live in hostile environments and tempt them to compromise with alien cultures (1:1-6). They threaten God's people with death if they do not conform (3:15; 6:7-9). These pagan powers strip God's people of their means to honor God and set up an appalling alternative that can only be described as an "abomination that causes desolation" (8:11-13; 9:27; 11:31). It is as if "the saints [have been] handed over" to the designs of evil men (7:25).

God's people are not merely victims in a world gone mad, though. They bear responsibility for the state of affairs as well. Daniel confesses that the people of the covenant "have sinned and done wrong" (9:5). They "have not obeyed the LORD" or "kept the laws he gave" (9:10). Therefore, God unleashed the forces of evil tyrants and "did not hesitate to bring the disaster" upon them (9:14). For continued disobedience God may extend judgment up to "seventy 'sevens'" in order "to finish transgression," "put an end to sin," and "atone for wickedness" (9:24). So the choices of God's people contribute to the course of events in this world. God responds to the response of people. Terrible affliction comes upon God's people because there are those who "forsake the holy covenant" and "have violated" its commands (11:30, 32). Ultimately a distinction is made between those who choose to serve God and those who do not. At the resurrection some awake to "everlasting life" and others to "everlasting contempt" (12:2).

Because human choices carry such weighty consequences, the book sets forth a major challenge to its readers. It urges them to be wise like Daniel and his three friends in the midst of an unfriendly, chaotic world. They should resolve "not to defile" themselves (1:8), to remain steadfast even if "thrown into the blazing furnace" (3:17), and to continue "praying and asking God for help" though forbidden by earthly authorities (6:11). Those who are wise must be ready to defy the king's command and "willing to give up their lives rather than serve or worship any god except their own God" (3:28). In the midst of persecution they need to "know their God" and "firmly resist" compromise with the world around them (11:32).

3. Hopeful Optimism for God's People, Not Pessimism

According to the book of Daniel, faithful living reaps rewards. The wise are vindicated for their steadfastness in the midst of affliction. Thus Daniel offers a profound word of hope that dispels the myth of pessimism. Evil does not have the upper hand. God and his people ultimately overcome both in this world and at the end of it.

The promise of Daniel is that those who are wise "will be delivered," either within this world or the next (12:1). God can rescue from defilement, a blazing furnace, or a lions' den (1:15-16; 3:26; 6:23). Though God's people suffer, they know rewards of a life well lived. Their afflictions draw them into a depth of spiritual relationship that only comes through such experiences. They are "refined, purified and made spotless" by their trials (11:35). When their suffering reaches unspeakable heights and their power is "finally broken," they are free to trust solely in the sovereignty of God (12:7). In such times, "those who are wise will understand" what the wicked do not (12:10). The violent world in which they live will still hold meaning and purpose. They will perceive that God remains in control, not humans, and trust in his sovereign power.

Daniel understands that salvation is neither earned nor deserved. Divine rescue is an act of grace. God does not intervene on the behalf of his people because they are so righteous but because of his "great mercy" (9:18).

But Daniel admits that God may not rescue within this present world. Some will perish in the heat of battle. They "will fall by the sword or be burned" (11:33). But those "who sleep in the dust of the earth will awake" on a day of resurrection and the value of living wisely will be proven at that time (12:2). They will rise to "everlasting life" and "shine . . . like the stars for ever and ever" (12:2-3). At the resurrection God vindicates the life of the wise and believers receive an "allotted inheritance" from God (12:3, 13).

The full manifestation of God's absolute rule awaits the final consummation of human history according to the book. At that point God will judge nations and exercise complete authority over this world (7:11-14, 26-27). Yet the hope of Daniel focuses more upon the present reality of God's rule rather than its future. God is at work in this world humbling kings and rescuing the faithful (3:26; 4:31; 5:30; 6:23). The forces of heaven arise to protect and defend God's people (1:9; 10:14; 12:1). Heaven responds to the prayers of the faithful and reveals his plans to them (2:20-23; 6:22; 9:23; 10:12-14). In the midst of trials, his faithful are purified and given understanding (12:10).

Therefore, faithful followers of God need not wait until the end of all things to know God's sovereign dominion. God is at work in the world right now "to will and to act according to his good purpose" (Phil 2:13). There is never a time when God's kingdom is absent from this world. For "his dominion endures from generation to generation" (Dan 4:3). "His dominion is an everlasting dominion that will not pass away, and his kingdom is one that will never be destroyed" (7:14).

COMMENTARY

I. STORIES FROM A FOREIGN LAND (1:1—6:28)

Overview

The first major portion of Daniel relates stories of Jewish captives in a foreign land. All six stories tell of life within an environment that is unfriendly toward God's faithful. These stories might be called court tales since their primary characters are kings and their attendants. Daniel plays a lead role in all of these stories except for one. In ch 3 three friends with whom Daniel is closely connected take center stage.

Each story in chs 1 to 6 has to do with a test. The three narratives in chs 1, 3, and 6 are tests of faithfulness, while chs 2, 4, and 5 relate tests of wisdom. Reading them from one perspective, they could emphasize Daniel's exceptional wisdom and faithful endurance. If the stories are about God more than Daniel, however, the emphasis shifts. These stories become tests of God's wisdom and faithfulness. The end result in each of these stories is the same. God proves trustworthy and knowledgeable, his servants are vindicated, and the world's most powerful monarchs acknowledge the sovereignty of Judah's God.

These stories prepare the reader for the visions that come in the second part of the book. They not only establish Daniel's credibility as a visionary but also present a model for faithful living in the midst of unfavorable circumstances. The visions, which portend unparalleled suffering for God's people under tyrannical oppressors, challenge readers to emulate the wisdom found in Daniel and his friends in such conditions. Both stories and visions combine to proclaim the same message: Regardless of how things might appear, God's people can trust that God remains absolutely sovereign over this world and live as if he is.

A. Food Defilement: The First Test of Faithfulness (1:1-21)

Overview

The first chapter of Daniel serves as a fitting introduction to the book. It presents the main characters of both the stories and the visions along with their Babylonian setting. The profile of the primary protagonist, Daniel, is drawn along with an initial sketch of a key antagonist, Nebuchadnezzar. The central theme of the book is also given preliminary form: God is always at work willing and doing his good pleasure. The dynamics of these characters, their setting, and the key theme create connections with ancient as well as modern audiences. Readers are drawn into the story because it is in some sense their story too.

BEHIND THE TEXT

The story that unfolds in ch 1 contains characteristics familiar to ancient audiences. Like each of the stories in the first six chapters of Daniel, it is a heroic narrative. Such stories focus on an individual or select group who embody the social and moral struggles of the community and overcome them. Episodes in the stories of Gideon, Samson, and David, for example, reflect this type of literature. Among extrabiblical material a popular Assyrian story of a righteous man named Ahikar provides several parallels in thought and expression (Pritchard 1969, 427-30).

Story of Ahikar and Daniel

The story of Ahikar has survived in several languages and versions. A Jewish version was discovered at Elephantine in Egypt where a community of Jews existed during the fifth century B.C. Ahikar was a high official in the court of an Assyrian king named Sennacherib (705-681 B.C.). Like Daniel, he was legendary for his wisdom. Because he was childless, Ahikar adopted his nephew and put him through a rigorous training in the wisdom literature of court officials. As a result of Ahikar's influence, the nephew secured a high position in the empire. The nephew, however, turned treacherous and devised a plot against his uncle that condemned him for treason. Ahikar miraculously avoided the king's death sentence like Daniel and his friends, was eventually vindicated and restored to his position. In the end the nephew dies a horrible death. The point of the story is made in the final lines: "he who digs a pit for his brother shall fall into it; and he who sets up traps shall be caught in them."

The Daniel stories also include features typical of dispersion and court tales. Dispersion tales give accounts of people, like those in the apocryphal books of Tobit and Susanna, who struggle to live faithfully outside the land of Israel. Court tales relate adventures of persons within the palace whose entertaining experiences edify audiences. The biblical stories of Joseph and Esther are this kind and bear a number of similarities with the stories in Daniel. Both are accounts of people who courageously survive the odds like Daniel. They face severe tests and emerge triumphant. There is poetic justice in each case as godly character is rewarded.

The romantic elements of these stories along with their archetypal plot motifs, patterns of repetition, and focus upon dramatic narration make them examples of great literature in the ancient and modern world. Like most biblical narrative there is a mix of realism with the mystery of the supernatural. High adventure with God is set within earthly existence. The point of each story is difficult to miss and yet deeper meanings emerge after extended reflection.

The tests of faithfulness in chs 1, 3, and 6 unfold in a similar pattern. They focus upon courage to maintain religious conviction in the midst of a hostile environment. In these stories Daniel and his friends are confronted with a threat of severe consequences for holding on to their beliefs. If they do not compromise, they risk rejection from the royal court (ch 1), facing a fiery furnace (ch 3), or being thrown into a den of lions (ch 6). In each case they choose the more difficult route and remain faithful to their convictions. They refuse to defile themselves by eating meat from the king's table, by bowing to an idol, and by ceasing to pray to God. The outcome of the test is the manifestation of God's faithfulness. The tests provide opportunity for God to prove

45

his sovereignty, and he does not disappoint. He intervenes and rescues his faithful servants, revealing his power among the pagans.

The ancient audience of Daniel held a store of memories associated with the characters and setting sketched in ch 1. Nebuchadnezzar, Babylon, and Babylonia, in particular, were symbols of hostility, oppression, and godlessness for people of Judah (vv 1-2).

The emergence of the Babylonian Empire during the seventh and sixth centuries B.C. profoundly affected the biblical story of Abraham's descendants. Judah, along with nearly every other political entity in the Middle East, was brought under its iron grip for approximately seventy years. The early days of this empire are the immediate milieu for the opening chapter of Daniel.

In 627 B.C. the death of Ashurbanipal brought to an end Assyria's dominance over the Fertile Crescent. Rebellion broke out across the empire, and a Chaldean prince named Nabopolassar led the resistance in Babylon. His military expertise and astute alliance with the Medes enabled him to dismantle the Assyrian Empire over the next twenty years. Asshur fell in 614 B.C. and Nineveh in 612 B.C. The final remnants of the Assyrian army were defeated in the summer of 605 B.C. at Carchemish.

At Nabopolassar's death in August of 605 B.C. the newly created empire passed into the very capable hands of his son Nebuchadnezzar (v 1). Babylonian influence rose to its greatest heights under the aggressive leadership of this master strategist. Further conquest and extravagant building marked his reign, which lasted from 605 to 562 B.C.

Nebuchadnezzar's status in biblical and rabbinic literature is almost legendary. He stands as a key antagonist to God's people throughout the OT. His name is mentioned more than any other foreign despot in Scripture, nearly ninety times. Throughout the book of Daniel Nebuchadnezzar's name is spelled with an *n* following the *d*. The Babylonian spelling of the name was Nebuchadrezzar with an *r* in place of the *n*. This spelling is preserved in several passages in Jeremiah and Ezekiel. Most of the time, however, the OT books prefer spelling the name Nebuchadnezzar. Whether or not this is a case of deliberate corruption of his name in order to mock the ruler is uncertain. The original Nebuchadrezzar probably means "Nabu protects the eldest son" while Nebuchadnezzar could be translated "Nabu protects the mule." Most scholars do not think it is intentional mockery. They suggest that the exchange of *n* for *r* was simply a normal kind of development as phonemes moved from one language to another (Wiseman 1985, 2-3).

Nebuchadnezzar was responsible for the ultimate humiliation of Abraham's descendants. After gaining control of Judah in 605 B.C., he systematically depleted its resources and squelched two major rebellions in 598 and 587 B.C. The latter event ended in the demolition of Jerusalem and the exile of a major portion of its population. This left the Jews without a king, temple, and homeland. It was a watershed event in OT history.

Supplied with the spoils of war and the annual tribute of subdued nations, **Babylon** became a spectacular city of beauty and wealth (v 2). Located along the banks of the mighty Euphrates River, its intimidating walls extended over seventeen miles around the city. Entrance was allowed only through imposing gates adorned with lions, bears, and dragons in colorful relief. A massive palace complex, the legendary hanging gardens, and more than fifty temples created the skyline for this remarkable city. The most impressive of the temples was dedicated to Marduk, the patron god of Babylon. It sat atop a ziggurat that measured approximately 300 x 300 feet at its base and rose to the same extent in height.

Babylon dominated the southeast portion of Mesopotamia during the first millennia B.C. Thus the region became known as **Babylonia** (v 2). The Hebrew behind this translation in Dan 1:2 is "land of Shinar" (*'ereṣ shinar*). This is a relatively rare phrase occurring only four times in the Hebrew Bible (Gen 10:10; 11:2; Zech 5:11; and here). Reference to Shinar occurs only four other times. The more common designation for the region of Babylonia, found mostly in Jeremiah and Ezekiel, is "land of the Chaldeans" (*'ereṣ kasdim*). The reference to Shinar evokes Gen 11, where humans displayed their misdirected aspirations by building the Tower of Babel. It was there that God rejected humanity's efforts to become like God. The author's use of the term further underscores the godless environment in which the events and visions of the book take place.

The book begins with a reference to **the third year of the reign of Jehoiakim** in which **Nebuchadnezzar king of Babylon came to Jerusalem and besieged it** (v 1). It refers to a time when the fortunes of Judah fell under the control of Babylon, around 605 B.C., and establishes the essential setting for this chapter as well as the book. This verse has been the subject of considerable debate among commentators over its historical reliability. In the third year of Jehoiakim Nebuchadnezzar was not yet king of Babylon, and the evidence of a siege of Jerusalem at this time is scant. After examining the evidence, many scholars believe it is not reliable history and assume the author of the book was simply not interested in historical accuracy (Hartman and Di Lella 1978, 128-29; Collins 1993, 130-33). Perhaps, some suggest, the author is merging the events of 605, 598, and 587 B.C. into one general statement (Goldingay 1989, 14; Seow 2003, 21). Other scholars, however, find reasonable basis to accept the reliability of the data (Baldwin 1978, 19-23; Archer 1985, 31-32; Miller 1994, 56-57; Longman 1999, 43-45). Still others withhold judgment because the evidence is not fully compelling in either direction (Lucas 2002, 50-52).

The reference to Nebuchadnezzar as **king of Babylon** is often explained as prolepsis. Thus it may be that Nebuchadnezzar is designated by the title for which he was best known later in life. Since the text seems to refer to events during the summer of 605 B.C., Nebuchadnezzar was not officially king as yet. His inauguration took place in September of 605 B.C. following his father's death in August.

Other data related to Dan 1:1-2 raises more difficult questions for the historian. When passages in Kings, Chronicles, and Jeremiah describe Babylon's initial takeover of Judah, they do not speak of **Jerusalem** being **besieged.** The record of 2 Kgs 24:1 is that "Nebuchadnezzar king of Babylon invaded the land, and Jehoiakim became his vassal for three years." In 2 Chr 36:6 the king of Babylon "bound him [Jehoiakim] with bronze shackles to take him to Babylon" and "took to Babylon articles from the temple." The reliability of these statements, especially the one in Chronicles, is also a matter of debate.

Jeremiah 25:1 and 46:2 complicate matters by connecting the event to the fourth rather than the third year of Jehoiakim. This is often accounted for, however, by assuming the use of different dating systems for reckoning the reign of a monarch. In Judah the typical approach was to begin counting years once the king took the throne. When the New Year was celebrated, records indicate that his second year began. In Babylon, the first year of ruling commenced only after the New Year. If Jeremiah reckoned according to Judah's system and Daniel followed the Babylonian system, then the discrepancy is explained. Historians are not sure this was the case however.

Nonbiblical evidence fails to mention a siege of Jerusalem as well. According to *The Babylonian Chronicles* the first siege of Jerusalem occurred in Nebuchadnezzar's seventh year, or 598 B.C., when Judah's revolt was squelched and Jehoiachin taken prisoner. *The Babylonian Chronicles*, however, do speak of Nebuchadnezzar subduing the region of Syria and Palestine following his victory at Carchemish in 605 B.C. Josephus may corroborate this by citing the fourth century B.C. Greek historian Berosus. According to this source, Nebuchadnezzar appears to have solidified his rule of the region before returning to Babylon to claim the throne. He "set the affairs of Egypt and the other countries in order, and committed the captives he had taken from the Jews, and Phoenicians, and Syrians, and of the nations belonging to Egypt, to some of his friends" (*Ag. Ap.* 1.19). Some scholars doubt the reliability of Berosus, however, or suggest he is referring only to mercenaries in the defeated Egyptian army.

The Babylonian Chronicles

The Babylonian Chronicles are a collection of clay tablets from ancient Mesopotamia that record key events connected to the Babylonian region. They begin with the earliest times down to the first century A.D. The material particularly focuses upon the first millennium B.C. and includes records of several events in Nebuchadnezzar's reign. Babylonian astronomers wrote these texts over a number of centuries. Modern translations in English are available in Grayson 2000.

Some scholars believe that the term translated **besieged** in Dan 1:2 does not demand an extended military action, although it is regularly used in this way. The basic meaning of the term is "to bind" or "secure" something. On the basis of 2 Chr 36:6 they suggest that Jehoiakim may have been rounded up with other despots in the region and brought before Nebuchadnezzar at Riblah in Syria. He likely swore allegiance to the Babylonians and presented enough booty from the temple treasury to convince them of his loyalty. In this proposal Dan 1:1-2 merely tells how Jehoiakim submitted to the overpowering forces of Babylon out of political expediency following the defeat of his Egyptian overlord at Carchemish.

Regardless of how the historical data of Dan 1:1-2 is understood, the subjugation of Judah to Babylon in the time of Jehoiakim provides the context for reading the story. Jehoiakim was the son of one of Judah's most devout kings, Josiah (640-609 B.C.). He did not follow his father's example, however, and steered a path toward the final demise of Judah. His blatant disregard for Israel's God earned him repeated warning and rebuke from Jeremiah the prophet (see Jer 22:13-23; 25:1-14; 26:1-6; 36:1-31).

The reign of Jehoiakim began after his father's death in 609 B.C. The Egyptian pharaoh Neco placed him in this position. Having defeated Judah's armies and killed Josiah at Megiddo, Neco first selected a younger son of Josiah, Jehoahaz, as king of Judah. Three months later he returned to Jerusalem, took Jehoahaz to Egypt, and authorized Jehoiakim to administer the kingdom. The victory of Babylonians and Medes over Egyptians and Assyrians at Carchemish in the summer of 605 B.C. changed the fortunes of Jehoiakim. The Babylonians laid claim to all of Judah and the surrounding states. At that point Jehoiakim came under the authority of the Babylonian Empire.

The narrative divides almost seamlessly into three sections: the setting (vv 1-7), the test (vv 8-14), and the outcome (vv 15-21). Each section is punctuated by reference to God's activity behind the scenes. God gives success to Nebuchadnezzar (v 2), then to Daniel (v 9), and finally to the young men (v 17).

The chapter unfolds in a chiasm. The focus upon training the young Israelites in vv 1-7 is balanced by an account of their successful training in vv 17-20. Then the desire to avoid defilement and take a test in vv 8-14 is balanced by the successful outcome of the test and avoiding defilement reported in vv 15-16. Temporal notations create an inclusion for the unit. **The first year of King Cyrus** in v 21 echoes back to **the third year of the reign of Jehoiakim** in v 1. These dates mark the extent of Judah's exile (605 to 539 B.C.), the primary setting for most events recorded in the book.

The hero of the narrative, Daniel, is gradually introduced. His name does not appear until v 6. By then, though, the reader has come to know something of his exceptional character and challenging circumstances.

IN THE TEXT

1. The Setting (1:1-7)

■ **1-2** Verses 1-7 establish the setting for the entire book as well as for the first story. These verses highlight three key features of the situation: God's people are (1) dominated by foreign powers, (2) forced to live in a foreign land, and (3) tempted to assimilate to the foreign culture. These three elements create the backdrop for the message of the book and each story or vision within it. The focus of these verses is on the fundamental tension over the clash of cultures, and they raise the central question of the book: "How can we sing the songs of the LORD while in a foreign land?" (Ps 137:4). In the context of Ps 137, this rhetorical question expresses the frustrating impossibility of living prosperously in exile. The answer to the question is, "We cannot sing." In the book of Daniel, however, the question is direct and the answers are positive. The "songs of the LORD" can be sung in a foreign land with passion.

This story is specifically dated to **the third year of the reign of Jehoiakim,** which refers to the critical year of 605 B.C. (Dan 1:1). One other story and each of the visions are introduced in reference to a particular year in the reign of a king (see 2:1; 7:1; 8:1; 9:1; 10:1). This shows a marked concern throughout the book for reading the material within a particular historical context.

Nebuchadnezzar king of Babylon is the subject of four verbs of aggression in these verses. He **came** (bô'), **besieged** (ṣûr), **carried** (causative of bô'), and **put** (causative of bô') (vv 1-2). It would seem that he is the one in control. Undoubtedly a powerful military force was deployed in order to subject Jerusalem. The author of Daniel, however, does not mention the strength of Babylonian armies as the key factor. These actions took place by the will of Judah's God. **The Lord delivered** (nātan also means "gave") them **into his hand** (v 2). This same language was used by Jeremiah when he predicted the downfall of Jerusalem (Jer 12:7; 21:10, etc.). Daniel agrees with Jeremiah. The circumstances behind the story of Dan 1 did not take place by accident. They were a fulfillment of prophecy. God had orchestrated these events. Jerusalem was given into the hands of Nebuchadnezzar as an act of divine judgment.

In Daniel God is designated by various names. The term used in Dan 1:2, **the Lord** ('ădōnāy), is frequently employed throughout the OT to highlight God's sovereign rule. It occurs eight other times in the book. These are found in the prayer of ch 9 as his favorite mode of addressing God (9:4, 7, 15, 16, 17, 19 [3 times]). Its appearance at this point subtly introduces a key theme of God's sovereign control over his people and their circumstances. This thought will be emphasized much more dramatically in subsequent passages.

According to the book of Kings, **Jehoiakim** represents the group of Judean rulers who "did evil in the eyes of the LORD" (2 Kgs 23:37). His political and spiritual incompetence appears to have hastened the end of Judah. In Daniel his role is limited to being the king who was subdued by Nebuchadnezzar. The mention of Jehoiakim in the opening verses is the only reference to a Jewish king in the book (Dan 1:1-2). Babylonian and Persian kings receive attention hereafter. This contrasts with most prophetic books where the activities of kings in Israel and Judah are prominent. The scope of Daniel is more international.

Babylonian policy included complete humiliation of their enemies. In order to reduce the prospects of rebellion, Nebuchadnezzar weakened those he conquered by depleting their resources. He accomplished this with Judah by: (1) taking **the articles from the temple of God . . . to the temple of his god** (v 2) and (2) seizing **some of the Israelites . . . to teach them the language and literature of the Babylonians** (vv 3-4). These two actions assured Babylonian control over Judah.

On the basis of 2 Chr 4 **the articles from the temple** might have included a variety of items used in its daily operations. These could be: sprinkling bowls, pots, shovels, meat fork, tongs, wick trimmers, dishes, and censers. According to Dan 5:2 goblets could be added to the list, though these might have been taken at a later time. These articles were all made of precious metals, such as gold or silver, and carried considerable value. They served as partial payment made to the overlord Babylon by the subdued vassal Judah.

The temple articles were national as well as religious treasures. They were symbols of Judah's strength and of her God's prestige. From the Babylonian perspective these articles functioned as idols representing the deity of Judah. By taking them **to the temple of his god** Nebuchadnezzar was making a statement of supremacy (v 2). This temple was likely one dedicated to Marduk, the patron god of Babylon. It was this god who enabled Nebuchadnezzar to prosper and for whom he fought his battles. The author of Daniel does not miss the point. The alignment of phrases and belabored wording of v 2 emphasize the stark reality for God's people. The power base had shifted **from the temple of God . . . to the temple of his god in Babylonia** (v 2). The initial tension in the story is more than political or cultural. It is religious. Babylon's god has seemingly subdued Judah's God. Marduk has overpowered Yahweh.

■ **3** The second element in Babylon's humiliation of Judah involved taking young men **from the royal family and the nobility** (v 3). This was part of the booty of war as well. These youths provided security for continued alliance with Babylon and could be trained to help administer the ever-expanding empire. They were, in a sense, hostages. Removing them from their homeland reduced any designs they might have had to restore Judah's freedom from Babylon. They would be trained and courted to be friends of the state.

The young men are identified as **Israelites,** literally "sons of Israel" (v 3). The author might have just as accurately spoken of "sons of Judah" since the northern kingdom no longer existed. By calling them sons of Israel the author ties this story to the bigger history of Abraham's descendents and heightens the tension between the cultural heritages of Israel and Babylon. This is the tension that underlies the drama being set up in these opening verses.

The king directed the **chief of his court officials** to oversee the training (v 3). His name is given as **Ashpenaz,** a name of Persian origin. His exact place in the hierarchy of palace personnel is difficult to determine. Some have suggested that **Ashpenaz** may be a title rather than a personal name. If so, it could mean "innkeeper." This would be fitting for the context since he seems to be in charge of accommodations for palace residents. The Hebrew term for **court officials** covers a broad range of roles in the palace. Later it came to designate eunuchs. At this point in history, though, there is no reason to assume he was a eunuch or that those under his charge became such. Whatever his precise position, the reference to his title as **chief** indicates the high level of training involved and serves to raise the stakes of the experience related in this chapter.

■ **4-5** The young men selected for training were exceptional in every way. They possessed above average physical and intellectual qualities that made them **qualified to serve in the king's palace** (v 4). The description **without any physical defect** is reminiscent of the attributes of priests and sacrifices that made them acceptable for Israel's God (Lev 21:16-23; 22:19-25). It subtly underscores further the point previously made with the temple vessels. That which should be dedicated to Yahweh is now dedicated to Marduk.

The young men's **aptitude for every kind of learning** recalls the qualities of the wise highlighted in Israel's wisdom literature (v 4). In Proverbs such persons possess both **aptitude** ("prudence," śākal) and **learning** ("wisdom," hokmâ) and are **well informed** ("know," daʿat) and **quick to understand** ("discerning," bîn). These qualities recall the description of Joseph's character in Gen 41:33 and 39. They connect Daniel and his friends with biblical wisdom tradition. Daniel in particular will display extraordinary ability within the tradition of Israelite wisdom beyond that which is found in Babylon. Daniel will be well trained in Babylonian ways. Yet the text clearly suggests that his most important preparation derives from his connections to Israel and her God.

The curriculum for training these outstanding young men was **the language and literature of the Babylonians** (v 4). The older English versions rendered **Babylonians** (*kaśdîm*) as "Chaldeans." The Chaldeans were a tribe from southern Mesopotamia that gained control over Babylon under the leadership of Nabopolassar in 626 B.C. The OT, however, refers to all people around the area of Babylon as *kaśdîm*. This was commonly done in Assyrian documents as well. Thus the translation **Babylonians** is appropriate.

In the book of Daniel *kaśdîm* refers to Babylonians three times (1:4; 5:30; 9:1). More often, though, the term is used to identify a class of learned wise men or priests (2:2, 4, 5, 10; 3:8; 4:7; 5:7, 11). The later usage is also found in the fifth century B.C. historian Herodotus (*Herodotus* 1:181-83).

The native **language** of the Chaldeans was Aramaic, the international language of the Middle East during this time. It is a close cognate to Hebrew, written with a similar alphabetic script. The official, literary language of the people of Babylon, however, was Akkadian. This required mastery of the ancient complicated system of writing known as cuneiform. The **literature of the Babylonians** also included ancient Sumerian texts copied from prior centuries and written in the same script as Akkadian. Archaeologists have unearthed a rich store of historical, economic, and religious texts in these languages. Among the religious texts are those that deal with the art of divination, a highly sophisticated profession in Babylonia. People were specially trained to decode the meaning of omens, which they believed were messages from the gods. Unusual natural phenomena, the movement of stars and even sheep livers provided insight into divine communications. The extent of this literature and intensity of instruction needed to master it is suggested by the fact that it took **three years** to become adequately trained (v 5).

Those selected for this specialized training enjoyed the benefits of eating **food and wine from the king's table** (v 5). This does not necessarily mean that they literally ate at the same table with the king. Only a select few enjoyed this privilege. The phrase simply indicates that the Israelites received the same kind of high-quality food as the king. Numerous persons in the large palace complex were provided **a daily amount** of food at state expense.

The outcome of the intense Babylonian education was to prepare these bright young men to **enter the king's service** (v 5). This could mean a variety of things. Based on the role fulfilled by Daniel in later chapters, it seems that this training prepared them to function as court sages, of which there were several categories (see comments on 2:2). The role of such persons was to act as advisers to the king. Their preparation fit them to access knowledge from the past in order to interpret and give advice for life in the present.

■ **6-7** With v 6 the hero of the book is finally introduced by name, along with three others who star in the story of ch 3. The technique of delayed introduction for the main character creates an initial suspense for the reader. A setting of conflicting cultures has already been dramatically sketched. Israelites in a foreign land are wined and dined and instructed in all the ways of the dominant culture. The threat of complete assimilation looms large. The arena is created for a hero to step forth from the oppressed community and defend the values of the group.

Four young men **from Judah** take the challenge (v 6). They are among the captives being enculturated into Babylonian society. The attention of the original audience would be drawn to the four, for they also were **among** those **from Judah** who lived under foreign domination. Could they champion the sacred beliefs of the Jewish community? How would they handle life in this hostile environment?

A final description of the process toward cultural compromise is given in v 7 and increases the drama considerably. The four Israelites are assigned **new names.** A person's name carried great significance in ancient Middle Eastern cultures. It reflected character, family relationships, and even religion. A change of name signified a significant reorientation of life. Abraham and Jacob in the OT and Peter and Paul in the NT may be the best examples of this in the Bible.

The four Israelites bore strikingly meaningful Hebrew names. **Daniel** means "my judge is God," **Hananiah** "Yahweh has shown grace," **Mishael** "who is what God is?" and **Azariah** "Yahweh has helped." Such names symbolize deep connections to the Jewish community and its God.

The **chief official** in charge of their training is presumably the same Ashpenaz from v 3. He **gave them new names** that reflect Babylonian associations (v 7). **Belteshazzar** means "protect his life" and seems to be a shortened form of either Bel-belteshazzar or Nebo-belteshazzar. Both Bel and Nebo are names of gods. Bel is another name for Marduk and Nebo (also Nabu) was his son. **Shadrach** most likely means "command of Aku." Aku was the moon god. **Meshach** appears to be the Babylonian equivalent to Mishael. It can be translated "who is like Aku?" **Abednego** may be a corruption of Abednebo, which means "servant of Nebo." Although modern knowledge of the exact meaning of each name contains some uncertainty, enough is known to reveal a pattern. The Israelites were given names that sought to identify them with the world of the Babylonians.

These Babylonian names were calculated to signify significant change in allegiance and direction for life. The import of this would not be lost on the original audience. A total loss of cultural identity, and thus religious convictions, was at stake.

Both the Hebrew and Babylonian names for the lead character of this book are appropriate. Daniel shows himself to be a man who lives as if he tru-

DANIEL

1:6-7

ly believes that God is his judge (**Daniel**). While demonstrating submission to the king and the state, he clearly holds himself ultimately accountable to God. As a result of this commitment, he becomes one whose life is divinely protected (**Belteshazzar**). His God, however, not Bel, rescues him time and again.

Throughout this section Babylonians are the primary subjects of the verbs. Nebuchadnezzar and his chief official call the shots. They **came** (v 1), **besieged** (v 1), **carried off** (v 2), **put** (v 2), **ordered** (v 3), **assigned** (v 5), and **gave . . . names** (v 7). On the other hand the Israelites are passive. The action is happening to them. The effect of this in the narrative is to underscore the subjection of Israel. This was the atmosphere of exile. On the surface, Babylon seemingly controlled the world of human events.

2. The Test (1:8-14)

■ **8** The stage is set in the opening verses for the test of vv 8-14. A gradual process of assimilation to foreign culture is described. The young men are taught the ways of Babylon and given Babylonian names. All of this is sketched in the context of absolute Babylonian domination.

In a dramatic move Daniel emerges from the midst of the Israelite trainees to take a stand for the values of the community he represents. No longer a passive pawn in the hands of an earthly tyrant, Daniel decisively takes the initiative. He lives up to his name and becomes accountable to God by resolving **not to defile himself** (v 8). The term **defile** ($g\bar{a}\,{}^{\jmath}al$) is used in the Hebrew Scriptures to indicate something or someone that is unfit for God. This may be the result of ceremonial pollution such as when a sacrifice is defective (Mal 1:7). The defilement also may be due to a breach of a moral law such as murder (Isa 59:3). In either case it is an action or condition that renders one unacceptable for fellowship with God.

The reason why Daniel determined that **the royal food and wine** would pollute his relationship to God is unclear (Dan 1:8). Some suggest that it is because of the food's association with Babylonian religion. Food at the king's table was regularly offered to Babylonian gods first. If this was Daniel's concern, though, it is difficult to explain why he accepted the vegetables. There is no evidence that these were excluded from the ritual offerings to idols.

Another suggestion is that refusing the food was Daniel's way of making a political statement. He would not cooperate fully with the Babylonian program. This position has problems as well. Throughout the book Daniel never displays anti-Babylonian views. He, in fact, seems fully loyal to his Babylonian hosts.

Several scholars conjecture that Mosaic dietary laws outlined in Lev 11 and other places may be at stake. Perhaps unclean animals were involved, preparation was inadequate, or blood was not drained. Unclean animals such as pigs and horses were certainly a regular part of Babylonian fare. Daniel's refusal of the king's food then could symbolize identification with Israel's heritage. This might explain Daniel's problem with the meat, but it does not indicate why wine is rejected. Israelite law does not forbid drinking wine unless it leads to drunkenness.

The refusal of **wine,** however, might be explained in light of Jer 51:7. In that text the prophet projects the image of Babylon as a cup of wine that "made the whole earth drunk." He warns, "The nations drank her wine; therefore they have now gone mad." Daniel displays a keen interest in Jeremiah, especially in ch 9. Perhaps refusing wine was symbolic of Daniel's desire to avoid drinking too deeply of Babylonian culture and becoming intoxicated with it.

A final proposal is that Daniel's refusal of the king's food was a way of identifying with the Judean exiles at large and mourning with them. Meat and wine were the food of the wealthy and those who celebrate. The vegetables and water requested by Daniel in v 12 is more in line with the daily fare of those at a lesser station of life. Perhaps Daniel's intent was to identify with the poverty and loss of his people in exile. Refusing the king's choice food was a sign of mourning with them.

At some later point the royal food apparently became part of Daniel's regular diet again. "In the third year of Cyrus," according to 10:3, Daniel indicates he was eating such food. He reports that he refrained from eating this food during a period of mourning, "I ate no choice food; no meat or wine touched my lips." This text suggests that the king's food was not necessarily inherently evil or contrary to Mosaic law. Abstaining from it was simply a part of the ritual of mourning.

Whatever the specific reason might have been for refusing the food, the text implies that it was an important symbol of his religious convictions. It was a determined move to avoid assimilation with the pagan culture. Daniel the Israelite chose to distinguish himself from Babylonian values and beliefs. Yahweh's hero stood against Marduk's world.

Refusing the king's fare was clearly a significant departure from the norm. Whatever Daniel's intentions might have been, it was likely interpreted as a political statement. As such his stance carried considerable risk. To highlight the severity of the situation, the narrator slows the action by relating dialogue between characters. In this way readers can feel the full implications of these events and experience the suspense as it builds. The text notes that Daniel needed to ask **for permission not to defile himself this way** (v 8). Certain things were expected of those in the training program, and the official diet was clearly one of them. To even question the food appears to be a perilous position for a trainee.

■ **9** Opportunity is provided for Daniel to take a stand because **God had** caused the official to show favor and sympathy to Daniel (v 9). This is the second time in the chapter that God's activity behind the scenes is mentioned (see v 2). **God** is credited with enabling the feelings of genuine care that Ashpenaz displayed. The official showed unusual kindness (**favor,** *hesed*) and a certain level of emotional attachment (**sympathy,** *rāḥam*) for Daniel. Through God's intervention a context was created that made faithful living possible for Daniel and his friends.

■ **10** Ashpenaz's efforts to dissuade Daniel give further indication of just how high the stakes were. He appealed to Daniel's logic as well as his emotions. They should rightly fear his **lord the king,** Nebuchadnezzar, who as absolute potentate might do anything at any time (v 10). The ruthless whims of Nebuchadnezzar are well documented in Babylonian history. He did not tolerate any appearance of disloyalty to the state. If Daniel and his friends ended up **looking worse than the other young men,** Ashpenaz could literally lose his **head.** The implication, of course, is that Daniel and his friends would fair no better.

Ashpenaz does not give Daniel a flat refusal. Instead he provides the criteria for possibly avoiding defilement. If Daniel could keep from **looking worse than the other young men,** then he would be able to have his way. Eating or not eating the king's food is not the issue. The concern is with health of the trainees. Thus a door is opened for a test that could prove that faithfulness to God will be rewarded.

■ **11** At this point Daniel turned to a lesser official, **the guard whom the chief official had appointed** over him and his friends (v 11). This **guard** (*melṣar*) apparently had direct supervision over the four Israelites, functioning as their guardian or overseer. Daniel picks up on the desire of Ashpenaz not to be involved and pursues a plan with a subordinate. This shows respect for Ashpenaz and distances him from the events should Daniel's plan fail.

■ **12-14** Daniel proposes a **test . . . for ten days** (v 12). This is a reasonable amount of time. It provides a duration long enough for the test to become valid. Over this period Daniel and his friends would eat **vegetables** and drink **water** instead of the regular provisions. The term for **vegetables** is literally "seeds" (*zērō'îm*) and could refer to anything grown from plants. This includes fruits and grains as well as vegetables. **Water** in the ancient world carried certain health risks since purification systems were not extensive. At the conclusion of the test period, the official was to make a judgment. He would compare the physical **appearance** of Daniel and his friends with that of the other trainees (v 13).

Daniel appears to submit his fate to the official. He humbly invites, **Treat your servants in accordance with what you see.** What might happen to them is suggested in Ashpenaz's words in v 10. Yet by this point in the story the reader has already come to expect the hand of God to overrule the hand of man. God has been at work in the actions of Nebuchadnezzar (v 2) and

1:9-14

Ashpenaz (v 9). One might anticipate the same divine activity for this circumstance. The official **agreed to this** (v 14), but he is only a pawn in the hands of a sovereign God.

3. The Outcome (1:15-21)

■ **15** The tension in the story has come to a climax and awaits resolution. Daniel has risked the favor of the Babylonian authorities and his place among them in order to avoid defilement. Ill health and even death could result as well. The outcomes of this test are encouraging for those who attempt the same: (1) Daniel and his friends maintain good health, (2) they avoid defilement, (3) they are given gifts of wisdom, and (4) they are brought into the king's service.

These outcomes bring resolution to the central question in the narrative: Can God's people remain faithful to their convictions in the midst of a hostile environment? The answer to that question is that it is possible not only to survive but to thrive. The outcomes are far better than expected. Daniel and his friends do not simply meet standards. They are superior to all others both physically and spiritually. Their reward is not just vindication but exaltation.

The diet of vegetables and water left the Israelites amazingly **healthier and better nourished than any of the young men who ate the royal food** (v 15). Literally they were ***better and fatter of flesh*** than the others. There is no indication in the text that such an outcome was based upon healthy eating habits. The point is not that vegetarians fair better than carnivores. In the context of this chapter, divine intervention is assumed. The health of the Israelites is miraculous. Their diet was inferior to the choice food of the empire. They should not have been healthier, but they were. The only explanation for this fact is God.

■ **16** As a result of the positive outcome of the test, the guard granted the request of Daniel and his friends. They avoided defilement by not eating the royal food. **The guard took away their choice food and the wine** (v 16). Thus they remain free from the corrupting influences of Babylonian culture. They continue to depend on God for their strength through the diet of **vegetables.** Those who seek to distinguish themselves as God's people can indeed remain free from the corrupting influences of the surrounding culture. It requires risk. But that is the nature of faith.

■ **17** At this point the test of food has been resolved. Daniel and his friends are vindicated for their faithfulness. But the narrator draws the story to a close by resolving another issue raised in vv 3-5. That is the concern of how the Israelites faired with their training. Just as they triumphed physically, they excel intellectually. By tying these two issues together in the narrative, the author accentuates the hand of God in both aspects.

The key to the intellectual superiority of the four Israelites is that **God gave knowledge and understanding** (v 17). The biblical tradition is unanimous that wisdom derives ultimately from the God of Israel (Dan 2:21; Ps 119:34; Prov 1:7; Jas 1:5). This is the third time God's initiative is highlighted in this chapter (see Dan 1:2 and 9). Each time the verb of which God is the subject is the same, **gave** (*nātan*). God gave Jerusalem to Nebuchadnezzar (v 2). He gave sympathy for Daniel to Ashpenaz (v 9). Now he gives wisdom (v 17). These three references to God's actions lift the story to a level beyond mere moral instruction. Good behavior works in concert with and under the dominion of God's gracious sovereign activity. Events unfold by divine will and not by human determination. As Prov 16:9 says, "In his heart a man plans his course, but the LORD determines his steps."

The four Israelites are divinely gifted in classic didactic wisdom, that is, in **knowledge and understanding of all kinds of literature and learning** (Dan 1:17). This included familiarity with collections of proverbs, wisdom stories, and lists of flora and fauna. Daniel, however, distinguishes himself among the four because of his gifts in mantic wisdom. That is to say, he has the ability to **understand visions and dreams.** This specialized area of wisdom involved skills in interpreting communications from the divine world. The stories in chs 2, 4, and 5 along with the visions in chs 7 to 12 demonstrate his abilities in this area.

■ **18-20** God's wisdom proved to be far more valuable than anything Babylon could offer. **At the end of the time set,** Ashpenaz **presented** his trainees to the king for an intense time of question and answer (v 18). According to v 5 "three years" was **the time set** for the training. During the interview Nebuchadnezzar uncovered something remarkable. There was **none equal** to the four Israelites (v 19). In fact he found them **ten times better than** anyone else in his kingdom (v 20). Their level of achievement is accentuated by the words **all** and **whole,** the same word in Hebrew (*kol*). The faithful Israelites showed themselves to be better than everyone else in the entire kingdom as a result of God's favor.

■ **21** The concluding verse of the narrative recalls the opening verse by referencing the reign of a king. The **first year of Cyrus** was 539 B.C. and marked the end of Babylonian power (v 21). This notation emphasizes two points: (1) Daniel had a lengthy tenure in Babylonian service and (2) he outlasted the empire. The first point suggests that one might expect further stories from the many years in the royal court. Thus the reader is prepared for additional stories in the following chapters. The second point reminds the reader that the faithful can outlive oppressive human institutions.

FROM THE TEXT

Chapter 1 explores several issues of theological and practical interest. The experience of life in exile, the conflict between convictions and culture, the risk of righteous living, and the God who overrules are some of the more prominent themes that emerge from the text.

The life of faith must be lived out in the context of exile. The book of Daniel describes a setting familiar to the people of God. It is the setting of exile, a foreign land of displaced peoples. Life in this environment must be lived among those who are hostile toward God. It is a world in which believers feel alienated from the mainstream of the surrounding culture. They do not quite fit. According to Jesus this is the lot of all who would be his disciples. They must live in a world that is not their home, a world at odds with the kingdom of God (John 17:14).

The first chapter of Daniel describes the nature of the exilic experience. Daniel and the other Israelite youth are swept into a world over which they have no control. Babylonians orchestrate the events of the day, and their hostility toward the faith is obvious. Sometimes it is overt, at other times more subtle. They attack and subdue the holy city, bringing humiliation upon God's people. Sacred vessels of God's temple are desecrated. These become treasures proudly displayed in the temples of false gods symbolizing the triumph of evil over good. The future hope of God's kingdom appears to be held hostage by unfriendly hosts. Israel's most promising youth are indoctrinated into the ways of the alien culture. They learn the vocabulary and worldview of its people. They are wined and dined on Babylon's best. Finally, those who hold the future of the kingdom in their hands are given names that strip them of any connections to their God.

Jesus warned his disciples that the world was a hostile environment. It would hate them as it had hated him (John 15:18-20). The world is at war with the ways of God, whether or not God's people recognize it. The prince of this world, represented by Nebuchadnezzar in our text, wages a constant battle against God's elect (Eph 6:10-11). All Christians, then, are in some sense persons who live life as aliens in a foreign country. They are far from home, in exile for the moment, facing hostile forces. Their true "citizenship is in heaven" (Phil 3:20).

Convictions of the faithful will often conflict with their culture. Living in an alien environment creates major challenges for those who would remain faithful to their convictions. Daniel found that his personal values brought him into direct conflict with the dominant Babylonian culture. This conflict did not remain only in the realm of ideas. It eventually found expression in the ordinary exercises of life, as all true convictions will. For Daniel eating certain food became the point of practical application of his beliefs.

Sociologists have documented the powerful influence of social knowledge upon personal knowledge. Some theorists even suggest that all individual beliefs and understandings are derived ultimately from our environment. The biblical concept of social freedom, however, suggests that people can choose ideas and courses of action that run contrary to the dominant culture. The heart of prophetic ministry in ancient Israel rested heavily upon this maxim. With this the book of Daniel clearly agrees.

How persons should interact with their surrounding culture presents believers with one of the most demanding questions of life. Jesus provided a basic principle for his followers in the directive to be in the world but not of it (John 17:15-16). He illustrated this teaching in his own life when asked about paying taxes to Caesar. "Give to Caesar what is Caesar's, and to God what is God's," he said (Matt 22:21). Paul and Peter also recognized the tension Christians face as citizens of two worlds. Each apostle admonished believers to practice good citizenship in this world (Rom 13:1-7; 1 Pet 2:12-16) while keeping their focus upon the other (Col 3:1-2; 1 Pet 2:9-11). Christians are to live fully engaged with their culture and yet avoid being squeezed into its mold (Rom 12:2).

Various strategies for applying the teachings of Jesus have been proposed by Christians over the centuries. One might interface with the surrounding culture by (1) rejecting and withdrawing from it, (2) identifying and embracing its best values, (3) living alongside it, and (4) working to transform it. Each might be a legitimate approach in the right circumstances.

Within the book of Daniel we can see several of these strategies employed. Daniel embraces some of the highest values of Babylonian culture by receiving training in its literature and languages. At the same time he lives with the paradox brought on by a new name. He continues to go by his Hebrew name Daniel most of the time, though he apparently answers to the Babylonian Belteshazzar as well. The text records no protest on this point and thus acknowledges the value of keeping a foot in both worlds.

At one point, though, Daniel draws the line and rejects the values of the dominant culture. The royal food represents a level of compromise he is not willing to make. Prudently the biblical text does not reveal the reason that the food was unacceptable. The ambiguity of the text communicates a principle rather than a particular. The point was not to establish an absolute standard with regard to certain foods that defile and others that do not. Such things are more often relative to the setting in which they occur. But the message of Daniel is clear: believers must distinguish an identity that is separate from the dominant culture at some point. They belong to another kingdom. Their values inevitably come into conflict with the cultures of this world.

In the end Daniel's rejection of particular values held by Babylonian culture provides a means for transforming it. The king takes note of the four Israelites and puts them in positions of influence within his realm. This point is more profoundly emphasized in later chapters when kings offer honor to the God of Daniel and bestow additional favors upon the Israelites (2:47-48; 3:28-30; 4:37; 5:29; 6:26-28).

Righteous living requires risk. As the story indicates, taking a stance against the dominant culture involves risk. For Daniel it meant misunderstanding, disfavor, and demotion at the least. At the most it could have resulted in ill health and his death. It also meant bringing other people into potential peril. Those in authority over Daniel were placed in jeopardy if he failed the test.

Daniel determined that holding to his convictions was worth the consequences, whatever they may be. The exchanges one must make to remain faithful can often carry a considerable price tag. Jesus taught that the cost of discipleship was high. His followers should count the cost and be ready to risk (Luke 14:26-32). Loss of a hand, foot, or eye is better than caving in to the world (Mark 9:43-46). In fact everything must become negotiable. In the end nothing can be held back (Luke 14:33). Subsequent stories in Dan 3 and 6 will make this point even more clearly.

In spite of outward appearances God rules. The book of Daniel examines the sovereignty of God from every angle and the implications of that truth for the life of the believer. Chapter 1 explores the realities of living faithfully on the underside of power. Daniel is subject to human forces beyond his control. Yet those forces do not ultimately determine the outcome. In reality God overrules Daniel's life. Being under the hand of Nebuchadnezzar does not mean being out of the hand of God.

At three significant junctures in the text God intervenes in Daniel's life. God allows the judgment of Jerusalem at the hand of Nebuchadnezzar (v 2), prompts the favor of Ashpenaz toward Daniel (v 9), and enables the learning of the four Israelite youths (v 17). Thus God proves to be faithful in the first test of faithfulness.

The implications of these three divine activities are profound. The first suggests that the circumstances of Daniel's life are no accident. God has placed him and his friends in the land of exile on purpose. They participate in a much larger story than simply their own. That which seems disruptive and overwhelming fits into the flow of the divine drama. Providence overrules. What people intended for evil, God intended for good (Gen 50:20).

The second intervention of God in Daniel's life reminds us that "God is faithful; he will not let you be tempted beyond what you can bear. But when you are tempted, he will also provide a way out so that you can stand up under it" (1 Cor 10:13). The potential for right living is divinely arranged for Daniel. Human determination is not enough to deal with a hostile world. God must provide opportunity for Daniel to take his stand. He causes Ashpenaz to feel favorable toward the young Israelite, which leads to Daniel's opportunity to do the right thing. Human effort combines with divine grace to keep Daniel from defilement. His righteousness is by grace not by works (Eph 2:8-9).

This truth makes the text something more than a simple moral teaching.

Daniel must choose well. But his choices alone do not determine the outcome. If God does nothing, then nothing is done. Those who would dare to be like Daniel need to be aware that they are working in concert with God. Apart from God there is no righteous person. Righteous living comes from God (Phil 3:9).

The third activity of God mentioned in this chapter suggests that the amenities of Babylonia do not serve as the key to success for Daniel and his friends. God is the true source for all that is good in life. Just as royal food from the Babylonian court proved unnecessary to nourish Daniel's health, so also Babylonian training was not essential to nourish his mind. Daniel "does not live on bread alone but on every word that comes from the mouth of the LORD" (Deut 8:3; Matt 4:4).

The provision of God is not just equal to that given by men, but it is far better. God's plan for nourishing the body produced youths much healthier than their counterparts. Likewise God's gift of wisdom made the Israelites ten times better. There is no comparison between human and divine provisions. "For the foolishness of God is wiser than man's wisdom, and the weakness of God is stronger than man's strength" (1 Cor 1:25).

All that Daniel and his friends accomplish in subsequent chapters is solidly placed in context by the opening chapter. Their achievements and promotion all come from God. They live "not by might nor by power, but by [God's] Spirit" (Zech 4:6). They are divinely resourced for their role among the exiles of Israel as are all believers in every age and every setting.

B. Dream of a Statue: The First Test of Wisdom (2:1-49)

Overview

The story of ch 2 narrates another test for the hero of the book and his God. This time it is a test of wisdom. Like chs 4 and 5 in the book, Daniel's gifts as an interpreter of divine signs are put on the line. Daniel is pitted against the other wise men of Babylon in a life-and-death contest devised by Nebuchadnezzar. The marked contrast between the wise men and Daniel provides the means to prove the wisdom of Daniel and, more importantly, his God.

BEHIND THE TEXT

Chapter 2 introduces the Aramaic section of the book. Beginning in v 4 the original language of the text shifts from Hebrew, the language of Jews, to Aramaic, the international language of the empire. This continues through ch 7, after which Hebrew is employed to finish relating the rest of the book. Precisely why this happens is difficult to determine, and scholars are divided about it. At the very least the phenomenon reflects the bilingual culture from which the literature emerged.

Whatever the original reason for the shift from Hebrew to Aramaic for six chapters, the feature is important to the design of the book and an understanding of its unity. Since the Aramaic section includes both stories and visions, it becomes a means of assuring that the reader will interpret the visions of chs 7 to 12 in reference to the stories of chs 1 to 6. The two sections of the book have been brought together by the use of Aramaic.

The Aramaic section itself is strongly bound together by a chiasmic structure. This structure signals the reader that chs 2 and 7, the beginning and ending of the chiasm, echo one another in some way. Both deal with four earthly realms that are subdued by divine intervention. Chapters 3 and 6 also balance one another in their focus upon divine rescue from oppressive powers. The central section of the chiasm, chs 4 and 5, emphasize God's humbling of earthly monarchs. The chapters are thus arranged as follows:

A—Ch 2: Dream of Four Realms
    B—Ch 3: Rescue from Furnace
        C—Ch 4: Humbling of Nebuchadnezzar
        C'—Ch 5: Humbling of Belshazzar
    B'—Ch 6: Rescue from Lions' Den
A'—Ch 7: Vision of Four Realms

The three couplets of the chiasm in chs 2—7 reflect the three interventions of God related in ch 1. This further unifies the book. In 1:17 God gave a gift of interpretation of dreams and visions to Daniel. This gift is employed in chs 2 and 7 to reveal the mysteries of the four realms. In 1:9 God works around reluctant royal authorities in order to provide deliverance. Similarly in chs 3 and 6 God trumps the plans of kings and miraculously rescues his people. Finally, in 1:2 God humbled King Jehoiakim by handing his city over to his enemy. So also in chs 4 and 5 God humbles kings, the Babylonian kings Nebuchadnezzar and Belshazzar. Thus the three interventions of God in ch 1 become programmatic for structuring the Aramaic section. This feature binds the work into an inextricable unity and reminds the reader that each story and vision should be understood in light of the whole.

The Use of Hebrew-Aramaic in Daniel

The use of two languages in the book of Daniel has caused considerable discussion among scholars. Some have suggested that the phenomenon is a clue to the development of the book. Perhaps the Aramaic section represents older material that was incorporated into the final work that eventually attached an introduction and the final five chapters in Hebrew (Montgomery 1927, 88-99). Others have proposed that the entire book was originally composed in Aramaic and only partially translated into Hebrew in order to be included in the canon of Judaism. The reason chs 2—7 were not translated into Hebrew, according to this theory, is that the considerable dialogue in this section would be more authentic if heard in the language in which it was originally spoken (Hartman and Di Lella 1978, 14-15). Still another proposal has been that the entire book was composed in Hebrew but an Aramaic version was developed for those who could not read Hebrew. When a portion of the Hebrew text was lost, the Aramaic version supplied the missing material (Bevan 1892, 26-28).

A more widely held view is that the text was originally written in two languages in order to highlight the content of the sections for Jewish and non-Jewish audiences. The Aramaic section would highlight material of particular interest to a broader audience, and the Hebrew section would focus more upon Jewish matters (Miller 1994, 47-48).

The simplest suggestion for a shift in languages is that it reflects the multilingual cultural setting out of which the book emerged (Driver 1900, xxii). Alternation between languages is a common feature in such cultures. The book of Ezra demonstrates similar tendencies in its use of Aramaic.

In many ways this narrative parallels a familiar patriarchal story of the Jews, that of Joseph interpreting Pharaoh's dream in Gen 41. Like Joseph, Daniel is a captive in a foreign land (v 12) called upon to interpret a king's troubling dream (v 14). Local experts in the art of interpretation fall short (v 8), but the Jewish captive comes through by the power and grace of his God (v 16). In the end he is honored with position and authority in the king's realm (vv 40-43).

Though there are these parallels between the two stories, ancient readers would likely notice significant differences as well. In particular Daniel's situation is more ominous than Joseph's. The king is unreasonable and suspicious, the wise men face the threat of death, and the dream itself carries a more far-reaching message. Thus the drama in the Daniel story is considerably more intense than that in the Joseph story.

The tension in the story of Dan 2 is accomplished through various scenes of the inner workings of the Babylonian royal court. While such glimpses of conversations and intrigues of the palace are entertaining, they are also calculated to heighten the emotional response of an ancient reader. The conflict between a king and his courtiers makes for a captivating drama.

Babylon's most famous and feared king, Nebuchadnezzar II (605-562 B.C.), becomes significantly animated in the story. He is portrayed as unreasonably demanding, unduly suspicious, and irrationally ruthless. This characterization fits well with what is known of him, and other ancient Near Eastern tyrants, from extrabiblical records. Kings ruled with unquestioned authority in the ancient world. Stories from biblical and rabbinic sources particularly accentuate Nebuchadnezzar's callous disregard for life. His capacity for unusually cruel treatment of captives is highlighted in 2 Kings where the fall of Jerusalem is recorded. The text notes, "They killed the sons of Zedekiah before his eyes. Then they put out his eyes, bound him with bronze shackles and took him to Babylon" (2 Kgs 25:7).

In the Daniel story Nebuchadnezzar declares that, if the wise men do not do what he wants, he will have them **cut into pieces** and their **houses turned into piles of rubble** (Dan 2:5). Both fates would have been horrifying to persons of the ancient world. Bodily dismemberment and the destruction of one's home were both dishonoring to individuals as well as to their families. Unfortunately, such treatment of subjects was typical for despots in ancient times. Cyrus gave a similar threat in one of his edicts recorded in Ezra 6:11, which reads, "Furthermore, I decree that if anyone changes this edict, a beam is to be pulled from his house and he is to be lifted up and impaled on it. And for this crime his house is to be made a pile of rubble."

The second year of Nebuchadnezzar's **reign** (Dan 2:1) would have taken place from Nisan (March/April) 603 to Nisan 602 B.C. At this early juncture, Nebuchadnezzar faced considerable opposition both inside and outside his empire. According to *The Babylonian Chronicles*, an insurgency in the western portions of his empire demanded a large-scale military action during this year.

Some scholars note a possible incongruity between the dates given in ch 1, which took place at the beginning of Nebuchadnezzar's reign, and those in ch 2. One might expect more time to elapse between the events recorded in these chapters. In ch 2 Daniel seems to be counted among the wise men of Babylon, but his training period, according to 1:5, was to be three years. To complicate the issue further, in 2:25 Daniel is introduced to the king as if he is unknown.

Efforts to reconcile the date with ch 1 have taken one of two tracks. One solution is to understand ch 2 taking place during the training period of Daniel. The events of ch 2 then would be a flashback. They would have occurred before 1:18-20, which was recorded earlier in order to provide an overview of Daniel's career. This helps explain why Daniel does not seem to be known to the king in 2:25, but it does not account for his status among the established wise men of the kingdom.

Another proposal is to take the story in ch 2 as occurring soon after the training period ends. This is possible because of the Hebrew practice of counting inclusively and the Babylonian method of computing the reigns of kings. On this basis the three years for Daniel's training can be reckoned within the first two years of Nebuchadnezzar. The first year of Daniel's training would correspond with Nebuchadnezzar's accession year from Elul (August/September) 605 to Nisan 604 B.C. According to the Babylonian system, the first year of Nebuchadnezzar's reign did not begin until the New Year was celebrated in the month of Nisan 604 B.C. Thus Daniel's second year of training would have taken place over Nebuchadnezzar's first year from Nisan 604 to Nisan 603 B.C. The third year of training would have occurred during Nebuchadnezzar's second year from Nisan 603 to Nisan 602 B.C. Thus, sometime during Nebuchadnezzar's second year the three years of training for the Jewish exiles would come to an end (1:18) and the events of ch 2 could occur.

Though this proposal allows for a natural reading of the text, it is not without its difficulties. The king's lack of knowledge of Daniel still remains unexplained. If this position is adopted, then one must assume that either the king has a short memory or formal introductions were obligatory before royalty.

Another way to deal with the text is to acknowledge that the dating is wrong and should be at least the fourth year of Nebuchadnezzar or later. One extant Old Greek manuscript of Daniel (*Papyrus 967*) does read "twelfth" in place of "second," but this reading is not likely original. According to scholars who take this position, the reason for the inaccuracy is that the author of Daniel was more concerned with the impact of the story than with historical details and may not have known his history very well.

Based on this incongruity and others, many commentators believe the story is primarily fictitious. They note several other implausible features in the text: (1) the absence of Daniel and his friends from the first scene (v 13), (2) the commander's deference to Daniel (vv 14-15), (3) Daniel's ability to access the king when others cannot (v 16), (4) the incredulous act of discovering another person's dream as well as interpreting it (vv 29-45), and (5) Daniel's remarkable promotion within the kingdom (v 48). These features convince a number of scholars that this chapter is essentially fiction (see, for example, Anderson 1984, 9-26; Fewell 1991, 23-37; Seow 2003, 33-42). Other scholars prefer to accept the historicity of the story and propose ways to reconcile incongruities (see, for example, Miller 1994, 75-105; Longman 1999, 73-93; Duguid 2008, 17-44). Regardless of one's view on the material's historicity, both kinds of interpreters can examine the text to discover its theological message.

This story ushers the reader deep into the world of Babylonian wise men. It is a world of **magicians, enchanters, sorcerers, diviners,** and **astrologers** (vv 2 and 27). While much information is available to scholars regarding wisdom in the ancient world, the groups mentioned in this story are not easily distinguished from one another. Each of them may have operated from a specialized body of knowledge and skills, but current knowledge allows scholars only to suggest certain tentative distinctions.

Magicians (*harṭummîm*) seem to have been Egyptian specialists in the art of exorcism. This is the same term used for the Egyptian magicians in the Joseph story of Gen 41. Assyrian and Babylonian sources speak of such foreign specialists being employed in their royal courts. The local Mesopotamian counterparts to the Egyptian magicians may have been the **enchanters**

(ʾaššāpîm). According to extrabiblical texts their skills included dealing with various illnesses in humans. They offered prescribed incantations to provide remedies for diseases. **Sorcerers** (mĕkaššĕpîm) may signify another group of conjurers, though the term could be a general designation that includes the first two terms. Their specialty may have been casting spells since their name could refer to the making of charms and potions from herbs. The only time these persons are mentioned in the book of Daniel is in 2:2.

Diviners (gāzĕrîn) might be identified as fortunetellers. Their name is related to the idea of "cutting" and "determining" as in determining a future. The final group, the **astrologers** (kaśdîm), apparently studied the stars to find answers to life's dilemmas. Throughout chs 2 to 5 this term refers to a class of wise men who take the lead in speaking to the king. The term originally designated a tribal group responsible for founding the Babylonian dynasty under Nabopolassar in 626 B.C. This usage is found in Dan 5:30 and 9:1 and possibly in 1:4 and 3:8. Eventually the term came to designate a group of priestly wise men. One might assume that the kaśdîm dominated the Babylonian priesthood and eventually gave their name to it. This would be similar to what happened with the Levites in Israel and the magi in Media.

Daniel's Usage of *Kaśdîm*

Some scholars have suggested that Daniel's usage of kaśdîm could provide evidence for dating the book. The term refers to Babylonians two times (5:30 and 9:1) and a class of wise men seven times (2:2, 4, 5, 10; 4:7; 5:7, 11). Twice the term could be translated either way (1:4 and 3:8). The use of kaśdîm to designate a group of wise men has been taken by some to indicate a late date for the book, since such technical usage might develop over time. Similar use of the term by Herodotus in the fifth century B.C., however, undermines this argument (*Herodotus* 1:181-83). In the end most scholars agree that the way that Daniel employs the term kaśdîm cannot be used to date the material.

The wise men of Babylon and of Israel shared much in common but also differed in important ways. Both were charged with knowing and preserving the collective wisdom of their culture. This included both didactic and speculative forms of literature. Proverbs, riddles, and a form known as "instructions" provided guidance for living in harmony with the order of the universe. Stories of innocent sufferers and other literature reflected upon the great mysteries of life.

Israelite wise men sought to understand the world that God had made and provided insight on how to live successfully within it. Babylonian wise men, however, moved beyond this point. They functioned from a different worldview. Theirs was a world filled with evil spirits and capricious gods. They employed their wisdom to interpret messages from the divine realm and to manipulate spiritual forces for their own advantage. The former is known as divination while the latter can be designated magic or sorcery. When Babylonian wise men explained the meaning of a dream or omen they also performed rituals to avert the evil portended in them. By contrast Daniel is able to interpret the dream, but he does not involve himself in any of the other practices of the Babylonians. The biblical record consistently condemns all forms of sorcery employed among Israel's neighbors (Deut 18:9-13) and in particular that which was found in Babylon (Isa 47:9-15).

Within this context the intense drama associated with the dream of a king is in no way overdone. Throughout the ancient world dreams were taken very seriously. They were understood as a primary means for divine communication with humans. Many times their messages were not positive, so Nebuchadnezzar's angst is understandable. Numerous texts from ancient Egypt and Mesopotamia provide a wealth of information regarding ancient understanding on this matter. Dreams and their interpretation were carefully recorded along with historical events that followed them. These were systematized and studied by persons specifically trained in the art of dream interpretation. Such are presumably some of the kinds of texts that Daniel and his friends might have studied in their training (1:4).

Within the book of Daniel two dreams of Nebuchadnezzar are interpreted. The other one is found in ch 4. Both are troubling and do not bode well for the king. In each case Daniel provides interpretation after the other Babylonian wise men fail to do so and Daniel's God is acknowledged as supreme among the gods by Nebuchadnezzar. Apart from these similarities the report of these dreams and their content are quite different. Chapter 4 is relayed mostly as a first person testimony from Nebuchadnezzar while ch 2 is a third person narrative. The king recounts his dream to Daniel in ch 4, but in ch 2 Daniel must discover what the dream is on his own. The dream in ch 4 focuses more upon events personally related to Nebuchadnezzar and his lifetime. The dream in ch 2 envisions things beyond Nebuchadnezzar's contemporary setting into the realms of his successors.

Dreams in the Hebrew Scriptures

Israelites took dreaming as seriously as other peoples of the ancient world. According to the biblical record, they believed that God might choose to communicate with them through dreams as well as by other means. In addition to the law of Moses, the prophets, the Urim, and even some forms of divination, it was believed that God sometimes spoke through dreams (see 1 Sam 28:6).

The Bible references two basic kinds of dreams. In one kind God speaks directly to the person who was dreaming. In the other a symbolic story is conveyed. Among those who heard God's voice in a dream were Jacob (Gen 28:12-15) and Solomon (1 Kgs 3:5-15). At times prophets are said to have received their messages from God through dreams (Jer 23:25-28). Dreams that consisted of symbolic stories needed interpretation. The two great interpreters of dreams in biblical literature were Joseph and Daniel.

Not every dream was considered a communication from God in the Bible. There are references to ordinary dreams that had no particular religious significance (Pss 73:20; 126:1). Also certain texts warn that some people might falsely claim to hear from God in a dream (Jer 29:8).

Of all the canonical connections to Dan 2 the message and images of Isaiah are most pervasive (see Seow 2003, 35-36). The God behind the action in Dan 2 is the one who "makes fools of diviners, who overthrows the learning of the wise" (Isa 44:25). He reveals "hidden things unknown" (Isa 48:6) to a troubled king. Like the pulverized world powers in Nebuchadnezzar's dream, the enemies of God become "like chaff" on a threshing floor. "The wind will pick them up, and a gale will blow them away" (Isa 41:16). The crushing rock in Nebuchadnezzar's dream grows until it becomes a "mountain" that dominates the landscape of earth (Isa 2:2-4). In the end Nebuchadnezzar did what Isaiah predicted all pagan kings would do when they "bow down before you with their faces to the ground" (Isa 49:23). These and other allusions to Isaiah prompt the informed reader to hear the story of Dan 2 in a particular way. Like Isaiah, Daniel's story is a message of hope and instruction for people functioning in a world dominated by foreign powers. God is "doing a new thing" through his servant Daniel. He is overruling the authorities of this world and "making a way in the desert" of Judah's exile (Isa 43:19).

A series of scenes of dramatic narration compose the story of Dan 2. These scenes are arranged in a chiasmic structure. Two extended dialogues involving the king and his wise men begin and end the story. Their structure and content serve to heighten the contrast between the Babylonian wise men in the first scene (vv 1-13) and Daniel in the final one (vv 26-49). Another couplet of scenes that offset one another includes those containing conversations involving Daniel, Arioch, and the king (vv 14-16 and vv 24-25). These couplets frame the central scene of the unit where Daniel and his friends seek and receive revelation from God concerning the king's dream (vv 17-23). The story's overall chiasmic structure focuses the reader's attention upon the central section. This scene climaxes with a hymn of thanksgiving extolling the character of God (vv 20-23). This hymn explicitly articulates the main point of the story, which is also the essential message of the dream. Thus the scenes in the story unfold as follows:

A—Scene 1 (vv 1-13): The King and His Wise Men
    B—Scene 2 (vv 14-16): Daniel, Arioch, and the King
        C—Scene 3 (vv 17-23): Daniel Before God
    B'—Scene 4 (vv 24-25): Daniel, Arioch, and the King
A'—Scene 5 (vv 26-49): The King and His Wise Man

I. Scene I: The King and His Wise Men (2:1-13)

■ **I** The first sentence of the story establishes a major character (**Nebuchad-nezzar**), a historical setting (**the second year**), and a problem (**dreams**) that needs resolution (v 1). The key character, the great Babylonian king Neb-uchadnezzar, is presented without much introduction. From ch 1 the reader knows that he was the king who had humiliated the Jews and dominated their lives as captives in his domain (1:1-5). In the current story his character takes on more definition as he interacts with other characters.

The setting for the story is early in the career of Nebuchadnezzar, **the second year** of his reign. As with most newly acclaimed kings in the ancient world, he faced considerable opposition at this time and was still solidifying his rule.

Whether or not the unsettled state of the empire has something to do with the king's troubling dreams the text does not say. What is clear is that the dreams got the king's attention. He **was troubled** and **could not sleep** (v 1). Literally the text reads *his spirit was struck.* The poignant term *struck* (*pāʿam*) suggests the alarming nature of the dreams. It is a word used to speak of a hammer hitting an anvil or bell. Ancient people paid close attention to their dreams since they were viewed as possible communications from the gods. Often the message contained in them was foreboding, so concern to have them interpreted is understandable. Anxiety increased when that message re-mained without interpretation.

The text speaks in the plural about Nebuchadnezzar's **dreams** (v 1), but only one dream is the subject of the story. The use of the plural in this case could indicate that the dream reoccurred or that the king was simply in a state of dreaming.

■ **2-3** Nebuchadnezzar's answer to his problem is to call upon the best wis-dom Babylon could offer. He summons **magicians, enchanters, sorcerers and astrologers** to his court (v 2). The possible meaning of each of these terms has already been discussed in *Behind the Text*. This list includes a portion of the various kinds of wise men available to him.

Kings in the ancient world surrounded themselves with numerous advis-ers whose job it was to provide input on matters of the state. The list here is not meant to be exhaustive or definitive but rather representative. A recurring literary technique of the book of Daniel is to pile up terms for dramatic effect. In this case the list of wise men accentuates the vastness of Babylon's re-sources. Nebuchadnezzar gathers Babylon's most accomplished experts to ad-dress his problem. Within the world at this time none could compare with the Babylonians in such matters.

DANIEL

2:1-3

The four groups mentioned all functioned in similar manner for the king. Their primary role was to interpret the meaning of various communications from the gods and to provide direction for dealing with threatening messages found in them. Their practical expertise lay in prescribing rituals and incantations that might diminish the evil effects conveyed by omens or dreams.

The king's purpose for calling the wise men together is so that they might **tell him what he had dreamed** (v 2). This hints at the uniqueness of the king's request and begins to build the drama of this section. Literally the king tells his advisers *I dreamed a dream and my spirit is troubled to know the dream* (v 3). The ambiguity of the king's request creates attention. It could be taken to mean that he wants to know either what the dream was or what it means. In fact he wants both. The king is not asking merely to have the dream interpreted. He wants his wise men to tell him what the dream was.

■ **4** The wise men assume he meant the former since that was the usual procedure. Dreams were told. Then interpreters searched their dream books for parallels and provided interpretation. So **the astrologers,** speaking on behalf of all the wise men, request the king to follow proper protocol, **Tell . . . the dream, and we will interpret it** (v 4).

The wise men began their speech showing appropriate honor, **O king, live forever!** (v 4). While this address is a typical respectful greeting for a monarch, it is also ironic in this context. As the dream will reveal, neither the king nor his kingdom will live forever, but God's kingdom will.

■ **5** The king makes it clear that he is determined to break with traditional procedures. He **firmly decided** to have them tell the dream and then interpret it (v 5). To add weight to his decision he utters a threat and a promise. If the wise men do not perform their duty, they will be treated as enemies of the king. They will be **cut into pieces** and their **houses turned into piles of rubble** (v 5). These were no idle threats. Dismemberment and destruction of one's house were regular penalties meted out by ancient monarchs. Both punishments were designed to bring dishonor on individuals as well as their families.

■ **6** On the other hand, if the wise men were able to grant the king's request, they were promised **gifts and rewards and great honor** (v 6). Such benefits might include fine clothing and jewelry (see 5:16-17) as well as promotion in the ranks of administrators (see 2:48).

■ **7** A second time the advisers request the king to follow normal procedures. They use almost the exact same words as before but place the object (**the dream**) before the verb in the Aramaic (v 7). This emphasizes their point. They must know the dream first before they can interpret it.

■ **8-9** The king's response is to accuse his advisers of treason and let them know he is not backing down from his demands. He suspects them of collusion. They are trying to **gain time . . . hoping the situation will change** (vv 8-

9). Perhaps in the interim, he suggests, they will feed him **misleading and wicked things** in order to pacify him (v 9).

■ **10** The final speech of the advisers closes the dialogue with the king and punctuates the point of the conversation. The demand is impossible. The advisers have no capacity to grant the request because there is **not a man** capable of such a thing (v 10). The demand has no parallel because **no king . . . has ever asked such a thing** (v 10). The question has no answer because it is **too difficult** (v 10).

■ **11** As the advisers finish their speech they ironically suggest the answer to their dilemma and foreshadow the resolution in the story. They confess that **no one can reveal it to the king except the gods** (v 11). Here is the central theme of ch 2. True wisdom comes from the divine realm. As far as the Babylonians could see, though, the gods **do not live among men** (v 11). That is, they do not readily share wisdom with humans. In stark contrast Daniel will demonstrate in this story that his God does reveal his wisdom to humans.

The cycle of three speeches between the king and his wise men in vv 3-11 highlights the unreasonableness of the king's demand. The technique of three repetitions effectively serves to heighten the drama of the impossible request.

Throughout this section some form of the verb *ḥăwah* occurs six times. It can be translated **tell** but conveys the idea of "show" or "explain." It is often coupled with *pĕšar* ("interpretation"), giving the sense of "reveal an interpretation" (2:4, 6*a*, 6*b*, 7, 9). Along with these the verb *yādaʿ* occurs twice in the causative form, meaning "make known" (2:5, 9). Also the term *nāgād*, "declare" or "reveal," occurs once in 2:2. These are words often associated with the reception or declaration of divine revelation. The concentration of these terms in this section emphasizes that the king's search is for divine understanding.

■ **12** The king's response to his advisers indicates how serious he was about the matter. He **ordered the execution of all the wise men of Babylon** (v 12). Nebuchadnezzar has been characterized throughout this scene as a typical ancient tyrant. He has been portrayed as troubled (vv 1-3), stubborn (v 5), selfishly magnanimous (v 6), suspicious (vv 8-9), and unreasonably demanding (v 10). Finally he becomes **angry and furious** and orders the murder of his advisers (v 12). Such was the portrait of the ancient monarch. The Persian king Darius the Great, for example, displayed many of these same qualities. He carried out a massacre of his wise men approximately a century later when he discovered insurrection among the ranks.

■ **13** At this point **Daniel and his friends** enter the story for the first time (v 13). The reason for their absence from the court exchange in vv 3-11 is not explained. Since 1:20 identifies these men as "ten times better than all the magicians and enchanters in his whole kingdom" one might assume they would

2:9-13

be present earlier. Some view this incongruity as a typical device in fictional works employed to dramatize a hero's entrance into the story. Others assume that only the more experienced leaders of the wise men were summoned earlier and that Daniel was not among those as yet.

In either case, the delay in introducing the Jewish exiles until the end of the opening scene is an excellent technique of the storyteller. It brings the tension of the story toward a climax. Their appearance in the narrative raises the stakes, for now the original readers have someone with which to identify. The threat of death takes on personal proportions.

The lack of introduction for Daniel and his friends indicates that the author is depending upon ch 1 for knowledge of these characters and their significance to the story. These Jewish captives, whom God had rescued in ch 1, are in danger once again. Their predicament was worse than before and for no fault of their own. They were in line for execution.

The opening scene of the story begins with the problem of a troubling dream that needs resolution. The tension builds steadily as no solution is found. Instead the problem becomes an insurmountable obstacle. The king is unreasonable. He sabotages his own quest by refusing to tell his dream. No answers and no resources among humans are available to resolve the issue. Lives of an entire population within the kingdom are threatened. Finally, and most importantly for the original readers, the survival of the Jewish exiles is in danger.

2. Scene 2: Daniel, Arioch, and the King (2:14-16)

■ **14-15** The second scene in the story provides a turning point in the action. The hero steps forward to champion the values of the community. Daniel deals wisely with Babylonian authorities and begins to move toward a resolution of the problem. Though this scene is brief, it is important to the flow and impact of the story. The contrast between Daniel and the other wise men of Babylon begins to take shape.

The king's men enforce the decree of Nebuchadnezzar by going out **to put to death the wise men of Babylon** (v 14). This means that those who were not present in the original conversation are rounded up for state execution. A man named **Arioch** leads the execution squad (v 14). Ironically his role in the story eventually becomes one of deliverer rather executioner. His encounter with Daniel transforms him. Because of his association with the hero the executioner becomes the rescuer of the wise men of Babylon.

Daniel's gifts apparently include diplomacy. He speaks to Arioch with **wisdom and tact** (v 14). That is, he selects his words well and presents them in good taste. Whatever else he says, the text records his question, **Why . . . such a harsh decree?** (v 15). The term **harsh** (*ḥăsap*) suggests urgency or haste, even audacity, which is certainly a fitting description of the decree. Arioch is not put out by Daniel's question. Perhaps he agrees with Daniel's assessment of the decree, for he takes time to explain **the matter to Daniel** (v 15).

■ **16** Following this Daniel **went in to the king and asked for time** to provide an acceptable response (v 16). The wording of the text does not demand a personal appearance before the king. It is unlikely that he could do this. There was specific protocol that prevented unwanted guests in the king's presence (see Esth 4:11). Probably a court official presented the request on Daniel's behalf and the time was granted. Why Daniel was given time when the other wise men were not is left unexplained. The reader might assume a parallel with Dan 1:9 where God intervened and caused the authorities "to show favor and sympathy" toward his people.

With these verses the differences between Daniel and the other wise men of Babylon begins to unfold. Daniel's successes accentuate the failures of the Babylonian wise men. Their speeches were strongly rebuffed by the king (vv 5, 8, 12), but Daniel was graciously received (v 15). The wise men of Babylon were not granted additional time (v 8), yet Daniel was (v 16). All of this affirms that the one who acknowledges God in all his ways will have his paths made straight (Prov 3:6).

3. Scene 3: Daniel Before God (2:17-23)

■ **17-18** The central scene of the story portrays Daniel coming before his God and finding a resolution to the tension. It is climactic in that it focuses attention upon the main message of the story: True wisdom is found only in the one true God who rules over all.

Daniel's plan of action includes gaining support from his fellow Jewish captives. The text introduces **Hananiah, Mishael and Azariah** by name at this point in the text (Dan 2:17). Their Hebrew names are used because they are being asked to invoke the Hebrew God, **the God of heaven** (*ʾĕlāh šĕmayyāʾ*, v 18). This name for Israel's God was common in postexilic books of the Bible, particularly Chronicles, Ezra, and Nehemiah. The only four occurrences in Daniel, however, are here and in vv 20, 36, and 44. The Persians also used this term to refer to the high god of Zoroastrianism, Ahura Mazada. It emphasizes the transcendence of God, which agrees with the assessment of the Babylonian wise men that deity "do not live among men" (2:11). Yet Daniel will prove that his God does connect with humans. He reveals mysteries to them. His God is both transcendent and immanent.

Daniel instructs his fellow Hebrew captives to engage in a traditional Hebrew spiritual exercise of prayer. They must **plead** (*bĕ ʿāʾ*) with God just as he had pleaded with the king for more time (v 18; see 2:16). Their petition was for **mercy** (*raḥămîn*), recognizing that God must freely choose to show compassion if the dream is to be revealed (v 18). They do not automatically

2:15-18

expect God to answer. This is the first emphasis on prayer in the book, but it will not be the last. Faithful servants come before their God regularly (see 6:11 and 9:3 in particular).

The focus of the prayer was to be upon revealing the **mystery** of the dream (v 18). Throughout this chapter the content of the dream and its interpretation is called a **mystery** (*rāz*, vv 18, 19, 27, 30, 47). Additionally the word is used three times to speak of God as the one "who reveals mysteries" (*gālēʾrāzin*, vv 28, 29, 47). The term *rāz* is a Persian loan word that refers to things that are secret or hidden. The community responsible for the Dead Sea Scrolls employed it as a technical term to designate things that are known only by divine revelation. That would seem to be its sense in the context of Daniel.

■ **19** The effect of the prayers of these Jewish captives is that **the mystery was revealed** (v 19). God came through for his servants. The revelation was made **in a vision** (v 19). This is the first of five visions of Daniel mentioned in the book. The other four provide the content of chs 7 to 12. Only this vision and the one in ch 7 are said to occur **during the night** (v 19).

■ **20** Daniel's response to the revelation was to honor God. He **praised the God of heaven** by means of a hymn of thanksgiving (vv 20-23). The structure of the hymn alternates between words of praise and reasons to praise. The progression is toward a more personal tone. The first words of praise (v 20) and reasons for praise are in third person (vv 21-22). The second section shifts to addressing God directly in second person. It parallels the first section by beginning with words of praise (v 23*a*) before moving to reasons for praise (v 23*b*). There is no invitation to praise, which is a typical feature of such hymns.

The opening words of the hymn establish its theme. All true **wisdom and power** derive from God (v 20). These are the predominant attributes demonstrated in this chapter. The **wisdom** to reveal mysteries comes from God, and the **power** to control kingdoms is in his hands. From a Babylonian perspective **wisdom** might be seen as the realm of sages and **power** as the provenance of kings. But Daniel affirms that neither belongs to them. They are gifts bestowed by the one whose they are. These two divine elements are tied together in other parts of scripture as well (Job 9:4; 12:13; 26:12; Isa 11:2; Jer 10:12; 51:15, 1 Cor 2:5; Rev 5:12; 7:12).

■ **21-22** God's **power** is displayed in his control over **times and seasons** and **kings** (Dan 2:21*a*). The dream profoundly illustrates the truth of this. It pictures the rise and fall of earthly kingdoms over time as God **sets up kings and deposes them** (v 21*a*). **Wisdom** also rests within the hands of God. He can make it available as a gift **to the wise** and **to the discerning** (v 21*b*). He **reveals** what humans cannot grasp by their own abilities, **deep and hidden things** (v 22*a*). Nothing lies outside God's comprehension, for he even **knows what lies in darkness** (v 22*b*). As the creation account testifies in Gen 1:3 and the vision of a new Jerusalem confirms in Rev 21:23, **light** has its origins in God (Dan 2:22*b*).

■ **23** These divine qualities found personal application for Daniel in the revelation of the dream and its interpretation. Therefore the hymn shifts to first person address and identifies Daniel's deity as **God of my fathers** (v 23*a*). This is another typical way to speak of God during the postexile period. It emphasizes the historic connections of the worshipper to Israel's past. As such it is a confession of faith in all that has been revealed about Israel's God throughout her history. The **wisdom and power** that belongs to God are shared with Daniel as a gift (v 23*b*). This happened when God responded to the prayer and **made known . . . the dream of the king** (v 23*cd*).

This piece of poetry sounds the central theme of the chapter. God possesses all wisdom and power and distributes them as he sees fit. With this pronouncement the stage is set for the dream to be revealed along with its interpretation. It will provide concrete illustration of the truth confessed in this hymn.

4. Scene 4: Daniel, Arioch, and the King (2:24-25)

Before the dream is revealed another brief scene prepares the reader for it. This scene serves to delay final resolution and thus maintains suspense. It balances scene 2 (vv 14-16), which includes the same three characters Daniel, Arioch, and the king. The roles are reversed however. Daniel seeks out Arioch and orders him to take him before the king. In scene 2 the king had issued an order that sent Arioch in search of Daniel. It is a subtle indication of how God overturns the designs of earthly rulers.

■ **24** The reader is reminded that Arioch is the one **appointed to execute the wise men of Babylon** (v 24). Verse 14 had made that quite clear, so its inclusion here is noteworthy. The phrase helps maintain intensity in the narrative by keeping the issue of life and death before the reader. This is further highlighted as Daniel mentions the phrase **execute the wise men of Babylon** again when he makes his request to Arioch.

Daniel is the one in control at this point. He employs imperative forms as he orders Arioch **not** to **execute** the wise men and to **take** him to the king (v 24). With an air of certainty he announces that he **will interpret his dream for him** (v 24). In Aramaic his words are arranged for the sake of emphasis. Literally he says, *the interpretation to the king I will show.*

■ **25** Arioch follows Daniel's orders and brings him to the king. He seems to take personal credit for discovering a solution to the king's problem and announces **I have found a man . . . who can tell the king what his dream means** (v 25). His description of Daniel as a foreign captive may seem demeaning. But it accentuates Daniel's humble origins and also helps the original readers identify more closely with the story. They understand what it means to be **among the exiles from Judah** (v 25).

5. Scene 5: The King and His Wise Man (2:26-49)

■ **26** The final scene of the story is the longest. Its dialogue between the king and a Jewish wise man parallel the opening scene of the king's dialogue with his Babylonian wise men (vv 1-13). Both scenes open with a speech by the king (vv 3 and 26) and close with a royal pronouncement (vv 13 and 48). These similarities draw attention to the marked contrasts between Daniel and the other wise men of Babylon that emerge in this section.

Even though the problem of discovering the dream and its interpretation has been solved and the wise men have been saved from execution, the story is not over. The content of the dream and its meaning has yet to be revealed. This technique of delaying knowledge of the dream's content increases suspense. The reader is all the more eager to hear what Daniel has to say.

The scene opens with further delay by focusing upon how the interpretation of dreams comes about. The king introduces the topic by asking, **Are you able to tell me what I saw . . . and interpret it?** (v 26). The question is straightforward and innocent enough. But the point raised is central to the story. The issue is who holds the keys to wisdom and how does one obtain it. The story is about a quest to find someone who can unlock the insight about life contained in the dream. Nebuchadnezzar is asking Daniel if he is the one who possesses this wisdom.

■ **27-28** Daniel understands the question and makes sure the king knows the truth. Human wisdom is derived. **No wise man** possesses the wisdom for which the king hopes (v 27). It does not matter if his specialty is **enchanter, magician or diviner.** This list accentuates the totality of all human wisdom much like it did in v 2. It is representative, not comprehensive. None of the experts in this realm can explain the dream.

By making such a statement Daniel agrees with his Babylonian colleagues, who admitted "there is not a man on earth who can do what the king asks" (v 10). He also agrees with them that true wisdom is found only in the divine realm. "No one can reveal it to the king except the gods," the Babylonian wise men said (v 11). But they did not think that the gods would share it because "they do not live among men" (v 11). In contrast, Daniel asserts that **there is a God in heaven who reveals mysteries** (v 28). This is the foundational understanding. God holds the keys to wisdom and dispenses it as he wills. In other words, the Babylonians believed humans must discover wisdom if they want it. Daniel declares, however, that wisdom is revealed. If God does not speak, there is no wisdom. God is the one **who reveals mysteries** (v 28, also vv 29 and 47). Therefore the only reason Daniel is able to reveal the dream and its interpretation is because God **has shown . . . what will happen** (v 28). Wisdom is a gift that God bestows.

The content of the dream involves **what will happen in days to come** (v 28). The phrase **days to come** (*bĕʾaḥărît yômayyāʾ*) literally means "in the following days." It refers to some unspecified time in the future. It does not necessarily indicate end-of-the-world events, though at times it can. Its Hebrew equivalent sometimes speaks of eschatological or end-time events (Isa 2:2; Ezek 38:16) but more often it references the unfolding of a more immediate future (Gen 49:1; Num 24:14; Deut 4:30; 31:29; Jer 23:20; 30:24; Hos 3:5). It is also used in contexts where its meaning could be taken either way (Jer 48:47; 49:39). The other usage of the phrase in Daniel occurs in 10:14 where it seems to refer to more immediate events. Within ch 2 a parallel phrase, "what is going to happen" (*ʾaḥărê dēnâ*), appears in vv 29 and 47. That phrase literally means "after this."

■ **29-30** With v 29 Daniel begins to reveal the dream. Yet he delays once more by clarifying what he just said about the origins of wisdom. Verses 29-30 essentially parallel the content of vv 27-28. Daniel confesses that even he is not responsible for true wisdom. **As for me,** he says, **this mystery has been revealed to me, not because I have greater wisdom** (v 30). Daniel does not receive insight because he consults certain books, performs the right rituals, or recites the proper incantations like his Babylonian colleagues. His wisdom is a gift of God's grace. God, **the revealer of mysteries** (v 29), has done this for the king so that he will **know the interpretation** and **understand** (v 30).

■ **31-35** The content of the dream is finally revealed in vv 31-35. It involved a large statue and a rock. The rock smashed the statue into pieces and grew into a huge mountain. The **statue** seems to be a human form since the various body parts mentioned include a **head, chest, arms, belly, thighs, legs,** and **feet** (vv 32-33). It was imposing in several ways. It was **enormous** in size and radiated a **dazzling** light (v 31). It was **awesome in appearance** in the sense that one might be terrified by it.

Four metals of great value were used in the statue, **gold, silver, bronze,** and **iron** (vv 32-33). These are arranged from head to toe in descending market value but ascending usefulness. While **gold** is the most costly, it is also the softest metal. **Iron** is the more durable metal of the four and most serviceable for tools and weapons. **Iron** replaced **bronze** in the history of humanity as the functional metal of choice around 1200 B.C. The idea of representing four successive eras with these same four metals occurs in the works of the eighth-century B.C. Greek poet Hesiod. A Zoroastrian text of uncertain date and the first-century A.D. Roman poet Ovid also made use of this scheme. Thus it appears to be a format familiar to ancient people.

The strength of the **iron** is compromised in the statue by mixing with baked clay (v 33). This becomes the point at which **a rock . . . struck the statue** and destroyed it (v 34). The entire statue crumbled into dust. The simile **like chaff on a threshing floor in the summer** vividly depicts complete destruction (v 35). **Chaff,** the inedible outer covering of grains, floats away in **the wind** during the threshing process.

The **rock** that brought the statue down **was cut out** ("of a mountain" according to v 45) **but not by human hands** (v 34). This suggests the involvement of a divine element, which the interpretation will emphasize more clearly in vv 44-45. That rock grew into **a huge mountain** that completely overtook **the whole earth** (v 35).

■ **36-38** Without confirmation that this was indeed the dream of the king, Daniel proceeds with its interpretation in v 36. The lack of response from the king at this point is a subtle indicator that the balance of power has shifted from Nebuchadnezzar to the man of God. The king who dominated the conversation in the opening scene (vv 1-13) remains quiet while Daniel speaks. This element supports the theme of the dream that earthly powers give way to the divine kingdom.

Verses 36-45 provide the interpretation of the dream. The interpretation begins by presenting a proper assessment of Nebuchadnezzar. Daniel identifies him as **the king of kings** (v 37), a title Nebuchadnezzar used of himself. His absolute sovereign control over the nations is emphasized by the fourfold **dominion and power and might and glory** (v 37). Daniel acknowledges that his realm extends over a vast region. The references to **mankind and the beasts of the field and the birds of the air** as well as **ruler over them all** allude to the creation story of Gen 1 and suggest world domination (v 38). This was the way Nebuchadnezzar saw himself. Inscriptions from his reign identify him as king of the entire world.

All Nebuchadnezzar's splendor, however, is viewed as a gift from God. **The God of heaven has given** the king this power (v 37). **He has placed** things under his control and **he has made** Nebuchadnezzar the ruler that he is (v 38). Daniel confirms what Jeremiah believed. Nebuchadnezzar is God's servant who does only what God allows him to do (Jer 25:9). Daniel also confirms a central message of the dream: the God of heaven always rules over earthly kings.

Thus **the head of gold** on the statue represents Nebuchadnezzar in all of his derived glory (Dan 2:38). He is as spectacular as earthly monarchs get. In many ways history bears this out. Though many powerful kings came before and after Nebuchadnezzar, he certainly ranks among the most impressive (see *Behind the Text* for ch 4).

■ **39-43** The interpretation continues by identifying each of the metals as representing kingdoms that would follow Nebuchadnezzar's. Little is said about the second and third kingdoms except that the second will be **inferior** and the third **will rule over the whole earth** (v 39). The **fourth kingdom** is described in greater detail (v 40). It will be like iron that stands as the strongest among metals. Like the strength of iron against other metals, this kingdom will be able to **crush and break all the others** (v 40). Yet the strength of this kingdom will be diminished because the iron is mixed with **baked clay** (v 41). This mixing of iron and clay represents **a divided kingdom,** a kingdom that is **partly strong and partly brittle,** a kingdom where the people **will not remain united** (vv 41-43).

■ **44-45** Verse 44 brings the interpretation to a climax with an explanation of the meaning of the rock. That rock is the kingdom of God. **The God of heaven will set up a kingdom** that is different from any other that has come before. This one will be indestructible. It **will never be destroyed** or even fall under the governance of **another people.** Just as the rock destroyed the statue in the dream, so God's kingdom will **crush** all human kingdoms and bring them **to an end.**

God will set up this kingdom **in the time of those kings** (*běyômêhôn dî malkaayyā*, v 44). This phrase suggests that God's kingdom does not break in after the earthly kingdoms have had their day. Rather the divine kingdom enters within the time of these earthly realms, overrules them, and outlasts them. This explains why Daniel's description of the dream mentioned that all the kingdoms were destroyed "at the same time" (v 35). Daniel is not suggesting that God's kingdom enters this world at one specific time but that it continues to emerge within the framework of human realms. Like Isaiah the remnant of God's people endures and eventually overtakes earthly powers (Isa 37:30-32). The kingdom of God flourishes in spite of apparent realities.

Daniel asserts plainly that **this is the meaning of the vision of the rock** (Dan 2:45). The kingdom of God supersedes human kingdoms. It endures whereas earthly kingdoms do not. These facts are **true** and **trustworthy** (v 45). The king, and any reader of this story, need not doubt them.

Commentators have traditionally sought to identify specific kingdoms known in history with the various metals on the statue. The rock is then correlated with a specific personality or group in history. The necessity of this move, however, is questionable. Daniel has already explained **the meaning of the vision** quite clearly (v 44). The point is that the kingdom of God will emerge in the midst of earthly kingdoms and outlast them.

No consensus exists among interpreters about the identification of the historical circumstances reflected in the metals. None fit all the details in the text perfectly (see the sidebar "Excursus: Historical Options for the Metals"). This alone might give a rise to caution in using such an approach to the text.

Interpretation of the Statue in Chapter 2

Some interpreters have found significance in the various body parts of the statue. The two legs or two arms, for example, are taken to suggest two parts of a kingdom. The ten toes, based on the association with the ten horns mentioned in ch 7, have been identified as ten kings who might rule over the final kingdom (Miller 1994, 97-98). The fact that ch 2 does not specifically refer to the number of arms, legs, or toes indicates that caution is needed in this matter. The interpreter runs the risk of saying more than the text intends at this point.

In all of the proposals the issue of literally identifying four particular historical entities seems important. Numbers in the Bible are often symbolic however. Four is used in biblical literature to suggest completeness. For example, the Bible speaks of the four corners of the earth and the four seasons of the year. Symbolic use of the number four is exactly what one should expect in the book of Daniel. It may well be that the four kingdoms of this dream indicate the totality of human kingdoms, whatever that number may actually turn out to be. The fourth kingdom would be the final kingdom of humankind, perhaps the one that readers of any age find themselves living in. The overview of human history begins with the contemporary king of Daniel. It makes sense to suggest that it ends with the end of human history. The final kingdom of this world, like the rest, will come to an end. Throughout the rise and fall of kingdoms the rule of God will continue.

Often an appeal is made to ch 7 in order to fill out details in ch 2. These two chapters are parallel, but their content is not necessarily synonymous. The vision in ch 7 deals with four kingdoms but does so in a very different way. Further reflection on the connections between the two chapters will come in the commentary on ch 7. Suffice it to say that one must be careful about overdrawing the connections between these two chapters. They do balance one another in the chiasmic structure of the Aramaic section. This does not mean, however, that every detail in them parallels.

■ **46-47** In vv 46-49 Nebuchadnezzar responds positively to Daniel's interpretation. The indication that his own kingdom would end does not seem to faze him. He honors Daniel, his God, and his friends. His actions in fact demonstrate the truth contained in the dream that earthly powers submit before God's kingdom.

Falling **prostrate,** offering **honor** and giving **an offering and incense** are all acts of worship (v 46). As his words indicate, such worship is not directed at Daniel but rather toward his God. The king extols Daniel's God for enabling Daniel **to reveal this mystery** (v 47). He seems to have understood the points that Daniel made at the beginning of his speech in vv 27-30. God is the only source for understanding the dream. So Nebuchadnezzar proclaims

Daniel's God **the God of gods and the Lord of kings and a revealer of myster-ies** (v 47). In other words, he is absolute sovereign over the affairs of the world. As **God of gods** he is the master of the heavenly realms. As **Lord of kings** he controls the destiny of nations. As **a revealer of mysteries** he possesses knowledge of the workings of the universe.

■ **48-49** Because he is God's representative, Daniel receives rewards from Nebuchadnezzar. He is given **a high position** in the administration of the em-pire **as ruler over the entire province of Babylon** (v 48). The province of Baby-lon was the central and most significant region in the empire. He was also **placed . . . in charge of all its wise men** (v 48). This made him the primary representative for this group of royal advisers. At Daniel's request his three Jewish friends were also given positions as **administrators** in the government (v 49). This apparently moved them to areas throughout the province of Babylon. Daniel, however, stayed at the heart of the kingdom within **the royal court** that is the massive palace complex itself (v 49).

Excursus: Historical Options for the Metals

Several theories have been proposed that attempt to match the four metals of the statue with kings or kingdoms in history. All of them begin with Nebuchad-nezzar or Babylon since that identification is made in v 38.

One theory has been that the four metals represent Babylon, Media, Persia, and Greece (Hartman and Di Lella 1978, 147-48; Collins 1993, 166-69). These em-pires ruled over various portions of the Middle East during the final centuries B.C. Since Media did not truly dominate the region like the others, this could be the reason the second kingdom is called **inferior** (v 39). The third kingdom would be Persia since it ended both the Median and Babylonian Empires. The fourth empire of iron would be the Seleucid branch of the Greek empire. The mixing of clay with iron might refer to the mixed marriages among the royalty that tended to weaken the kingdom. In this scenario the rock would be identified either as Judas Mac-cabeus or a pious group of Jews such as the Hasidim. These orchestrated a suc-cessful rebellion against the Seleucids in 164 B.C. and established an independent Jewish state. Of course this kingdom did not last forever and so the prediction of the dream would be in error.

Another way of identifying the metals has been especially popular among many groups of Christians from the earliest times until the present. They have seen the metals representing Babylon, Persia, Greece, and Rome (Archer 1985, 46-48). These were clearly the four dominant empires that successively ruled the Middle East. If Rome is the final empire, then the rock that crushes it is Jesus Christ. He establishes a kingdom that lasts **forever** during the reign of the Roman Empire (v 44). This position is given additional support by correlating the four beasts of ch 7 with the four metals. The strength of Rome might be readily com-pared to iron and its moral failures as the weakening influence of clay. Greece with its extensive conquest under Alexander the Great corresponds well with the third kingdom that **will rule over the whole earth** (v 39). Persia, however, does not fit the character of the silver kingdom. Its extent, wealth, duration, and even moral fiber were in no way inferior to Babylon.

A variation of this theory suggests that the fourth kingdom also represents the last kingdom of the earth (Miller 1994, 97-98). Since the Roman Empire in some sense still exists and the kingdom of Christ has not yet culminated its rule over the earth, the final fulfillment of this vision may remain in the future.

Still another approach to interpreting the metals is to view them as representatives of kings rather than empires. Nebuchadnezzar himself is identified with the **head of gold** (v 38) and the text refers to **those kings** (v 44). The term **kingdom** (*malkû*) can be translated as either "realm" or "reign" (v 39). Therefore one suggestion would be to understand the metals as Nebuchadnezzar and his successors in the Babylonian Empire (Davies 1985, 48). The three other kings would be Amel-Marduk, Neriglissar, and Nabonidus. The nine-month reign of Neriglissar's son Labashi-Marduk would be overlooked in this scheme, perhaps because it was so short. The **divided kingdom** of the fourth king would reflect the years of Nabonidus's absence from Babylon and his son Belshazzar reigning in his stead (v 41). In this scenario the rock would be either Cyrus or the Jewish exiles that returned to Judah to rebuild the temple and their community. The sixth-century B.C. context of the book tends to support this theory.

Another option for a series of kings would be the four kings mentioned in the book of Daniel (Seow 2003, 46; Goldingay 1989, 49-51). These are Nebuchadnezzar, Belshazzar, Darius, and Cyrus. While the latter two may in fact be the same person, the book of Daniel does identify these two separate names. According to this theory, the rock would be either the remnant of Jewish exiles who return to Judah or a more spiritualized kingdom of God emerging in the midst of the Persian Empire.

FROM THE TEXT

As the discussion above shows, the dominant theological themes in this chapter center around the **wisdom** and **power** of God highlighted in v 20. These elements rest in the hands of an almighty God who disperses them at will. No earthly expert or authority can claim control over them. In the crucial test of wisdom, God and his servant win out over the most impressive collection of knowledge humans could assemble.

God holds the keys to wisdom and shares it as he pleases. Wisdom is insight into the workings of the universe. It is about knowing what is really going on in the world, understanding what things mean, how they are ordered, and the ways a person can live in harmony with it all. The story of ch 2 is about a king's quest to discover wisdom contained in his dream. In the end he finds out that Daniel's God is the one who is **a revealer of mysteries** (v 47). This God possesses the wisdom that he seeks.

The story of ch 2 emphasizes that true wisdom belongs to God, while human wisdom is limited. This emphasis is brought out through the contrast between Daniel and his Babylonian colleagues. The Babylonians understood the nature of wisdom much like the Israelites. But they differed on how to obtain it. The Babylonians needed to know the dream so that they could interpret its meaning. This is why they press the king twice to **tell his servants the dream** (vv 4 and 7). Once they heard the dream they could examine their books of dreams to find a corollary. Based on parallels with what had been dreamed before and what happened after it, the wise men could determine the interpretation. Their wisdom was discovered through observation of life.

Daniel's wisdom came by means of a vision from God. His wisdom was not discovered. It was derived from the Source of wisdom. This is the heart of the issue in this story. Babylonian wisdom was impersonal and disconnected from a relationship to the divine. They believed that the gods **do not live among men** (v 11). Daniel's wisdom, on the other hand, depended upon a vital relationship to God. He received his insight **in a vision** following or perhaps in the midst of prayer with his God (v 19).

Wisdom is given to those who are **wise** and **discerning** according to v 21. From the biblical perspective, the wise are persons who undertake their search for wisdom in "the fear of the LORD" (Prov 1:7). In other words, they are persons who follow the admonition to "trust in the LORD with all your heart and lean not on your own understanding" (Prov 3:5-6). The wise have a vital relationship to the origin of all wisdom, God himself.

The book of Ecclesiastes agrees with the book of Daniel about the limits of human wisdom. "All the things done under the sun," that is, within the realm of humans, "are meaningless, a chasing after the wind" (Eccl 1:14). It makes no sense. Only in relationship to God does one discover true wisdom for living (Eccl 12:13-14). Job also discovered this truth. After he and his friends exhausted their minds in trying to understand life, God broke in to ask, "Where were you when I laid the earth's foundation?" (Job 38:4). The implication of God's speech is that humans cannot fully grasp the intricacies of life. Wisdom lies beyond their understanding.

The Apostle Paul confirms the assessment of wisdom found in the Hebrew Scriptures (1 Cor 1:18-31). Human wisdom comes up short in the most important issue of life. Through it people have not been able to come to know God. Human wisdom, in fact, looks like foolishness next to God's wisdom. To put it another way, Paul said, "The foolishness of God is wiser than man's wisdom" (1 Cor 1:25).

The rest of the Bible also affirms Daniel's belief that God is willing to share his wisdom as **the revealer of mysteries** (Dan 2:29). The story of Solomon declares that it was God who gave the king "a wise and discerning heart" (1 Kgs 3:12). James puts it most clearly in his instruction, "If any of you lacks wisdom, he should ask God . . . and it will be given to him" (Jas 1:5).

Two Types of Wisdom

Scholars like to differentiate between traditional wisdom that focuses upon skill for living and mantic wisdom that focuses upon more esoteric knowledge, such as dream and omen interpretation. The story in ch 2 deals with the latter in particular. Yet it does not distinguish between the two kinds of wisdom. God's provenance over wisdom is not restricted to one sphere or the other. He controls both. In the end both kinds of wisdom are about the same thing. They are about how the world works and how one should live in relationship to it.

The power of God's kingdom is greater than the kingdoms of this world. The king's dream portrayed earthly kingdoms in all their glory and strength. There were gold kingdoms and silver kingdoms of great wealth, as well as bronze kingdoms and iron kingdoms of great strength. Their appearance struck fear into the hearts of humans because they were so **enormous** and **dazzling** (v 31). For all their apparent power and strength, however, they had feet of clay. As with all kingdoms of earth, there was weakness within them. They were **divided** and **brittle** because of the **mixture** of people who bred internal disunity (vv 41-43). They were all destined to fall. Not of their own accord but by divine will. Their destruction will come at the hand of God. His kingdom, a **rock cut out of a mountain,** will crush them (v 45). That kingdom will become what no earthly kingdom could. It will fill **the whole earth** (v 35) and **never be destroyed** (v 44). While earthly kingdoms rise and fall, the kingdom of God will **endure forever** (v 44).

This is the kind of kingdom Jesus spoke about. He told Pilate that his kingdom was not of this world (John 18:36). It was unlike any earthly kingdom. Jesus' kingdom was a dominion of the heart. As Jesus declared, "The kingdom of God is within you" (Luke 17:21). It will outlast all other kingdoms, for in the end "every tongue [will] confess that Jesus Christ is Lord" (Phil 2:11).

God controls the future of human history. The theme of God's sovereignty over the future takes on greater proportions in the latter half of the book and dominates it. It is introduced in Dan 2 in preparation for those chapters. Daniel's God in this story is the one who **changes times and seasons** (v 21). The temporal elements of earth remain in his hands.

The king's dream is about **what is going to happen** (v 29; see also v 45). It tells of the rising and falling of kingdoms throughout the history of humanity. Beginning with the contemporary kingdom of Nebuchadnezzar a series of realms unfolds thereafter even to the final one. **God has shown the king** these things (v 45). The one who oversees their development is the one who revealed them. **He sets up kings and deposes them** as he wills (v 21). Thus he is **the Lord of kings** who orchestrates the history of humans (v 47).

The foreknowledge of God described in this chapter does not necessarily suggest a rigid foreordination of events. The details of history are vague enough to allow many turns in the road. The only specific historical figure mentioned in the text is Nebuchadnezzar. Beyond this the subsequent kingdoms are generic enough, as interpreters over the centuries have proven, to suggest a variety of possible kings or empires in this world. The essential point is that God remains in control of history. He has not necessarily prescribed its every detail, but he has determined its outcome.

C. Fiery Furnace: The Second Test of Faithfulness (3:1-30)

Overview

One of the most entertaining stories in the book of Daniel is that of Shadrach, Meshach, Abednego, and the fiery furnace. It is a well-told story conveyed with elements of humor, irony, and other literary devices to heighten its affect. Like ch 1, it describes a dangerous circumstance for the faithful that becomes an opportunity for God to prove his faithfulness. Fortunes are reversed as the accused become the acclaimed and the oppressor becomes the protector of God's people.

BEHIND THE TEXT

The most natural way to read ch 3 is as a sequel to ch 2 and not as a story that stands alone. The absence of a specific date for Nebuchadnezzar's reign initially suggests this strategy for reading. Moreover the relationship between characters and concepts found in both chapters supports the connection. Importantly ch 3 fulfills the prediction of the dream in ch 2. The power of God's kingdom overrules a powerful kingdom of this earth like a rock crushing a statue of metals.

The main characters in ch 3 are familiar to the reader from previous stories. Nebuchadnezzar the king, his Babylonian advisers, and the Jewish captives Shadrach, Meshach, and Abednego appear once again. Their entrance into the text at each point implies that the writer is depending on their introduction in other stories for understanding. In particular the status and role of the three Jewish captives relies upon 2:49, which notes their promotion as officials in the province of Babylon.

Nebuchadnezzar is the only fully developed individual character in the story. The advisers and the captives are presented as groups and thus as types of persons. The Babylonian advisers represent hostile pagans who endanger the lives of the faithful. The Jewish captives depict God's faithful servants in an unfriendly environment. Nebuchadnezzar initiates most of the action in the story. He makes the image, sets it up, summons officials to its dedication, receives a report on the Jewish captives, interrogates them, orders their execution, observes their rescue, directs their release, decrees honor for their God, and promotes them in his empire. The dominance of Nebuchadnezzar's character throughout the story signals that the conflict is not between Jew and Babylonian but rather between the king and the God of the captives.

Daniel is missing in this tale. This is the only chapter in the book where he does not play a role. The association between the three heroes of this story and Daniel, however, is well established in the preceding two stories (1:6, 11, 19; 2:17, 49). In a sense Daniel is connected with this story by means of proxy of his three friends.

Still Daniel's absence provokes questions for commentators. Why does the hero of the book not take a stand along with his friends? Some scholars see this element, along with other qualities of the narrative, as a clue to the fictional character of the story. They understand the story as a traditional tale of the Jews invented for the sake of inspiration and encouragement. If so, reconciling Daniel's absence from the story is unnecessary. Other scholars assume the story relates real events. As such, they propose that the persecution of only three Jews from among all the exiles in Babylonia was selective. The accusation in vv 8-12 indicates that personal political jealousy, and perhaps ethnic bigotry, motivated **some astrologers** to denounce **some Jews.** Surely other Jews, such as Daniel, did not comply with the king's edict either.

The plot of the story in ch 3 recalls that of chs 1 and 6. These are all stories that test the faithfulness not only of God's servants but also of God. A major concern is whether or not Jewish captives will remain true to their convictions in the midst of a hostile environment. Overshadowing this concern is the tension over God's ability to rescue his faithful servants. The question of God's power and trustworthiness among world powers is the fundamental focus of these three stories.

The content of ch 3 parallels most closely that of ch 6. In many ways the ordeal of Shadrach, Meshach, and Abednego in the fiery furnace is similar to Daniel's ordeal in the lions' den. Within the chiasmic structure of the Aramaic section of the book, these two chapters balance one another (see *Behind the Text* on ch 2). They both deal with a decree of a king that creates a religious dilemma for the Jewish faithful. State officials inform the king of the Jews' noncompliance and a death sentence is issued. Miraculously God rescues and the king honors the accused and their God.

The story of ch 3 also needs to be read in light of the dream in ch 2. The message of that dream underscored God's absolute sovereignty over the history of nations and over Babylon in particular. Nebuchadnezzar's ostentatious grasping for control in ch 3 stands in greater relief against this backdrop. Clearly Nebuchadnezzar did not comprehend the message of the dream. In many ways the story of ch 3 illustrates how the dream of ch 2 finds fulfillment within the contemporary Babylonian context. The kingdom of God continues to break into the kingdoms of this world and overrules their designs.

Chapter 3 is also connected directly to ch 2 by the colossal **image** set up by the king (v 1). It reminds the reader of the statue in the king's dream of ch 2. The golden head of the dream statue represented Nebuchadnezzar's extensive domain. The golden image in ch 3 likewise symbolizes the king's great wealth and power.

Ancient kings regularly erected images of themselves, their gods, or other figures to communicate authority over an area. Images of gods and kings were normally found in temples. Other kinds of images were set up at various sites to serve as propaganda for the state and a reminder of its power. Assyrian kings demanded that governing officials throughout their empire swear an oath of loyalty before these images. **The dedication of the image** in ch 3 appears to be a similar kind of ceremony (v 2). Such an event may be why Zedekiah king of Judah and a chief official, Seraiah, were called to Babylon in about 594 B.C. (Jer 51:59).

The pomp surrounding such ceremonies in ancient Babylon is well known. Annual religious festivals, victory celebrations, and other kinds of spectacles have been preserved in documents from this era. Processionals, rituals, and dramatizations at these events were accompanied by **all kinds of music** (Dan 3:5). Babylonians were fond of such events because they provided a means to promote the power of the state and insure continued allegiance. Such events were always religious in nature in order to further legitimate the state's plans to the populous.

Persons from throughout the empire were required to attend such pageants to show loyalty. The administrators who were called to the dedication of the image represented a wide range of officials throughout the kingdom. These included **satraps, prefects, governors, advisers, treasurers, judges, magistrates and all the other provincial officials** (v 2). This list includes a mixture of Persian and Akkadian terms. It appears that they are listed according to rank, with **satraps** administering large regions and **magistrates** responsible for lesser domains. The number of officials suggests the complexity and sophistication of the Babylonian governance system.

The story never explicitly describes the features of the image, whether it is of the king, a god, or something else. The demand to **fall down and worship** it suggests a god since these are religious actions (v 5). The king, however, might require the similar honoring of himself or another figure. The term **worship** (*sĕgid*) means to prostrate oneself before another, an act of submission and honor. This is what Nebuchadnezzar did before Daniel in 2:46. Whether the image was a god or something else, falling before it symbolized the same thing. Proper respect for the image implied allegiance to Babylon, and loyalty to Babylon implied submission to her gods. Political and religious loyalties went hand in hand in the ancient world.

The size of the image is exceptional, though not beyond reality. The dimensions of **ninety feet high and nine feet wide** are given in cubits in the Aramaic text as "sixty" and "six" (v 1). This reflects the numerical system of the Babylonians that used a base of sixty. The unusual feature of these dimensions is the slender width for such a tall structure. It suggests instability. Typically the width of a statue would be about twenty-five percent of its height in order to provide adequate base. Part of the height would likely include a pedestal, however, which could be as much as half the overall height. Thus the actual image would be more in proportion to its width. The Greek historian Herodotus describes two large golden statues in Babylonian temples in the fifth century B.C. The size of one representing Zeus was given at eighteen feet. The famous colossus of the Greek god Helios rose to over one hundred feet as it guarded the harbor at Rhodes in the third century B.C.

The furnace used in manufacturing this statue may well be the one into which the three Jews were thrown. Furnaces were used for baking food, for firing pottery and bricks, and for metalworking. These were often dome-shaped structures with openings in the top and along the sides. They were not normally a means for execution although occasionally ancient texts refer to such. Jeremiah does mention two prophets, Zedekiah and Ahab, who were burned in a fire by Nebuchadnezzar (Jer 29:21-22). Charcoal, pitch, brush, and manure were used to create and stoke the fire. Bellows made from animal skins forced air into the furnace in order to increase its temperature. While no gauges were available, ancient craftsmen were skilled in knowing the level of heat. The maximum range of a furnace at this time was approximately 1,800 degrees Fahrenheit.

A major piece of the background for this story is not explicitly mentioned in the text. That is the biblical injunctions forbidding honoring other gods and idolatry. The dynamics of this story do not make sense unless one understands these demands of biblical faith. The first two of the Ten Commandments are at issue. The three Jewish captives are tempted to break the first commandment by placing "other gods before" their God (Exod 20:3). The king demanded priority for the image that he set up. The language contained in the second prohibition of the Ten Commandments is more directly echoed in the story: "You shall not make for yourself an idol (*pesel*)" and "You shall not bow down (*šāhâ*) to them or worship (*'ābad*) them" (Exod 20:4-5). Though the precise terms differ between the commandment and the Daniel story, they agree conceptually. Nebuchadnezzar broke the first part of the command when he **made an image** (*ṣĕlēm*) **of gold** (Dan 3:1). Then he directly required the breaking of the second part when he commanded his subjects to **fall down** (*nĕpal*) **and worship** (*sĕgid*) the image (v 6). The issue of idolatry, so prevalent throughout Israel's history, came to a crisis during the exile. The temptation to honor the gods of Judah's captors was great. After all, they had triumphed in every way—militarily, politically, and economically. In Daniel's story, however, the words of Isaiah find fulfillment. "All who make idols are nothing . . . he and his kind will be put to shame . . . Let them all come together and take their stand; they will be brought down to terror and infamy" (Isa 44:9, 11).

The structure of the story in Dan 3 unfolds in a manner similar to that observed in ch 1. There is a description of the setting (vv 1-7) followed by the drama of the test (vv 8-23). The narrative comes to a climax when the outcome of the testing is disclosed (vv 24-30). This is the typical structure for the three tests of faithfulness found in chs 1, 3, and 6.

A chiasmic structure also overlays the material. The story begins (vv 1-7) and ends (vv 28-30) with a decree of the king that promotes obeisance to deity. An accusation and interrogation of the Jews (vv 8-15) is balanced by an order for their execution and subsequent vindication (vv 19-27). The fulcrum of the chiasm is the confession of faith by the Jewish captives (vv 16-18). This structure highlights the significance of the confession, which stands as the theological climax of the story.

IN THE TEXT

I. The Setting (3:1-7)

■ **1** The description of the setting for this story focuses upon establishing the social and religious environment. The context is one of pretentious power and overwhelming conformity. Various details in the text make the narrator's sketch of the setting especially entertaining to a Jewish audience.

The text says little about historical connections. The reference to **Nebuchadnezzar** locates the story within Babylon's most dominant era of power (v 1). Nebuchadnezzar's reign (605-562 B.C.) was unequalled among the monarchs of Babylon. (See *Behind the Text* on ch 4 for additional description of his accomplishments.) No particular year in his reign, however, is identified in the Aramaic text. The Greek versions supply "in the eighteenth year," but this is not likely original. That date would connect these events to the fall of Jerusalem in 587 B.C.

The geographical description for the story is also brief and nonspecific.

The plain of Dura in the province of Babylon cannot be located with any precision (v 1). The entire **province of Babylon** lay on a flat plain. **Dura** refers to a "walled area" or "fortification" and many places in antiquity carried this designation. The best suggestion for this place to date is Tulul Dura, located about sixteen miles south of Babylon.

The social and religious context of the story is obviously the narrator's main concern. At the center of this setting is **an image of gold** (v 1). In essence this image symbolizes the overwhelming power and wealth of Babylon and its builder Nebuchadnezzar. The term **image** (*şĕlēm*), in both Aramaic and Hebrew, often refers to a physical representation of a god, an idol. Other times it is used to speak of the likeness of other things, including "the image of God" that is reflected in humanity (Gen 1:26-27). Whether or not the image represented a god or something else, it is a sacred object to be reverenced in this story. It embodies Babylon's power.

The size and substance of the image serve to highlight its importance. At **ninety feet high** it would tower over an open plain and be seen from a great distance (Dan 3:1). It was nearly one-third the height of the awe-inspiring ziggurat temple Etemananki that punctuated the skyline of Babylon. **Gold** was the most costly of metals in the ancient world. The amount needed to construct an image of this size, even assuming it was gold plated, would be staggering. The extensive conquests and subsequent plundering of Nebuchadnezzar made such an impressive structure possible.

As the builder of this magnificent image, Nebuchadnezzar himself assumes great significance. The object of worship was **made** (*'ăbād*) and **set up** (*qûm*) by him (v 1). Of this fact the reader is reminded eight more times in the story (vv 2, 3, 5, 7, 12, 14, 15, 18). The point is clear. Nebuchadnezzar wields absolute power in this world. For the Jewish reader, however, a subtle irony is contained in these references. The Aramaic term **made** (*'ăbād*) also conveys the idea of service, as it does in Hebrew. One might also read the opening line as "King Nebuchadnezzar served an image of gold." The one who thinks he commands power through his creation may in fact be subservient to that very creation. The term **set . . . up** is also a faint reminder of Isaiah's satire of the deluded idol maker who "shapes a god" with his own tools (Isa 44:12-20).

■ **2-3** A sense of overwhelming conformity to the whims of Nebuchadnezzar emerges in a description of the image's dedication service. The ceremonies surrounding **the dedication of the image** served to promote the empire and its king (Dan 3:2). A long list of **provincial officials,** noted twice, accentuates the vast group of significant persons who fall under Nebuchadnezzar's authority and aura (vv 2-3). From the powerful **satraps,** whose influence extended over large regions of the empire, to the **magistrates** who governed at the local level, they all come when summoned by the king (v 2). Absolute allegiance to Nebuchadnezzar is indicated by their response. Ironically they imitate the image that the king had **set up** (*qûm*) as they **stood** (*qûm*) **before it** (v 3).

■ **4** Emphasis upon widespread compliance continues as the king's command regarding the image is put forth and response to it described in vv 4-7. The **herald** not only proclaims the decree but also does so **loudly** (*ḥāyil*), literally *with great strength* (v 4). All the **peoples, nations and men of every language** receive it and obey it just as the governing official had done in the previous verse. This list reflects the wide scope of the Babylonian conquest that incorporated numerous language groups into its empire. Again, the length of the list and its repetition (vv 4 and 7) serves to enhance its meaning. Every person on the face of the earth conforms to the king's directive. No one is exempt.

■ **5** The list of musical instruments further enhances the pomp surrounding this event. Included are wind (**horn, flute, . . . pipes**) and stringed instruments (**zither, lyre, harp**) commonly used in public ceremonies in the ancient world (v 5). The spectacular sight of the image and the vast crowds are joined by the spectacular sounds of **all kinds of music.** This description serves to impress the reader further with the intimidating grandeur of the event.

Compiling lists of similar items is a stylistic device used throughout the book of Daniel. Such lists were characteristic of the wisdom tradition in the ancient Middle East. The device is employed to its greatest extent in this chapter. Besides heighten the affect of those things listed, this device also slows readers down. It allows them time to feel the impact of all that is being said. An additional effect of these lists may be mocking humor. For the Jewish reader, the list of musical instruments in particular suggests the mindless ritual of empty pagan worship. This list is repeated again in vv 10 and 15.

When the music plays, all people are required to **fall down and worship** the golden image (v 5). This injunction is at the heart of the story. The word pair **fall down and worship** appears no less than five additional times after this verse (vv 6, 7, 10, 11, 15). In addition the word **worship** (*sĕgid*), which means to prostrate oneself out of respect for another, occurs five more times in the text (vv 12, 14, 15, 18, 28). In four of those occurrences the term is paired with "serve" (*pĕlaḥ*), which means to submit to a deity (vv 12, 14, 18, 28). Clearly the issue at hand is a religious one. The command of Nebuchadnezzar is to show loyalty not only to his gods but also to the state.

■ **6** Anyone who does not submit to the image faces severe penalty. More than being identified as a nonconformist or countercultural rebel, they are marked as traitors to the empire. Treason has one punishment in most societies, death. Therefore those who go against overwhelming odds and reveal their disloyalty will **be thrown into a blazing furnace** (v 6). The Aramaic expression translated **blazing furnace** (*'attûn nûrā' yāqidtā'*) is a redundant construction that serves to increase the terrifying image of the furnace. Literally the words read *a furnace of burning fire.* The horror of such a death adds to the drama of the story. Aside from the excruciating suffering involved in being burned alive, death by fire meant no honorable burial. One of the greatest fears for ancient people comes true. The body is not properly interred. Thus the spirit never finds rest and succeeding generations do not appropriately honor the deceased.

■ **7** Everyone in the kingdom seems to follow Nebuchadnezzar's decree to the letter. Verse 7 confirms that **they heard the sound of . . . all kinds of music, and all the peoples . . . fell down and worshiped the image . . . Nebuchadnezzar had set up** (v 7). The laborious repetition of previous phrases mocks the pomp of the ceremony. It also adds to the impression of widespread compliance.

The stage is dramatically set for a test of faithfulness. The context is pretentious power that commands overwhelming conformity. The odds are thoroughly against anyone who would stand against the tide. Should one venture defiance it would surely mean death. Will someone rise up in the midst of such a context and defy the powers of Babylon? Will any of God's people take a stand for the values of the community of faith? If they stand, will God stand with them? Can the God of the Jews stand as tall as the image Nebuchadnezzar has set up? These are the questions the narrator has prompted by his sketch of the setting.

2. The Test (3:8-23)

■ **8-12** As the reader might expect, a test for God's faithful people emerges out of this oppressive setting. An accusation by devious colleagues provokes the test (vv 8-12). An audience with the king confirms the convictions of God's people (vv 13-18) and a plan for their execution is carried out (vv 19-23).

In this story, as in ch 6, the Jewish captives do not initiate confrontation. Their piety is observed and reported by **some astrologers** (v 8). The hostility involved in the report of these persons is revealed in the term **denounced** (v 8). The word literally translates an Aramaic idiom "eat their pieces," which suggests malicious motives. The term translated **astrologers** (*kaśdāʾîn*) can designate either a class of professional wise men or Babylonians in general. The former group represented all the wise men of Babylon who came before the king in 2:4-11 and would have been colleagues of the three Jews who are betrayed. The identification of the accused as those **whom you have set over the affairs of the province of Babylon** suggests political motives for the accusers (v 12). Labeling them **Jews** may also imply an issue of ethnic bigotry. The conflict may have been more than a professional one. It could have been racial as well.

It is worth noting that not all *kaśdāʾîn* are involved in this malevolent plan. Only **some** of them are (v 8). Further not all Jews are targeted directly. Only **some Jews** are identified in particular (v 12). Both these details suggest that the rivalry is personal and restricted to certain persons. Yet early readers of this story would feel the broader implications of an attack upon all those who maintain their convictions in a hostile culture.

The informants approach the king respectfully with the traditional greeting of honor, **O king, live forever!** (v 9). They remind the king of his decree by essentially repeating the herald's pronouncement in vv 5-6. Once again the list of musical instruments is replicated with the command to **fall down and worship the image of gold** and the threat of **a blazing furnace** for those who do not comply (vv 10-11).

The allegation is that three specific individuals **pay no attention** to this decree (v 12). They ignore what the king has spoken. This is evidenced by their refusal to **serve** the Babylonian gods or **worship the image of gold** (v 12). Serving and worshipping identify the same activity. To **serve** (*pĕlah*) literally means to be involved in rituals that honor a god. **Worship** (*sĕgid*) connotes falling prostrate before a god and acknowledging its authority. Thus the point of **the image** is further clarified. Honor for the image was a statement of faith. Therefore not honoring it was also a way of communicating beliefs.

This is the first time that **Shadrach, Meshach and Abednego** are named in the story (v 12). Their position is acknowledged as those whom the king had **set over the affairs of the province of Babylon** (v 12). This also connects them to the previous story, specifically 2:49 where they are first promoted to their positions. Though they have Jewish names (1:6), their Babylonian names are used to underscore their ability to remain faithful in spite of hostile influences. Accommodation to the Babylonian culture at one point did not demand complete surrender of all convictions. The three will be specifically named eleven more times in this story (vv 13, 14, 16, 19, 20, 22, 26*a*, 26*b*, 28, 29, 30). The fact that they are always presented as a group emphasizes the corporate nature of the story. They stand as representatives of all those who choose to remain firm in their faith.

The overall tenor of the accusation is personal. The Jewish captives are portrayed as more than traitors to the state. They have personally affronted the king. Thus the accusation begins with the emphatic second person pronoun ʾantâ in Aramaic, **you have issued a decree** (v 10). It closes with four second person references in v 12. The accused are identified as those whom **you have set** in positions of authority and yet **pay no attention to you**. They do not honor **your gods** and they ignore the idol **you have set up**. The accusers have gone to the heart of the matter. Nebuchadnezzar is the reality behind the image. Honor for the image and his gods is about honoring him. Idol worship is worship of human strength.

■ **13-15** The accusation against the Jews produced the desired result. The king became **furious with rage** just as he had in ch 2 with his incompetent wise men (v 13). Acting the part of an absolute monarch Nebuchadnezzar exercises his uncontested authority. He summons the offenders, proceeds with an inquiry, follows with an ultimatum, and ends with a taunt. Using the terms employed in the accusation in v 12, the king asks if it is **true** that they did not **serve** or **worship** as decreed (v 14). The personal tone of the infraction is maintained. The king employs first person forms and refers to **my gods** and the image that **I have set up** (v 14). He then offers an ultimatum that repeats the herald's pronouncement in vv 5-6 one more time. **Fall down and worship** or be thrown **into a blazing furnace** (v 15). The three Jews are provided opportunity to demonstrate their loyalties. To increase the drama the king adds the word **immediately** to the decree's demands (v 15). There is no time to ponder a response or to change one's mind. Execution comes swiftly if the wrong choice is made.

The king's speech ends with a taunt that clearly focuses the key issue of the story. Once the three Jews are in the fire, he asks, **then what god will be able to rescue you from my hand?** (v 15). This question defines the crucial challenge and signals a potential resolution. The conflict is between the abilities of God and of humans. As the most powerful man in the world, Nebuchadnezzar apparently controls the destiny of all those in his domain. He even holds the power of life and death over the three Jewish captives. The only hope for them is a god who is **able to rescue.** Subsequent events prove that the God of Shadrach, Meshach, and Abednego is just such a god.

■ **16-18** The taunt is a rhetorical question for the king, but for the three heroes it is a direct question begging for an answer. The speech of Shadrach, Meshach, and Abednego concentrates its response on the rescuing character of God. The tone of the speech contrasts sharply with that of their accusers. Gone is the polite opening address and feigned loyalty to the king. Gone also is the mindless repetition of lists. Rather the speech speaks directly to the king's speech, even following a similar pattern of double contingency. This is much clearer in the Aramaic text. The king literally says, *if you . . . but if not* and the Jews say, *if there is . . . but if not.*

Shadrach, Meshach, and Abednego, speaking as one, feel no necessity **to defend** (*tûb*) themselves (v 16). Literally the term means, *return an answer* or *give a comeback.* There is no room for discussion. Their decision has been made. Whether or not God chooses to rescue them, they **will not serve** other **gods or worship the image** (v 18). The first two of Israel's key commandments will be kept. They will have "no other gods before" their God, and they will "not bow down" to an idol (Exod 20:3-5).

The reason for their decisive answer is the character of their God. According to the three Jews **the God we serve,** literally ***our God*** (*'ĕlāhanā'*, v 17), does not compare to **your gods** (*'ĕlāhāyik*, v 18). In direct response to the king's question in v 15, they affirm that their God is **able to save** (v 17). He does not lack capacity to overrule the affairs of humans. In fact, they confidently assert, **he will rescue** them (v 17). This last phrase might be better rendered ***he may choose to rescue*** in light of what follows. The very next statement qualifies their faith, **but if he does not** (v 18). This leaves the outcome in God's hands. They do not presume to decide their own fate. God will do that. Thus their position is that God is capable of delivering, but he is completely free to choose whether or not he will do so. Their lives rest in the hands of the sovereign God, not in the **hand** of the king (v 17).

The words **save** and **rescue** in v 17 are different forms of the same root, *šêzib*. It is a key word throughout the story, occurring elsewhere in vv 15 and 28. A synonym *nĕzal* also occurs in v 29. Each of these terms conveys the fundamental idea of being delivered or snatched from danger.

Verse 17 could be translated another way. The first words in Aramaic, *hēn 'îtay*, literally mean, "if there is" or "if it be so." Normally these words have been read as referring to Nebuchadnezzar throwing the Jewish captives into the furnace. Some translators, however, have taken the contingency to refer to God. Thus the verse would read, "If our God whom we serve is able to deliver" (NRSV and similarly TNIV). According to this translation the three Jews would be questioning God's ability to save. Some interpreters adopt this reading and suggest that the Jews are merely making the statement for the sake of argument. Though this translation is possible, it is not demanded by the grammar. Many argue that it does not fit well in the context. The story seems to be about three believers who trust unreservedly in the providence of God.

The ambiguity of the text is interesting. Perhaps it is a device employed to raise suspense in the story. One way of reading the text insinuates that the Jews are not only unsure of their fate but also uncertain of God's ability to save. If this is true, then their deliverance does not depend on their faith in any way, as if it ever did. On the other hand, if the text is understood as a confirmation of faith, the tension still remains. The three believe in God's ability but remain unsure if he will choose to intervene. In either case, the fate of the three Jewish captives is left in question. Not even Shadrach, Meshach, and Abednego know if God will rescue them.

■ **19-23** At this juncture the story takes an unexpected turn and the drama intensifies as the execution of Shadrach, Meshach, and Abednego is swiftly carried out. If the reader hoped for rescue, that does not happen. Orders for execution move rapidly forward. The admirable righteous stance of God's faithful does not produce positive results for them. It, in fact, evokes further fury.

In order to allow the reader time to ponder the full impact of this event, the narrator supplies extended detail. The king's anger and the furnace's heat rise significantly together. The king becomes full of rage (**furious**) and alters **his attitude** (v 19). Ironically the term for **attitude** is the same word used for "image" (*ṣĕlēm*). Literally the phrase reads *the image of his face was changed.* The furnace is heated **seven times hotter than usual,** which was a way of saying that it was brought to its maximum temperature (v 19). The intensity of the heat became so great that it **killed** the executioners, who were **the strongest soldiers** in Nebuchadnezzar's army (vv 20 and 22). The irony is that Babylon's best perish at the king's command, not God's best.

Three times the narrator notes that the three men were tied up (*kĕpat*) as they went into the fire (vv 20, 21, 23). This emphasizes their sense of helplessness, but also evokes the image of a sacrifice similar to that of Isaac (Gen 22:9). The reference to their clothing, **robes, trousers, turbans and other clothes,** underscores the urgency with which the execution was carried out (Dan 3:21). Both the binding and the clothes help set the stage for the extent of the miraculous deliverance. One of Nebuchadnezzar's first observations is that the three men are "unbound" in the fire (v 25). After they emerge from the fire the fact that "their robes were not scorched" is also noted (v 27).

The narrator points out that the three **fell into the blazing furnace** (v 23). The term **fell** (*nĕpal*) is the same one translated "fall down" in previous verses. It is a subtle irony that, though they had refused to fall before the image, the three must fall into the fire.

At this point in the text, the Greek versions of Daniel include the apocryphal selections known as The Prayer of Azariah and the Song of the Three Young Men. These materials are fitting for the context but are undoubtedly later additions to the book. They include a prayer for vindication and praise for deliverance.

The Prayer of Azariah and the Song of the Three Young Men

The Prayer of Azariah and the Song of the Three Young Men were attached to the book of Daniel sometime in the first or second centuries B.C. The first part of this material, The Prayer of Azariah, is a corporate lament 22 verses long voiced by Azariah, also known as Abednego. It exalts God as a righteous judge, recounts his judgment upon Israel, and confesses their sins. The plea of this lament is to "deliver us" and to "put to shame" those who harm his people.

The last part of this material, the Song of the Three Young Men, continues for another 46 verses. It begins with a description of the experience in the furnace that explains how the Babylonians kept stoking the fire but the angel of the Lord "drove the fiery flame out of the furnace." Then an extended hymn of praise follows. Nearly every line begins with "bless the Lord," exhorting the various elements of creation to "sing praise to him and highly exalt him forever." Toward the end of the song Hananiah, Azariah, and Mishael are called upon to praise God for their deliverance "from the midst of the burning fiery furnace."

3. The Outcome (3:24-30)

■ **24** The trial of the three Jewish captives did not turn out as believers might have hoped. Their steadfastness did not produce positive outcomes. Rather it provoked the king to set in motion events designed to bring about death. Their convictions led to execution.

Though the narrative might have ended as a martyr story with v 23, it is not over. Verses 24-25 signal a dramatic turning point in the story. The narrator allows suspense to build as a clear statement of what happens is delayed by conversations between the king and his advisers. The king initiates the turn of events by rising quickly from his seat **in amazement** and questioning **his advisers** (v 24). The question he poses is curious, **Weren't there three men that we tied up and threw into the fire?** The answer to this question should be obvious. The three names were recounted three times in the account of their execution in vv 19-23. The fact that they were bound was also repeated three times in those verses. So the advisers confirm the accuracy of the facts.

■ **25** The king's eyewitness report reveals the remarkable turn that the story has taken. He sees **four men** who are **walking . . . , unbound and unharmed** (v 25). These details announce the miraculous reversal that has taken place. The bound have become **unbound,** the harmed are **unharmed,** and the three have become **four.**

Most amazing to Nebuchadnezzar is **the fourth** person. He identifies this person as one who **looks like a son of the gods** (v 25). This phrase could be, and has been, translated as "the Son of God" (KJV). If translated this way, the phrase might indicate an appearance of Christ before his incarnation. But this is likely assuming too much for the context. The word **like** (*dāmēh*) suggests the king saw something representing deity to him. Later, in v 28, he identifies the being as an "angel" or messenger of God.

A significant point of the king's observations is that this all takes place **in the fire** (v 25). Shadrach, Meshach, and Abednego were not delivered from the fire. They were delivered in the midst of the fire.

■ **26-27** Final confirmation of the miraculous deliverance is delayed further by Nebuchadnezzar's command to **come out** of the furnace (v 26). The king who has summoned people and been obeyed throughout the story (vv 2-3, 13) once again beckons and is obeyed. But this time the command runs counter to his original intentions. The absolute monarch orders something he did not plan. This is an indication that he is no longer in charge of events. His reference to **the Most High God** signals who is in control (v 26). This title is used several times in Daniel to refer to the God of the Jews (3:26; 4:2; 5:18, 21; also "the Most High," 4:17, 24, 25, 32, 34; 7:18, 22, 25, 27). It identifies God as supreme among the gods but does not necessarily confess monotheism. Its use in this context accentuates the shift of power that has taken place. The God above all gods is above Nebuchadnezzar as well.

Following the king's command **Shadrach, Meshach and Abednego came out of the fire** (v 26). This statement finally confirms their deliverance. To add further testimony to their rescue, Nebuchadnezzar's officials **crowded around them** and gave witness (v 27). The list of officials is not as extensive as the one in v 2 but serves the same purpose of representing the entirety of Nebuchadnezzar's administrators. They observe that **the fire had not harmed** the bodies of the three (v 27). **Not harmed** (*lā šělēṭ*) literally translates *had no power or sovereignty over.* This further underscores the exchange of power that has taken en place. The threatening power of the state, the fire in the furnace, has been thwarted. Those who came to witness the power embodied in the image now see the power of God displayed in his servants. In addition to **their bodies,** the officials notice **their heads** and **their robes** remain untouched. With each observation the miracle becomes more remarkable. Finally the officials witness that there was not even the **smell of fire on them** (v 27).

■ **28-30** Nebuchadnezzar's response to the miracle is to offer praise (v 28), pronounce a decree (v 29), and promote the three Jews (v 30). He praises **the God** who revealed himself in the obedient actions **of Shadrach, Meshach and Abednego** (v 28). Two things done by that God gain Nebuchadnezzar's admiration. He **sent his angel and rescued his servants** (v 28). In brief summary these elements demonstrated the power of God to the king.

Nebuchadnezzar also commends the three men. They displayed the ideal qualities of loyal servants: trust, defiance, and sacrifice. They (1) **trusted** in God, (2) **defied** human directives, and (3) **were willing to give up their lives** rather than compromise their convictions (v 29). Nebuchadnezzar had desired to see such loyalty exhibited toward himself. The ceremonies surrounding the dedication of his image had been designed to accomplish this. Now he finds it among those who refused to demonstrate allegiance by means of the image.

The king who began the story uttering a **decree** ends with one (v 29). It is addressed to **the people of any nation or language** much like the decree in v 4 was directed to "peoples, nations and men of every language." It also includes a threat like the earlier one. The punishment for disobeying this decree is not a burning furnace, though. Rather it involves being **cut into pieces** and having **houses . . . turned into piles of rubble.** This is the same sentence given the incompetent wise men in 2:5.

The parallels between the opening and closing decrees accentuate the differences. The first decree called for honor for the image while the second calls for respect for **the God of Shadrach, Meshach and Abednego**. No one may **say anything against** this God (v 29). This declaration provides protection for worship of God, but it does not demand allegiance. Another difference is the motive for the decree. None is given in the first decree. The second, however, points out that the reason for this decree is that **no other god can save in this way** (v 29). This is an acknowledgment of the uniqueness of Israel's God and an allusion to the first commandment. It also affirms once more the ability of God **to save** (*nĕzal*). This has been the central issue in the chapter. Nebuchadnezzar raised it in v 15. The God he asked about in that context revealed himself through Shadrach, Meshach, and Abednego.

Nebuchadnezzar's final action is to reward the three Jews. The term **promote** (*zĕlah*) means "to prosper" (v 30). So the precise nature of their promotion could have included monetary gifts as well as added influence. The final irony of the story is noted here. Those who were thrown down are now raised up. In the end steadfast conviction did bring blessing.

FROM THE TEXT

The issues raised in ch 3 clearly indicate that it is more than a children's story. While it may be read at a surface level with great interest and benefit, the story evokes profound theological ideas. Among these are the power of idols, deliverance within the fire, the witness of ordeals, and the ethic of conviction.

The power of idols is a formidable force for the faithful to encounter. Humans are prone to be idol makers. The setting of ch 3 is a world where people pursue substitutes for the reality of God. They construct an image designed to promote their own exaggerated sense of importance and to produce an illusion of control over life. Whether the image in the story took the form of a god or some other entity, it is an idol, a figure embodying a power other than God.

The story of Shadrach, Meshach, and Abednego reveals that honor for Nebuchadnezzar's image, in effect, meant worship of the king. Nine times the text reminds the reader that it was he who **set up** the image. The real power behind the image was Nebuchadnezzar. Refusal to honor the idol signaled disloyalty to the king. The indictment against the Jews was that they **pay no attention to you, O king** when **they neither serve your gods nor worship the image of gold** (3:12). As with all idols, in the end they are concretized humanism. They glorify human creation and its achievements in place of God.

As the story unfolds it becomes clear that this image was a means to another end. It was a way for Nebuchadnezzar to gain a measure of control over his world. Many commentators have suggested that the disturbing dream in ch 2 may have provoked Nebuchadnezzar to make the golden image in ch 3. It was perhaps a representation of the golden head of the dream statue, which

Daniel had said symbolized Nebuchadnezzar's reign (2:38). The dream suggested that his reign would end like all others. Thus the image of ch 3 may be Nebuchadnezzar's way of trying to gain control over that which was out of his hands. In truth this is the practical function behind all idolatry. Idols are an attempt to manage life apart from God.

Idols function best when they can produce an illusion of power. In order to maintain this illusion radical measures must be taken. In the story uncompromising royal decrees filled with threats of death are needed to assure recognition of the idol. Pompous ceremonies with pretentious music and grand gatherings of important officials must be generated as well. All of this was calculated to overwhelm the populous and draw them to submission.

The ostentatious power of idols, however, need not overwhelm the believer. As the story reveals, three faithful followers of God stood strong against its power and won. They were rescued, vindicated, praised, and promoted.

The power of idols is a familiar feature in every culture and generation. Like Nebuchadnezzar people are looking for ways to manage life and enhance their own significance apart from God. The Bible thoroughly warns against such. In addition to the second commandment, numerous other texts prohibit making and worshipping idols (Exod 20:3-5; 1 Kgs 14:9; Acts 15:20; 1 John 5:21). Clearly God has set his own image on earth in the crown of his creation (Gen 1:26-27). No representation of God could adequately capture his magnificence. All images of the divine fall short of the reality. Idolatry is absurd from the perspective of biblical writers (Isa 44:9-20; 46:1-7; Rom 1:22-23). It is deception at its worst, for in the end it blocks a real relationship with the God of the universe.

God delivers in the midst of the fire as well as from it. The drama of Dan 3 takes an ugly turn that readers may not be fully prepared to absorb. The three faithful witnesses of God are actually thrown into a burning furnace, helpless and hopeless. They are bound by Babylon's strongest men and pitched into an inferno heated to its maximum temperature. Burning flesh, anguished cries, and excruciating pain are images that pass through the mind of the reader as their execution is meticulously portrayed.

God did not save his servants from the blast of flames. He did, however, come to them in the midst of the furnace. Miraculously Isaiah's word picture takes on literal reality. "When you walk through the fire, you will not be burned; the flames will not set you ablaze" (Isa 43:2). God chooses to step into the fire with the three Jewish men in the form of an **angel** (Dan 3:28). Nebuchadnezzar said it looked **like a son of the gods** (v 25). An apocryphal addition to Daniel tried to imagine what this must have been like. It says that the angel "drove the fiery flame out of the furnace, and made the inside of the furnace as though a moist wind were whistling through it" (Sg Three 26-27).

The irony of the fire is that this is the very element that is so often associated with the God of Israel. From the midst of fire God spoke to Moses (Exod 3:2) and to Israel (Deut 4:12). Fire indicates God's presence on Mount Sinai (Exod 19:18) and even describes his nature (Deut 4:24). God exercises absolute authority over fire by employing it for judgment (Gen 19:23) and to display his power among pagans (1 Kgs 18:38). Even God's appearance is described in terms of fire (Ezek 1:27).

A popular metaphor for God's greatest act of deliverance, the exodus from Egypt, is that of being brought "out of the iron-smelting furnace" (Deut 4:20; 1 Kgs 8:51; Jer 11:4). The exile is also described as a fire experience. It is called "the furnace of affliction" where God refines his people (Isa 48:10). Perhaps the reader should not be surprised that the rescue took place in the midst of fire.

God's promise to the faithful is that he will "be with" them (Exod 3:12; Ps 23:4-5; Isa 43:1-3; Jer 1:8; Matt 28:20). It is not to keep them away from all harm and danger. He may protect them from unpleasant things in life, or he may come to them in the midst of them.

The ordeals of life provide opportunity for witness to God's power in the world. The story of Dan 3 fulfills the message of the dream in ch 2. "In the time of those kings," such as Nebuchadnezzar, God sets up his kingdom that will not be destroyed (2:44). Like a rock smashing a statue, the unmatched power of God's kingdom overrules the pretentious power of Nebuchadnezzar. Three representatives of that kingdom are delivered from the furnace of an earthly kingdom. The ostentatious display of magnificence by Nebuchadnezzar is revealed for what it is, a statue with clay feet.

A very impressive and broad audience witnesses the dramatic rescue of Shadrach, Meshach, and Abednego. It all takes place in a grand public forum. Nebuchadnezzar and his entire entourage of government officials are present. These not only witness the uncompromising faith of three Jews but, more importantly, witness the unassailable faithfulness of God.

Unwittingly the king provided the elaborate stage for the display of God's power. He summoned **all the peoples, nations and men of every language** (v 7). Nebuchadnezzar precipitated the crisis with his decree, interrogated the three, and ordered their execution. He is also the first to observe the miracle of **four men walking around in the fire, unbound and unharmed** and testify to it (v 25). His highest courtiers provide additional eyewitness testimony as they examine the **bodies, heads,** and **robes** of the three Jews and find no trace of fire (v 27).

To his credit Nebuchadnezzar is also the first to acknowledge the faithful character of the three Jews and the divine workings in his midst. He identifies three essential characteristics of a convincing witness. These are unshakable trust in God, defiance of the opposition, and willingness **to give up their lives** rather than compromise their convictions (v 28). Nebuchadnezzar also testifies to the faithfulness of the God of these men. He acknowledges that **no other god can save in this way** (v 29).

Such testimony does not emerge without trial. The scripture affirms that the testing of one's faith is of great value. It is a key to personal faith development moving people toward maturity and a deeper life with God (Rom 5:3-5; Jas 1:2-4). More than that, though, tests reveal the power of God to the world. This is what the early Christians understood as they admonished one another to "rejoice that you participate in the sufferings of Christ, so that you may be overjoyed when his glory is revealed" (1 Pet 4:13). God often unveils his power in the most trying times of life. His greatest revelation to the world came in the agony of crucifixion.

Faithful people function from an ethic guided by conviction. The steadfast stance of the Shadrach, Meshach, and Abednego is as remarkable as it is refreshing and admirable. These men remain unmoved by the overwhelming conformity to secular power surrounding them. Their speech to the king in Dan 3:16-18 reveals an unwavering conviction that determines their actions. This is the focal point of the story as the chiasmic structure of the passage indicates.

The three offer no defense for their actions. They do **not need to defend** themselves (v 16). They are guilty of trusting God and defying the king as charged. Clearly their decision is determined by an inviolable faith in the absolute commands of their religion. It is not based on any certainty that they will be delivered from death. They know God **is able to save** and may **rescue . . . but even if he does not,** their position stands (vv 17-18). They are committed to the Torah and the life it prescribes. They will not break the expressed command of their God and **serve . . . or worship the image** (v 18).

The bold belief of the three is all the more amazing because it does not assume resurrection to life after death. There is no reference to such in this passage. They are **willing to give up their lives** for their beliefs (v 28). The reward for standing by their convictions is having done the right thing. As Nebuchadnezzar observed, they simply **trusted in** God (v 28). John Wesley commented, "They were resolved to suffer rather than sin, and leave the cause to God" (Wesley 1990, 366).

The Bible calls people to an ethic of conviction grounded in the directives of God. The continual challenge of Hebrew law is to "observe the commands of the LORD your God" (Deut 8:6). Wisdom books state this a little differently, "Trust in the LORD with all your heart" (Prov 3:5). While such admonitions regularly include a notice of reciprocation, the Bible knows that rewards for faithful living are not always direct or immediate. The book of Job acknowledges this when the main character asks, "Shall we accept good from

God, and not trouble?" (Job 2:10). In the Letter to the Hebrews the author recounts the suffering of the OT faith heroes and notes that "they did not receive the things promised; they only saw them and welcomed them from a distance" (Heb 11:13). The deepest faith is that faith which stands alone without hope of reward. Such is the kind of faith that guides actions in the moment of crisis as it did for Shadrach, Meshach, and Abednego.

D. Dream of a Tree: The Second Test of Wisdom (4:1-37)

Overview

The most surprising story in Daniel may be the one found in ch 4. Nebuchadnezzar, who has been the primary antagonist of God and his people in the first three chapters, suddenly testifies to a profound working of God in his life. In his final appearance in the book, the king speaks as if he is a convert to the God of the Jews. While Nebuchadnezzar's words of praise at the end of chs 2 and 3 might have prepared the reader for this to some degree, nothing suggested the kind of personal testimony found in ch 4. Remarkably, one of the most powerful kings of the ancient world bows out of the drama with weighty words of praise for Daniel's God on his lips. He has learned the truth of Proverbs regarding God's ways with humans. "He mocks proud mockers but gives grace to the humble" (Prov 3:34).

BEHIND THE TEXT

Nebuchadnezzar comes across as a humble and spiritually sensitive monarch in Dan 4. He relates a dramatic personal experience, which he acknowledges unfolded at the hand of Daniel's God. Initially this characterization appears to contrast with the overall impression of an unbending, impetuous, pagan tyrant found in chs 1 to 3. Yet ancient Babylonian documents reveal a personality every bit as complex as the one put forth in the book of Daniel. He was both unwaveringly decisive and open-minded, materially motivated and spiritually sensitive, ruthless in his judgments and morally concerned.

The *Babylonian Chronicles* and other texts confirm that Nebuchadnezzar possessed exceptional organizational and leadership skills both militarily and politically. He ruled one of the most dominating and prosperous empires of the ancient world for forty-three years. Under his guidance the empire was well organized and continued to expand its influence.

While Nebuchadnezzar ruled with tight-fisted precision, inscriptions and actions also reveal a man who was concerned with spiritual and moral matters. His many building projects included numerous religious sanctuaries dedicated to various gods and goddesses. In royal texts Nebuchadnezzar declared that his kingship was a gift of the gods and that he regularly sought their guidance for the empire. During religious festivals he participated in the ceremonial rituals prescribed by temple priests.

Nebuchadnezzar also claimed to have a deep concern for justice in his kingdom. In one inscription he bemoaned mistreatment of the poor and bribery in the law courts found throughout his empire prior to his rule. City governments were regulated within his kingdom, according to this inscription, so that they would be more equitable in their dealings with people.

Though such actions and statements were typically designed as propaganda to legitimate the rule of the king, in Nebuchadnezzar's case their cumulative effect indicates something more to scholars. Nebuchadnezzar's religious and moral interests appear to possess a certain genuine quality. Daniel's portrait of the king then corresponds well with what is known of him otherwise. He was a complex personality with unusual gifts for leadership (see Wiseman 1985, 98-102).

Nebuchadnezzar in Babylonian Inscriptions

Royal Babylonian inscriptions claim Nebuchadnezzar possessed deep spiritual and moral sensitivity. In a text addressed to Marduk, the patron god of Babylon, Nebuchadnezzar declared, "You begot me and entrusted me with the rule over all peoples." Thus he testified, "When I was born and created I continually sought the guidance of the gods and followed the way of the gods." With regard to moral issues Nebuchadnezzar believed he improved things with his system of governance. Before his rule Nebuchadnezzar noted, "The strong used to plunder the weak who was not equal to a lawsuit. The rich used to take the property of the poor" (Wiseman 1985, 99-100).

Some scholars doubt that Nebuchadnezzar was originally the subject of the story in ch 4. Babylonian records of the king do not corroborate either his illness or his acknowledgment of the Jewish God. Official documents from Nebuchadnezzar's last thirty years are sparse, however, and one debated fragment may reference the kind of illness that could have rendered Nebuchadnezzar incapable of ruling as ch 4 describes. Nevertheless, certain commentators posit that the events of ch 4 may refer to Nabonidus, a successor of Nebuchadnezzar who ruled Babylon from 556 to 539 B.C. Nabonidus was known to have separated himself from Babylon for a ten-year period, suffered a major illness, and been bothered by dreams on a regular basis. Evidence from the Dead Sea Scrolls seems to support this conclusion to some extent. A fragmentary document titled "The Prayer of Nabonidus" provides interesting parallels to the story conveyed in ch 4. This material speaks about an illness of Nabonidus that lasted for seven years. The illness came to an end with the assistance of a diviner who was a Jewish exile. This document has suggested to some scholars that Daniel's story may be a confused or elaborated variation of one originally about Nabonidus. The differences between the two stories, however, make such a conclusion tentative. While themes and some details are similar, the two stories depart considerably from one another. A firm line of relationship cannot be drawn between the two.

The Prayer of Nabonidus

The Prayer of Nabonidus displays interesting connections to the story of ch 4. This document has been reconstructed from four fragments found in Cave 4 at Qumran. The document is known as 4QPrNab, 4QOrNab, or 4Q242. Only the introduction is preserved, and the actual prayer is broken off. The text parallels Dan 4 in several ways. It mentions (1) the king's illness for seven years, (2) restoration to health, (3) mediation of a Jewish exile diviner, and (4) honor offered to God Most High. In addition (5) the text is narrated in first person.

In several ways the text differs from ch 4 however. These include (1) the name of the king, (2) the nature of the illness, (3) the reason for illness, and (4) the geographical setting. Significantly (5) the role of the Jewish exile, who is not named, is quite different. He admonishes the king to make a public testimony but does not interpret a dream.

The story of ch 4 portrays Nebuchadnezzar boasting over **the great Babylon** that he built (v 30). Ancient texts and archaeological excavations have confirmed that Nebuchadnezzar and his father made Babylon into a showcase city as the capital for the empire. They poured the major portion of the resources gained from their conquests into it. Massive building and refurbishing projects caused Babylon to become one of the greatest cities of the ancient world.

4:1-37

Babylon was located along the Euphrates River, the main communications and transportation artery of the Mesopotamian region. From **the roof of the royal palace** Nebuchadnezzar could overlook the city from the north (v 29). On his right ran the impressive Euphrates lined with retaining walls and spanned by a prominent bridge approximately four hundred feet long. Between the river and the palace probably lay the terraces of the strikingly beautiful royal gardens filled with the most remarkable collection of species of flora known in the ancient world.

Looking southward the king would see the city spread out over a flat plain with a skyline punctuated by over fifty temples. One of them, a ziggurat known as Etemananki, reached nearly three hundred feet in height. Streets of burnt brick laid in bitumen wound throughout the city along with broad promenades of limestone slabs. A system of underground canals provided fresh water to its inhabitants. Massive double walls enclosed all this and stretched over seventeen miles around the city. Magnificent gates were decorated with colorful enameled brick reliefs of lions, dragons, and bulls and secured by spectacular bronze doors. A gate dedicated to the goddess Ishtar rose to over forty feet and provided an imposing entrance on the north side of the city.

The primary literary form of ch 4 is that of a royal proclamation. It is a public document addressed to the entire kingdom, which Nebuchadnezzar unashamedly describes as **peoples, nations and men of every language, who live in all the world** (v 1). Such proclamations are well known from ancient inscriptions. Ezra 1:1-4 preserves one of these from the Persian king Cyrus. What is unusual about the decree in Dan 4 is its very personal and less than flattering nature. More typical of royal decrees are themes and language that heighten the image of the monarch. Part of the impact of this chapter is realized by employing this familiar royal form to convey a story of humiliation and faith. The strength of the personal testimony gains force as a result of the authoritative genre of royal decree.

Another unusual feature of this chapter is the shift from first person testimony to third person narrative and back again to first person. The first person accounts (vv 1-18 and 34-37) frame the third person section (vv 19-33). In many ways the alternation of narrative perspectives is natural and goes almost unnoticed. The third person account picks up at a crucial juncture when Daniel interprets the king's dream. It continues through a report of the dream's fulfillment. The first person narration of Nebuchadnezzar returns again with a testimony acknowledging God's power.

The affect of the move from first to third to first person is to underscore a central theme of the chapter: Nebuchadnezzar is not sovereign. Control of the story rests in the hands of the omniscient third person narrator, not Nebuchadnezzar. While the king relays the bulk of his experience, the external narrator assures the reliability of this account. The third person narrative conveys the way in which God overrules Nebuchadnezzar. The king's humiliation at the hand of God was not a subjective experience. A third party witnessed its reality and told about it. The advantage of this literary technique is to preserve the convincing force of a personal testimony while guarding its integrity.

Chapter 4 is closely connected to the other stories of the book and must be understood in relationship to them. Since the story involves the interpretation of divine communications, ch 4 is a test of wisdom like chs 2 and 5. Like the stories in those chapters, ch 4 poses a challenge to the wisdom of Daniel and his God regarding present and future realities that need explanation. The wise men of Babylon cannot help. But Daniel and his God can. In ch 4 the element of contest between Daniel and the Babylonian wise men is not as pronounced as it was in ch 2. In this way it is more like ch 5. The emphasis lies rather upon the fulfillment of the dream and the king's response to it. Chapter

5 also includes a brief element of fulfillment. Chapter 4 also differs from chs 2 and 5 by not mentioning any honor or promotion for Daniel.

Connections between chs 4 and 5 are significant. Both chapters deal with the humbling of a Babylonian king and form the central couplet of chapters in the chiasmic structure of the Aramaic section of the book. Together they form a fulcrum for this section that focuses attention upon the key theme of God's sovereignty over earthly rulers. The bond between the two chapters is made explicit when Daniel briefly rehearses the story of ch 4 as an object lesson for Belshazzar in 5:18-21. Chapter 5 also mentions God as "the Most High God" in the same manner as ch 4. This title is used more often between 3:26 and 5:21 than anywhere else in the book.

The relationship between chs 3 and 4 is important as well. In both chapters Nebuchadnezzar is the dominant character, and the issue of his arrogance in relation to the God of Daniel is addressed. In addition, both the beginning of ch 4 and the ending of ch 3 contain words of praise spoken by Nebuchadnezzar. This feature may lay behind the different versification of the Hebrew Bible and other versions. The Hebrew Bible includes the first three verses of ch 4 as part of the end of ch 3. Thus 4:1-3 in the English Bible is equal to 3:31-33 in the Hebrew Bible. Such division of chapters was not original to the Hebrew Bible since it came about in the thirteenth century. But it does recognize the close association between the two chapters.

Greek Version of Chapter 4

The Old Greek version of ch 4 varies considerably from the Aramaic of the MT. The Old Greek lacks some verses found in the Aramaic and adds others. For example, the Old Greek version does not begin with Nebuchadnezzar's confession in vv 1-3 but rather the announcement of a disturbing dream noted in v 4. It also omits any reference to the king summoning wise men in vv 6-9 and proceeds with a description of the dream. Other lesser variations occur until the fulfillment of the dream is recounted. At that point the Old Greek provides additional description of Nebuchadnezzar's experience. When the time of illness draws to an end, the Old Greek tells of an angel coming to address Nebuchadnezzar again. Then the final praise and vow of Nebuchadnezzar is given at greater length than that found in the Aramaic.

Chapter 4 also makes connections with other portions of the Hebrew Bible. In the book of Job Elihu describes one of the values of dream visions, which is illustrated in Nebuchadnezzar's experience. The terrifying affects of such visions are meant "to turn man from wrongdoing and keep him from pride, to preserve his soul from the pit, his life from perishing by the sword" (Job 33:17-18). In the end this is just what Nebuchadnezzar's dream accomplished.

The vision also alludes to Gen 1—3 by recalling references to an idyllic

109

garden scene where **beasts of the field** and **birds of the air** find nourishment and protection from a life-giving tree (Dan 4:10-12). The enormous height of the tree whose **top touched the sky** (v 11) evokes images of the tower of Babel in Gen 11. Both stories speak about the issue of arrogant grasping at divinity as well as a judgment of scattering.

The metaphor of a **tree . . . large and strong** has numerous other parallels in both biblical and nonbiblical literature (Dan 4:11). Israel's prophets regularly employ the imagery associated with trees to convey messages of hope and judgment (Isa 10:33-34; 11:1; Hos 14:5-7; Amos 2:9). Ezekiel, in particular, likens the Davidic dynasty (ch 17), Jerusalem (ch 19), and Pharaoh (ch 31) to flourishing trees that will be cut down. The language of Ezek 31 parallels Dan 4 in several ways. For example, the prophet speaks of "all the birds of the air nested in its boughs, and all the beasts of the field . . . under its branches" (Ezek 31:6) much like Dan 4:12.

The tree imagery found in the Hebrew Bible is shared within the larger context of ancient Near Eastern literature and iconography. A recurring motif in this material is the sacred cosmic tree. It was a way of envisioning the unity of creation and its provision for life. The roots of this tree reach down to the waters beneath and its top to the heavens drawing the major elements of the cosmos together. In some texts the king embodies the reality of the tree and stands as its personification. Thus the tree described in the dream of ch 4 was a familiar concept to its ancient audience.

The Tree Imagery in the OT

The tree is a symbol of abundance and life throughout the Bible. The scarcity of trees in some parts of Israel makes it a particularly poignant image of vitality. Trees symbolize God's provision and care for his creation (Ps 104:16-17). They can be symbols of beauty (Song 7:7), of longevity (Isa 65:22), of well-being (Zech 3:10), of protection (Ezek 31:6), and of a well-lived life (Ps 1:3). Their majestic height can signify pride (Isa 2:12-13) and their destruction judgment (Ezek 19:12-14). The tree of life in the Garden of Eden emerges as a special symbol for eternal life. It stands as an image of God's original design for humans that became lost as well as an image of hope for the future (Rev 2:7). The splendor of God's ultimate renewal of creation is pictured finally with abundantly fruitful trees (Ezek 47:12).

Chapter 4 is a royal proclamation testifying to God's working in Nebuchadnezzar's life. It begins (vv 1-3) and ends (vv 34-37) with the king's confessions of praise. These declarations create an inclusion that draws the material into a coherent unit. Within this frame a story is told of a disturbing dream (vv 4-18), of its interpretation (vv 19-27), and of its fulfillment (vv 28-33). Suspense is created for the reader by delayed explanation. Outcomes of events and responses to them are announced before details are described.

IN THE TEXT

1. Opening Confession (4:1-3)

Unlike other stories in Daniel, ch 4 begins with a hymn of praise for God. These words provide a glimpse of the outcome of the story that will be told. The intended effect of such an introduction is to create immediate interest for the reader who must wonder why a Babylonian king such as Nebuchadnezzar is praising God.

■ **1** The words of praise and the story that follows are couched in the language of public proclamation. Nebuchadnezzar introduces his announcement in typical form for official Babylonian and Persian correspondence. He identifies himself and those he addresses and wishes them prosperity. The designation of his audience as **the peoples, nations and men of every language, who live in all the world** tends to heighten Nebuchadnezzar's own importance (v 1). He is king not only of Babylon but also of **all the world.** Such claims were typical for Assyrian and Babylonian monarchs. The description of the audience is similar to that of 3:4, where another royal decree called for worship of a statue. This similarity tends to accentuate a contrast between the two proclamations. In ch 3 Nebuchadnezzar was arrogantly seeking honor for himself while in ch 4 he humbly gives honor to God.

The typical salutation **may you prosper greatly** introduces the motifs of prosperity and greatness that become central to the story (v 1). The concept recurs several times throughout the chapter by means of different terms to highlight a key point (see vv 3, 11, 20, 22, 24, 30, 36). Human prosperity and greatness truly comes only from the hand of God.

■ **2** The events that Nebuchadnezzar will speak about are summarized as **miraculous signs and wonders that the Most High God has performed** (v 2). The expression **signs and wonders** (*'otayyā' wĕtimhayyā'*) refers to signature events, either natural or supernatural, that testify to the reality of God in this world. Israel's exodus experience is frequently described in such terms (*'ot wĕmôpēt* in Exod 7:3; Deut 4:34; Neh 9:10; Jer 32:20, etc.). Daniel's deliverance from the lions' den is also classified among God's dramatic "signs and wonders" (Dan 6:27).

Nebuchadnezzar calls God **the Most High God** (v 2). This expression, along with the shortened form "the Most High," is concentrated in this chapter (4:2, 17, 24, 25, 32, 34). It is appropriate in this context since it emphasizes God's superiority over all other authorities. It helps to underscore the key theme of God's absolute sovereignty over human monarchs, even the world's most impressive potentate Nebuchadnezzar.

DANIEL

4:1-2

111

The Most High God

The expressions "the Most High God" and "the Most High" occur thirteen times in the book (3:26; 4:2, 17, 24, 25, 32, 34; 5:18, 21; 7:18, 22, 25, 27). These occurrences are concentrated in chs 4 and 7. These designations for God do not affirm monotheism, but they do emphasize God's superiority in the divine realm. God stands above all other spiritual forces. The related phrase "God Most High" (*'el 'elyon*) or simply "Most High" (*'elyon*) occurs another thirty-six times in the Hebrew Scriptures. In the NT God is called by the equivalent Greek term (*hupsistos*) nine times.

■ **3** Nebuchadnezzar's words of praise reflect the language of Israel's worship literature. Psalm 145:13, for example, is almost an exact parallel to the latter half of Dan 4:3. Similar expressions, however, may be found in Babylonian ritual as well. So the king is not necessarily quoting Hebrew scripture, though the Jewish reader might hear it that way. Nebuchadnezzar extols God for revealing his sovereign authority with a series of word pairs. The words in each couplet (**signs** and **wonders; great** and **mighty; kingdom** and **dominion**) may be taken synonymously and serve to heighten the effect of praise (v 3).

The greatness of God's **signs** and **wonders** make known **his dominion,** which impresses the king because of its stability and present reality. It has no ending and no absence. The rule of God remains present in this world because it **endures from generation to generation.** People do not need to wait until the end of time to experience the kingdom of God on earth.

2. The Disturbing Dream (4:4-18)

The reason for Nebuchadnezzar's hymn of praise is explained in what follows. A disturbing dream (vv 4-18) was interpreted by Daniel (vv 19-27) and brought to fulfillment in the king's life (vv 28-33).

Nebuchadnezzar begins his story by describing a dream that came to him. He delays conveying the content of the dream (vv 10-18), however, by first describing his circumstances prior to the dream (v 4), his reaction to it (v 5), his attempts to have it interpreted (vv 6-8), and his words of confidence in Daniel (v 9). This delaying technique effectively raises suspense in the story.

■ **4** The dream came to Nebuchadnezzar unexpectedly. He was **at home . . . , contented and prosperous** (v 4). These conditions suggest a time in Nebuchadnezzar's reign when most hostilities were under control. Literally, the text says he was **at ease** (*sĕlēh*) and **flourishing** (*ra'nan*). The latter term can describe healthy, productive plants. It foreshadows the dream in which a fruitful tree symbolizes the king.

The surprising nature of the dream is further highlighted by Nebuchadnezzar's reference to receiving the dream while **lying in my bed** (v 4). Two more times he will emphasize this location (vv 10 and 13). If the king had been seeking communication from the divine realm, he might have been in a temple engaged in rituals designed to accomplish such ends.

■ **5-7** The unexpected vision not only made the king **afraid** but also **terrified** him (v 5). The use of both words accentuates the dread felt by the king. In the ancient world dreams were considered special communications from the gods and often their messages were ominous. (See *Behind the Text* for ch 2 for additional background on dreams.) Therefore **wise men of Babylon,** whose role it was to interpret such messages, are brought to the king (v 6). This included **magicians, enchanters, astrologers and diviners** (v 7). This list of experts is similar to the ones in 2:2 and 2:27. (See *Behind the Text* for ch 2 for possible distinctions between these groups.) Their job was to consult the vast collections of dreams and omens that had been preserved for centuries. If a corresponding dream was found, they would be able to make an interpretation. Apparently no match was discovered because **they could not interpret it** (v 7).

■ **8** After the other wise men exhausted their resources, **Daniel came** into the king's presence (v 8). As in chs 2 and 5 the contrast between Daniel and the Babylonians is emphasized. Traditional Babylonian wisdom cannot compare to Daniel's wisdom. Daniel possesses a gift of interpretation that the others do not. He is different and this time the king knows why. Daniel has a unique connection with the divine world, **the spirit of the holy gods is in him** (v 8). Two more times the king will underscore this observation (vv 9 and 18). While the phrase *rûaḥ ʾĕlāhîn qadîšîn* could possibly be translated "the spirit of the Holy God," such words do not seem likely on Nebuchadnezzar's lips. Jewish readers, however, may note the irony of the king's words. Daniel is like Joseph, "one in whom is the spirit of God" (*rûaḥ ʾĕlōhîm*; Gen 41:38). The point is that Daniel's wisdom derives from the heavenly realms. Thus the phrase acknowledges the truth highlighted in Dan 2; God holds the keys to real wisdom.

The king mentions that Daniel's Babylonian name is **Belteshazzar** and notes its connection to **the name of my god** (v 8). He is likely referring to Bel who is also known as Marduk, the patron god of Babylon. While Nebuchadnezzar is aware that Daniel's gift derives from the divine world, he understands things from the perspective of his polytheistic worldview. In the context of the Hebrew Scriptures, though, readers know that the God of Israel is Daniel's source of wisdom.

As Nebuchadnezzar begins to address Daniel directly, he confirms his confidence in him. The king will close his speech in like manner in v 18. He calls Daniel by his Babylonian name, **Belteshazzar,** as one might expect. The king's multiple uses of this name (vv 8, 9, 18, 19) in this context may have special meaning. It translates "protect his life." Perhaps repetition of the name offers some comfort to a troubled king.

■ **9** Nebuchadnezzar identifies Daniel as **chief of the magicians** (v 9). This is the position to which he had been promoted after interpreting the king's statue dream (2:48). Perhaps this is the reason Daniel was last to speak with the king in this instance. Lesser diviners may have tried their hand at interpretation before the master came forth. In any case, the king is quite sure that **no mystery is too difficult for you** (v 9). This phrase further identifies Daniel's wisdom with God's, though the king may not know it. Israel's faith confessed that God's wisdom had no restraints (Dan 2:22; Job 11:7-9; Ps 139:11-12; Isa 55:8-9; Jer 23:24).

■ **10-12** The content of the disturbing dream is finally described in Dan 4:10-17. It involves a large tree that is cut down and turns into a person who takes on animal characteristics. As might be expected of a dream, the transition from tree to human is not clearly defined or entirely logical.

Nebuchadnezzar explains that he saw a surreal tree abounding with life. Four qualities accentuate the greatness and prosperity of this tree. The greatness of the tree rests in (1) its placement and (2) it size. The prosperity of the tree can be seen in its ability to (3) nourish and (4) protect creation. It is of central importance to the earthly realm because it is located **in the middle of the land** (v 10). From there it grew so large that it **touched the sky** and **was visible to the ends of the earth** (v 11). Its branches produced so much **fruit** that it could nourish all creation. There was enough **food for all** and **from it every creature was fed** (v 12). Its abundance drew both **beasts of the field** and **birds of the air** who also found protection under its branches (v 12). Like the tree of life and the tree of the knowledge of good and evil in the middle of the Garden of Eden, this tree is surrounded by the pulsating life of creation (Gen 2:9).

■ **13** Abruptly a heavenly being enters the dream and disrupts the idyllic garden scene. This being is called **a messenger** (*ʿîr*), literally "a watcher" (Dan 4:13). The term refers to an angel, as the accompanying parallel term **holy one** (*qadîš*) indicates. The use of the term "watcher" became more frequent in Jewish literature during the Greek and Roman periods. It suggests a role for heavenly beings of watching over the affairs of God on earth.

■ **14-16** The angel's words are in the form of a royal proclamation. Like the official herald in 3:4, he calls out in **a loud voice** (v 14). Four vivid verbs command the complete devastation of the tree: **cut down, trim off, strip off,** and **scatter** (v 14). As a result fauna that had been nourished and protected by the tree take off. The tree is not completely destroyed, however. **The stump and its roots** are allowed to **remain in the ground** and are **bound with iron and bronze** (v 15). The metal binding could have at least two meanings. It may refer to a metal band placed around a tree stump to protect it from further deterioration. This practice is not attested in ancient horticulture, however, and is only a conjecture by modern scholars. Another possibility is that the band refers to a metal fetter used to restrain animals. The description of a wild animal in the following verses supports this understanding.

The decree of the messenger continues with a message of devastation. This time, however, it is for a person. In the midst of v 15 the subject shifts from a tree to a human. This is the first hint that the tree is a metaphor for a human being. That person will live **with the animals** unprotected from the early morning **dew** (v 15). More than that, even **his mind** (literally, "his heart" or "inner person") will become like that of **the mind of an animal** (v 16). All of this will have a set duration. Precisely how long, however, is not delineated. **Till seven times pass by for him** is a way of saying that a certain amount of time is allotted (v 16). The number **seven** symbolizes completeness, while the term **times** ('*iddānîn*) varies in its meaning from days to seasons to years. Thus the phrase designates an unspecified period of time.

■ **17** The messenger concludes his pronouncement by underscoring the authority of the dream and giving its purpose. He confirms that the dream is a **verdict** communicated through divine **messengers** (v 17). The language reflects royal communication and accentuates the decisiveness of the dream's message. The heavenly king has issued this decree in dream form through his heralds.

The intended effect of the dream's message is to gain recognition for God's absolute sovereignty in the human sphere. Those who must concede this are **the living,** that is, those to whom the king's proclamation is being addressed. These are "the peoples, nations and men of every language, who live in all the world" (v 1). What they must acknowledge is **that the Most High is sovereign over the kingdoms of men** (v 17). In other words, God rules over earthly affairs as well as heavenly affairs with absolute freedom. He exercises his authority over human kingdoms in two ways: (1) he **gives them to anyone he wishes** and (2) he **sets over them the lowliest of men** (v 17). The audience is challenged to **know** (*yĕda*') this truth. The Aramaic term might be better translated *learn.* In any case it suggests more than head knowledge. The understanding must be heartfelt. Fulfillment of the dream will illustrate this truth dramatically. Nebuchadnezzar will gain the kind of knowledge that only experience can give. He will become one of **the lowliest of men** whom God sets over a kingdom. God will rescue him from a dreadful disease and restore his rule to him (see v 36).

Poetry in Chapter 4

The king describes his dream in poetic fashion. The rhythm of Semitic poetry becomes obvious in the Aramaic text (Aramaic verse numbers in brackets) of vv 10-12 [7-9] and 13-16 [10-12]. The beginning of the poetry is signaled by the phrase **and there before me** (*wa'ălû*) in both instances (vv 10 [7] and 13 [10]).

115

Counting words in thought units, one may observe the pattern of lines as follows in vv 10-12 [7-9]: 2+2+2, 3+3+3, 2+2+2, 4+4+3. In vv 13-16 [10-12] the pattern emerges as: 2+3, 4+4+4, 3+2, 3+2+3+3, 3+2+2, 3+2+2, 2+2. The overall irregularity of the beat is typical of biblical poetry, but a rhythm is distinguishable.

Aside from the hymnic praises in vv 2-3 and 34-35, other verses in ch 4 reflect poetic qualities. Parallelism, rhythm, and balancing are evident at different points throughout the story. For example, v 17 [14] introduces the purpose of God's judgment with a line that exhibits internal parallelism. Literally it reads "By decree of watchers the sentence, and a word of holy ones the decision." Only vv 2-3 [3:32-33], 10-12 [7-9], 13-16 [10-12], and 34-35 [31-32] have been laid out in poetic structure by the standard Hebrew text *BHS*. The NRSV and some other English translations have followed this lead.

■ **18** Nebuchadnezzar closes his address to Daniel as he began it. He expresses confidence in Daniel because **the spirit of the holy gods** is evident in him (v 18). This factor sets Daniel apart from **the wise men** of Babylon. It is the reason they are not able to interpret the dream. They belong to Nebuchadnezzar's kingdom, while Daniel has connections with another dominion.

3. Interpretation of the Dream (4:19-27)

Another narrator takes control of the story at this point. The first person testimony of Nebuchadnezzar gives way to a third person perspective in order to relay the interpretation of the dream (vv 19-27) and its fulfillment (vv 28-33). As noted previously, the change of perspective at this juncture in the text suggests that things are no longer in Nebuchadnezzar's hands. His story is now told by another to ensure its fidelity and to prove the point of God's sovereignty that the story intends to emphasize.

The literary technique of delayed explanation is employed once again. Daniel's reaction to the meaning of the dream is described (v 19) before his interpretation is given (vv 20-26). Then the section closes with a prophetic warning (v 27).

■ **19** Daniel reacts to the dream much like Nebuchadnezzar did. He is deeply troubled by it. It is the same kind of response he would have to other visions (7:15, 27; 8:27). In those cases his unrest was because he did not fully understand the meaning of the visions. In this case it is because he did. The dream so **perplexed** and **terrified** him that an awkward silence ensues **for a time** (4:19). Though this does not bode well for the king, he encourages Daniel to remain calm. He takes on a role often performed by angels and admonishes Daniel, **Do not let the dream or its meaning alarm you** (v 19). Undoubtedly he determines that it is better to know details of bad news than to surmise about them.

Daniel effectively distances himself from the dream by sharing Nebuchadnezzar's dread. He expresses a desire that the message be for the king's **enemies** and not for him (v 19). By this statement he communicates that the message of the dream is not his message. Daniel is only relaying it.

■ **20-22** Most of the description of the tree in the dream is repeated in vv 20-21 before Daniel finally confirms that **you, O king, are that tree!** (v 22). Like Nathan before David, Daniel forthrightly declares, "You are the man!" (2 Sam 12:7). Only Nebuchadnezzar possesses the **greatness** and kind of **dominion** signified in the tree. The extent of Nebuchadnezzar's power is emphasized by reference to both **sky** and **earth**.

Heaven and Earth

The terms **heaven** and **earth** are used significantly throughout the chapter. **Heaven** (šěmayin), which is also translated "sky" and "air," occurs sixteen times (vv 11, 12, 13, 15, 20, 21, 22, 23a, 23b, 25, 26, 31, 33, 34, 35, 37). **Earth** (ʾǎraʿ) occurs ten times (vv 4, 10, 11, 15a, 15b, 20, 22, 23, 35a, 35b) and may be translated "land," "ground," or "world" depending on context. The concentration of these terms throughout this chapter highlights the contest between earthly and heavenly realms. God's heavenly kingdom contrasts sharply with Nebuchadnezzar's earthly domain. Though the king exerts remarkable influence throughout the earth and even touches the heavens, in the end he is overpowered by the powers of heaven. God "does as he pleases with the powers of heaven and the peoples of the earth" (v 35). Clearly the God of Daniel is sovereign over both realms and Nebuchadnezzar is not (see Jer 10:11-12).

■ **23** In light of the identification of the king with the tree, the second section of the dream becomes even more foreboding. The messenger's command to **cut down the tree and destroy it** refers to Nebuchadnezzar (v 23). He will **live like the wild animals** for a period of time.

■ **24-26** This interpretation is made clear in vv 24-26 where Daniel details the implications of living like an animal of the fields. It means the king will (1) **be driven away from people,** (2) **live with the wild animals,** (3) **eat grass like cattle,** and (4) **be drenched with the dew of heaven** (v 25). Saturation with dew may indicate more than outdoor exposure. The phrase is specifically repeated four times in the story (vv 15, 23, 25, 33). Among the ancients **the dew of heaven** was thought to come from the stars and bring either sickness or healing. In this case it brings sickness. Thus the dew signifies the dominion of heavenly forces.

The irony of this judgment is obvious. The one who attempted to be seen as more than human will become less than human. The mightiest will become the lowliest. The one who nourished others with abundant fruit must find nourishment in grass. The protector will become the unprotected. The king will lose his place in the cosmos.

The duration of the judgment is clarified in v 25. It will last until the king confesses **that the Most High is sovereign over the kingdoms of men.** Once he concedes that God's sovereignty is so absolute that he can assign kingdoms **to anyone he wishes,** Nebuchadnezzar's ordeal will end. The purpose statement from v 17 has become a contingency statement in v 25.

At this point Daniel does not mention that God "sets over them the lowliest of men" as was noted earlier (v 17). The omission of this phrase and others that were included in Nebuchadnezzar's original dream description, suggests that Daniel may be exercising restraint as he interprets the dream. He does not repeat the entire description of the tree in vv 20-21 or all the details of the tree's destruction in v 23. Such seems appropriate since the details are already known. The blow of judgment does not necessarily diminish because of these omissions. It is still a foreboding sentence.

The hope offered the king through the image of the **stump** and **roots** is reminiscent of messianic references to the same (Isa 11:1). These remnants of the tree signify that Nebuchadnezzar's **kingdom will be restored** to him (Dan 4:26). It will happen only upon the condition that he concedes **that Heaven rules,** however. The statement confirms what had just been said in v 25. The end of Nebuchadnezzar's judgment will come when he submits to God. This use of **Heaven** to refer to God is unique in the Hebrew Bible. During the Second Temple period in Judaism this became common practice among the rabbis as a means of avoiding trivializing God's name and breaking the third commandment.

■ **27** Daniel finishes his dream interpretation with a respectful but strong word of warning. One task of Babylonian diviners was to divert the ill effects of dreams and omens through various incantations. Daniel does not resort to these means, however. He calls for ethical conversion in the tradition of Israel's prophets. He challenges the king to **renounce** his **sins** and **wickedness** (v 27). **Renounce** (*pĕruq*) implies a radical break from current behavior. **Sins** (*ḥăṭāy*) and **wickedness** (*ʿāwāyâ*) correspond to the typical terms used throughout the Hebrew Bible to describe unacceptable behavior before God. **Sins** refer to actions that miss the goal God has set for a person, while **wickedness** refers to the perverted tendencies that characterize a life that displeases God.

Evidence of genuine repentance includes (1) **doing what is right** and (2) **being kind to the oppressed** (v 27). These actions reflect a mandate issued to kings of Israel. They were to preserve justice and righteousness (1 Kgs 10:9; Isa 9:7; Jer 9:24). Daniel holds the Babylonian king to the same standards as the kings of Israel. He must do more than avoid unfair practices. He must actively show kindness to **the oppressed,** those who lack resources to obtain justice on their own. With these words Daniel sounds a recurring note of Israel's prophets. Like Amos he calls for "justice [to] roll on like a river, righteousness like a never-failing stream" (Amos 5:24).

Daniel closes his admonition with a word of hope. Genuine repentance might allow the king's current **prosperity** to continue (Dan 4:27). The reference to **prosperity** (*šĕlēh*) employs the same word used to speak of the king's "contented" condition before the dream came (v 4). Daniel does not guarantee this result but offers it as a possible motive for change.

4. Fulfillment of the Dream (4:28-33)

■ **28** In ch 2 a similar kind of story concludes rapidly once the interpretation of the dream is given. It finishes with a note of praise for God and promotion for Daniel. The story here, however, is concerned to relay the fulfillment of the dream. The narrator explains that **all this happened** (v 28) and then proceeds to describe the circumstances that led up to the fulfillment (vv 29-32) before detailing the actual realization of the dream (v 33). This is the most extensive description of fulfillment of a vision within the book. It serves, therefore, to highlight an implied message of the book as a whole. The divine revelations recorded here will be realized.

■ **29-30** Fulfillment of the dream came **twelve months** after Daniel's interpretation of it (v 29). This would be a little less than a solar year since Babylonians used a lunar calendar with about 354 days in the year. The length of time suggests grace on God's part to allow Nebuchadnezzar adequate opportunity to heed Daniel's counsel in v 27. This temporal reference also alludes to God's sovereignty over time, which is firmly declared in 2:21.

The scene for Nebuchadnezzar's demise is appropriately set **on the roof of the royal palace of Babylon** (v 29). This setting might easily evoke pride as the king overlooked one of the most impressive cities of the ancient world. (See *Behind the Text* for description of the city.) Nebuchadnezzar's feelings of self-importance are evident in his free use of the first person personal pronouns **I** and **my** (v 30). The subject of the verb **built** is punctuated by the emphatic use of the first person personal pronoun *'ănâ*. The overall tenor of the statement is summarized well by Daniel in ch 5. Speaking to Belshazzar in that context he explained that Nebuchadnezzar's "heart became arrogant and hardened with pride" (5:20).

Wholesome pride over his achievements may have been appropriate for the king, but his arrogance was not. He erred in two ways. First, he believed that he had built the fabulous city by means of his own **mighty power.** His victorious armies had brought tremendous wealth to the city and enabled the massive building projects. Yet, according to Daniel, this all transpired by the will of God. Earlier the prophet had explained to Nebuchadnezzar, "The God of heaven has given you dominion and power and might and glory; in your hands he has placed mankind and the beasts of the field and the birds of the air" (2:37-38).

Nebuchadnezzar's other mistake was thinking that the beauty of the city was for **the glory of** [his] **majesty** (v 30). The word **majesty** (*hādar*) derives from a term that means swollen or enlarged. Nebuchadnezzar felt that the purpose of all his accomplishments had been to make him more important. In fact achievements of the creature should only point toward the Creator's glory.

■ **31-32** The divine response to Nebuchadnezzar's arrogant statement was immediate. **A voice . . . from heaven** pronounced judgment (v 31). This **voice** could belong to either God or an angelic messenger. God has been identified already in this story by reference to heaven in v 26. Whether or not it is God's direct voice, the message comes with the authority of the One whose abode is above and beyond the earth.

The words of the voice are spoken in the form of a royal decree, much like the words of the heavenly messenger in the dream (see vv 14-17). The one who normally makes decrees now must ironically submit to an edict from a higher authority. The pronouncement follows much of what was revealed in the dream, but it both omits and adds things. The statement **your royal authority has been taken from you** is new (v 31). It succinctly summarizes the effects of Nebuchadnezzar's judgment. He would not be able to rule when he is struck by an illness that causes him to be **driven away from people, live with the wild animals,** and **eat grass like cattle** (v 32). Being drenched with dew is not mentioned at this point.

The condition for ending the curse is given for the fourth time in the story (see vv 17, 25, 26). The illness will cease when the king is ready to **acknowledge that the Most High is sovereign** (v 32). The statement here is identical to the one in v 25.

■ **33** The fate predicted for Nebuchadnezzar befalls him **immediately** (v 33). He becomes like an animal of the fields who is **driven away from people,** eats **grass,** and is **drenched with the dew of heaven** (v 33). The result of such living is unkempt **hair** and **nails** that look like bird **feathers** and **claws** (v 33). This aspect of the king's condition is new. It provides a visual of Nebuchadnezzar's distraught appearance. The term for **grass** (*'ăśab*) includes vegetables and other herbs. So Nebuchadnezzar likely subsisted on a variety of edible plants.

The best guess of modern scholars is that Nebuchadnezzar's condition reflects a person with lycanthropy. This is a mental disorder in which people believe they are animals and act accordingly. Whatever the precise diagnosis might be, it is clearly a debilitating illness that renders Nebuchadnezzar unable to function as a king. He becomes like one of the dependent creatures that he was designed to nurture (see vv 12 and 21).

5. Closing Confession (4:34-37)

The story concludes with a resolution to Nebuchadnezzar's plight. The king regained his understanding (v 34*a*) and his position (v 36). This restoration provokes a confession of praise (vv 34*b*-35) and a final confession of faith (v 37). The interweaving of restoration and confession in this section highlights the interdependence of these two concepts. The king's restoration rests upon his acknowledgment of God as sovereign.

The notes of praise here echo back to the opening of the story. The return to first person testimony does the same. The story ends with the perspective from which it began.

■ **34** Nebuchadnezzar testifies that his condition changed when he **raised** [his] **eyes toward heaven** (v 34). These simple words form the turning point of the story. They describe the uncomplicated act of a person expressing faith in God, much like is found in the psalms of Israel (Pss 121:1; 123:1-2). Lifting one's eyes toward God signifies trust in him. The result of this basic act of faith was that the king's **sanity was restored** (Dan 4:34). This phrase could be translated *my knowledge returned to me* (*mandĕʿî*). What Nebuchadnezzar now knows is "that the Most High is sovereign" (vv 25, 32). This is what he was supposed to learn from the experience according to the messenger and the voice from heaven. These had said the illness would last until he acknowledged this truth.

Putting feet to his faith, Nebuchadnezzar extols God with a hymn of praise. Precisely when the hymn begins and the introduction to it ends is difficult to determine. Successive lines and verses are connected by conjunctions. The narrative simply flows into a poem, which conveys feelings of ecstasy appropriate for the moment. The beginning of the poem may start with **Then I praised,** or it could begin with **His dominion** (v 34). The former seems more appropriate for a hymn, which often starts with a word of praise before providing the reason to praise. If this is so, that line could be literally translated *Now the Most High I praise, and the one who lives forever I honor and glorify.*

The collection of three parallel terms—**praised, honored,** and **glorified**—also communicates emotion (v 34). The king is bursting with awe for God. The appellative **the Most High . . . who lives forever** appropriately acknowledges the worth and character of the one he praises (v 34). It also confesses the sovereignty and eternality of God, the two central themes of the hymn. **His dominion is an eternal dominion** captures the essence of these two themes while the remaining lines repeat or elaborate upon it. This line and the next replicate almost verbatim lines from the opening hymn of this chapter (see v 3). The terms **dominion** and **kingdom** are exchanged between the two versions, however, which indicates that they are to be taken as synonymous. The rule of God is not limited like that of earthly kings. His domain is **eternal,** lasting **from generation to generation.** That is to say, God's kingdom is past, present, and future. It is never absent from this world. Absolute sovereignty would require this, and that is exactly what God possesses.

■ **35** God freely exercises authority over two realms, **the powers of heaven and the peoples of the earth** (v 35). **The powers of heaven** (*hêl šĕmayin*) could refer to either the sun, moon, and stars or the army of angels or to both (Pss 33:6; 103:20-21). The latter seems most likely since the phrase is parallel to **the peoples of the earth.** Within both realms God can do what monarchs of the ancient world ordinarily did, **as he pleases. No one,** not even the mighty Nebuchadnezzar, can keep God from doing what he wants to do. A king's **hand** could signal judgment upon the guilty, direction for a nation, or advance of armies. Whatever God chooses to do will be done. Nebuchadnezzar had thought **all the peoples of the earth** were under his authority (see Dan 4:1), but in fact they are under God's. They are **regarded as nothing** in the sense that they have no power to challenge God. They cannot question his actions.

■ **36** As Nebuchadnezzar confessed God's sovereignty, he found his position restored to him (v 36). Like David, his faith and fame went hand in hand (see 1 Chr 14:8-17). All his former **splendor** and more returned. His **advisers and nobles,** who likely continued to run the kingdom in his absence, reestablished him as ruler of the empire (Dan 4:36). He describes his restoration in terms similar to those used in v 30 where he was condemned for arrogance. Again he makes free use of the first person personal pronoun and speaks of **glory** (*yĕqār*) and **honor** (*hădar*), translated "majesty" in v 30. The circumstance is entirely different here, though, and he receives no condemnation. The king speaks in the context of the faith he has just confessed. Human authority and achievement is not denied or condemned, for it now functions appropriately under the sovereign hand of God.

■ **37** The chapter closes with one more confession of faith, which assures the reader that Nebuchadnezzar's boast in the previous verse is understood rightly. As in v 34 a trilogy of terms express his worship. **Praise** and **glorify** are used again (v 37). **Exalt** is a new term that means to lift up or promote. It is the same term Daniel uses in 5:20 to express Nebuchadnezzar's arrogance prior to his illness. Its use emphasizes the transformation that took place in Nebuchadnezzar. The one who had lifted up himself was transformed into one who lifted up God.

Nebuchadnezzar acknowledged God as **the King of heaven** (v 37). This title for God is found only here in Scripture. It affirms the sovereignty of God. It can be compared to the title "God of heaven," which Daniel and others used to refer to Israel's God during the Persian period (for example, Ezra 1:2; Neh 1:4; Dan 2:37). That title was used to refer to the chief god of Zoroastrianism, Ahura Mazda. Addressing God as **the King of heaven** is fitting for this context because it brings together two key motifs of the chapter: kingship and heaven. It affirms the biblical perspective that heaven is the proper locus for true kingship.

The motive for Nebuchadnezzar's worship is twofold: God's justness and his power. **Everything he does is right** means the same thing as **all his ways are just** (v 37). Both phrases express God's righteous justice, which is what kings should possess ideally. By contrast, Nebuchadnezzar had lacked these qualities and was judged for them (see v 27). In these affirmations the king is confessing that God's judgment of him has been fair. His misdirected arrogance deserved rebuke.

The power of God is confirmed once more in the final phrase of the chapter, **those who walk in pride he is able to humble** (v 37). These words concisely summarize the moral and theological lesson illustrated by the story. God's absolute sovereignty over the world enables him to bring its most powerful rulers to their knees. Such control is a practical demonstration of God's sovereignty within the realms of human beings. This key theological statement stands at a significant juncture in the book. It is midpoint in the chiasmic structured Aramaic section of chs 2—7. All material in this section has led up to this point and will lead away. Readers should take note then. The message of Daniel applies directly to a common human situation, arrogant tyrants. The kingship of God means this world's most threatening and powerful personalities bow before the divine sovereign will.

FROM THE TEXT

Chapter 4 explores the nature of human pride and its interface with the sovereign God of the universe. The story illustrates the admonitions of Proverbs, which teach, "A man's pride brings him low, but a man of lowly spirit gains honor" (29:23). The discussion, however, is not restricted only to the effects of pride upon the individual. Something much greater comes into view. Human pride affects cosmic designs. As such it receives divine rebuke and provides a signal opportunity for heaven to exercise absolute control over earthly affairs once again.

Human arrogance disrupts God's purposes for his creation. The cosmic tree and other motifs in the text evoke images of God's creation. The dream pictures a well-designed world functioning in perfect order. A luxuriant tree nourishes and protects creatures of earth and sky. That tree, who is Nebuchadnezzar, is endowed with an abundance of resources so that he might share it with his world. This is his God-ordained role in God's world. He is given plenty in order to supply others. Daniel admonishes the king to fulfill his divinely determined destiny by **doing what is right** and **being kind to the oppressed** (v 27).

The story reveals, however, that pride deludes the king and leads him to relinquish his place in the cosmos. In the end he loses more than position in a kingdom. He abdicates his God-given vocation among humans. Nebuchadnezzar comes to believe that his position and power is about something other than it is. He thinks the accumulation of resources is for the purpose of his

glory and that his achievements were the result of his **mighty power** (v 30). The king entertains false notions of self-importance and self-sufficiency. Worse, he identifies with the aspirations of those who built the tower of Babel (Gen 11) and strives for divine status. Pride completely disorients the king. As a result he is no longer allowed to function in his God-given role. God will not allow the order of creation to be utterly upset.

Petty jealousy and unwillingness to share glory are not the reasons why God reacts to Nebuchadnezzar's arrogance. The king's achievements, power, and influence do not intimidate God. The issue runs much deeper. The problem with his pride is the damaging effects it produces upon himself, his fellow human beings, and his relationship to God. Pride disturbs the harmony of God's created order.

Human beings were never designed to function as gods and exercise absolute autonomy. They cannot manage their world alone. According to scripture humans were created to live in mutually supportive relationships with others. "It is not good for the man to be alone," God said (Gen 2:18). The illusion of pride is that humans can somehow live disconnected and arrange for life themselves. Pride pulls people away from one another and, in particular, away from their Creator. It pushes them toward independence rather than interdependence.

Pride was at the heart of the first sin. Adam and Eve were taken by their own self-importance. They questioned their need for God's wisdom and ventured out from there. God's strong response in that case parallels his response to Nebuchadnezzar. The curse that fell upon them connected them more to the realm of creatures, **wild animals** and **cattle,** than that of the Creator (Gen 3:17-19; Dan 4:32). They were brought low in order to once again discover their proper place within creation. God intended for them to be "a little lower than the heavenly beings," yet function as "ruler over the works of [his] hands" (Ps 8:5-6). They are servants of the Creator who have been "crowned . . . with glory and honor" (v 5).

God acts against the proud. The events that unfolded in Nebuchadnezzar's life do not transpire by accident. His fall from greatness is not a result of random circumstances or even of natural law. They happen by divine initiative. The hand of God rises against the king and judges his arrogance.

Proverbs 16:18 points out that "Pride goes before destruction, a haughty spirit before a fall." This maxim may suggest a principle of natural consequences. Pride can set into motion circumstances that lead to disaster. The testimony of Nebuchadnezzar makes clear, however, that in this case God handles pride personally. The king's arrogance provokes God's displeasure, and God initiates a dramatic response to it. In so doing God displays his sovereign reign among humans.

Daniel 4 attests to God's absolute sovereignty. The struggle between heaven and earth turns out to be no real contest. God's ability to bring down the most powerful monarch in the world demonstrates his complete control over the affairs of this world. The testimony of the psalmist is confirmed, "I have seen a wicked and ruthless man flourishing like a green tree in its native soil, but he soon passed away and was no more; though I looked for him, he could not be found" (Ps 37:35-36).

This story agrees with the rest of Scripture by affirming that pride is extremely offensive to God. Of the several things that God detests, pride is near the top of the list (Prov 8:13; 16:5). Thus, wherever it is found, arrogance evokes divine indignation. A frequent threat of Israel's prophets is that God "will put an end to the arrogance of the haughty" (Isa 13:11).

Throughout the Bible God confronts humans in their pride. He rebukes the arrogant (Ps 119:21), takes away their strength (Isa 10:12-19), destroys their accomplishments (Jer 50:30-31), disrupts their lives (Ezek 7:24-27), frustrates their plans (Hab 2:9-14), removes them from positions of power (Zech 10:11), and makes them objects of taunting (Isa 14:4-21). The arrogant are not permitted to stand in God's presence (Ps 5:5; Zeph 3:11). In the end God envisions a perfect world where "the eyes of the arrogant man will be humbled and the pride of men brought low; the LORD alone will be exalted in that day" (Isa 2:11).

God resurrects the lowly to new life. The rule of God is constructive as well as destructive. It may bring down, but it also raises up. God is free to act as he pleases in all matters. He gives the kingdoms of this world **to anyone he wishes and sets over them the lowliest of men** (Dan 4:17). This is the positive side to God's sovereignty. He not only humbles the proud but also lifts up the humble.

Nebuchadnezzar fell to the lowest level among humans. He was **driven away from people** and became like one of **the wild animals** (v 32). He ate as they ate, lived as they lived, and even took on some of their appearances. Whatever the precise diagnosis of his disease, he is pictured as **the lowliest of men** (v 17). In a sense he died to his human existence. Yet God took him from that state and raised him up to rule over his kingdom. He restored his **honor and splendor** as king of Babylon (v 36). This restoration is a glimpse of God's most dramatic act of sovereignty, resurrection.

A major theme of biblical literature is God's transformation of the humble. It is the primary image of resurrection in the OT. First Samuel 2:8 asserts, "He raises the poor from the dust and lifts the needy from the ash heap; he seats them with princes and has them inherit a throne of honor." God seems drawn to those of humble station in life. Isaiah 61:1-3 identifies the objects of the Messiah's ministry as "the poor," "the brokenhearted," "the captives," "the prisoners," "all who mourn," and "those who grieve." These are the ones the Messiah will transform to new life.

The most dramatic illustration of God's transforming resurrection power comes in Jesus Christ. It is this "incomparably great power" that Paul prays believers will realize in their lives (Eph 1:19). That power was "exerted in Christ when he raised him from the dead and seated him at his right hand in the heavenly realms, far above all rule and authority, power and dominion, and every title that can be given, not only in the present age but also in the one to come" (vv 20-21). In the death and resurrection of Jesus Christ God demonstrated his absolute sovereign rule over this world once and for all. The story of Nebuchadnezzar foreshadows this truth.

God reigns on earth. As the previous statements demonstrate, Dan 4 affirms that God expresses his sovereignty within this world. While God oversees the affairs of the heavenly realms, he also directs earthly dominions. **He does as he pleases,** not only with **the powers of heaven,** but also with **the peoples of the earth** (v 35). God strips the most powerful king on earth of his authority and brings him lower than any person in his kingdom; he becomes like an animal. Then God restores him to his throne again.

God's design is that life should be "on earth as it is in heaven" (Matt 6:10). Jesus instructed his disciples to pray for this. The justice and righteousness that characterizes God's kingdom is the model for earthly rulers. So Daniel admonishes Nebuchadnezzar to rule as God intended **by doing what is right** and **by being kind to the oppressed** (Dan 4:27). When he does not respond, God judges him. The reason Nebuchadnezzar falls from his position of power is that he does not **acknowledge that the Most High is sovereign over the kingdoms of men** (v 32). In short, he does not recognize that God reigns on earth. Once he does this, though, God restores him.

For those living under oppressive authorities, this is good news. Whether or not God appears to be in control at the moment, this chapter affirms that he is. When he chooses, God can reverse the powers of this world, for "he sets up kings and deposes them" (2:21). He can raise the lowly and bring down the powerful (1 Sam 2:5-8). Therefore, people of God live in the hope that God will rise up among the nations and exert his authority over them. This hope is not only for "the last days" when "the mountain of the LORD's temple will be established as chief among the mountains" (Isa 2:2). It is also for the present. God's people know that **his dominion endures from generation to generation** (Dan 4:3). They look forward to a day within human history when God will bring "an end" to unruly rulers "at the appointed time" (11:27). This thought will become much clearer in subsequent chapters of Daniel. So in the interim, God's people can remain hopeful and "say among the nations, 'The LORD reigns'" for "he will judge the peoples with equity" (Ps 96:10).

E. Writing on the Wall: The Third Test of Wisdom (5:1-31)

Overview

Chapter 5 presents another story of a king humbled by Israel's God. It is a sequel to ch 4 and should be read along with it. It is the third and final test of wisdom in the book. As in chs 2 and 4 Daniel and his God are challenged to reveal mysteries that no one else can decipher. Since the wisdom of God has been well established in previous stories, that element does not receive as much emphasis in this one. The abilities of Daniel are highlighted, however, but only insofar as they serve to exalt his God. In this chapter Daniel takes on a role more like that of the classical prophets in Israel. The absolute free rule of God over human affairs still remains a central theme.

BEHIND THE TEXT

The setting for ch 5 can be dated very specifically. It occurred on the day that **Belshazzar, king of the Babylonians, was slain** and the city of Babylon fell to the Persians (v 30). According to ancient sources, this event happened in 539 B.C. on the sixteenth day of Teshrit, which corresponds to October 12 in current calendars. The fall of Babylon marked the end of the Babylonian dominance in the Middle East and the ascendancy of the Persians.

A few days before this momentous event the Medes and Persians had defeated the Babylonian army at Opis. They crossed the Tigris River and, without a fight, took Sippar, located only fifty miles from Babylon. The end of the empire was eminent as troops moved to take the capital.

The Cyrus Cylinder and *The Babylonian Chronicles* report that the Persians took the city of Babylon without a battle. According to the Greek historian Herodotus, the Persians diverted the Euphrates from flowing through the city and entered the city by this means. Xenophon, another Greek historian, adds that the Babylonian king and his retinue were killed in the takeover.

The king who died that night was likely **Belshazzar,** as Dan 5 suggests. But ancient historians are not entirely clear on this point. He was the eldest son of Nabonidus who was officially Babylon's last king and apparently away from the city at the time of its fall. The son of Nebuchadnezzar, Amel-Marduk, assumed control of the empire following his father's death in 562 B.C. Neriglissar cut short Amel-Marduk's rule, however, when he assassinated him and took over the empire only a few years later. Neriglissar's son Labishi-Marduk reigned at his father's death in 556 B.C., but only for a few months. Nabonidus and Belshazzar led a coup that placed them in power for the next seventeen years. Around 550 B.C. Nabonidus left most of the affairs of the kingdom in the hands of his eldest son and retreated to Teima in Arabia for religious reasons. Thus,

Belshazzar functioned as king over the Babylonian Empire for a number of years even though his father Nabonidus was the ruler of record.

Whether or not Belshazzar continued to function as king until the fall of Babylon is uncertain. None of the records of Babylon's conquest mention Belshazzar by name or his fate. According to the *Nabonidus Chronicle*, Nabonidus returned to Babylon in time for the new year festival in the spring of 539 B.C. That fall he engaged Cyrus in a losing battle at Sippar and fled just before the Persians took Babylon. After Babylon fell the *Nabonidus Chronicle* says the Persians captured Nabonidus when he returned to Babylon. Berosus adds that he was deported to Carmania. Xenophon records that "the king" and his entire retinue were killed the night of the invasion, but the name of the king is not given. Many scholars assume that Belshazzar is the king Xenophon says was murdered and that Nabonidus was captured and deported as the other sources indicate.

According to Herodotus and Xenophon, a feast was taking place when Babylon fell. Both Isa 21:5 and Jer 51:39 appear to predict that this would be the context of defeat. The story of ch 5 unfolds around such an event, which the text calls a **great banquet** (v 1). The purpose for the feast is not clear. In a preface to the story, the Old Greek (Septuagint) identifies it as "the inauguration of the palace." This might suggest Belshazzar was celebrating an addition to the massive palace complex. The reliability of the Old Greek on this point cannot be confirmed. Another reason for the feast may have been to rally support for the crumbling empire. The recent victories of the Persian armies and their advances toward Babylon necessitated solidifying the remaining loyalties of the kingdom. Some commentators have conjectured that Belshazzar was simply throwing one last party in the awareness that the end was near or as a diversion from impending doom. It is also possible that this was the regular time for some annual feast and Belshazzar carried it out so as not to overly alarm the populace of the city.

Whatever the reason for the feast, it was the kind of affair typical of ancient monarchs. References to **a thousand of his nobles,** the presence of the king's **wives and his concubines** and freely consuming **wine** are not overdone (vv 1-4). Numerous sources document lavish feasting by oriental kings, especially among the Persians. Though documentation is lacking for the Babylonians, scholars assume they followed practices of other kingdoms in this regard. Within the Hebrew scriptures Esth 1 provides an illustration of the kind of extravagant festivals royalty enjoyed.

The feast took place at **the royal palace** located in the northern section of Babylon (v 5). This massive complex sat along the Euphrates River and consisted of three ornately decorated palaces. The main palace was an extensive structure designed to present an opulent impression worthy of a mighty empire like Babylon. It included a throne room extending over one hundred seventy feet long and fifty feet wide. This was the most likely venue for the feast of Dan 5. Some of its walls were covered with dark blue enameled bricks and others with white gypsum **plaster** (v 5). Columns of yellow glazed bricks topped by blue Ionic capitals and a frieze of white rosettes above them provided a dazzling display of color. Animal motifs, including scorpions, serpents, panthers, lions, and mythological monsters, punctuated the décor of the room.

An important historical background issue is raised when the final verse of the chapter relates that **Darius the Mede took over the kingdom** (v 31). Ancient sources describing the capture of Babylon indicate that Cyrus the Great took the city by means of his general Gubaru. No mention is made of a person named Darius the Mede. Complete discussion of this issue has been reserved until ch 6. (See *Behind the Text* section for that chapter.) The outcome of that discussion does not bear significantly upon interpretation of this chapter.

Chapter 5 contains numerous literary connections with other stories of Daniel. As a test of wisdom within the context of the royal court, it bears resemblances to chs 2 and 4 in several ways, but also differs in certain respects. In all three chapters the plot unfolds around a king who receives an ominous communication from the gods that his wise men cannot interpret. In chs 2 and 4 the communication came in a dream, while in ch 5 it is by means of a hand inscribing words on a wall. God's hero, Daniel, shows up in each case to bring resolution to the tension by providing an interpretation. In chs 2 and 5 he is duly promoted for this service, but in ch 4 no promotion is mentioned. Chapters 4 and 5 note the fulfillment of Daniel's interpretation, but ch 2 does not. Most of these literary features are typical of a genre known throughout the ancient world. Scholars sometimes call it a "court contest of wise men." This form is reflected in the stories of Joseph (Gen 41).

The story of Dan 5 is clearly intended as a sequel to ch 4. Understanding the full impact of ch 5, in fact, depends upon one knowing the content of ch 4. The central theme of a Babylonian king humbled by Israel's God obviously suggests this close relationship. Yet many other features in the two stories assure that the reader will not miss the connection. The most explicit link is 5:20-21 in which Daniel summarizes Nebuchadnezzar's experience in ch 4. This makes clear the marked contrast between Nebuchadnezzar and Belshazzar that is key to unlocking the message in ch 5. Comparison of the kings is referenced in numerous ways throughout ch 5. In addition, various other verbal features create connections between the two chapters. For example, descriptions of Daniel are similar in both chapters. He is described as one who has "the spirit of the holy gods" (4:8, 9, 18; 5:11, 14) and "chief of the magicians" (4:9; 5:11). These phrases are found only in these chapters. Thus, these two chapters form a couplet that must be read together.

As was noted earlier (see *Behind the Text* for ch 2), chs 4 and 5 form the central couplet of the Aramaic section of the book. This section (chs 2—7) follows a chiasmic structure that places these two chapters at its fulcrum. The point of this structure is to focus readers upon the theme of God's ability to humble earthly monarchs and effect human affairs. This is the most tangible evidence of God's sovereignty in a world of oppressive foreign powers.

The relationship between chs 3 and 5 is more subtle, but no less important. Both stories begin abruptly in very similar manners. Without any reference to temporal setting they begin "King Nebuchadnezzar made" and "King Belshazzar gave" (3:1; 5:1). In each case the king made something spectacular, the leading citizens gathered, the king commanded something, and the command was carried out. In the end both groups end in worship of idols. Repetition of the lists of those attending the king's convocation is also a feature in both introductions. These parallels suggest that the narrator of ch 5 wants to evoke an atmosphere similar to that of ch 3. The pretentious practices of pagans, which was sketched so well in ch 3, is integral to the setting of ch 5. By recalling the story of ch 3, the narrator of ch 5 creates this environment with a greater economy of words. The effect of the paralleling also sets up the comparison between the two kings of the story. As the story of ch 5 unfolds, the linkage between Nebuchadnezzar and Belshazzar becomes a significant component of the message.

Chapter 5 also has particular relationship to chs 2, 7, and 8. Chapters 2 and 7 contain visions projecting the eventual end of the Babylonian Empire. The fulfillment of this aspect of those visions occurs in 5:30-31 when Belshazzar is killed and the kingdom passes to the Persians. The visions in chs 7 and 8 are the only other two chapters in the book connected to the reign of Belshazzar. They are dated specifically to his first and third years, which were approximately 550 B.C. and 548 B.C. (7:1; 8:1). As noted earlier, ch 5 takes place in 539 B.C.

Three significant images embedded in this story are worthy of special notice because they serve to heighten its dramatic effects for ancient audiences. The **goblets . . . taken from the temple of God in Jerusalem** represented an important connection to Israel's sacred past (v 2). Once Solomon's temple was destroyed, these goblets and other sacred vessels provided tangible evidence of this significant structure, which had stood as a seminal symbol of God's covenant relationship with Israel. The Hebrew Scriptures carefully chronicle David's plans for the temple vessels (1 Chr 28:13), Solomon's creation of them (1 Kgs 7:48-51), Nebuchadnezzar's taking of them (2 Kgs 24:13; 25:14; 2 Chr 36:7, 10, 18; Dan 1:2), and their return with the exiles (Ezra 1:7; 5:14-15; 6:5). Drinking from the goblets, then, portrays blatant blasphemy of Israel's God. Desecrating sacred vessels was no trifling matter for any group of people in the ancient world. Few would risk provoking the wrath of heaven in this way.

The most haunting image of the text is the disembodied **human hand** whose finger writes upon a wall (Dan 5:5). The description in the text suggests only a hand appeared without an arm or other body parts. Its sudden ghastly appearance not only evoked dread but also conveyed an image of defeat and judgment. Typical military practice of the day included cutting off hands of enemy troops killed in battle. They were displayed as trophies of war. The hand also stands as a symbol of the power of God in this world. The **finger** that writes recalls images of God's hand at work in creation and the Exodus (Ps 8:3; Exod 7; 31:6; Dan 9:15). Within the book of Daniel the hand of God directs human history. It is indirectly referenced when kingdoms are destroyed, "but not by human hands" (2:45; 8:25).

References to **scales** and weights also carry special meaning in the text (5:26-28). The words written on the wall, **mene, tekel,** and **parsin,** were names for weights used on measuring scales and, by extension, of units of money. These terms evoke images of merchandising and justice. The scale was a common feature of the marketplace where merchants counted and weighed their commodities in order to insure fair exchange. Thus scales were associated with doing what is just and right. Dike, the Greek goddess of moral justice, was said to carry scales. Egyptians spoke of their lives being weighed in the afterlife. The Hebrew Scriptures picture God weighing the hearts of persons (Prov 16:2; 21:2; 24:12). In addition, scales and weights serve to heighten the element of providence in the story because the scale image was particularly appropriate for announcing judgment upon Babylon. According to the zodiac calendar, Babylon fell in the month of Libra (September 23—October 22). Ancient astrologers represented the alignment of stars in Libra with a scale and weights. The connection of this astral sign with the fall of Babylon underscores the divine mystery behind these events and further enhances the drama of the story.

Greek and Hebrew Versions of Daniel 5

As in ch 4, the Old Greek (Septuagint) and the Masoretic versions of ch 5 differ considerably. In general the Greek is shorter. It omits several details found in the Aramaic, such as the queen's description of Daniel in vv 11-12 and Daniel's rebuke of Belshazzar in vv 18-22. The Greek adds some minor details as well, however. These include a preface, which summarizes the story. The point of the story in both versions remains the same but subtle shifts in emphases do occur.

Chapter 5 relates a story of a king in crisis over a divine communication (vv 1-9) who finds hope for an answer in Daniel (vv 10-16). Daniel does not disappoint. He delivers God's message to the king (vv 17-28), which finds immediate fulfillment (vv 29-31). A chiasmic structure overlays the story and serves to highlight the contrasts contained in it. The exalted king who dishonors Jews in the opening verses (vv 1-4) becomes a humbled king who honors a Jew in the closing verses (vv 29-31). The writing that Babylon's wise men fail to understand (vv 5-9) is interpreted clearly by God's wise man in the end (vv 25-28). The queen's recommendation of Daniel (vv 10-12) is balanced by Daniel's rebuke of the king (vv 18-24). At the center is the king's request of Daniel to interpret the dream (vv 13-17). This central speech lays down the challenge of the chapter by rehearsing Daniel's competence along with the Babylonian wise men's incompetence.

IN THE TEXT

I. The King's Crisis (5:1-9)

The first nine verses set up a dilemma that begs resolution. In the midst of a pretentious party (vv 1-4) the king receives an ominous message from heaven (vv 5-6). None of the king's wise men, however, is able to explain the meaning of the divine communication (vv 7-9).

■ **1-4** King **Belshazzar** shows up in the book of Daniel for the first time without the honor of an appropriate introduction (v 1). This befits him because he is a petty pretender to the throne. Historically he was the son of the true king of the Babylonian Empire, Nabonidus. During his father's absence from the city, he functioned as ruler. The narrator of ch 5 must have known this, for he clearly intends to characterize Belshazzar as a second-rate ruler. Throughout the story he sketches an image of Belshazzar as a poor imitation of **Nebuchadnezzar his father** (v 2). Whether **father** refers to actual blood relative, such as "grandfather" or simply "predecessor," cannot be determined based upon present evidence. Belshazzar's mother may have been a daughter of Nebuchadnezzar, but this cannot be confirmed.

In any case the story makes clear that Belshazzar compares unfavorably to Babylon's greatest king Nebuchadnezzar. In view of Nebuchadnezzar's testimony in ch 4 the contrast is that much greater. The introductory verses of the story subtly point out that Belshazzar attempts to raise his status by using goblets that Nebuchadnezzar obtained through conquest. Perhaps he is trying to outdo Nebuchadnezzar by trivializing his accomplishment. Whatever his motive, this arrogant act backfires upon him.

A great banquet is the setting for the drama of this story (v 1). Though such feasts were common in ancient oriental courts, the narrator's description of this event serves to convey an atmosphere of arrogant pretense. Several parallels to ch 3 evoke the pompous air of that story (see *Behind the Text* above). The guest list, which is repeated twice, included **a thousand of his nobles** along with the king's **wives and his concubines** (vv 1-3). Besides providing an image of opulence, this list underscores the public nature of the event and assures that the unusual omen was not merely an illusion.

An emphasis upon wine consumption adds to the picture of frivolity.

Five times in four verses the text mentions **drinking** (vv 1-4). Intoxication does not seem to be the issue, though. **While Belshazzar was drinking** may simply refer to the moment in the meal when the wine was being served and not that he was inebriated (v 2). The reason for the several references to drinking is twofold. They indicate that all the elements were in place for a grand affair and also focus attention upon the decisive act of pretense, drinking from the temple goblets.

The climactic act of arrogance is violating the **goblets that had been taken from the temple of God in Jerusalem** (v 3). These goblets were part of the booty that Nebuchadnezzar secured when he subdued Jerusalem. According to Dan 1:2 Nebuchadnezzar had at least treated these special vessels with respect and placed them in a sacred space, the temple of his god. Belshazzar, however, shows his contempt for Israel's God, and Nebuchadnezzar as well, by drinking from them. He increases the offense by including them in worship of **the gods of gold and silver, of bronze, iron, wood and stone** (v 4). They are, perhaps, used to make ritual libations to these gods. The long list of materials used for making idols suggests Belshazzar is trying to impress his nobles with his power. Collecting idols of conquered people was a way of showing strength. There is some irony in the fact that both goblets and gods are made of **gold and silver.**

■ **5** The ostentatious affair comes to an abrupt halt when an ominous omen appears. A disembodied **human hand** materializes and its **fingers** write words upon a wall (v 5). What the hand wrote is not revealed at this point. For the Jewish audience images of the finger of God inscribing stone tablets on Mount Sinai (Exod 31:8) or creating the heavens (Ps 8:3) may come to mind. The hand of God symbolizes the creative and sustaining power of God at work in this world.

The public nature of this vision is underscored again by reference to details such as **the plaster of the wall, the lampstand,** and **the royal palace** (v 5). Writing on **plaster,** made of white gypsum, in front of a **lampstand** should allow for clear visibility for all guests. Mention of **the royal palace** provides a location for the banquet but more importantly identifies a significant audience for the omen. To add further clarity and allow the reader to feel the impact of this vision, the narrator notes that **the king watched the hand as it wrote** (v 5). As one might expect, the vision had gotten the king's attention.

■ **6** The king's response to the apparition is predictable, but it may also highlight his inferior character. Turning **pale,** being **frightened, knees** knocking, and **legs** giving way might be expected (v 6). Others who saw visions experienced some of these symptoms (Isa 21:3-4; Ezek 21:6-7; Dan 2:1; 4:5; 10:8). The listing of all of these at once, however, suggests weakness of character. The phrase **his legs gave way** literally translates "his joints loosened." Some commentators have suggested that this could indicate he lost control of his bodily functions. The phrase **his face turned pale** literally translates "his splendor changed." The word for "splendor" (*zîw*) is used to describe Nebuchadnezzar's return to power in 4:36. Belshazzar's loss of splendor portrays his true status before God and also foreshadows the ultimate message of the writing on the wall. This will be referenced once again in 5:9 and 10.

■ **7** In desperation **the king called out** for his wise men to come and interpret this unusual message (v 7). The Aramaic text says he did so "loudly." This suggests a panic-stricken scream from a man who is losing composure. The list of advisers is similar to ones given in previous stories (2:2, 27; 4:7). The royal court retained these **enchanters, astrologers and diviners** for just such occasions. Their role was to interpret communications from the gods and provide incantations to offset their evil effects.

The rewards offered to the interpreter of this omen indicate the level of significance the king felt this message must have. Belshazzar offered gifts fitting for royalty (Gen 41:42; Esth 8:15), which included **purple** clothing and **a gold chain** (Dan 5:7). These would be appropriate to one promoted to **the third highest ruler in the kingdom.** The king appears to refer to a position of authority just after his father and himself. The term **third** (*talfî*), however, might refer to a high-ranking position such as personal attendant to the king much like a similar term in Akkadian. In the Hebrew Scriptures the term "third" (*šalîš*) can be translated this way as well in certain contexts (2 Kgs 7:2, 17, 19; 9:25; 15:25).

■ **8** None of Babylon's wise men could collect on the reward, though. They could neither **read the writing** nor explain **what it meant** (v 8). When Daniel reads the inscription later in v 25, the words are clearly Aramaic. Why the Babylonians could not at least read the words is a mystery and only adds to the contrast between them and Daniel. It may be that they could actually decipher the words but were unable to determine their significance. Perhaps they denied being able to read the words because they could not understand their meaning.

■ **9** The incompetence of his experts leaves Belshazzar even more distraught. As in v 6, he is **terrified** and **pale,** but this time the text employs participial and intensive forms of the verbs to express his increased state of dismay (v 9). In addition, the king's **nobles were baffled.** They have no answers for the puzzle either. The inabilities of all of Belshazzar's resources produce a picture of utter hopelessness. Yet, there is a resource he has not considered.

2. The King's Hope (5:10-16)

With the king and his officials completely helpless to understand the divine communication, hope for an answer arrives from an unexpected source. The queen enters the story for the first time, bearing words of promise. Chapter 5 is a story of sudden appearances. A king, a disembodied hand, and now a queen all appear without introduction. This sets up a contrast with the hero, Daniel, who will enter the story only after a dramatic buildup by the queen. It also prepares the reader for the ending of the story, which ends with the sudden death of Belshazzar "that very night" (v 30).

■ 10 The queen is likely the queen mother since Belshazzar's wives were already in attendance at the banquet (v 10). Such women were powerful figures in royal courts in ancient times. She is likely the wife of Nabonidus, but a wife of Nebuchadnezzar is not out of the question. Josephus thought that she was Belshazzar's grandmother. In her speech, she recommends Daniel to the king; her speech also enhances the contrast between Belshazzar and Nebuchadnezzar.

That the queen comes **into the banquet hall** without permission and gives orders to the king suggests her high status (v 10). It also reveals Belshazzar's lack of authority. No one entered an ancient monarch's court or advised the king without invitation (Esth 4:11). She ironically addresses the king in typical respectful fashion, **O king, live forever!** The irony is that he will not live past "that very night" (Dan 5:30). She also instructs him to quit displaying the weakness of his character. She tells him, **Don't be alarmed** or **look so pale** (v 10). Both conditions describe Belshazzar in vv 6 and 9. **Alarmed** is the same term translated "frightened" in v 6 and "terrified" in v 9.

■ 11 The king's hope lies in **a man** within his own kingdom with exceptional abilities (v 11). That man is not named until later, for dramatic effect. First his attributes and skills are listed in order to impress the king and raise interest for the reader. He has **the spirit of the holy gods in him** (v 11). This phrase is exactly how Nebuchadnezzar described Daniel in 4:8, 9, and 18. It highlights Daniel's divine connectedness, which has been thoroughly clarified in ch 2. Daniel does not work like other wise men. His ability to interpret depends upon God, not human ingenuity.

God was the source of Daniel's unusual gifts of **insight and intelligence and wisdom like that of the gods** (5:11). According to the Hebrew Scriptures, such attributes are ones pursued by the truly wise and only acquired by those who reverence God (Prov 1:1-7). **Insight** (*nahîrû*) refers to receiving divine illumination into a matter. **Intelligence** (*śākĕtānû*) includes prudent speech and actions as well as intellectual competence. **Wisdom** (*hokmâ*) is applying the right truth at the right time in the right circumstance. This person excelled so much in these areas that **Nebuchadnezzar . . . appointed him chief of the magicians** (Dan 5:11). The same title is also used of Daniel in 4:9.

■ 12 At this point the queen dramatically announces the name of **this man**. It is **Daniel,** the hero of three previous stories in the book (v 12). As if his résumé is not impressive enough, the queen continues with a list of three more attributes and finishes with a trilogy of skills. Daniel's gifts also included **a**

5:10-12

keen mind and knowledge and understanding (v 12). The phrase **a keen mind** (*rûaḥ yattîrâ*) could also be translated "an excellent spirit," which points to his divine connections once again. **Knowledge** (*mandaʿ*) could refer to possessing information about various things, but it also included awareness gained by personal experience. **Understanding** (*śākletānû*) is the same word translated "intelligence" in the previous list of v 11. When applied to specific situations these attributes produce skills highly coveted by wise men of old. Such are **the ability to interpret dreams, explain riddles and solve difficult problems** (v 12). Daniel has already shown his mastery of dreams in chs 2 and 4. The skill of explaining riddles will be used in the current chapter. The skill of solving difficult problems carries an irony because of its verbal connections with Belshazzar's condition. The phrase **solve difficult problems** literally translates as "loosen knots" (*mĕšārēʾqiṭrîn*). Verse 6 spoke of weakness in the king's legs, which is more literally "the knots of his loin were loosened" (*qiṭrê ḥarṣēh mištārayin*). When Daniel "loosens the knots" of the writing on the wall he will likely further "loosen the knots" of the king's body.

The effect of the queen's speech is to introduce Daniel into the story. It also serves to contrast Belshazzar with Nebuchadnezzar once more. The queen emphasizes **your father** three times in v 11. One of those times it occurs in an emphatic phrase **your father the king.** The point is that Nebuchadnezzar knew the importance of Daniel, but Belshazzar did not. A truly great king identifies the valuable resources in his kingdom. Belshazzar had not done so. Why he did not is left for speculation. Some scholars suggest Daniel was too old to be involved anymore. He would likely be in his eighties at this point. Yet his role in the Persian Empire that follows these events does not support this idea (6:3). It seems most likely that Belshazzar had purposefully severed relationships with Daniel. Perhaps this was because of Daniel's connections to a previous regime or because Belshazzar preferred his own counselors.

The queen closes her speech by urging the king to act and by expressing confidence in Daniel once again. She recommends that the king **call for Daniel** (v 12). He is the one who can solve the king's problem, according to the queen, by telling him **what the writing means.**

■ **13** Influenced by the queen's speech, Belshazzar invited Daniel into his court. His questions and statements, however, reveal that he has not been entirely convinced of Daniel's abilities. He remains arrogant and acts demeaning toward Daniel. The overall tone of his speech is skeptical. This contrasts with Nebuchadnezzar's conversation with Daniel in 4:9-18. Nebuchadnezzar showed respect and expressed great confidence in the man of God.

Belshazzar opens with a question intended to set Daniel in his place. He identifies him as **one of the exiles my father the king brought from Judah** (v 13). Reference to Daniel as a captive of war is calculated to lower Daniel's status before Belshazzar. For the Jewish audience, however, the same words serve to heighten his standing. He is a survivor, not merely a captive. He is a man of Judah, not a man of Babylon. The details of this description of Daniel betray the fact that the king has known of Daniel. The queen had not mentioned that Daniel was an exile.

■ **14-16** The king expresses his skepticism in the phrase **I have heard,** which he says twice (vv 14 and 16). What he has heard is what the queen just said about Daniel. He has a special connection with heaven and possesses the qualities and skills of a superb wise man. While rehearsing Daniel's credentials, Belshazzar also acknowledges that his wise men **could not explain** the meaning of the writing on the wall (v 15). Unwittingly he highlights the contrast between his advisers and Daniel. So he offers Daniel the same rewards of royal position for successfully interpreting the writing as before. His final statement to Daniel divulges doubts about the possibilities of success, though. He says **if you can** (v 16). Such uncertainty contrasts severely with Nebuchadnezzar's words to Daniel in 4:18, "you can, because the spirit of the holy gods is in you."

As the central section of the chiasmic structure of the story, this speech performs an important function. It puts forth the challenge to Daniel's wisdom and his God's. The speech itself is arranged in chiasmic form. The reference to Daniel's low status in v 13 is offset by reference to the possibility of high position in v 16. The king's rehearsal of Daniel's credentials in vv 14 and 16 also balance one another. The center of the chiasm is v 15, which highlights the Babylonian wise men's inabilities. Thus the speech focuses attention upon the contest of wisdom. As the story reveals, only the one in whom "the spirit of the gods" dwells possesses wisdom to truly interpret divine messages.

3. God's Message for the King (5:17-28)

At this point in the narrative, Daniel takes control. His speech is the longest one in this chapter. He begins with a refusal of the gifts (v 17), moves to a rebuke of the king (vv 18-24), and ends with a reading of the writing on the wall (vv 25-28).

The tone of Daniel's speech is different from his previous speeches before monarchs. He dispenses with polite protocol and unleashes a prophetic tirade on Belshazzar before giving the interpretation of the omen. Contrast with ch 4 is again significant. Daniel's response to Nebuchadnezzar was very respectful, even somewhat protective. He was deeply troubled by the message he must convey and almost apologetic for bearing such unpromising news. "My lord, if only the dream applied to your enemies and its meaning to your adversaries!" he said (4:19).

■ **17** Daniel responds to the king's deprecating speech with conviction and authority. In defense of his integrity, Daniel refuses the king's **gifts** and tells him to **give your rewards to someone else** (v 17). Such words undoubtedly offend the king. They also clarify Daniel's motives and confirm his commitment to larger purposes in life. Like other genuine prophets, he could not be bought (Num 22:18; 2 Kgs 5:16-17). Neither would he allow himself to be too closely identified with the regime of Belshazzar. He understood that his role was **to read the writing for the king and tell him what it means** (v 17). That was the reason he had agreed to stand before the king, and he would do it.

Before explaining the writing on the wall, though, Daniel expounds the reason for it. In this section he sounds more like a prophet of Israel than a sage (see, for example, 1 Sam 12; 1 Kgs 21; and Jer 38). His speech includes a lengthy invective (vv 18-23) before pronouncing a brief judgment (v 24).

■ **18** Daniel begins with a history lesson from the life of Nebuchadnezzar, the one Belshazzar has been subtly compared with throughout the story. This lesson succinctly summarizes the story of ch 4, even using specific language from that story. Daniel launches into this speech with the same words he has used before when speaking to Nebuchadnezzar (2:37; 4:22). Literally he says, "You, **O king**" (v 18). In previous speeches he describes the glory God had given the king. One might expect the same again. But this time Daniel speaks of the greatness God has given to Nebuchadnezzar, not to Belshazzar. Nebuchadnezzar was divinely gifted with **sovereignty and greatness and glory and splendor** like the large, luxuriant tree in the dream of ch 4 (v 18; see 4:22). **God gave** him this role in the universe. His power was a gift from God. Daniel refers to God as **the Most High God.** This was also done throughout ch 4 and served to emphasize God's sovereignty over his creation and particularly Nebuchadnezzar.

■ **19 All the peoples and nations and men of every language** came under Nebuchadnezzar's authority just as the birds and animals gathered under the branches of the great tree (v 19; see 4:21). The breadth of his sovereignty meant that he had the ability to affect the lives of people in powerful ways. He could **put to death, spare, promote,** or **humble** as he pleased (v 19). This portrait of Nebuchadnezzar's extensive power differed considerably from Belshazzar's limited influence. It also describes the kind of power one might expect only of God (Ps 75:7-8). Yet God overrules even one who wields such dominating sovereignty among humans.

■ **20** Nebuchadnezzar's splendor was stripped from him, however, **when his heart became arrogant and hardened with pride** (v 20). A literal translation of the phrase would read, ***when his heart was lifted up and his spirit was hardened.*** This occurred, according to 4:28-30, when he boasted in his achievements in Babylon as if they were his accomplishments and for his glory. His opinion of himself was ***lifted up*** beyond where it should be. He became **hardened** toward the reality of God's grace in his life. Nebuchadnezzar's problem was an issue of the inner person, **his heart** and ***his spirit.***

■ **21** As a result Nebuchadnezzar was **driven away from people** and lived among animals (v 21). This description of the king's state is almost identical to that in the story of ch 4 (see 4:25 and 33). The main difference is a reference to **wild donkey,** which further accentuates his debased condition. The king continued in this way until **he acknowledged that the Most High God is sovereign over the kingdoms of men and sets over them anyone he wishes** (v 21). This is precisely the condition laid down in 4:17, 25, and 32. He had to confess that God freely reigns over the affairs of humans, even those within the Babylonian Empire.

■ **22** With the history of Nebuchadnezzar rehearsed, Daniel turns to an indictment of Belshazzar. He points out that Belshazzar has not learned what Nebuchadnezzar learned. Nebuchadnezzar's story had taught Belshazzar nothing, which is what the narrative of ch 5 hints at throughout. His pride was of a different sort than Nebuchadnezzar's, for it expressed itself in contemptuous disregard for truth. Belshazzar distanced himself from Nebuchadnezzar to his own peril. He could have benefited from Nebuchadnezzar's experience but instead determined to outdo him.

Daniel holds Belshazzar fully accountable for his actions because he **knew all this** and chose not to let it affect his behavior (v 22). He was undoubtedly old enough to witness the events of ch 4 since he served as a high official in the empire only two years after Nebuchadnezzar's death.

■ **23** Daniel charges that Belshazzar chose rather to **set** himself **up against the Lord of heaven** (v 23). The term **set up** (*rûm*) is the same one used to describe Nebuchadnezzar's pride in v 20, which led to his humbling. It is a posture of arrogant defiance. Daniel refers to God as **Lord of heaven** in this context to emphasize God's sovereignty over the realms of both heaven and earth, a key theme of ch 4. Belshazzar has taken on the most formidable force in the universe.

The specific actions that demonstrated Belshazzar's defiance were (1) when he **had the goblets from his temple** made available for drinking, (2) when he **praised the gods of silver and gold** with them, and (3) when he **did not honor the God** who is truly sovereign (v 23). These are all acts of utter disrespect for God. Drinking from the goblets is a blatant act of blasphemy. It devalued the sacred and thus, by extension, the God to which they were connected. Praise for other gods is also an act of sacrilege that derives from determined ignorance as far as Daniel and other prophets are concerned (Isa 44:9-20). Such gods are impotent. They have no capacity to engage life or exert control over it. They **cannot see or hear or understand** (see Isa 44:18).

Failing to honor God was an act of irreverence that comes from confusion about sovereignty in this world. Belshazzar did not imitate Nebuchadnezzar's acknowledgment of **the God** who reigns over all (v 23; see 4:34-35).

5:21-23

Every aspect of the cosmos falls under God's dominion. **In his hand** rests Belshazzar's very **life** (literally "breath") and all his doings. But Belshazzar does not concede this.

The use of the second person personal pronoun in Daniel's denunciation of Belshazzar is notable. Nine times the pronoun appears in vv 22-23. Two of those times it is an emphatic usage. In addition four times the second person verbal form is used. Clearly Daniel intends to hold Belshazzar personally responsible for his actions. He, and no one else, is accountable for his sins against God.

■ **24** Having made his accusation of Belshazzar, Daniel announces God's judgment upon him. It is brief and to the point. God **has sent the hand that wrote the inscription** (v 24). These words confirm what the king had suspected. The message of the inscription was not good news. These words also emphasize the divine origin of the writing. Literally the Aramaic reads, *from his presence was sent the palm of the hand.* Like a messenger dispatched from a sovereign ruler, the ominous hand had gone forth with its tidings. The use of the word **hand** in these verses highlights the sovereignty of God. A hand that announces death through an inscription on a wall (v 24) comes from the hand that holds Belshazzar's life in it (v 23).

■ **25** With the reason for the writing clarified, Daniel is finally ready to give a reading (v 25) and interpretation (vv 26-28) of the writing on the wall. For the first time the audience hears the content of that writing. Since v 5 the mysterious writing has been known about, but only now is it given. This delaying technique has helped sustain suspense in the story.

The words that had been written on the wall were MENE, MENE, TEKEL, PARSIN (v 25). In Aramaic the conjunction precedes the final word and is pronounced "u." Thus many translations have "uparsin" (or "upharsin") for the final word. The first word is repeated presumably to increase the sense of decisive authority. These three Aramaic words can be understood as either nouns or passive participles. As nouns they designate measures of weights or units of money. The **mene** (Hebrew *mina*) is the largest and **tekel** (Hebrew *shekel*) next in size. In Babylon, the mina equaled sixty shekels at this time. **Parsin,** a plural noun, stands for "halves" and could refer either to half-mina or half-shekel. The latter is more likely in this context. The order, then, is in descending value, which fits the thrust of their message and the movement of the story. It might also be a veiled allusion to the effectiveness of Babylonian kings. The *mina* might represent Nebuchadnezzar, Nabonidus the *shekel*, and Belshazzar the half-shekel.

■ **26-28** Daniel explains that the message from these three words comes through the verbal forms related to each of them. **Mene** suggests the verb *měnâ*, which means **numbered** (v 26). Thus the message is that **God has numbered the days** of Belshazzar's rule. His time is up and his reign over Babylon is finished. **Tekel** evokes the verb *těqal*, which means **weighed** (v 26). The message from this is that Belshazzar has not measured up to expectations. As Daniel's indictment made clear, when placed **on the scales** he is **found wanting** over against Nebuchadnezzar. He did not humble himself, learn from Nebuchadnezzar, and acknowledge "that the Most High God is sovereign" (see vv 21-22). Thus he comes up short in spiritual things. He lacks a right relationship with God. **Parsin** calls to mind two words, the verb *pĕras*, which means **divided,** and *paras*, which means **Persians** (v 28). The message in this case is that Belshazzar's kingdom will be parceled out **to the Medes and Persians,** the two dominant groups of the great Persian Empire.

The three words of the inscription evoke a picture of a merchant counting, weighing, and sorting products to determine value. When weighed against the humbled and God-honoring Nebuchadnezzar of ch 4, Belshazzar is deficient. He is **found wanting** spiritually. Thus the transaction between divine and human domains is terminated. The God who supplied Nebuchadnezzar's splendor is ending the deal with the Babylonian kingdom. The message of this image is one of imminent judgment for Belshazzar and the Babylonians. In short, time is up, the verdict is reached, and the sentence awaits execution.

4. God's Fulfillment of the Message (5:29-31)

The story ends as abruptly as it begins. Two kings fulfill their pronouncements. Belshazzar rewards Daniel for his interpretation (v 29), and God rewards Belshazzar for his pride (vv 30-31). Daniel gains promotion while Belshazzar receives demotion.

■ **29** Belshazzar responds to the interpretation of the inscription by honoring Daniel as promised. Daniel is given royal clothing and adornment and **proclaimed the third highest ruler in the kingdom** (v 29). Each of the other stories in chs 1—6 ends in like manner, with the prosperity of God's people. In contrast to four of these stories (chs 2, 3, 4, and 6), however, Belshazzar does not speak positively about Daniel's God at the conclusion of his ordeal. This befits the character of this king sketched throughout the story. He has not valued God's vessels, his spokesman, or his royal example. It is not surprising that he will not honor God now. Thus he reaps the appropriate reward.

■ **30-31** This story ends, then, in judgment. The message of the three words find immediate fulfillment **that very night** (v 30). Belshazzar was killed and the Persians **took over the kingdom** (v 31). According to ancient records, the momentous event of Babylon's fall occurred on October 12, 539 B.C. The term **took over** (*qĕbēl*) can also be translated "received." This could be a subtle reminder of a key point made earlier that "the Most High God is sovereign over the kingdoms of men and sets over them anyone he wishes" (v 21). The Persians did not take the kingdom; they received it from God. This was also a major theme of ch 4.

The story ends with a curious reference to the age of the conquering ruler as **sixty-two** (v 31). While this might be an incidental detail to confirm the historicity of Darius, it is more likely something else. It bears connection to the value of the three words written on the wall. A mina equals sixty shekels. If the ending of *parĕsîn* is taken as dual, then the word could be understood as two half-shekels. Thus the numerical value of the three words, *mene, tekel,* and *parsin,* would be sixty-two shekels. The point of this reference may simply be that all aspects of this event are divinely orchestrated. The convergence of even minor details, such as the number sixty-two, confirms this. The sovereign God of heaven has been in control of every detail.

FROM THE TEXT

The story of ch 5 is more complex than might appear at first. More is happening than simply the announcement of judgment through surreal writing upon a wall or the contesting of Babylonian and Israelite wisdom. Significant connections to ch 4 with its comparisons between Belshazzar and Nebuchadnezzar lead the reader to consider other issues.

Chapter 5 assumes the same themes put forth in ch 4 and builds upon them. The theme of human pride and its consequences, for example, is explored further. Pride takes different forms and impacts national as well as personal outcomes of life. Along with ch 4, and the other stories in Daniel, ch 5 focuses upon the sovereignty of God. Yet it extends the discussion to consider additional aspects of that subject. In particular the personal implications of God's sovereignty and the responsibility of humans before the supreme Ruler of the universe are emphasized.

The arrogance of sacrilege provokes divine judgment. God's response to Belshazzar's mishandling of the sacred was decisive and dramatic. God does not allow his sovereignty to be trivialized for long. The hand appeared **suddenly** while Belshazzar and his company toasted their gods with God's goblets (v 5). The text suggests an immediate response to the king's profane act. It is not unlike the prompt divine response to Nebuchadnezzar's arrogant boast in ch 4. "The words were still on his lips when a voice came from heaven" (4:31). Fulfillment of God's judgment upon Belshazzar also came swiftly. **That very night** the message of the writing on the wall was accomplished and his life ended (v 30).

The swiftness of God's response is related to the nature of the offense. Belshazzar's actions were a direct challenge to God's sovereign rule of this world. The goblets were remnants of the most tangible symbol of God's powerful presence in this world, the temple in Jerusalem. They may have only been symbols, but the reality behind them was of utmost importance. When Belshazzar took the sacred goblets and used them to honor other gods, he denied their significance. The sovereignty of the one to whom they were dedicated was disputed. The text makes this clear when Daniel accuses the king of setting himself up **against the Lord of heaven** (v 22).

Belshazzar's offense was similar to Nebuchadnezzar's and yet different. They both denied the grace of God at work in their lives. They were unwilling to acknowledge that their power was derived and not achieved. The added offense of Belshazzar was that he remained defiant even though he **knew** of Nebuchadnezzar's experience (v 22). While Nebuchadnezzar's pride in some sense might be understandable in light of all his accomplishments, Belshazzar's was not. His was an act of frivolous defiance. He had little to boast about except what had come to him through his predecessor Nebuchadnezzar.

God's impatience with blasphemy is consistent throughout Scripture. The Ten Commandments warn against treating God's name lightly (Exod 20:5). Instructions for priests and the rituals of worship were designed to preserve proper reverence for the majesty of God. When Uzzah touched the ark as it was being taken to Jerusalem, God struck him down (1 Chr 13:9-10). The point of that story, and of this one as well, is that God will not permit humans to treat him casually. God is holy. He is not like anything in the human realm and must be treated accordingly.

God's response to Belshazzar's blasphemy is also an act of mercy, as are all of God's judgments. Human beings who do not appropriately respond to the sacred are lost in this life. They do not know their origins or their destiny and thus how to live rightly in this world. They must understand the truth about God. Salvation depends on getting it right. Thus, in mercy, God calls people to acknowledge his holy sovereignty.

God's sovereignty carries personal implications. Earlier chapters of Daniel emphasize the affects of God's sovereign rule upon nations. Chapter 2, in particular, voiced this theme by relating the dream of four kingdoms crushed beneath the indomitable power of God. This theme gained further confirmation in ch 4 as Nebuchadnezzar was challenged to acknowledge "the Most High is sovereign over the kingdoms of men and gives them to anyone he wishes" (4:25). Chapter 5 affirms this concept when it quotes this same verse (5:21) and reports the demise of Babylon and the ascendancy of Persia by the hand of God.

A hint of the cosmic implications of God's sovereignty can also be detected in ch 4. As "King of heaven" (4:37), God exerts influence over all creation. He endows earthly kings with resources to sustain "the beasts of the field" and "the birds of the air" (4:12). "The dew of heaven" is employed to demonstrate God's dominating power.

God's sovereign reign not only impacts humans on the macro level of nations and creation, however, but bears upon the individual as well. Chapter 4 introduced this concept in its descriptions of God's personal dealing with

Nebuchadnezzar. God exercised his sovereignty over the king by bringing affliction and restoration to him personally. The king suffered and benefited directly from God's rule.

Chapter 5 brings greater focus to the personal implications of God's sovereignty. God is specifically identified as the one **who holds in his hand your life and all your ways** (v 23). These words were spoken expressly to Belshazzar. The very breath he breathed and the activities of each day were under the scrutiny and control of an omnipotent God. The character of his life, not that of Babylon's, was **weighed on the scales and found wanting** (v 27). Again, the days of his reign and not of Babylon's rule were numbered and **brought . . . to an end** (v 26). In the end God's judgment cost Belshazzar his life as well as the fortunes of Babylon. He **was slain** and the kingdom was taken over (v 30).

The personal repercussions of God's sovereignty recall various passages from the Hebrew Scriptures. Israel's sages maintained, "In his heart a man plans his course, but the LORD determines his steps" (Prov 16:9). Job is an illustration of this. He experienced God's absolute control over his personal life and acknowledged it when he asked, "Does he not see my ways and count my every step?" (Job 31:4). As well as any portion of scripture, Ps 139 articulates the impact of God's control over every part of an individual's life. Following a dramatic poetic description of God's omniscience, omnipresence, and omnipotence, the psalmist confesses, "All the days ordained for me were written in your book before one of them came to be" (v 16).

Belshazzar received God's judgment because he did not recognize the implications of God's sovereignty for his life. God controls the cosmos and nations, but he also rules over individuals. Belshazzar learned the hard way that, "If it were his [God's] intention and he withdrew his spirit and breath, all mankind would perish together and man would return to the dust" (Job 34:14-15).

Humans are responsible for their actions before a sovereign God. The emphasis on God's absolute freedom in ch 5 could be misread. Human actions might appear to be ineffectual up against the designs of the Most High God. God overturns Belshazzar and his powerful kingdom. The king who could throw a feast for a thousand Babylonian officials, collect numerous gods of defeated enemies, and scoff at the God of Israel was dramatically brought to an end. Connecting back to ch 4, the story recalls that God even exercised control over one more powerful than Belshazzar. God humbled the legendary Nebuchadnezzar who **put to death, spared, promoted,** and **humbled** whomever he pleased (v 19). Almost like a god, Nebuchadnezzar wielded authority in his kingdom. But the God of Israel subdued him.

Belshazzar seems to have no recourse against the sovereign God who sent a disembodied hand with a message. The writing on the wall, however, only announced the demise of Belshazzar and Babylon. It did not determine it.

The message of judgment came as a response to Belshazzar's actions. His deeds were justly **weighed on the scales and found wanting** (v 27). Those deeds were the reason for the unhappy ending to his life. As Daniel made clear, Belshazzar, and no one else, **had the goblets . . . brought** to him and his nobles, his wives and his concubines (v 22). He honored false gods instead of the living God. Belshazzar did all this with full knowledge. He knew what had happened to Nebuchadnezzar, but he repeated the same offense. Just as Nebuchadnezzar had done, Belshazzar set himself up **against the Lord of heaven** (v 22). The text makes clear that no one is to blame for Belshazzar's fate except Belshazzar. He bears responsibility for the outcome of his life under the hand of a sovereign God.

The rest of Scripture knows this truth. The very basis of prophetic preaching rested upon a belief that human action matters in a world governed by a sovereign God. The prophetic summons to repentance challenged people, "Seek the LORD and live" (Amos 5:6). If they did not change, then God promised, "my wrath will break out and burn like fire because of the evil you have done" (Jer 4:4). Ezekiel drives the point home to an audience who wanted to blame others for their adversity. They quoted the proverb, "The fathers eat sour grapes, and the children's teeth are set on edge" (Ezek 18:2). But Ezekiel reminded them, "The soul who sins is the one who will die" (v 4). The sovereignty of God does not trump personal responsibility. God holds people accountable for their actions within his dominion.

The sin of an individual affects a nation. The personal nature of one's relationship to God does not mean an individual's sin has no corporate effects. Sin always affects the community. It does so in direct proportion to the level of influence that a person has within that community. Thus the sin of leaders bears heavy consequences for the group under their influence.

Belshazzar's pride led to the overthrow of Babylon. In the end the empire is brought to an end along with Belshazzar. Yet the king is the focus of Daniel's rebuke, not Babylon. The sin enumerated by Daniel is Belshazzar's. Little reference is made to the sins of the people. When the nobles, wives, and concubines drink from the goblets, they are identified in connection with the king. They are described to the king as **your nobles, your wives and your concubines** (Dan 5:22). Though they apparently joined Belshazzar in praising the false gods according to v 4, Daniel only notes that the king did this. **You praised the gods of silver and gold,** he said (v 22). **You did not honor the God who holds in his hand your life.** It is Belshazzar's pride that concerns Daniel and is the reason given for the judgment upon Babylon.

In some sense the king stands as representative of Babylon as a whole. Other prophets of Israel indicted the nation for its pride and predicted Babylon's downfall because of it (Isa 13:11, 19; Jer 51:31-32). Chapter 5 marks the fulfillment of these predictions. But in this story the pride of Belshazzar is the issue. One cannot get around the fact that the prophecies against Babylon came to realization because of one man's failure before God. Belshazzar's incorrigible actions tipped the scales toward final judgment.

God oversees the details of human life. The convergence of images surrounding this event is more than coincidence. As the text suggests, they indicate that God's sovereignty extends to the minutest details of a situation. The connections of the message to Libra, the number sixty-two, and the Persians highlight God's interest in details. The mystery of God is, in some ways, not so mysterious. All elements point toward One in whom "all things hold together" (Col 1:17). God is at work in all aspects of life, if one will but notice.

Jesus indicated that God's interest in details even extends to the number of hairs on a person's head (Matt 10:29-30). God directs the care of the most common facets of his creation, birds and lilies (6:26-29). Psalmists agree. God "makes grass grow for the cattle" (Ps 104:14) and knows when a person sits and rises (139:2). God's knowledge of people, nations, and his world is very particular and personal.

This is a fundamental concept in the book of Daniel. As the visions will attest, God rules with precision. He manages at both the macro and micro levels of life.

F. Lions' Pit: The Third Test of Faithfulness (6:1-28)

Overview

Daniel and the lions' den may be the most popular story in the book. The drama about a God-fearing man rescued from the jaws of lions and the uncomplicated moral of faith finding reward appeals to audiences of every age in every generation. The story is about much more than lions and dramatic rescues, however. Like previous stories in Daniel, it focuses upon kingdoms in conflict. The narrative unfolds around three royal edicts, two from Darius and one from God. In the words of the text, "the law of his God" challenges "the law of the Medes and Persians." In the end Darius issues a new law that acknowledges the supremacy of God's rule. The conflict between the two realms of lawmakers provides the venue for another test of faithfulness for Daniel and his God. Once again God and his servant come through in spectacular fashion.

BEHIND THE TEXT

Chapter 6 reads as a natural follow-up to ch 5. The final verse of ch 5 links the two chapters. It is actually employed as the first verse of ch 6 in the

Hebrew Bible. Therefore the verse numbers in the Hebrew Scriptures vary by one from the English versions throughout the chapter. Daniel 5:31 in English is 6:1 in Hebrew and so forth. This verse announces the Persian takeover of Babylon and introduces Darius the Mede. The connection to ch 6 is logical, but the division of the English versions is more appropriate. The reference to the age of Darius makes it a better conclusion to ch 5 than introduction for ch 6. The number sixty-two seems to reference the numerical value of the words on the wall inscription of ch 5.

The content of 5:31 prepares the reader for the new setting in ch 6. A fresh kingdom replaces an old one. A mature, benevolent monarch sits in authority in exchange for a young, frivolous, antagonistic pretender to the throne. Finally, a distinguished administrator whose gifts are recognized by his king emerges in place of an ignored and disrespected sage whose abilities were nearly forgotten.

The Persian court provides the sociopolitical setting for ch 6. This is different from previous chapters, yet familiar in some ways. The first five chapters of Daniel take place in the context of the Babylonian court during the time of Nebuchadnezzar (604-562 B.C.) till Belshazzar (550-539 B.C.), the co-regent with Nabonidus (560-539 B.C.). In 539 B.C. the emerging empire of Medes and Persians solidified their control of the Middle East by taking Babylon. This is the event Dan 5:30-31 notes. Persia's king, Cyrus the Great, had systematically built his empire since rebelling against his Median overlord in 550 B.C. He subdued Lydia and eastern entities before moving upon Babylon. Once conquered, Babylon became his winter residence. The reader may assume this to be the location for the events of ch 6, but the text does not state it explicitly.

The ruling monarch of ch 6 is identified as **Darius.** He is called "Darius the Mede" in 5:31 and "Darius son of Xerxes (a Mede by descent)" in 9:1. According to 5:31 he "took over the kingdom" of the Babylonians "at the age of sixty-two." In 9:1 he is described as the one who "was made ruler over the Babylonian kingdom." These references present a historical problem. No one known by this name in extrabiblical sources fits this description. The name Darius first appears in the lists of Persian kings with Darius I (522-485 B.C.). Others to take the name were Darius II (423-404 B.C.) and Darius III (336-330 B.C.). Each of these persons is too late to be associated with Daniel.

Scholars have suggested several ways to deal with this historical issue. One approach is to consider Daniel's Darius a fictitious character invented for the sake of good storytelling. He may represent a composite picture of several Persian kings such as Cyrus, who actually conquered Babylon, and Darius I, who is noted for organizing the empire into satrapies. Those who hold to a second-century B.C. date for the book often take this view. They assume historicity of characters and events are not important to the message of the stories in Daniel. These scholars also note that the appearance of Darius the Mede before Cyrus the Persian in the book seems to fit the author's confused understanding of history. The final editor of Daniel, they say, believed there was a Median Empire prior to the Persian Empire.

Another approach is to look for a known historical personage who fits the description of Darius. This view suggests that Darius is an alternative name, most likely a royal title, for someone mentioned in secular texts. Dual names and titles were not uncommon in ancient times. While several possibilities have been suggested, the two leading candidates for a historical figure behind Daniel's Darius are Cyrus and Gubaru.

Cyrus the Great was the Persian king credited with conquering Babylon in 539 B.C. He was about sixty-two years of age at the time and was half Median. His mother was a daughter of the Median king Astyages. His father Cambyses was also of royal blood, which may account for the reference in Dan 9:1. This verse calls Darius "the son of Xerxes." Xerxes (Ahasuerus in Hebrew) was also a royal title meaning "he who rules over men." Though there is no documentation to support this, some scholars suggest that Xerxes may be an alternative title for either the father or a grandparent of Cyrus. Clearly 9:1 cannot be referring to Xerxes I (485-465 B.C.), who was the son of Darius I, unless the reference is taken as confused history.

That Cyrus might carry two titles could make sense in his context. The power base for his kingdom depended upon both Medes and Persians. The title Darius the Mede, then, would appeal to his Median subjects and Cyrus to the Persians. Daniel 6:28 may well support this connection. It is possible to translate the verse: "So Daniel prospered during the reign of Darius, that is, the reign of Cyrus the Persian." The conjunctive *waw* can function as an explicative in both Aramaic and Hebrew. Thus, 6:28 may be clarifying that Darius and Cyrus are the same person.

The other possible identity for Darius is Gubaru, also called Gobryas by Greek historians. Gubaru served either as commander in charge of the conquest of Babylon or as its ruler following the fall. If Gubaru is the same person as Ugbaru, then he functioned in both these roles. Daniel 5:31 states that Darius "took over the kingdom," and 9:1 declares he "was made ruler." Both fit the description of one such as Gubaru who would have been authorized to rule by Cyrus. According to the Greek historian Xenophon, he was a man "advanced in years" when he took control of Babylon.

It is possible, then, to identify Darius with a real historical figure, either Cyrus or Gubaru. Both men fit within the context of events in ch 6. As the text suggests, these were the early days of organizing governance over newly acquired lands following the fall of Babylon. The reference to the appointment of **120 satraps to rule throughout the kingdom** most likely reflects these beginning stages (v 1). Later, under Darius I (522-485 B.C.), the empire would develop its well-designed system of 20 to 29 satrapies or provinces for which the Persian Empire came to be known. An official called "satrap" administered each of these provinces and was directly responsible to the king. At this point "satrap" took on a technical meaning along with its more generic sense of "protector of the kingdom." In ch 6, a large number of these "protectors" were given responsibility for various regions of the kingdom. Esther 1:1 and 8:9 mention 127 satrapies at the time of Xerxes I (485-465 B.C.). First Esdras 3:2 and the Old Greek of Dan 6:1 mention this number as well.

In order to protect the king's interests, **three administrators** managed the many satraps (v 2). This element of Persian governance cannot be directly supported by any extant documents from the empire. Under a later system at the time of Darius I, three persons bore equal responsibility before the king for each province. These included a satrap, a military commander, and a civil servant. If Dan 6 refers only to the organization of the Babylonian province, then the system under Darius I provides a good parallel to Dan 6:2. Otherwise Ezra 7:14, Esth 1:14, and the Greek historians Herodotus and Xenophon refer to seven key advisers to the kings of Persia in the fifth century B.C. The three administrators of Daniel could reflect an early development of these advisers.

The system was obviously flexible at this point because Darius contemplated putting Daniel **over the whole kingdom** (Dan 6:3). This indicates a position as the king's most trusted adviser, which was not unknown throughout the ancient world. In the book of Esther Haman held such status under Xerxes and was replaced by Mordecai in the end (Esth 3:1; 10:3). Joseph rose to a similar level under the pharaoh in Egypt (Gen 41:41-43).

Darius makes two decrees in this story. Esther 8:9-10 describes the process by which this was done. Scribes made copies of the edict in various languages in order to communicate with each people group in the kingdom. The king signed and sealed them with his signet ring. Then couriers on horseback delivered them to the various regions throughout the empire.

The nature of the first decree approved by Darius has raised questions among scholars. It prohibited making requests **to any god or man** except the king (v 7). If this suggests deification of the king or exclusive worship, then it is totally out of character for Persian kings, especially Cyrus. Texts are unanimous that Cyrus and his successors encouraged worship of all gods and did not see themselves as divine. The Cyrus Cylinder illustrates this stance by proclaiming freedom for displaced captives to return to their homelands and rebuild temples to their own gods. Ezra agrees with this official Persian policy and chronicles the state support for rebuilding of the temple in Jerusalem (Ezra 1—6). If the edict in Dan 6 is authentic, then it cannot be understood as an attempt to make the king a deity or restrict worship of other gods. It would have to be about designating the king as the sole representative before the gods. Perhaps he would perform the primary priestly duty of mediator between the gods and the people. In this way the legitimacy of his rule would be acknowledged. Such a requirement would have particular appeal to a monarch in the early days of his kingdom. Thus allegiance to the state was the central point of the decree.

Those unwilling to acknowledge loyalty to the king in this way must face the ordeal of a **lions' den,** according to the decree. Execution by this method is not documented in contemporary documents. However, Assyrians and Persians were known to hunt and cage these animals. They certainly present a logical option for capital punishment. The language of Daniel indicates that the lions' den could be understood as a trial by ordeal. He says he was **found innocent in his sight** (v 22). Trial by ordeal was widespread in the ancient world. The practice placed accused victims in some peril designed to prove their innocence or guilt. One such tactic was to bind persons and throw them in the river. Those who survived these ordeals were proclaimed innocent because by miraculously sparing them the gods had judged them so.

The immutability of **the laws of the Medes and Persians** creates another issue for scholars (vv 8, 12, 15). Apart from Esth 1:9 and 8:8, the idea is not strongly attested by secular sources. It might be assumed as a reasonable standard for royalty, though. A monarch who changed his mind too often would find his authority undermined. Persia's last king, Darius III, reportedly felt he could not change a death sentence once it was issued. Also, the ancient Code of Hammurabi made it a crime for a judge to change a decision. Nevertheless, some monarchs are known to have altered decrees. Perhaps this is why the conspirators of the story press the issue with the king. By tradition laws were unchangeable, but some monarchs made up their own rules as they went along. Persian kings attained one of the most stable empires the world has known, as their longevity attests. The firmness with which the Medes and Persians normally held to their laws likely inspired the references to unalterable laws that **cannot be repealed** (vv 8, 12, 15).

The inviolable nature of Medo-Persian law sets up the conflict in the story. The tale is told by means of a familiar genre called court conflict and intrigue. In particular it exhibits traits of a well-known plot in ancient times of the fall and rehabilitation of a court official. Conspirators scheme against a good person who somehow triumphs in the end. Proverbs 24:15-16 succinctly summarizes the moral of such stories when it warns, "Do not lie in wait like an outlaw against a righteous man's house, do not raid his dwelling place; for though the righteous man falls seven times, he rises again, but the wicked are brought down by calamity." Examples of this genre include the story of Joseph in Gen 39—41, the book of Esther, the apocryphal addition to Daniel called Bel and the Dragon and the Assyrian tale Ahikar. Daniel 3 also illustrates this genre.

The apocryphal story of Bel and the Dragon shares some interesting connections to ch 6. In this story Daniel was a favored administrator to a Persian king, who is Cyrus. His opponents convince the king to throw Daniel into a lions' den from which he is miraculously delivered. Other than these features the stories are quite different. The main theme of Bel and the Dragon is the futility of idol worship.

Connections between chs 6 and 3 are more striking. Both speak of jealous colleagues, plots and accusations against Jews, impossible peril, rescue by an angel, royal decrees, and in the end, prospering Jews. Several specific terms are shared by both stories. For example, lists of court officials, which consist mostly of terms borrowed from Persian and Akkadian, are very similar (3:2; 6:8). Also, the descriptions of conspirators includes "eating pieces" of the accused (translated "denounced" in 3:8 and "falsely accused" in 6:24) and decrees are addressed to all the "peoples, nations and men of every language" (3:4, 29; 6:25). Clearly these two stories were designed so that they might be read in reference to one another. They form balancing stories in the chiasmic structure of the Aramaic section of the book framing the central couplet of chs 4 and 5. (See *Behind the Text* for ch 2.)

Several differences between chs 3 and 6, however, highlight the uniqueness of each story as well as changes in setting. The issue challenging Shadrach, Meshach, and Abednego centered on public worship, whereas Daniel's focused upon private worship. The role of the conspirators is more highly developed in ch 6. In ch 3 they act merely as catalysts to set off Nebuchadnezzar's tirade against the Jews. In ch 6 they are colorfully characterized through their actions and speeches. They manipulate and prod the king into action. The role of the kings in these stories also is quite different. Nebuchadnezzar initiates the decree that poses a problem for Jewish captives, while Darius is manipulated into issuing such a decree. More startling is the attitude of the kings toward the captives and their God. Nebuchadnezzar acts with pompous disregard toward both and lays down a direct challenge to divine authority. Darius, on the other hand, exhibits genuine concern for Daniel and openness toward his God. This latter point undoubtedly reflects the contrasting atmosphere in each empire. The Persians were more open to religious diversity within their empire than were the Babylonians.

Greek and Hebrew Versions of Chapter 6

The differences between the Old Greek (Septuagint) and Masoretic texts of ch 6 are less than in chs 4 and 5. Nevertheless there are significant variations. In general the Greek tends to add statements that clarify details left out in the Aramaic. The motives of characters, for example, are described. The Greek also leaves out certain nuances found in the Aramaic. For example, it does not translate "the law of the Medes and Persians" each time the phrase is repeated in the Aramaic. This, and other alterations, shifts the focus of the story more toward Darius than the conflict between human and divine laws. In the end, Darius explicitly confesses personal faith in Daniel's God in the Greek, something that does not take place in the Aramaic.

Daniel is characterized in this story as a highly capable bureaucrat. This is somewhat different from his roles in previous stories, which noted his ability to interpret divine communications. He was, however, designated as "chief of the magicians" (4:9 and 5:11), which implied administrative duties. The association between the wisdom tradition and state governance was significant in the ancient world. As the biblical tradition reflects, throughout the ancient world sages were more than appendages to the governing system. Their contribution was integral. Curriculum for administrators included the collected proverbs and other wisdom works of the sages. Many proverbs of the Hebrew Scriptures deal with the conduct of kings and their officials (for example, Prov 25:1-10). Thus, Daniel's role in this chapter is fitting for his training and expertise.

The general structure of ch 6 follows the same progression found in the tests of faithfulness in chs 1 and 3. The setting is described (vv 1-3), a test devised (vv 4-18), and the outcome reported (vv 19-28). These components can be further refined into various scenes of the drama. These would include: the conspiracy (vv 1-9), the offense (vv 10-15), the execution (vv 16-18), the deliverance (vv 19-23), and the conclusion (vv 24-28).

As with many other stories, a chiastic structure can be observed throughout the narrative. The success of Daniel reported in the opening verses (vv 1-3) returns in the final verse (v 28). The plotting of the conspirators and their contrived edict (vv 4-9) are off set by the demise of these conspirators and a second edict that replaces the first (vv 24-27). Daniel's faithful actions (vv 10-11) find reward with his rescue from the pit (vv 19-23). The conspirators anxiously pressing for Daniel's execution (vv 12-15) balance the king reluctantly sealing his fate (vv 17-19). At the center of this chiasm stands the order for execution along with the king's prayer for Daniel (v 16). The chiastic structure tends to focus attention on this dramatic moment when the only hope for Daniel is a miraculous deliverance by his God.

IN THE TEXT

I. The Conspiracy (6:1-9)

The narrative begins with a brief sketch of the setting (vv 1-3) and a description of the intrigue that creates tension in the story (vv 4-9). All the main characters are introduced. These include the protagonist Daniel along with his antagonists, both witting and unwitting. Daniel's colleagues oppose him intentionally, but the king does so unwillingly. Unlike previous stories, Daniel's introduction into the text is not delayed. Awareness of his exceptional abilities is needed early on in order to develop the plot. The reader may notice, however, that Daniel does not speak until late in the story. These features tend to move attention away from Daniel and toward the fourth main character in this story, God.

■ **1-2** The circumstances of ch 6 are unique among the stories in Daniel. This tale takes place in the context of a Persian court rather than Babylonian. A Persian ruler named **Darius** is now in charge (v 1). According to Dan 5:30-31, this is the person who "took over" the Babylonian kingdom following the death of Belshazzar. Contemporary sources do not identify this early ruler of Babylon by the name Darius, but at least two persons fit the description. Darius may be an alternative name or title either for a commander named Gubaru or for Cyrus the Great himself. (See *Behind the Text* above.)

The text describes Darius's plan for governing the newly acquired territory. The kingdom was divided into 120 regions, each overseen by an official called a satrap. These **120 satraps** in turn reported to **three administrators** (vv 1-2). Ironically the narrator notes the reason for this elaborate system was **so that the king might not suffer loss** (v 2). In fact, it is this very system that leads toward intrigue and nearly causes the loss of one of his most trusted advisers. In a subtle way, a main theme of the story is introduced: all the careful planning of humans cannot bring about the stability they desire.

■ **3** Darius noted that Daniel excelled in administration. As a professional wise man, Daniel would be well versed in the proverbs and wisdom stories that were part of the training for administrators. More than that, though, he displayed **exceptional qualities** (v 3). Literally this phrase translates "an excellent spirit was in him." It recalls Nebuchadnezzar's observation that "the spirit of the holy gods" was in Daniel (4:18). The source of Daniel's excellence was his connection with God.

Daniel **so distinguished himself** among the government officials that the king planned to promote him further (v 3). He would be **set . . . over the whole kingdom,** which suggests a position like that of Haman and then Mordecai later under Xerxes (Esth 3:1; 10:3). It was this consideration by the king that precipitated the crisis of the story. The other officials in the kingdom saw this move as a threat and sought to avert it. Their motives are not explained at this point, but comments in v 13 will reveal them.

■ **4** Certain high-level officials conspired against Daniel in order to block his promotion. Most likely not all 122 **administrators and satraps** were involved (v 4). The Old Greek identifies only the two other administrators as the oppo-

DANIEL

6:1-4

nents, though the Aramaic includes at least some of the satraps along with the administrators. At first they looked for some sort of wrongdoing in **his conduct of government affairs** so that they might have **grounds for charges against** him (v 4). This proved fruitless since they discovered **no corruption in him.** What they found instead was faithfulness, honesty, and diligence, the same kinds of qualities he would demonstrate in his private religious life (see v 10). A **trustworthy** person is one who can be relied upon to follow through. A person who is **neither corrupt nor negligent** cannot be bought off from his or her core values or distracted from his or her duties.

■ **5** Since Daniel's public life was above reproach, his opponents looked elsewhere. They determined that his loyalty to **the law of his God** could provide opportunity (v 5). **The law** referenced here encompasses the entirety of Hebrew practice articulated in the Torah. It is succinctly summarized in Deut 6:4-5, "Hear, O Israel: The LORD our God, the LORD is one. Love the LORD your God with all your heart and with all your soul and with all your strength." This sets up the primary issue of the story. Daniel's allegiance to God will be brought into conflict with his commitment to the state. The law of God and "the law of the Medes and Persians" will stand in tension to one another (Dan 6:8, 12, 15).

The description of the conspirators' dilemma in vv 4-5 includes the term **find** (*šākaḥ*), a significant word in the story. Daniel's opponents try to "find" misconduct, but they "find" none. What they "find" is faithfulness. They realize they have not been able to "find" what they were looking for so they turn to "find" something in his religion. They will "find" him faithfully praying as they expected (v 11). In the end, they will "find" him to be innocent (v 21) and without harm because of his faithfulness (v 23). The discoveries of the conspirators lead the reader through the story. Those who pay attention will uncover the same truth about Daniel as his antagonists.

■ **6** The plan of Daniel's detractors was to persuade the king to issue a decree that would force Daniel to decide his allegiances. He would have to choose between loyalty to the state and loyalty to his God. **The administrators and the satraps** who were involved in the scheme **went as a group to the king** to make their proposal (v 6). The phrase **went as a group** (*rĕgaš*) mocks the frenzied activities of the conspirators. It conveys a picture of a commotion or uproar like a swirling ocean. Three times the conspirators are described this way (vv 6, 11, 15).

There is some intended ambiguity in how the group came **to the king** (v 6). Ordinarily persons are said to come "before" the king (see 2:2; 3:13; 4:6; 5:13). The preposition used here is "to" (*'al*), which can also be translated "over" or "against." Thus the narrator might be suggesting that the conspirators were making a commotion "over" the king in order to flatter him and win his approval. Additionally one could hear the text saying they were stirring up a commotion "against" the king.

The conspirators begin their proposal with appropriate respectful address for royalty, **O King Darius, live forever** (v 6). Then they give the false impression of widespread support for their proposition by claiming that a long list of high-ranking government officials had "all agreed" (v 7) on it. The list of officials is similar to that found in 3:3.

■ **7** The group's proposal was for the king to issue a decree that would solidify allegiance to him. No one could pray **to any god or man during the next thirty days** other than to the king (v 7). Though the wording might imply deification of the king, such a concept does not fit well with what is known of Persian propensities. (See *Behind the Text* above.) More likely the point of the decree was to make the king the only representative of the gods during this brief period. Those who followed the decree would be affirming the sovereignty of the king as well as their allegiance to him and the state. The penalty for not following the decree was a certain and gruesome death by **lions.** Those who do not bow to the king of the state must face the king of beasts. The image of such ferocious animals raises the intensity of the drama. The stakes are high.

■ **8-9** The conspirators urge the king to **issue the decree and put it in writing** (v 8). Putting injunctions in writing included sealing them with the king's signet ring, which protected them from tampering. Of paramount importance to Daniel's opponents is that the decree **cannot be altered** or **repealed.** No modifications or revisions can be permitted. **The laws of the Medes and Persians** is evoked as the standard for irrevocable regulations. This reflects the firmness and consistency with which these two groups of people apparently carried out their decisions. Verse 9 reports that the king yielded to the proposal presented to him.

The emphasis upon immutability of the decree underscores the impossible circumstances presented to Daniel. There is no alternative. He must confront this decree. Thus the tension in the story increases considerably. The stage is set for a dramatic confrontation between Daniel and the decree.

2. The Offense (6:10-15)

With the plan in place, the conspirators need only that it play itself out. Daniel does not disappoint them. He acts with conviction (vv 10-11) and his opponents press for a conviction (vv 12-15).

■ **10** The same qualities Daniel displays in public life he demonstrates in private. He is faithful, honest, and diligent before his God. His unusual devotion is evidenced by the reference to the place, times, and posture of his prayer. In full knowledge of the decree, Daniel neither flaunts nor hides his convictions. He goes to his **upstairs room** to pray (v 10). This is likely an apartment on top of the typical flat-roofed home set aside for such a purpose. Having the latticed **windows opened toward Jerusalem** indicate Daniel's focus is upon the God whose temple had been there. Solomon had suggested such an orientation for prayer (1 Kgs 8:35), and it became more and more popular after the temple was destroyed in 587 B.C. Thus Daniel's petition is made directly to God and not to Darius, as the decree demands.

His practice of praying **three times a day** signals not only diligence but also spiritual discipline and urgency beyond the ordinary (v 10). Praying three times daily may have been a Persian custom but was not prescribed by biblical faith. Prayer twice a day is most often mentioned in the Hebrew Scriptures, though three times—morning, noon, and evening—is mentioned in Ps 55:16-17 when the need was pressing. Getting **down on his knees** may also indicate fervency. Standing was the more typical posture. Probably with arms stretched out and lifted toward heaven he comes before his God **giving thanks.** None of this was contrived or for show. Daniel simply did **as he had done before.**

Perhaps Daniel utters the words of Ps 22:21, "Rescue me from the mouth of the lions." But no record of what Daniel actually said is given at this point. Readers are told what he did, not what he said. The effect of this within a narrative filled with speeches is to emphasize Daniel's actions. His faith is demonstrated by what he does rather than by what he says (Jas 2:18).

■ **11** Daniel's colleagues witnessed his faithfulness to God. They saw him doing exactly what the king's edict had forbidden, **praying and asking God for help** (v 11). Praying (*bĕ'ā'*) is the same word used in the decree. The two actions they observe describe essentially the same thing, which is making petition or supplication. They are a hendiadys that functions to intensify Daniel's offense.

■ **12** Armed with evidence, the conspirators proceed to the royal court. Rather than begin with accusations, they get the king to confirm his edict. They ask, **did you not publish a decree** (v 12)? The king affirms that it stands and is unchangeable according to the standard of **the laws of the Medes and Persians.** It is a clever tactic to solidify the inviolability of the decree. It is also a poignant reminder to the reader that Daniel will have no way out of his predicament.

■ **13** The accusation of Daniel's colleagues is telling. By identifying him as **one of the exiles from Judah** they reveal more about themselves than Daniel (v 13). Their motive becomes clear. Daniel is a second-rate foreign captive who does not deserve a position of authority over them. He is not one of them. The accusers portray Daniel as a traitor to the king by punctuating their invective with second person personal pronouns. They maintain he **pays no attention to you, O king, or to the decree you put in writing.** It is a masterful attack upon the integrity of Daniel. The actual offense is stated simply, **he still prays three times a day.** By mentioning **three times a day,** even Daniel's attackers ironically acknowledge his diligent faithfulness to his God. They may skew the facts about his commitment to the state, but they cannot misread his devotion to God.

■ **14-15** The king's response to the accusation is surprising. At first it seems to parallel Nebuchadnezzar's angry response to the treachery of Shadrach, Meshach, and Abednego in 3:13. The narrator describes Darius's condition as **greatly distressed** and **determined to** do something about it (v 14). One might assume he was furious and intent on expunging this treason from his kingdom. But Darius had set his heart **to rescue Daniel,** not exterminate him. He worked all day trying to find some way **to save him.** His efforts fail, though, and stand in contrast to what God is able to do later. In the end Darius must recognize that only God is the one who truly "rescues" and "saves" (see v 27).

Time for the king and Daniel runs out at **sundown** (v 14). This must have been the prescribed period for justice to be served on this edict. The accusers come once again to hold Darius accountable for his decree. They remind him that **no decree or edict that the king issues can be changed** (v 15). For the third time **the law of the Medes and Persians** looms as the force directing events. The law stands as if it were a divine power controlling the king. By implication Daniel is doomed by this sovereign force. There appears to be no escape from its dominating power, for not even a Persian king can deliver him from it.

3. The Execution (6:16-18)

The narrative slows down at this point to allow readers to absorb the impact of Daniel's execution. More than the death of a man is portrayed. The picture of a world under the dominion of oppressive human law emerges. The only hope in such a world is voiced in the words of the king who wonders if Daniel's God can make the difference. Events are told from the king's perspective throughout this section. He gives the order (v 16a), offers a word of hope (v 16b), seals Daniel's fate (v 17), and spends a restless night (v 18).

■ **16** Daniel's execution is ordered according to the rule of law. With appropriate cold royal dispatch he is brought and thrown **into the lions' den** (v 16a). Once again the king surprises the reader when he speaks to Daniel, **May your God, whom you serve continually, rescue you!** (v 16b). The ambiguity of these words leaves one wondering if the king has offered a challenge, a wish, or a conviction. They can be translated in any of these three ways. This ambiguity is reminiscent of the reply of Shadrach, Meshach, and Abednego to Nebuchadnezzar (3:17). Whatever the precise intent of Darius's comment, it is a flicker of hope in the midst of a dismal scene. The king had tried to rescue Daniel but could not. Now he speaks of the only hope left, which will turn out to be enough.

■ **17** As a note of finality, the den is literally sealed by the king and his nobles. **A stone was brought and placed over the mouth of the den** (v 17). This suggests that the place where the lions are caged is a pit in the ground with a bottled neck, something like a cistern. Sealing the pit involved a cord fastened across the stone with soft clay. Into the clay the king and each noble would impress his personalized **signet ring.** This assures that the den will not be disturbed or, if it is, authorities will know. These measures are taken so that Daniel's fate will **not be changed** (*šānâ*), just like the king's edict (see v 15). Daniel seemingly has no escape. The irony is that while the Persians are closing **the mouth of the den** God is closing "the mouths of the lions" (see v 22).

■ **18** The scene describing the night in the palace portrays a man deeply distressed by the unwanted outcome of his own authority. Ironically his power does not determine the situation. He is oppressed by the unseen power of a law to which he has relinquished control. The result of this abdication is a night **without eating, entertainment,** and **sleep** (v 18). Physically, mentally, and emotionally he is distraught. His body cannot gain strength from food. His mind cannot be distracted by amusements. His emotions will not permit him rest. The depressing effects of oppressive human law bear heavily upon him.

4. The Deliverance (6:19-23)

The action continues to unfold slowly so that readers can ponder the significance of Daniel's deliverance. The king comes to the den (v 19) and questions if Daniel has been rescued (v 20). Daniel confesses that he has (vv 21-22) and the king confirms it (v 23). The scene moves in a chiasmic design from the king to Daniel and back to the king again. This focuses attention upon Daniel's testimony of deliverance, which is a theological highpoint in the chapter.

■ **19-20** The anxious concern of the king for Daniel's situation is evident. As soon as the darkness of the oppressive night lifts, he hastily runs to the den. **At the first light of dawn** conveys the idea of the earliest possible moment (v 19). At the den he speaks in **an anguished voice** (v 20). This could be translated *with a painful cry.* He is obviously hopeful but expecting the worst.

The king's question articulates the central question of the story: Will God be faithful to rescue a faithful man? Reference to Daniel as a **servant of the living God** along with the phrase **serve continually** emphasizes Daniel's exemplary faith (v 20). This is the second time the king has mentioned the latter characteristic (see v 16). He has noticed Daniel's devotion. The king also highlights the dynamic and personal nature of Daniel's God. He is **the living God** and **your God.**

At the heart of the question of the king is whether or not God is **able to rescue.** This is a question not only of effectiveness but also of trustworthiness.

The issue is whether or not God cares to make a difference in this world as well as whether or not God can make a difference.

■ **21-22** Daniel speaks for the first time at this juncture in the story. This feature of the narrative underscores Daniel's quiet faithfulness. He has not been forceful, but everyone seems to know where he stands. The activity of God in his life appears more pronounced because of this. Daniel's first words acknowledge his loyalty to the king. **O king, live forever** is not simply polite protocol (v 21). It affirms loyalty, just as the final words of this short speech do (**nor have I ever done any wrong before you, O king,** v 22).

Daniel testifies that God is able and willing to affect human circumstances. He has intervened in a dramatic way. **God sent his angel, and he shut the mouths of the lions** (v 22). As with Shadrach, Meshach, and Abednego, God dispatched a messenger to accompany his devoted servant in the midst of his trial (3:28). The promise of Ps 91:11 finds fulfillment in this case, "For he will command his angels concerning you to guard you in all your ways." Daniel emphasizes the point that his rescue came from God. It did not result from good fortune, random chance, or even a divine messenger. The **angel** was **sent** from God. The primary explanation for his preservation is the saving initiative of God.

Daniel's deliverance, however, is not only the result of God's faithfulness but depends upon Daniel's faithfulness as well. The devotion of Daniel provides opportunity for the faithfulness of God to be manifest. Daniel displayed loyalty in two ways: before God and before the king. He was **found innocent** in God's eyes and proven not to have **done any wrong** to the king (v 22). Allegiance to God did not make him disloyal to the king. Daniel illustrates that commitment to the state and commitment to God do not need to conflict.

■ **23** Only at this point is Daniel removed from the pit. The king gives **orders** and Daniel is **lifted from the den** (v 23). Like a man brought "up from the grave" (Ps 30:3) Daniel rejoins the land of the living. The fact that **no wound was found on him** confirms Daniel's testimony. The reason for his deliverance is once again articulated. It is Daniel's devotion to God. This time his faithfulness is described by the phrase **he had trusted in his God** (v 23). As the story illustrates, this means he believed in God so much that he was willing to place his political position as well as his physical life in God's hands. This kind of faith literally brought him life.

The result of God's intervention is that Daniel is "not hurt" (v 22) and he has **no wound** (v 23). These descriptions suggest that Daniel has become the visible representation of the kingdom of God. That kingdom "will not be destroyed," according to v 26. The same Aramaic root *ḥăbāl* is behind the translation of "hurt" (v 22), **wound** (v 23), and "destroyed" (v 26). Daniel's endurance illustrates the everlasting quality of God's kingdom.

5. The Conclusion (6:24-28)

The story concludes with two commands that confirm Prov 14:35, "A king delights in a wise servant, but a shameful servant incurs his wrath." The king orders the execution of Daniel's accusers (Dan 6:24) and the worship of Daniel's God (vv 25-27). The second command is the theological climax of the chapter. A final note about Daniel's prosperity closes out the story (v 28).

■ **24** The story contains poetic justice as Daniel's accusers receive the judgment planned for him. They were **thrown into the lions' den** (v 24). This follows Israelite custom (Deut 19:18-19) as well as Persian (Esth 7:10). The inclusion of the **wives and children** assures loss of legacy as well as loss of life. It may also eliminate family retaliation. This practice was normally prohibited in Israelite law (Deut 24:16) but at times was permitted among them (Josh 7:24-25). The description of the accusers' demise includes irony. The phrase **falsely accused** literally translates *eaten his pieces* and **crushed** literally translates *broken in pieces.* Thus the ones who ate Daniel's pieces had all their bones broken in pieces and presumably eaten. The scene also underscores Daniel's miraculous deliverance. The lions were not passive or overfed. They were so ravenous that they attacked their victims **before they reached the floor of the den.**

■ **25** The other command of Darius replaces his first edict and highlights the main theological points of the story. These points provide an excellent summary for the story section of Daniel and thus a fitting conclusion to this unit in the book. They recall specific language from the royal praises that concluded several of the chapters thus far (2:47; 3:28-29; 4:34-35). The king uses hendiadyses in his speech in order to add emphasis to his thoughts. These include "fear and reverence," "he rescues and he saves," and "signs and wonders."

Darius addresses his new edict **to all the peoples, nations and men of every language throughout the land** (v 25). The audience is all-encompassing and reflects the language of Nebuchadnezzar's decrees in 3:4 and 4:1. The edict follows typical proclamation form and begins with a wish, **May you prosper greatly** (see 4:1).

■ **26** The decree specifies that everyone must **fear and reverence the God of Daniel** (v 26). This injunction is in keeping with Persian practice of giving honor to all deities throughout the empire. From the Israelite perspective it calls people to become truly wise, for "the fear of the LORD is the beginning of wisdom" (Prov 9:10).

The reason Daniel's God must be honored is because of his character, which Darius saw displayed in Daniel's life. He had observed a living God, an eternal God, a saving God, and a miracle-working God. These same points are highlighted in the previous stories of the book (see *From the Text* below). **The living God** references God's capacity to truly engage human life (v 26). Jewish readers would hear the contrast to idols, which cannot see, hear, or speak (see Isa 44:18; Dan 5:23).

The steadfastness of God strikes at the heart of the conflict in this story. Thus it receives the greatest attention from Darius. That God **endures forever** stands in direct opposition "to the laws of the Medes and Persians." Human law proved to be anything but unchanging as the pronouncement of the second edict proved. Though the laws of Darius's kingdom may alter, terminate, and reverse, God's **kingdom will not be destroyed,** and **his dominion will never end.**

■ **27** Through the lions' den ordeal Darius saw that Daniel's God **rescues** and **saves** (v 27). Darius himself was not able to do this. He hoped that Daniel's God could (see v 16) and questioned if he was able (see v 20). Now he knew that God was a savior because he had seen it with his own eyes. He confesses that God **has rescued Daniel from the power of the lions** (v 27).

The hand of God at work in Daniel's experience showed that God **performs signs and wonders,** not only **in the heavens** but also **on the earth** (v 27). Nebuchadnezzar testified to the same realization (4:3, 35). This emphasizes the universality of God's rule and, in particular, its manifestation within the realm of humans. God is not distant. He is near. God does not hide. He reveals himself.

The final notation of the chapter hearkens back to its beginning as well as the opening story of the book. Daniel once again "prospered" under the rule of a powerful king (v 28). According to 1:21 he served in royal courts, beginning with Nebuchadnezzar until "the first year of Cyrus." In ch 6 he is apparently restored to his position in Darius's court. The connections between the opening and closing stories of Dan 1—6 remind the reader that Daniel has outlasted the transition of kingdoms. As God's representative of the divine kingdom, Daniel proves the truth of ch 2 and the affirmation of Darius, "his dominion will never end" (v 26).

■ **28** The phrase **during the reign of Darius and the reign of Cyrus the Persian** may attempt to make a connection between Darius and Cyrus (v 28). The conjunction **and** can be translated as an explicative. Thus one could render, *during the reign of Darius, that is, the reign of Cyrus the Persian.* If this is the correct meaning, then it clarifies the relationship between Cyrus and Darius. If **and** is taken as a conjunctive, then it simply relates Daniel's continued success under two different rulers. In whatever manner one chooses to translate this phrase, the theological point of the sentence should not be missed. God's faithful servant thrives in the midst of foreign powers.

FROM THE TEXT

Chapter 6 is more than a captivating story about hungry lions endangering one of God's best. As the final installment in the stories of Daniel, ch 6 brings things to a fitting conclusion. It summarizes key points from previous stories but explores new dimensions of them. Key themes examined are the effects of faithful service, the human search for stability, the interface between state and divine law, and the implications of God's sovereignty for individual human life.

Faithful people reveal a faithful God. Darius defined God on the basis of what he saw in the life of Daniel. In effect Daniel became a theology book for Darius. Thus the king confessed in vv 26-27 that God was a living God, an eternal God, a saving God, and a miracle-working God.

The active hand of God manifested in Daniel's life convinces the king that his God was **a living God.** Daniel's consistent devotion, praying three times a day and serving continually, testifies to the reality of God for everyday life. Since Daniel remained unharmed throughout his ordeal, the king reasons that God's kingdom **will not be destroyed** either. He also observes that God's rescue of Daniel from the pit proved that God **saves.** The accompanying **signs and wonders** of shutting mouths of hungry lions illustrate that God is a miracle-working God, not only in the heavens but also on the earth.

These very points are the same ones that the previous stories had highlighted. As ch 1 suggested, Daniel's God was not defeated at the fall of Jerusalem. He is **a living God** actively at work on behalf of his people. His presence may not be as tangible as that of idols, but it is more real in the effects produced. As ch 2 emphasized, Daniel's God **endures forever.** He is a king whose kingdom outlasts all other kingdoms. Earthly kingdoms will rise and fall, but **his dominion will never end.** As ch 3 illustrated, Daniel's God **rescues** people from disasters. He intervenes on behalf of his faithful servants and **saves** them from impossible perils like lions and furnaces. Finally, as chs 4 and 5 pointed out, Daniel's God reveals himself within the realm of humans. **He performs signs and wonders in the heavens and on the earth** to get their attention (6:27). He does not remain at a distance or disconnected. Earthly affairs are God's affairs.

Darius knew these things about God because of Daniel. He saw them demonstrated in his life. As Heb 11:33 confirms, Daniel's faith made a difference in his world; it "shut the mouths of lions." Through Daniel's devotion God was revealed to those who would notice. In a dramatic test of faithfulness, God showed himself faithful through a faithful servant.

Stability is found in God laws, not the laws of humans. Chapter 6 exposes the illusion of human legislation. While laws are necessary for an orderly society, it is easy to expect too much of them. People often hope for more than human governance can deliver. The main conflict in the story develops between **the law of his God** (v 5) and **the laws of the Medes and Persians** (vv 8, 12, 15). The latter claimed permanence. It was thought that they **cannot be al-**

tered or **repealed** (vv 8, 12, 15). As such they seemed to promise a sense of stability and security for human life. These laws appeared to be useful tools for managing life, but in the end they prove to be oppressive.

Darius was fooled into thinking law could fulfill the human longing for stability. For thirty days all petitions in his kingdom would be brought under his control. A feeling of order and consistency would prevail. Darius was not alone in his hope, however. The conspirators also saw promise in the laws of humans. Just the right decree could solve their dilemma and help them gain an advantage. Ironically they undermined the essential value of human law by trying to use it for personal advantage rather than for corporate service. Laws are for community, not individual, gain. The conspirators also revealed the fatal flaw of human law. When it serves the few, it ceases to fulfill its God-ordained role (Rom 13:1).

The search for complete security through laws is shown to be faulty on two counts in the text. On the one hand, the unchangeable **laws of the Medes and Persians** prove to be changeable. The conspirators must have suspected this option. Their continual affirmations of immutability and pressing the king regarding it betray uncertainty on this point. In the end Darius does issue a second decree that sets aside the first. A law demanding **fear and reverence** for **the God of Daniel** replaces one that called for exclusive reverence for Darius (v 26). By proclaiming the second decree Darius demonstrates the impermanence of human laws. The conspirators' worst fears came true. Human law gave way to a greater power.

On the other hand, the laws of God do not bend. As the psalmist says, "The law of the LORD is perfect, . . . the statutes of the LORD are trustworthy, . . . the precepts of the LORD are right, . . . the ordinances of the LORD are sure and altogether righteous" (Ps 19:7-9). Daniel lives by them and proves their truth. He not only survives but also prospers in the end. They do bring him to the brink of disaster. He is thrown into a lions' pit as a result of living by these laws. But he is also rescued from that pit unharmed **because he had trusted in his God** (Dan 6:23). The rule of God brought about his deliverance.

The illusion of law is that it will establish a system that somehow will **not suffer loss** (v 2). It promises a security it cannot grant. The story shows that human law can, in fact, produce grave losses. The king's favored servant is nearly lost to its power, but more than that occurred. The king himself lost peace of mind and even authority to act at will under its dominance. The conspirators lost their integrity and eventually their lives because of it. **The law of the Medes and Persians** takes on an almost divine quality in the story. It is an external force that controls earthly events. That law overpowers all the characters in the story, except God. Proverbs 14:12 might be applied to human laws when it says, "There is a way that seems right to a man, but in the end it leads to death." As Dan 6 illustrates, people sabotage their own designs for the good life when they place too much confidence in their laws.

Those who desire a life well ordered must look to the God who **endures forever,** as Darius puts it. The place where God rules **will not be destroyed** and the sphere of his authority **will never end.** True stability and security are only found in God's kingdom. The everlasting God holds such gifts in his hands. He is like a rock and a fortress that "will not be shaken" (Ps 62:6). "Though the earth give way and the mountains fall into the heart of the sea" God remains steadfast and sure (Ps 46:2).

The best citizens of the state are God's people. The conflict in this story goes beyond opposing laws. At another level it is about religion versus the state. Allegiance to God comes into tension with allegiance to the state. Yet, Daniel maintains that he has never **done any wrong** to the king (v 22). Though he violated the decree by petitioning his God, Daniel claims his loyalty to the state remains.

One might argue from this story that Daniel proved to be more loyal than those subjects who kept the letter of the law. By devising the first edict the conspirators encouraged and enabled the state to follow illusions. Their insistence on the inviolability of the law perpetrated the delusion that law can somehow create absolute stability. They also advanced the beliefs that loyalty can be legislated and that people can be vested with power only God should have.

When the state follows such delusions, its best citizens will protest. The protest of Daniel's prayer was mild but effective. It called upon the king to question his decree and look for ways to save Daniel from it. In the end he is unable to rescue Daniel from the tyranny of the edict, but God can. As the scenario plays out and God's power becomes manifested through it, the king moves toward a healthier position. His second edict leads the state in the right direction by demanding **fear and reverence** for God (v 26). Daniel's loyal citizenship prompts the empire to do the right things.

New Testament writers understood Daniel's dilemma and confirmed his position on allegiance to the state. Jesus taught his disciples to "give to Caesar what is Caesar's" (Matt 22:21), and Paul admonished believers to "submit . . . to the governing authorities" (Rom 13:1; Titus 3:1). The motives for good citizenship are several. They include avoiding reprimand from the state as well as providing a witness to nonbelievers (Rom 13:2-7; 1 Pet 2:13-22). More importantly, though, NT writers understood all authority deriving from God (Rom 13:1). Thus rebellion against the state is like rebellion against God. Therefore Christians must obey the laws of the state "for the Lord's sake" (1 Pet 2:13). However, when conflict emerges between God's law and human laws, Christians understood that they answered to a higher authority. As Peter said, "We must obey God rather than men!" (Acts 5:29).

God holds power over death. Chapter 6 is a story about deliverance from death. Being thrown into the lions' pit spelled Daniel's demise. No human could be expected to survive this execution. But he did. As the text reports, **God sent his angel, . . . shut the mouths of the lions,** and delivered Daniel unharmed (v 22). God's power extends to the preservation of life. Thus, the sovereignty of God includes ability to overrule not only kings and decrees but also humanity's greatest enemy, death.

The story does not indicate that every person should expect to be rescued from danger. Biblical faith knows that suffering and death come to the faithful. Stephen, James, Paul, Peter, and nearly all the other original twelve disciples of Jesus suffered martyrdom for their faith in those early years. Since then countless others have joined them, even unto today. God, for reasons known only to him, does not always preserve life in this world. Yet, as Daniel's experience testifies, God brings life where death reigns. He is **the living God.** God is the giver and sustainer of life (Gen 2:7; John 1:4).

God's resurrection power is faintly reflected in this story. As such it anticipates the final vision of the book, which announces, "multitudes who sleep in the dust of the earth will awake" (Dan 12:2). It also foreshadows the story of Jesus. Parallels between Jesus and Daniel are remarkable. Both are victims of betrayers and found praying before their arrests. During their trials the chief authority sees the fallacy of the proceedings and labors to free them. In the end they are condemned under misguided human law. A rock covers over their underground chamber and is sealed by authorities. No hope for their survival can be found within the human realm. At the break of day, though, with great joy it is discovered that they are, in fact, alive.

II. VISIONS FROM A FOREIGN LAND (7:1—12:13)

Overview

The second major section of the book records four visions that Daniel receives while serving in the courts of Babylon and Persia. They are arranged in chronological order beginning within the time frame of the stories in chs 1—6 and moving beyond them by a few years. Like Ezek 1, they affirm that God continues to speak to his people in a foreign land.

167

These visions connect integrally to one another. Common themes, subject matter, structural elements, and key words create a sense of interdependence and unity. All four visions deal with the subject of kingdoms in conflict. As they progress, each vision tends to become more particular and detailed than the previous one. The first vision in ch 7 sketches a general overview of world history in broad strokes. The other three visions in chs 8—12 concentrate upon a specific time of turmoil within that scheme. They focus upon a period of affliction surrounding an event called "the abomination that causes desolation" (9:27; 11:31; see 8:13). The images of the visions also display a movement from the surreal toward the more familiar. Fantastic animals in ch 7 give way to more realistic animals in ch 8. These are exchanged for numerical images in ch 9 and finally for specific activities of kings in chs 10—12.

As a unit the visions reaffirm the central themes put forth by the stories in the first portion of the book and explore their implications further. The sovereign God experienced by Daniel and his friends remains fully in control. His dominion extends over all the kingdoms of this world and even beyond it. Those who are wise like Daniel can expect deliverance from God, if not in the present, then in the future. Faithful living is always ultimately rewarded. So as believers await the full manifestation of God's rule in the future, they are challenged to remain unwavering in their commitment to his kingdom in the present.

A. Vision of Four Beasts (7:1-28)

Overview

Chapter 7 serves as the focal point of the book. All that has gone before and all the follows converge in its verses. In some ways everything is new. In other ways much remains the same. A new genre is employed to sketch a fresh image of God's sovereignty over this world. Yet, at the same time, an overall narrative frame remains, and the language and motifs of the stories reappear. These elements combine to paint a memorable picture of "the appointed time" when the Lord "will arise and have compassion on" his people (Ps 102:13). The centrality of this chapter must not be missed.

BEHIND THE TEXT

Several features mark ch 7 as pivotal in the book. Language, themes, and motifs link this chapter to both the stories (chs 1—6) and the visions (chs 7—12). Structural elements and genre also cause the chapter to function as a hinge between the two major portions of Daniel. As a vision ch 7 introduces the final section of the book. Yet it also serves as a conclusion to the stories.

At the end of ch 7 the Aramaic section of Daniel (chs 2—7) comes to completion. This portion forms a distinct unit within the book that is held together not only by language but also by other features (see *Behind the Text* on ch 2). Its conclusion signals something significant to the reader. The themes and motifs have come full circle and a climactic concluding point is reached.

Even though the Aramaic section is dominated by narrative, ch 7 is integrally related to them. Verbal and thematic connections between ch 7 and these stories are evident on several levels. Most obvious is the relationship to ch 2 and its comparable dream of the four kingdoms. The theme of divine judgment upon earthly kingdoms dominates both chapters. Visions through the medium of dreams, the rising and falling of four kingdoms, and the terrifying iron-like strength of the last kingdom are some of the similar motifs. As the beginning and ending of the Aramaic section, these two chapters form an inclusion for the material in this section.

The descriptions and interpretations of four world kingdoms in chs 2 and 7 tend to complement each other. They supply details that may be lacking in one or the other. The way in which earthly kingdoms afflict God's people, for example, is not mentioned in ch 2 but is given considerable emphasis in ch 7. The two versions also provide contrast in perspectives. The imposing metal statue of ch 2 portrays the kingdoms of this world from a human standpoint in all their glitter and glory. The grotesque beasts of ch 7, on the other hand, convey the animalistic character of earth's kingdoms from God's point of view. The appearance of two similar visions within the book underscores the significance of the messages contained in them. The motifs have been repeated to alert the reader to take notice.

Links with other stories in the book are also significant. Some examples include the following. Reference to execution by a "blazing fire" (7:11) recalls the ordeal of Shadrach, Meshach, and Abednego in ch 3. The description of the beasts in 7:4-8 alludes to Nebuchadnezzar's pride and beast-like appearance in ch 4. The setting of Belshazzar's reign (v 1) and the descriptions of the boastful "little horn" (vv 8, 25) evoke the story of Belshazzar's humbling in ch 5. The lion-like appearance of the first beast (7:4) recalls the lions that threatened Daniel in ch 6.

While ch 7 is closely associated with the stories, it also commences the second half of the book. A new genre, the apocalyptic styled vision report, is employed, which will dominate the final chapters. Four personal visions of Daniel are recorded in chs 7—12. They employ typical apocalyptic motifs and language such as symbolic animals and numbers along with heavenly beings who act as guides to the visionary.

The general form of chs 7—12 is that of a prophetic vision report. Typical of vision reports among the prophets is a two-part structure: (1) an account of what is seen followed by (2) its interpretation (see Jer 1:11-16). This is the pattern followed here in ch 7. Other elements often found in this genre include: (1) an indication of circumstances, (2) a request for understanding, and (3) a concluding statement about the visionary's response. An additional feature of heavenly beings assisting the one receiving the vision is found in some exilic and postexilic prophets (Ezek 40—48; Zech 1—6) and becomes common in noncanonical apocalypses. Prior to the exile prophets typically reported God conversing directly with them and explaining meanings (Isa 6; Amos 8:1-2).

Like ch 8, the visionary of ch 7 reports seeing animals that represent human kingdoms. Thus these two visions can be distinguished from those in chs 9—12, which do not include such images, as symbolic vision reports. The animals in ch 8 are different from those in ch 7 however. There are only two of them, and they are not hybrids. Yet, they are ferocious animals with horns. The second one has a terrorizing small horn much like the little horn of ch 7. The setting for both visions is identified in relation to the reign of Belshazzar. There are other connections, but these will be considered in comments on ch 8.

Aside from common genre, the final chapters of the book are linked by a new chronological sequence that breaks with the earlier chapters. The stories in chs 1—6 moved sequentially from the time of Nebuchadnezzar to Belshazzar to Darius. Chapter 7 reverts to the first year of Belshazzar, which places it chronologically between chs 4 and 5. Then the visions in chs 8 and 9 are related to the reigns of Belshazzar and Darius, while the final vision in chs 10—12 is connected to the third year of Cyrus. There is also a pattern of "first year" then "third year" in these notations that creates another bond for these visions.

Except for the first verse, the vision of ch 7 is relayed from a first person perspective. A third person introduction is not unusual for these kinds of reports (see 10:1). Though this feature could indicate a secondary hand in the material, it does not necessarily mean that. Third person comment is a typical literary device employed in postexilic material (see Ezra 7 and Neh 1). It tends to highlight the eyewitness effect of the first person perspective.

The historical setting given for the vision of ch 7 is significant. It identifies a time of unrest and emerging empires like those envisioned in Daniel's dream. **The first year of Belshazzar** was around 550 B.C. (v 1). This was the year that the Babylonian king Nabonidus relinquished daily control of the empire to his eldest son, Belshazzar, and retreated to the Arabian desert for a period of about ten years. Nabonidus preferred worship of the moon god Sin to the patron god of Babylon, Marduk. These factors created a religious and political struggle among various factions in Babylon and threw the empire into disorder.

The year 550 B.C. also marks the time that Cyrus the Great rebelled against his Median overlord Astyages and united the forces of the Medes and Persians. By so doing he established one of the most enduring empires of world history, the Persian Empire. It lasted for over two centuries from 550 B.C. to

331 B.C. and became one of the largest empires the world has ever known (see *Behind the Text* for ch 8 for more information).

Though many of the ideas and images employed in ch 7 are unique to it and the book of Daniel, interconnections with other texts in the Hebrew Scriptures are many. Especially noteworthy are passages that refer to God as creator and judge. Such texts establish essential background for the worldview underlying this vision. God forming and subduing monsters from the sea is a significant image reflected in the vision (Gen 1:20-21; Isa 17:12-13; Jer 46:7; Job 40—41; Ps 74:12-14; Ezek 29:3; 32:2), as is the picture of God sitting as judge over nations (Pss 9:7-8; 96:10-13; 110:1-7). Psalm 2 is particularly instructive because it mentions God installing his "Son" the king to rule over the nations. Similarly Ps 89 speaks of God ruling from his throne and investing a Davidic ruler with authority. This psalm also includes reference to God crushing the sea monster Rahab. Prophetic visions of the final consummation of human history on the day of the Lord provide additional backdrop to Daniel's vision (Isa 2:1-5; 66:17-24; Zech 14:1-21). The depictions of God's people sharing in the dominion over their former oppressors (Isa 14:1-4) and all nations worshipping God (Isa 2:2) are particularly applicable. The appearance of God on his throne is consistent with other throne room visions of the Hebrew Scriptures (1 Kgs 22:19; Ezek 1:4-28).

The ideas and images of ch 7 are also at home within the context of the ancient Middle Eastern world (see Lucas 2002, 168-76, and Collins 1993, 280-94, for extended discussions). Mythology, iconography, and wisdom texts of Mesopotamia and Canaan provide a number of general parallels to the elements found in Daniel's vision. Though no exact correspondences to what Daniel envisions can be discovered in this material, a context for processing bizarre images and the pattern of relationships between characters is established. For example, the Mesopotamian creation myth *Enuma Elish* relays Marduk's struggle with the sea and its monsters. Texts from Canaanite Ugarit provide a similar episode with Baal as champion. Reliefs and statues of winged lions were regular motifs in palaces of the ancient world. Omen texts recorded births of malformed hybrid animals. These were considered messages from the gods and analyzed with extreme care. Such parallels do not indicate that Daniel borrowed these elements to construct his vision. They do, however, provide background for the visual and conceptual effects of the vision upon its original audience. Daniel's vision was not an entirely unique collection of images and ideas without reference to the thought world of his audience.

The vision of ch 7 follows a simple structure. A report of the vision (vv 2-14) is followed by its interpretation (vv 15-27). These two major sections are enveloped by a brief introduction (v 1) and an even briefer conclusion (v 28).

The report and interpretation parallel one another. The report moves from a description of the four beasts (vv 2-7) to a focus upon the little horn (v 8) to the throne scene in heaven (vv 9-14). The interpretation follows the same order by explaining the meaning of the four beasts (vv 17-18), the little horn (vv 19-25), and then the throne scene (vv 26-27).

IN THE TEXT

I. Introduction (7:1)

■ **I** The opening verse does more than provide a setting for the vision. It also establishes links with other parts of the book. **Daniel** is introduced without any description of his background, position, or abilities. The vision report obviously relies upon information from the first six stories to provide background for this main character. His role has changed from that in the narratives, however. He is now a recipient of dreams rather than an interpreter of them.

The historical setting for the vision also connects it with the stories. Reference to the Babylonian king **Belshazzar** locates Daniel's vision chronologically between chs 4 and 5. This alerts the reader to additional background for understanding the drama of ch 5. Daniel apparently knew where things were headed even before the writing on the wall appeared. He had received a personal revelation regarding the unfolding of events in his world. **The first year of Belshazzar,** about 550 B.C., is significant in the flow of world history. It references a time of confusion in the Babylonian Empire and the entire Middle East. New nations were emerging while others were waning. It was a crucial era of transition (see *Behind the Text* above).

Daniel receives the **visions** through the medium of **a dream.** This parallels Nebuchadnezzar's experiences in chs 2 and 4 (2:28; 4:5). Daniel's later visions do not come in the context of dreams (8:1; 9:21; 10:1). The vision happened **as he was lying on his bed.** This also recalls Nebuchadnezzar's experience in ch 4 (4:5, 10, 13). The location may indicate the unexpected nature of the vision. Persons intentionally seeking communication with the divine world would more likely do so in a temple setting.

In order to ensure its perpetuity, Daniel **wrote down the substance of his dream.** Putting a divine message into writing marked it for fulfillment and gave it the authority of a royal decree (Isa 8:1; Hab 2:2). It also made possible the continuing affects of the message for subsequent generations (Jer 36:2-3; Ezek 43:10-11). The phrase **substance of** (*rēš*) literally translates *beginning of.* The implication is that Daniel records the dream in the sequence in which it came to him, starting at the beginning.

2. Report of the Images (7:2-14)

The account of Daniel's vision is conveyed in a chiasmic structure that focuses attention upon God seated in judgment upon his throne in vv 9-10. The final scene in which a divine figure comes on the clouds in vv 13-14 balances the opening portrayal of beasts emerging from the sea in vv 2-3. Reference to the fate of the three beasts in v 12 offsets their initial descriptions in vv 4-6. Similarly judgment upon the fourth beast in v 11 stands over against its first appearance in vv 7-8. Besides highlighting God's role as judge over earthly kingdoms, this structure dramatizes the effects of divine rule. The contrast could not be more pronounced between the chaos prior to vv 9-10 and the order following. Before the throne of God both cosmic and human realities are significantly altered.

For the first time in the book Daniel conveys his experience in first person. This perspective dominates the remainder of the book. The impact of this feature is to highlight the eyewitness aspect of the material and thus enhance its sense of authority. The reader is also able to live the experience with Daniel more tangibly.

■ **2** The report is punctuated with formulaic sayings such as **I looked** (*ḥăzēh ḥăwêt*; vv 2, 4, 6, 7, 9, 11*a*, 11*b*, 13) and **there before me** (*ʾărû/ʾălû* literally means "behold"; vv 2, 5, 6, 7, 8, 13). These phrases intensify the drama by focusing the audience upon the key scenes. They also accentuate the personal aspect of this experience. Daniel further underscores the ominous character of his dream by noting it took place **at night** (v 2). Three times he emphasizes this setting, thereby alerting readers to the gravity of his dream (vv 2, 7, 13). Night visions carry additional emotion (Gen 46:2; Job 33:15; Zech 1:8).

Daniel's dream begins with a scene of great terror, a violent ocean storm. The picture of **the four winds of heaven churning up the great sea** depicts chaos and the cosmic proportions of the dream (v 2). Reference to **the four winds of heaven** suggests hurricane conditions with wind coming from every direction—north, south, east, and west. Since the term "wind" (*rûaḥ*) also translates as "spirit," the phrase **winds of heaven** could subtly suggest divine involvement. These winds stir up threatening waves from the ocean. **The great sea** (*yammāʾ rabbāʾ*) might refer to the Mediterranean Sea (see Josh 1:4; *hayyām haggādôl*) but also evokes the primordial waters of biblical imagery and Mesopotamian mythology. "The great deep" (*tĕhôm rabbâ*) lies above the firmament and beneath the earth (Gen 7:11; Amos 7:4; see also Gen 1:7). Throughout the Bible the **sea** symbolizes uncertainty and disorder (Rev 21:1). The whole scene recalls Gen 1:2, which describes chaos before creation when "the earth was formless and empty, darkness was over the surface of the deep [*tĕhôm*], and the Spirit [*rûaḥ*] of God was hovering over the waters [*māyim*]."

■ **3** Out of the chaotic ocean tempest emerge **four great beasts** (v 3). Though they share common oppressive characteristics because of their origins, each has distinguishing marks. They are **each different from the others** in their appearance and the terror they evoke. Biblical writers frequently envision the sea teeming with intimidating serpent-like monsters known as Leviathan or Rahab (Pss 89:9-10; 104:25-26; Isa 51:9).

■ **4** The first beast looks **like a lion** with **wings of an eagle** (v 4). The combination of the king of beasts with the king of the birds makes this beast exceptional. Yet the creature experiences both highs and lows of life. Having its **wings . . . torn off** suggests loss of ability and status. Gaining qualities of **a man,** however, indicates a move in the other direction. The language recalls ch 4, where Nebuchadnezzar falls and rises in power. In his demise he was given "the mind of an animal" (literally, "the heart of a beast," 4:16) and grew hair that looked like "the feathers of an eagle" (4:33). The beast of Daniel's vision knew the reversal of these effects and was **lifted from the ground** like Nebuchadnezzar (7:4; see 4:36).

■ **5** The second beast looks **like a bear** that is deformed (v 5). The description of being **raised up on one of its sides** is ambiguous. It could indicate that the bear is raised up in an attacking stance. More likely, though, it portrays a disproportioned growth on one of its sides. Grotesque animals are a common feature of apocalyptic works. The **three ribs** in its mouth could be understood as "tusks" or "fangs" rather than body parts of another animal. In any case, the beast is instructed by an unidentified voice to **get up and eat your fill of flesh.** The ravenous character of this animal is being emphasized.

■ **6** The third beast looks **like a leopard** with **four wings** and **four heads** (v 6). The leopard is known for speed and agility and the reference to **four wings** only increases this image. The **four heads** suggest extended influence over the world, which is confirmed by noting **it was given authority to rule.** This creature recalls the four living creatures with four faces and four wings in Ezekiel's vision of heavenly realms (Ezek 1). These creatures possessed the ability to move in any direction at any time in absolute synchronized harmony.

The first three beasts resemble some of creation's most imposing predators. The **lion, bear,** and **leopard** occur in biblical texts, sometimes together, to evoke dread (Jer 5:6; Hos 13:7-8). The architects of ancient Mesopotamian palaces commonly employed these same animals for similar effects. Animals with wings was a typical motif of ancient royal artists. Winged lions in particular decorated thrones and court entrances. The hybrid character of such animals, including those in this text, only adds to their horror for an ancient Jewish audience. Certain kinds of creatures were appalling to Israelites (Lev 11:9-12, 23) and the mixing of species was contrary to the created order (Gen 1:24-25; Lev 19:19).

■ **7** The order in which the first three beasts appear is descending in terms of how ancient writers traditionally perceived their strength and terror. But the fourth beast reverses this trend and becomes the most imposing of all. The shift is marked by the use of active verbs to describe this beast. By contrast the first three beasts are depicted with passive verbs. Daniel adds dramatic affect to the fourth beast's introduction by pausing to remind the audience once again that this occurs **in my vision at night** (v 7; see vv 2 and 13 also).

The description of the fourth beast is more extended than that of the others, indicating its special significance. A trilogy of horrific attributes **terrifying and frightening and very powerful** is matched by a trilogy of oppressive actions **crushed and devoured . . . and trampled** (v 7). The actions depict an animal killing and feasting on prey. With powerful jaws the beast crushes its victim and tramples on the carcass while consuming its flesh. The increased terror associated with this beast is emphasized by the comment that **it was different from all the former beasts.** If a lion, bear, and leopard are terrifying, this beast is more. It is so horrifying that no earthly beast compares to it. Thus it remains unnamed, incomparable, and more mysterious. Terms such as **powerful, iron,** and **crushed** recall vocabulary describing the fourth kingdom in the dream of ch 2.

As a symbol of its superiority, the beast dons **ten horns** (v 7). Throughout the Hebrew Scriptures **horns** signify status, strength, and at times pride (1 Sam 2:1; Pss 75:4-5; 112:9). The number **ten** suggests a full amount, such as is associated with the Ten Commandments or ten fingers (Gen 32:15; Exod 34:28; 1 Sam 1:8). The fourth beast possesses unmatched strength. Since some animals might normally have two horns, this beast is five times greater than normal.

■ **8** As the description of the beast continues, additional details are given about its horns. Among the ten horns emerges **a little one** that uproots **three** others (v 8). The little horn **came up** (*sĕlēq*) **among them** in a manner resembling the emergence of the beasts who "came up out of the sea" in v 3. Similar to the first beast, this horn possesses some human qualities. Its eyes are **like the eyes of a man.** It also has **a mouth that spoke boastfully.** Notice of the beast's **eyes** and **mouth** focus attention upon its character. In biblical tradition these particular body parts reveal the inner person (Ps 19:14; Prov 4:23-25; Matt 12:34). Often they are associated with pride and foolishness (Prov 6:16-17; 15:2). The term translated **boastfully** literally means *great things* (*rabrĕbān*), which could be taken either positively or negatively. The interpretation of the vision clarifies a negative meaning is intended. The little horn speaks arrogantly "against the Most High" (v 25). It reflects the character of those kings God humbled in chs 4 and 5.

■ **9** The dream report continues with a dramatic shift in atmosphere. An orderly scene of divine beings invades the chaotic stage of grotesque beasts. The author signals this shift by moving to poetic verse in vv 9-10 and 13-14. Parallelism, rhythm, metaphor, simile, hendiadys, assonance, and repetition are employed to heighten the effect of this scene.

A court coming to order is envisioned by **thrones** being **set in place** and **the Ancient of Days** taking **his seat** (v 9). The judgment hall is a palace throne room. The king, his throne, a body of water, and the royal attendants are described. Within Hebrew Scriptures the divine title **Ancient of Days** is only found in this chapter (vv 9, 13, 22). It reflects the Ugaritic reference to Baal as "father of years" and emphasizes God's age. Ancient cultures revered older persons. So the point of the name is to underscore God's authority to rule. God can sit as judge of nations because he is eternal. God has been before anything else from the beginning, so he has a perspective that no one else can have. **Clothing** that is **white as snow** and **hair** that is **white like wool** adds to this image. These are features associated with someone respected and wise.

The whiteness of God's **clothing** and **hair** signifies more than age, however (v 9). It also conveys unmatched purity and alludes to God's holiness. Reference to a **throne** that is **flaming with fire** and **wheels** that are **all ablaze** adds to the impression of God's holy otherness. Fire functions as a catalyst in the purifying process of metals and thus evokes an image of separation and purification throughout the Hebrew Scriptures (Exod 3:2; 19:18; Zech 13:9; Mal 3:2). The chariot-like appearance of a throne with **wheels** is common imagery for divine thrones in the ancient world. It recalls Ezekiel's vision of God by the Kebar River once again (Ezek 1). In that vision God moves quickly and freely in all directions as a result of the wheels beneath the throne. Thus the description of God in these verses accentuates his holiness. God is not like the beasts of earth or anything else in creation. **His clothing,** his **hair,** and **his throne** set God apart.

■ **10** Before the throne flows **a river of fire** (v 10). One might imagine a reflecting pond, which was sometimes used in ancient temples. In any case, this feature portrays divine judgment. Throughout Scripture God deals with evil like "a consuming fire" (Deut 4:24). Thus fire is frequently used as a symbol for God's judgment (Isa 66:15-16; Ezek 21:31-32; Amos 5:6). Typical of ancient royal courts, the king is attended by a large number of courtiers. **Thousands upon thousands** and **ten thousand times ten thousand** poetically express incalculable numbers (v 10). God's throne is surrounded by "a great multitude that no one could count" (Rev 7:9).

While the attendants remain standing, the divine judge is **seated** and the proceedings begin (v 10). **The books** that are **opened** might be a record of things that have taken place within the king's domain. Based on the context, one could assume these are the deeds of the four beasts. Royal records were typical among ancient monarchs (Ezra 4:15; Esth 6:1), and the tradition of God keeping records of human behavior within his realm runs deep in the Hebrew Scriptures (Exod 32:32; Ps 56:8; Mal 3:16). Yet the contents of **the books** could also be God's purposes for the future. Within Daniel the idea of God sealing such plans in a book is particularly emphasized (8:26; 9:24; 10:21; 12:4, 9).

■ **11** The poetry of vv 9-10 and 13-14 is briefly interrupted by prose description of judgment for the four beasts in vv 11-12. This prosaic interlude draws attention to this moment in the scene and helps contrast it with the more positive components that precede and follow it.

God executes judgment upon the four beasts. First, the fourth beast is **slain** for his offenses (v 11). **The boastful words the horn was speaking** are the primary reason given for this sentence. As in chs 4 and 5, God does not tolerate insolence within his domain. Execution by means of a **blazing fire** indicates the severity of the crime. The most heinous offenses were handled in this way (Lev 20:14; 21:9; Josh 7:25; Dan 3:6). With **its body destroyed** the condemned has no hope of further existence according to ancient mentality. This dramatic picture reflects the vision of Isaiah regarding "that day" when God "will slay the monster of the sea" (Isa 27:1).

■ **12** After dealing with the fourth beast, God turns to the other three. God's judgment is discriminating for **the other beasts** are not treated as harshly as the fourth beast (v 12). They are **stripped of their authority** and **allowed to live for a period of time.** The difference in the treatment of the beasts suggests that the evil perpetrated by the fourth beast is more offensive to heaven than that of the other three. As v 25 will make clear, it is the blasphemous behavior of the fourth beast that is judged so severely. This agrees with the stories in chs 4 and 5. The arrogant sacrilege of Belshazzar also exacts the death sentence, while the pompous pride of Nebuchadnezzar is given a chance to change. Perhaps the three beasts are offered the same grace that Nebuchadnezzar had in ch 4 when they are **allowed to live for a period of time.**

The fact that judgment of all four beasts occurs at one time agrees with the dream of ch 2. There the statue representing four kingdoms is destroyed by one crushing blow (2:34, 43). This suggests that God's kingdom breaks into the various realms of earth throughout history. God's people do not have to wait for the culmination of history before the kingdom of God manifests itself among them. Yet, focus upon the last beast and its demise indicates that final judgment on the ultimate day of the Lord is also in view. Similar to what Israel's other prophets perceived, this vision anticipates both historical and eschatological events. God deals with nations and establishes his kingdom on earth within history as well as at its end (Isa 2:1-5; Zech 14:1-21).

■ **13** The final episode in the throne scene is the climax of the vision. An extended introduction signals the significance of these verses. Daniel notes once again that his experience took place in a **vision at night** when he **looked** and saw remarkable things **before** him (v 13). These three elements constitute the same formulaic introduction used at the beginning of the report (v 2) and when the fourth beast was described (v 7). Thus the main character of this scene is set over against the four beasts and in particular the fourth beast. The contrast between the two could not be greater.

177

The key figure of this dramatic scene is **one like a son of man** (*kĕbar'ĕnāš*, v 13). The Aramaic phrase *bar 'ĕnāš* corresponds to the Hebrew *ben 'ĕnôš* and *ben 'ādām*, which literally translate "a son of a man" or "a descendant of a human being." It can be used in an indefinite sense to indicate "someone" and often designates "humanness" (Pss 8:4; 144:3; Jer 49:18; Ezek 2:1). Thus it simply means "a human being."

The figure here is said to be **like** a human being, which suggests an essence other than human. Since this person comes **with the clouds of heaven,** deity is implied. Clouds were typically the vehicle of divine transport within Israelite and Canaanite thought. Baal, the god of thunderstorms, is called "Rider on the Clouds" in myths from Ugarit. In the Hebrew psalms and prophetic literature God rides the clouds like a king in a chariot (Pss 18:9-12; 68:4; 104:3; Isa 19:1). Therefore the "son of man" figure displays both human and divine qualities.

This person comes before **the Ancient of Days** to be invested with authority (v 13). The language evokes ancient enthronement ceremonies as the "son of man" figure moves through the throne room led by a royal entourage into the **presence** of **the Ancient of Days.**

■ **14** To this person God grants **authority, glory and sovereign power** (v 14), the same kinds of things Nebuchadnezzar had received from God (2:37; 5:18). These are gifts only divinity can bestow, for they are God's by nature according to the book of Daniel (4:3, 34; 6:26). **Authority** (*šālṭān*), also translated **dominion** in this verse, is repeated throughout this chapter (vv 6, 12, 14 [3 times], 26, 27 [2 times]). The divine right to rule, which was stripped from the beasts (v 12), is given over to the "son of man" figure in this verse and also, according to v 27, "the saints."

Now vested with authority, the "son of man" figure becomes an object of worship. The term for **worshiped** (*pĕlaḥ*) recalls ch 3 where the dilemma for the Hebrews was whether or not they would bow before a statue (3:12, 14, 18, 28). In this vision all people do what Nebuchadnezzar had hoped they would do before his idol. They pay ultimate reverence to one worthy of such. An eschatological scenario envisioned by the prophets of Israel unfolds here (Isa 2:2; Zech 14:16). The entire world, **all peoples, nations and men of every language,** fall before "the one like a son of man" (v 13). This list recalls the royal decrees of Nebuchadnezzar and Darius that called for worship of Daniel's God (4:1; 6:25). So also does the declaration that **his dominion** is **everlasting, will not pass away** and **never be destroyed,** which is identical with the language of the secular kings (4:3; 6:26). These three expressions of the indestructible nature of the kingdom underscore its present reality as well as its assured continuance. This contrasts sharply with the fate of the beasts just noted in vv 10 and 11.

An interpretation for the "son of man" figure is not offered in the vision's explanation of vv 15-27. Thus readers are left to interpret this person in light of other scriptures. Both Jewish and Christian interpreters have observed similarities between the "son of man" figure and portraits of messianic personalities in other prophetic books. The prophets proposed a Davidic descendent who would exercise authority over the kingdom of God much like Daniel's vision portrays (Isa 9:1-6; 11:1-5; Mic 5:1-5; Zech 9:9-10). The major element that is different in Daniel is the combination of divine and human features. Of the several possible identifications proposed for the "son of man" figure, the best option is Jesus Christ. He fits the description of a divine-human person who is invested with universal authority and worshipped by all peoples at the end of time. New Testament writers clearly understood Jesus in this way. In one of Paul's letters, for example, Jesus is described with the features of the "son of man" figure in Dan 7. He is the one "who, being in very nature God" was "made in human likeness" and yet was exalted by God so that "at the name of Jesus every knee should bow . . . and every tongue confess that Jesus Christ is Lord" (Phil 2:6-7, 10-11).

Son of Man in Daniel 7:13

Scholars have offered numerous proposals for the identification of the "son of man" figure in Dan 7:13. The most prominent include: (1) Judas Maccabeus, (2) the people of God, (3) an angelic being, and (4) Jesus of Nazareth. Some of those who view the book as a second-century composition have favored Judas Maccabeus. He is the messianic figure who led the revolt that freed the Jews and established the Hasmonean Kingdom in 164 B.C. The book's lack of support for violent resistance like that of the Maccabees, however, argues against this idea.

The people of God have been proposed because "the saints of the Most High" are said to receive the kingdom in vv 18, 22, and 27. Scholars propose that the "son of man" individual in v 13 symbolically embodies the whole. This proposal might be acceptable if worship of the "son of man" figure were not described in v 14. According to biblical tradition only God should be honored in this way. Thus a distinction between the "son of man" figure and the people of God should be maintained. It is reasonable to understand, then, that the "one like a son of man" will lead "the saints" as they inherit the kingdom of God.

The worship of the "son of man" figure in v 14 also preempts the angelic being option proposed by some scholars. Both Gabriel and Michael, who are mentioned later in Daniel (8:16; 9:21; 10:13, 21; 12:1), have been suggested. Neither human beings nor angels, however, can be the legitimate objects of worship from the biblical perspective.

Jewish and Christian traditions over the centuries have been dominated by the understanding that the "son of man" figure is messianic. Jewish interpreters have looked for a future personality yet to come, while Christians naturally identified Jesus of Nazareth as that person. The favorite title of Jesus for himself throughout the Gospels was "the son of man," which he clearly associated with Dan 7:13 (Matt 13:26; 24:30; 26:64; Mark 14:61-62). The early Christian community picked up on this and advanced the same connection (Rev 1:13; 14:14; see *From the Text* below for more discussion).

3. Interpretation of the Images (7:15-27)

Like the dreams of chs 2 and 4, interpretation follows description of the images. This time, however, Daniel does not provide the interpretation. He is the recipient of the vision and must rely on another person to interpret for him. Suspense is built by presenting Daniel's reaction first (vv 15-16), then a summary interpretation (vv 17-18) before the detailed explanation (vv 19-27). The vision concludes with a note on Daniel's final response (v 28).

The interpretation essentially follows the sequence of scenes in the dream reported in vv 2-14. Only v 18 jumps ahead to summarize the meaning of the last scene. Otherwise explanation of the four beasts is given (v 17), then the fourth beast (vv 19-25) and finally the throne scene (vv 26-27).

■ 15 Daniel's initial response to what he saw is similar to that of others who received visions (Gen 41:8; Dan 2:1; 4:1) and that he himself experienced on another occasion (4:19). It is not as intense as what Belshazzar felt (5:6, 9), however, or even what he would experience in later dreams (8:27; 10:8-17). A sense of apprehension along with some positive anticipation is expressed by the phrases **troubled in spirit** and **disturbed** (v 15).

■ 16 He who knew the meaning of such things in previous chapters must now rely upon another to interpret. So Daniel asked **one of those standing there** for help (v 16). This person is apparently a heavenly being, perhaps the archangel Gabriel based upon the notation in 9:21, which identifies him as "the man I had seen in the earlier vision." Zechariah also experienced the assistance of angels during his visions (Zech 1—6). It is a common feature of non-canonical apocalypses, which tends to add authority to the interpretation of the vision by asserting that it was also of divine origin.

■ 17 The angel gives a brief summary interpretation of the vision's two key scenes: the beasts emerging from the sea and the court sitting in judgment. According to the heavenly interpreter **the four great beasts are four kingdoms that will rise from the earth** (v 17). The term **kingdoms** (*malkin*) can also be translated "kingships" or "kings." It is a feminine noun expressing the idea of royalty or reign. Since a kingdom is embodied in its king and vice versa either meaning is possible in the context.

The identification of these kings or kingdoms with specific historical entities has been a matter of scholarly debate. By reference to the characteristics described of each animal in the vision, several schemes have been proposed.

Comparisons with the statue of ch 2 and the beasts of ch 8 also add to each argument. The point of the vision, however, may not be to identify precise kingdoms or kings. The description of each beast is general enough to allow several applications. The features of the four-headed leopard, for example, might fit with the Persian Empire, the Greek Empire, or the Babylonian king Neriglissar. The nature of vision material suggests caution in this regard. The goal of such material is to paint a picture, not to sketch details. Vision images are symbols of general realities, not necessarily specifics. Interpreters must be careful not to overanalyze symbolism in such material.

The number **four** is best taken symbolically rather than as a designation for a particular quantity. It is clearly significant in this vision. There are four winds, four beasts, four wings, and four heads. The vision of the bear includes the numbers three and one, which add up to four. The fourth beast has three horns and then a little horn. As was noted in ch 2, the number four traditionally symbolizes universality or completeness (Exod 25—39; Prov 30; Amos 1—2). A list of four things denotes comprehensiveness. The subject has been covered in its entirety when four are mentioned.

The scheme of **four great beasts,** then, most likely intends to present an image of the entire scope of human history. **Four kingdoms** symbolize all the kingdoms of this world in their totality. The final fourth beast represents the last political power in history from the perspective of the audience. That is to say, the last kingdom is the realm under which the current audience lives, whenever that may be. The first beast logically represents the realm of the Babylonian kingdom or Nebuchadnezzar. This is the time in which the vision claims to have originated. The second and third kingdoms, to which the text gives little attention, could stand for any significant political entity between the first and last kingdoms. Their oppressive beastly qualities could fit any number of kingdoms throughout human history. Thus for Daniel the beasts might represent the four kings Nebuchadnezzar, Amel-Marduk, Neriglissar, and Nabonidus. The little horn that grows from the fourth beast would be Belshazzar, the contemporary despot for the vision. The imprecise nature of the vision's images, however, does not restrict the historical referents only to Daniel's time. Later audiences are invited to understand the fourth kingdom as the contemporary power at work in their day. This kingdom is different from all the rest because it is present. Its terror is greater because the audience feels it firsthand.

Historical Referents for the Four Kingdoms

Many commentators attempt to associate each beast with a specific world power or person. As in ch 2, two primary views dominate the discussion. Scholars suggest the kingdoms are either (1) Babylon, Media, Persia, and Greece or (2)

Babylon, Persia, Greece, and Rome. Those who hold to a second-century B.C. date of composition typically follow the first position while those who argue for a sixth-century B.C. date of composition more readily assert the second. A modification of the latter view is to understand Rome in terms of a modern confederacy of European states (Miller 1994, 196-203). Another less prominent theory is that the four beasts represent four individual kings. These kings might be the Babylonians Nebuchadnezzar, Amel-Marduk, Neriglissar, and Nabonidus.

Numerous specific points may be made for each of the four empire views (see Lucas 2002, 187-91, for Babylon to Greece view; see Archer 1985, 85-87, for Babylon to Rome view). All positions essentially agree on the identification of the first beast as either Babylon or Nebuchadnezzar. This understanding is based upon links with chs 2 and 4 and the fact that the vision logically might begin with the contemporary kingdom.

The bear can be viewed as representing either the Median or Persian empires. The connection of the bear with the Median Empire rests upon the assumption that the author of Daniel believed the Medes ruled the Middle East between the Babylonians and the Persians. Following this line of argument, the three ribs are thought to signify either three kings or nations the Medes subdued. Perhaps the three are Ararat, Minni, and Ashkenaz, based on Jer 51:27-29. If the bear is taken to represent the Persian Empire, though, the three ribs can be connected to kings or nations overrun by them. One common suggestion is to identify them with the three great conquests of the Persians, which were Babylon, Lydia, and Egypt. The description of the bear with one side raised up also fits with the Persian Empire. According to some, this feature could represent the two-part character of the empire, Medes and Persians, of which the Persians were the more dominant.

The speed and agility indicated by the winged leopard can describe either Persia or Greece. Both boasted highly efficient military operations. The remarkable sweeping conquest of the Middle East by Alexander the Great is the most compelling comparison, however. The reference to "four heads" in this case fits well with the fourfold division of the Greek Empire at Alexander's death. On the other hand, if the leopard is taken to represent Persia, then the "four heads" might apply to the rule of four Persian kings implied by Dan 11:2, though Persia certainly had many more kings than this.

The fourth beast has been identified as either Greece or Rome. For those who view the book as a second-century B.C. composition, the fourth beast represents the contemporary oppressive political power of the Seleucids. This empire sprang from the Greek Empire and was ruled by a series of kings from Seleucus I to Seleucus IV that might represent the "ten horns" of v 7. Actually there were only seven kings in this time frame, but three contenders for the throne following the death of Seleucus IV would bring the number to ten. These contenders could be considered "three of the first horns" uprooted by "the little horn" (v 8). The "little horn" who succeeded to the throne then was Antiochus IV Epiphanes, a person who certainly spoke "boastfully" (v 8) and intentionally oppressed "the saints" (v 25; see *Behind the Text* on 11:2—12:4).

The association of the fourth beast with Rome is based upon the sequence of empires in world history. If the third beast is Greece, then Rome was the next world empire. Its dominating hold over the Mediterranean world could appropriately be described with "iron teeth" that "crushed and devoured its victims" (v 7). The coming of "one like the son of man" during the Roman era naturally fits with the birth of Jesus Christ in the days of Augustus Caesar. No identifications for the ten horns, three horns, or the little horn has received wide acceptance, though. Because of this, some scholars suggest that the fourth beast also speaks of the final kingdom of the earth. They project a federation of ten European states from which an antichrist figure will emerge before Christ comes to establish the kingdom of God on earth.

The theory that the four beasts represent four Babylonian kings moves the vision's primary reference into the time frame of Daniel. Nebuchadnezzar can be as easily associated with the first beast as the Babylonian Empire at large. How Amel-Marduk and Neriglissar might reflect the second and third beast is uncertain since little is known of them. The disruptive fourth beast could represent Nabonidus because of the way he took over the kingdom and ruled it so carelessly. In this scheme the little horn would be Belshazzar who, according to ch 5, rose up to speak "boastfully" (v 8) and set himself "against the Most High" (v 24).

■ 18 A key message of the vision is that **the saints of the Most High will receive the kingdom and will possess it forever** (v 18). This point is made three times in the interpretation with increasing clarity (see vv 22 and 27). **The saints of the Most High** could refer to either heavenly beings or the people of God. Most likely it is the latter, referring to those on earth who identify with a holy God by their commitment to holy living. The term **saints** (*qaddîšîn*) is an adjective that translates literally as *holy ones.* It derives from the term *qaddîš* (Hebrew *qāddaš*), which means to set something apart for divine purposes. The adjective form typically refers to heavenly beings in other chapters of Daniel (4:13, 17, 23; 8:13). Yet the saints in 7:22 and 25 are clearly people of earth because the ruler of the fourth kingdom attacks and oppresses them.

Saints

The Hebrew equivalent to saints (*qāddôšîm*) often denotes heavenly beings like the Aramaic term, but not always (see Ps 34:9). Frequently God challenges people to be "holy ones" just as he is a holy one (Lev 11:44; 19:2; 20:8, 26). Noncanonical Jewish literature uses the term to refer to both heavenly beings and human beings (for heavenly beings see Sir 42:17 and Wis 10:10; for human beings see *1 En.* 100:5 and Wis 18:9). (See further discussion in Collins 1993, 313-17.)

The saints are said to **receive the kingdom** and **possess** it (v 18). The term **kingdom,** as noted previously, refers to the idea of reign or royalty. In this context it undoubtedly refers to God's kingdom described in v 14. The emphasis there, as here, is upon its stability. It will last **forever—yes, for ever and ever.** The threefold repetition of **forever** (ʿālam) underscores its permanence. This is not only a future reality but also a present one. The kingdom of God in this world continues despite the rising and falling of human kingdoms. To say that the saints will **receive** and **possess** the kingdom is a way of indicating significant participation in that realm. What that means precisely is not articulated. This idea resonates with the rest of the prophets who assert that God's people will rule over their former oppressors (Isa 14:1-4; 49:22-23; 60:10-12).

The relationship of **the saints** to the "one like a son of man" in v 13 is an important question. Since both are said to receive the kingdom, some scholars have suggested that they must be the same. Perhaps the "son of man" figure is the embodiment of Israel or God's people as a whole. The worship of the "son of man" figure in v 14, however, argues against this. Within biblical tradition only God is to be worshipped (Exod 20:3), not human beings or even heavenly beings. Therefore the "son of man" figure must be distinguished from the saints in this verse and later (vv 22, 25, 27). This implies that the "son of man" figure heads up this kingdom and the saints participate in the rule of it. New Testament writers project just such a scenario with regard to Jesus and his followers (Matt 24:30-31; 1 Thess 4:16-17; Rev 20:4-6).

■ **19-20** The summary interpretation is not enough for Daniel, nor for the reader. The brief interpretation only whets the appetite to understand more of the vision. Daniel wants to know details, in particular, **the true meaning of the fourth beast** (v 19). This beast received special attention in the report of the vision (see vv 7-8). The interpretation now confirms its significance by focusing upon it as well. The narrative builds suspense further at this point by rehearsing the description of this beast given in vv 7-8 along with some omissions and additions. The new elements include reference to **bronze claws** and the fact that the little horn is **more imposing than the others** (vv 19-20). Both features increase the sense of terror associated with this beast.

■ **21-22** The most important addition to the description of the fourth beast is that **this horn was waging war against the saints and defeating them** (v 21). The significance of this point is signaled by the introduction **I watched,** the same formula that occurred at seminal junctures in the report of the images (vv 2, 6, 7, 9, 11, 13). This new information describes **the saints,** God's people on earth (see discussion above), engaged in battle with the horn that came from the fourth beast (v 22). Worse yet, they are losing. This detail exposes the particular evil in which the beast is involved. He is opposed to God's people. Verse 25 will articulate further aspects of the horror.

The people of God may become involved in a dramatic struggle with the ferocious fourth beast, but they emerge as victors. The text describes **the Ancient of Days** intervening and pronouncing **judgment in favor of the saints of** the Most High (v 22). The ruling of the divine judge regarding the struggle between the beast and God's people shows preference for the people. They come to possess **the kingdom** that holds authority over the beasts of this world. All this occurred when **the time came** for it to happen. The inference is that the timing of things is out of the hands of the saints. They cannot determine it. The information at this point provides additional context for understanding some of the drama behind the throne scene in vv 9-14. The fourth beast is not sentenced to death only because he is boastful. He is singled out for the severest punishment among the beasts because he attacks the people of God. Also the information indicates that the saints will join the "one like a son of man," presumably under his leadership, in ruling God's kingdom. The explanations coming in the next verses will make these things clearer.

In response to Daniel's request, the heavenly being finally provides a more detailed interpretation. He elaborates on the fourth beast (v 23), the ten horns (v 24a), the little horn (vv 24b-25), and the court scene (vv 26-27). In order to signify the importance of the interpretation, the text once again reverts to poetic verse throughout vv 23-27 (see *BHS* and NRSV).

■ **23** The heavenly interpreter clarifies what was previously said in v 17: **the fourth beast is a fourth kingdom that will appear on earth** (v 23). It is **different from all the other kingdoms** in the extent of its domination and terrorizing. **The whole earth** will feel the effects of this kingdom. The three beast-like actions mentioned in the vision report are reiterated (see v 7). Like a ravenous animal this kingdom will exploit the world by consuming its resources and **trampling** them underfoot.

■ **24** **The ten horns** are explained as **ten kings** who rule over the fourth kingdom (v 24). While these kings might refer to specific historical figures, their number is likely symbolic. The number **ten** signifies a full amount. Thus this kingdom will endure for what might seem to be a full cycle for earthly kingdoms. At this moment, though, when people might hope that this kingdom is coming to an end, **another king will arise.** This is the "little one" of v 8. His prowess is indicated by his ability to **subdue three kings** in order to secure the throne. Again the number could refer to three particular kings, but it is more likely symbolic of extra strength. **Three** things create a strong bond (Eccl 4:12). Yet the final king is able to overcome such. This may be why he is described as "more imposing than the others" in v 20.

■ **25** The terror of this final king is made plain in a list of his evil deeds. Blasphemy and religious persecution are his trademarks. He is in direct opposition to the things of God. This king will (1) **speak against the Most High,** (2) **oppress his saints,** and (3) **try to change the set times and the laws** of the faith (v 25). Like Belshazzar in ch 5 this king arrogantly sets himself "up against the Lord of heaven" (5:23). He is also like Belshazzar in the way he trivializes the sacred. Belshazzar handled the consecrated goblets of the temple with contempt (5:2-4). Similarly the king of Dan 7 treats the holy ones of God and his sacred institutions with disregard. The word **oppress** (*bāla'*) literally means "to wear out," indicating the king's attacks upon the faithful will be relentless. **The set times and the laws** likely refers to prescribed worship practices outlined in the laws of Moses. These include such things as Sabbath observance, sacrifice rituals, and annual festivals. While this sort of thing has happened at various times throughout history, 1 Macc 1:41-50 records a particular time when Antiochus IV (175-164 B.C.) issued a decree restricting Jewish worship practices (see also Dan 8:11-13; 9:27; 11:31; 12:12).

The continual assault of the king will result in God's people being **handed over to him** (v 25). Just as Jerusalem fell to Nebuchadnezzar (1:2) so they will come under the control of this king. The expression literally reads ***given into his hands,*** which implies divine action. The people of God are not overpowered by the evil king but are permitted to fall into his hands. Like Shadrach, Meshach, Abednego, and Daniel in chs 3 and 6, God's people are not delivered from their ordeal but rather in it.

This time of affliction will not go on forever. An ending has been predetermined. It will last **for a time, times and half a time** (v 25). Many commentators suggest that this phrase refers to three and a half years, even though the term **time** (*yiddān*) does not necessarily mean "year" but rather "a period of time." Also **times** (*yiddānîn*) is not dual but simply plural. Based upon other references in Daniel and the NT, however, this seems to be the best understanding. Daniel 12:7 connects the phrase to 1,290 days and 1,335 days, which approximate but do not match three and a half years. The NT links it with 1,260 days, which is three and a half years on a 360-day lunisolar calendar (compare Rev 12:6 with 12:14). Revelation 11:2 also refers to forty-two months for the trampling of Jerusalem.

This does not mean the phrase must be taken as a literal calculation. Three and a half is half of seven, the perfect number. The phrase thus symbolizes the imperfect duration of the final evil king. It also suggests that his reign comes to an abrupt halt. The faithful will endure a seemingly unending oppression **for a time** and **times,** but then it will suddenly cease as it is cut in **half.** Therefore the phrase is a symbolic expression for an unspecified amount of time that quickly ends. The point is that the saints will not suffer endlessly. God has marked a time for its conclusion.

■ **26** At the appointed time the divine **court will sit** in judgment of the evil king (v 26). God executes the sentence by deposing the king and bringing his reign of terror to an end. His authority is **taken away** and **completely destroyed.** The utter elimination of the king's realm is emphasized in the Aramaic, which literally reads, ***annihilated and destroyed to the end.*** Verse 11 carried the same emphasis when it pictured "his body destroyed and thrown into the blazing fire."

■ **27** By contrast, all the imposing power wielded by the evil king and more is transferred to the people of God. They inherit **the sovereignty, power and greatness of the kingdoms under the whole heaven** (v 27). This expression, which uses three words with similar meanings, accentuates absolute sovereign control. The authority of God's kingdom encompasses all the power of all the realms of the four beasts portrayed in the vision. These beasts represent all **the kingdoms under the whole heaven.** Thus the new kingdom is greater than anything ever known within human history.

Those who receive the new kingdom are **the saints, the people of the Most High** (v 27). Literally this phrase translates, "the people of the saints of the Most High" (so RSV, ESV, and others). The meaning of the phrase depends on whether one takes **the saints** as possessive or explicative. Accordingly it can also be translated either "the people who belong to the saints of the Most High" or as the NIV has it. In light of references to the saints in vv 18, 22, and 25, the rendering of the NIV seems most appropriate. The text is explaining that **the saints** are **the people of the Most High.**

The kingdom that **the saints** receive can be described as **his kingdom,** meaning God's kingdom (v 27). The text could be translated "their kingdom," however, referring to the people (so NRSV). The antecedent for the pronominal suffix on **his kingdom** could be either the masculine singular noun **people** or the masculine plural noun **Most High.** The latter is more likely since the verse goes on to speak of worship and obedience given to **him.** Ultimately God holds authority over this kingdom and is the only one appropriately worshipped. Therefore it is properly referred to as **his kingdom,** not their kingdom.

The new kingdom is characterized by permanence and universal worship. It will be **an everlasting kingdom,** a point well emphasized before in vv 14 and 18. **All rulers** who serve in this kingdom bow before the central authority. They **will worship and obey** the true leader of this kingdom. The scene is reminiscent of numerous biblical visions of the final kingdom of God. It is a time when "all kings will bow down to him and all nations will serve him" (Ps 72:11).

4. Conclusion (7:28)

The chapter concludes with another note about Daniel's response to the vision. This echoes back to v 15, which began the interpretation section of the vision. So also the phrase **the end of the matter** (*sôpā' dî millĕtā'*) balances ***the beginning of the matter*** (*rē'š millîn*) in v 1 and creates an inclusion for the entire vision (v 28).

Daniel remains **troubled** as he was before in v 15. This time his countenance is affected, however, and his **face turned pale.** Like Belshazzar (5:6, 9), Daniel's "splendor changed," which denotes intense anxiety.

The emphasis on Daniel's response highlights the significance of this vision. Such strong emotion surely indicates something worthy of consideration. It invites readers to take the time to ponder the vision's meaning.

FROM THE TEXT

The dramatic images of the vision of ch 7 portray theology that is central not only to the book of Daniel but also to the entire Bible. The chaos perpetrated by ungodly governance is powerfully portrayed in all of its horror. Yet divine subjection of this human upheaval is equally envisioned. God will bring judgment upon earth's evil institutions and individuals. While God's authority over this world is assured, its final manifestation awaits a time appointed by heaven itself.

The rule of human beings apart from God creates chaos. The vision in ch 7 captures the essence of secular human kingdoms in a poignant portrait. It is an insightful political observation sketched with powerful images that emphasize the cosmic dimensions of earthly governments. **Winds** from every direction churn up deep oceans that spit out grotesque **beasts** (vv 2-3). These horrifying animals represent human kingdoms that terrify and devour the world into which they come. Their attempts at creating order through domination only yield more chaos. They move swiftly, stealthily, and determinedly, each more fearful than the other. The final beast embodies all the worst of its predecessors and produces the most brazen ruler of all. Wielding unparalleled power, he arrogantly blasphemes heaven. He emerges from obscurity, overthrows the strength of three, speaks **against the Most High,** and trivializes the sacred (v 25).

The scene forms a striking impression of life in utter confusion. Contrast with the well-designed, peace-filled paradise of Gen 1—2 is marked. Also missing are the ideals of the luxuriant cosmic tree in Nebuchadnezzar's dream of Dan 4. Images of care and protection for God's creation, birds nesting in fruitful branches and animals gathering for shelter (4:12), are foreign to the vision of ch 7. In their place are descriptions of exploitive predators crushing, devouring, and trampling their prey. They abuse rather than preserve the bounty and beauty of God's creation.

Such disorder disrupts, oppresses, and terrorizes those living under the realm of these kingdoms. Especially vulnerable are persons who try to live connected with God. **The saints,** as the text calls them (vv 18, 21, 22, 27), are worn out from the assaults of secular despots. Eventually they are **handed over** to the whims of evil tyrants (v 25). Like Shadrach, Meshach, Abednego, and Daniel (chs 3 and 6), they experience the full force of the insanity of human decrees before they are delivered.

Chaos is one of the most consistent manifestations of evil. All that opposes or ignores God moves toward confusion, disorder, and meaninglessness (Gen 11:7; Isa 24:1-13; Lam 1:1-6; Eccl 1:14). It reverses the order of creation. As Gen 1 makes plain, God's creative actions produce a well-arranged, purposeful world. That which was formless and void takes on meaningful design in the hands of the biblical Creator. "God is not a God of disorder but of peace" (1 Cor 14:33).

Within the earthly sphere human kingdoms often become the prime perpetrators of chaos in this world. While they are not the only source of disorder, they are a major expression of its presence in God's creation. They miss the truth that order has divine origins and attempt to control by human law. They do not understand that there is one who "judges the earth" (Ps 58:11) and in whom "all things hold together" (Col 1:17). The story of Daniel's lion pit ordeal highlighted the illusion of human law. The chaotic affects of earthly approaches to peace are as far ranging as a nation's dominion. People, especially God's people, suffer under such regimes. As this text shows, evil states affect more than the lives of its individual subjects. They disrupt the creative purposes of God. Their evil actions carry cosmic implications. Decisions by governments are more than political, social, economic, or even moral issues. They are spiritual ones.

The vision affirms that ungodly rulers design ungodly states. Evil is not only corporate but also personal. The text comes to focus upon one individual leader, **a little one** (Dan 7:8). This person is responsible for speaking blasphemy, oppressing God's people, and altering sacred traditions (v 25). While the evil state may have created such a person, his wickedness embodies the character of that kingdom. The nature of the horrific beast is ultimately located within the hearts of individuals.

Throughout history Christian interpreters have connected the little horn of ch 7 with an end-time figure known as "the antichrist." New Testament writers employed the images and motifs of ch 7 when describing rebellious figures such as "false Christs" (Mark 13:22), "the man of lawlessness" (2 Thess 2:3-9), "the antichrist" (1 John 2:18, 22; 4:3; 2 John 7), and "the beast" (Rev 13:1-10). These persons manifest both a present and a future reality. They will appear within and at the end of human history, according to the early Christians. Like the little horn of Dan 7, they stand for everything opposed to God and lead a rebellion against heaven. Yet in the end they are subdued by Christ and brought to judgment (Rev 19:20-21).

God judges evil states and brings new order out of chaos. The turbulence of raging nations ceases before God's court. The beasts of chaos are **slain** and **stripped of their authority** before the heavenly throne (Dan 7:11-12). **Authority, glory and sovereign power** are placed within the hands of an anointed one and his people and a new kingdom is established (v 14). This kingdom will be one of perfect order because **all rulers** will fulfill their God-ordained roles and give reverence to God (v 27). The original purposes for creation will finally be accomplished. With God at its center, this kingdom will be secure and stable. It will last forever. It **will not pass away** or **be destroyed** (v 14).

The image of God judging nations in order to restore creation is fundamental to the biblical worldview. Prophets and psalmists agree on this point. One day God will come to "judge the world in righteousness and the peoples in his truth" (Ps 96:13). The result of divine judgment will be a world of God's choosing. Biblical writers envision "new heavens and a new earth" where "the sound of weeping and of crying will be heard in it no more" (Isa 65:17, 19), "mountains will drip new wine" (Joel 3:18), "the LORD will be king over the whole earth" (Zech 14:9), "peoples will stream" to the mountain of God to worship (Mic 4:1), and "God himself will be with them and be their God" (Rev 21:3). It will be a world filled with abounding joy (Isa 24:14). Therefore creation looks forward to God's judgment with great anticipation. "Let the rivers clap their hands, let the mountains sing together for joy; let them sing before the LORD, for he comes to judge the earth" (Ps 98:8-9).

Psalm 2 affirms the same picture found in Dan 7 with a more earthy description. That poem envisions earthly rulers rising up and plotting against God and his purposes like the beasts emerging from the sea. But "the One enthroned in heaven laughs; the Lord scoffs at them. Then he rebukes them in his anger and terrifies them in his wrath, saying, 'I have installed my King on Zion, my holy hill'" (Ps 2:4-6). The kingdom of the Lord's anointed will transform the chaos perpetrated by nations just as the kingdom of the "one like a son of man" will. Isaiah also reflects this thought when he writes, "He will judge between the nations and will settle disputes for many peoples. They will beat their swords into plowshares and their spears into pruning hooks" (Isa 2:4).

The text makes clear that the new order is a divine act. The role of God's people is not emphasized. They simply receive the kingdom and give honor to God. Neither faithful living nor persistent resistance is explicitly admonished. The vision even remains silent about the actions of the "son of man" figure. These features tend to underscore the divine origins of the kingdom and its authority. God takes the initiative over the forces of chaos in this vision as he does throughout Scripture. Genesis 1:1-2 first confirms it and Job 40—41 agrees. Turbulent storms and sea monsters do not intimidate or thwart God's purposes. He "rides on the wings of the wind" (Ps 104:3), cosmic waters obey his commands (v 7), and all creatures of the sea, even Leviathan, come under his control (vv 25-26).

The full manifestation of God's authority in this world awaits the end of human history. The events portrayed in Dan 7 are both historical and eschatological. Like Israel's other prophets, Daniel sees God's kingdom entering this world within the frame of human history as well as at the end of it. That kingdom is never absent, for it **will never be destroyed** (v 14). It is forever.

The court scene of ch 7 portrays God's judgment of all human kingdoms. Together earthly realms are sentenced, some to death and some to diminished authority. This corporate verdict implies both ongoing and final judgment. Treatment of the three beasts indicates judgment within history. These kingdoms are **stripped of their authority** and **allowed to live for a period of time** (v 12). The execution of the fourth beast, the symbol of earth's last kingdom, conveys final judgment. The dominion of human kingdoms ceases when the beast is **slain** and **its body destroyed** (v 11).

The authority of these beasts, according to the vision and its interpretation, is handed over to **one like a son of man** and **the saints** (vv 13-14 and 18, 22, 27). The new kingdom over which they reside is eschatological. Verse 22 references **the time** when God's people **possessed the kingdom.** That moment is concurrent with events that can only take place at the end of human history. It is when the "son of man" figure comes **with the clouds of heaven** and is **given authority** (vv 13-14). Then, **all peoples, nations and men of every language,** including **all rulers,** will fall down in worship before God (vv 14 and 27).

The scene portrayed in ch 7 provided NT writers with images to describe the work of Christ within this world and at the end of human history. These writers allude to the patterns, motifs, and images in this chapter more often than any others in the book. According to the Gospels, Jesus' favorite way of referring to himself was as "the Son of Man." While this designation could convey only the fact that Jesus was human, the contexts in which he uses it suggest more. Scholars are divided on the issue, but it seems likely that Jesus was identifying himself with the "son of man" figure in v 13. His use of the definite article could communicate "that particular son of man," meaning the one mentioned in Daniel.

When Jesus describes his second coming he envisioned "the Son of Man coming on the clouds of the sky" (Matt 24:30; Mark 13:26). Before the high priest at his trial he proclaims, "In the future you will see the Son of Man sitting at the right hand of the Mighty One and coming on the clouds of heaven" (Matt 26:64; Mark 14:62). Following his resurrection Jesus states, "All authority in heaven and on earth has been given to me" (Matt 28:18). Thus Jesus claims that God "has given him authority to judge because he is the Son of Man" that Dan 7 speaks about (John 5:27).

These images of Christ and the culmination of human history lie behind the descriptions of final victory in the writings of Paul (1 Thess 4:16-17; 2 Thess 2:1-12; 1 Cor 15:50-57). The picture of the way God will judge world powers, however, is most vividly expressed in the book of Revelation. A beast with horns rises from the sea and terrorizes the world in Rev 13. This creature speaks "proud words and blasphemies" like the little horn in Dan 7 (Rev 13:5). It makes "war against the saints" and extends its authority throughout the earth (Rev 13:7). Eventually the beast is slain in the final judgment. It is thrown into "the fiery lake of burning sulfur" (Rev 19:20). Its judge and conqueror is Jesus Christ, who finally reigns absolute over this world along with those who have remained faithful to him (Rev 20:1-6).

The vision of Dan 7 then, according to the NT, found realization in the person of Jesus Christ. It still awaits its final fulfillment in his second coming.

B. Vision of Two Beasts (8:1-27)

Overview

Chapter 8 begins the final major movement within the book of Daniel. It relays the first of three closely related visions recorded in chs 8—12. These three visions focus upon a period of intense persecutions for God's people that occur after the lifetime of Daniel. With increasing detail they concentrate upon a particular era of oppression by ungodly forces like that briefly sketched in ch 7. These visions offer concrete examples of the terror human tyrants perpetuate in this world, but more importantly how such kingdoms still remain under the sovereignty of God.

BEHIND THE TEXT

A change in language signals the shift that is taking place within the book. Beginning with 8:1 the text returns to Hebrew after an extended use of Aramaic that began in 2:4. Many commentators have observed that the alternation of languages corresponds to wider or narrower interests of the material. The Aramaic section of chs 2—7 has greater international appeal, while the Hebrew portions of chs 1 and 8—12 relate more directly to Jewish concerns.

The shift in language also alerts the reader to significant differences between chs 7 and 8. Though these two chapters share common features, they diverge from one another at several points. Both chapters indicate that Daniel experienced visions during the reign of Belshazzar, ch 7 in his first year and ch 8 in his third year. Each vision contains animals that represent human kingdoms and references to horns that symbolize rulers. The animals of ch 8, however, are less bizarre than those in ch 7 and are specifically identified in the text with known kingdoms of world history. Both visions speak of a small horn that denotes an oppressive ruler who threatens God's people. The small horn emerges from ten horns in ch 7 but comes forth from one of four horns in ch 8. Chapter 8 provides much more detail about the specific activities of the small horn than ch 7. The divine judgment of earthly kingdoms so prominent in ch 7 is only briefly alluded to in ch 8. Finally, the formal structure of these visions is quite similar. Elements of setting, vision report, vision interpretation, and recipient response are included in both. Overall, though, the style of ch 7 is more poetic than ch 8. The ponderous chains of synonymous terms as well as rhythmic verses found in ch 7 are gone from ch 8 (see further in Goldingay 1989, 201).

Scholars differ on how to assess the relationship between the two chapters. Clearly ch 8 stands as a further clarification of ch 7. But the question is, in what way is this true? Various responses to this question relate to how ch 7 has been interpreted. Since ch 8 clearly identifies the two kingdoms symbolized by animals as **kings of Media and Persia** and **of Greece** (vv 20-21), the issue is which kingdoms in ch 7 represent these two kingdoms. Some scholars identify them as the third and fourth kingdoms of that vision while others view them as the second and third kingdoms (see *In the Text* of ch 7 for various views). One's position on this issue also affects how the small horn is understood. Since the small horn is related to the fourth kingdom in ch 7, those who understand the third and fourth kingdoms of ch 7 to symbolize Persia and Greece identify the small horn of both visions as one and the same personality, usually the Seleucid ruler Antiochus IV (Goldingay 1989, 174). Other interpreters, who understand the second and third kingdoms of ch 7 to be Persia and Greece, view the small horn as representing a different personality in each vision. Typically the small horn is seen as an antichrist at the end of the age in ch 7 and as Antiochus IV in ch 8 (Miller 1994, 225).

As this commentary has pointed out, specific identification of kingdoms in ch 7 may not be the best approach to interpreting that chapter (see *In the Text* on ch 7). The portrait of human history sketched in ch 7 might be better understood as an overview of all human history from Babylon to the end of time. The first kingdom seems to reference the Babylonian kingdom contemporary with the vision and the fourth kingdom the final kingdom of human history. The middle two kingdoms, however, do not necessarily intend to reference particular historical entities but rather stand as representatives of the kinds of kingdoms this world will experience. From this perspective the kingdoms of ch 8 can be understood as specific examples of the kinds of intermediate kingdoms sketched in ch 7. Of the many kingdoms that will rise and fall on the stage of world history, ch 8 focuses upon two particular powers, Persia and Greece.

Connections to chs 9—12 are also important. These chapters, along with ch 8, focus upon a particular era of upheaval in Jewish history. The three visions contained in these chapters each climax with a critical event when the sacrifice in the temple ceases and "the abomination that causes desolation" happens (8:10-13; 9:27; 11:31; 12:11). In each case a time limit regarding the duration of this crisis is announced (8:14; 9:24-27; 11:33-35; 12:11-12). The means by which each vision reaches these points is different, and the details vary. But the common climactic element binds the three final visions of the book into a unit that must be read as a whole.

The chiasmic structure of chs 8—12 also unites these visions. The focus on two kingdoms in ch 8 is echoed in a more detailed portrait of the same two kingdoms in chs 10—12. Both visions include dramatic encounters with angels that affirm the involvement of the heavenly realm in earthly struggles. Each vision highlights a particularly ruthless oppressor of the second kingdom. The central vision of ch 9 clarifies that the extended period of upheaval reviewed in the other two visions results not only from evil nations but also from Israel's sin.

Events related to the Persian and Greek kingdoms from the sixth to second centuries B.C. form the historical background for various allusions in these final three visions. The Persian Empire emerged around 550 B.C. to become one of the most dominating and expansive empires the ancient Middle East has ever known. It was also known as the Achaemenid Empire, named for Achaemenes, an ancestor of its founder, Cyrus. It stretched from the Greek states in the west to the Indus Valley in the east and from Egypt in the south to the Caspian Sea in the north. The empire's architect was Cyrus the Great, the son of a Persian king and a Median princess. Part of his genius rested in his ability to unite the resources of both Medes and Persians to establish his kingdom. The latter of these two was the more prominent. The empire was one of the most enduring in human history, lasting over two hundred years.

The Greeks, led by Alexander the Great, brought the Persian Empire to a swift and decisive end. They engaged the Persians first at the Granicus River in northwest Asia Minor in May 334 B.C. and struck the final blow on the plains of Guagamela east of the Tigris in October 331 B.C. Alexander continued expanding the empire eastward to the Indus River until 326 B.C. He did not enjoy the fruits of his vast conquest long, however. He died in 323 B.C. at age 32 in the palace of Nebuchadnezzar in Babylon. Following his death, the empire fragmented into several major and minor political entities. By 301 B.C. four dominant kingdoms emerged. One was centered in Macedon under Cassander, a second in Thrace under Lysimachus, a third in Egypt under Ptolemy, and a fourth in Mesopotamia under Seleucus. The last of these kingdoms seems to be the primary focus of the final three visions.

The Seleucid Kingdom administered the largest portion of the Greek world. It extended from Syria to the Indus River. In 198 B.C. the land of Israel fell under its domain. Seven emperors ruled before Antiochus IV gained control by intrigue in 175 B.C. He displaced several claimants to the throne, including the rightful heir Demetrius, who was his nephew, in order to establish

194

his rule. His sense of self-importance is highlighted by the additional name he took, Epiphanes, which means "Illustrious" or "Shining One." His erratic behavior, however, earned him a less flattering name from his opponents, Epimanes, which means "mad man."

Antiochus sought to expand and support his empire by conquest. In 169 B.C. he invaded Egypt and in 166 B.C. he turned his forces against the Persians and Parthians to the east (1 Macc 3:27-37; 6:1-7). His lack of success against Egypt fueled an aggressive policy of persecution against the Jews. The temple treasury seems to have been his main interest, but other reasons are possible as well. According to 1 and 2 Maccabees, he is responsible for the deaths of thousands of Jews over a seven-year period from 171 to 164 B.C. This era begins with removal of Onias III from the office of high priest and his eventual assassination in 171 B.C. (2 Macc 2—4). In both 169 and 167 B.C. Antiochus cruelly attacked the land of Israel, massacred portions of its population, and pillaged the temple (1 Macc 1; 2 Macc 5—6). He eventually forbade Sabbath observance, circumcision, and other practices of Judaism. For over three years regular offerings to the God of Israel ceased at the temple. In December 167 B.C. this Seleucid king committed his most detestable act of sacrilege by setting up an altar to Zeus in the temple courts and sacrificing swine upon it (1 Macc 1:54-59; 2 Macc 6:2-5).

The policies of Antiochus provoked intense opposition from the Jews, sparking a revolt led by Judas Maccabeus and his brothers (see 1 Macc 2—6 and 2 Macc 5—10). This struggle brought about the liberation of Judah from Seleucid control and initiated the Hasmonean Kingdom in that land. A climactic moment occurred on the twenty-fifth day of Kislev 164 B.C. when the Jewish rebels reclaimed the temple precincts, cleansed it of pagan elements, rededicated the altar, and relit the sacred lampstand (1 Macc 4:36-58). Since that time Jews rehearse these events annually at the Feast of Lights or Hanukkah.

In Jewish literature, Antiochus IV is remembered as one of the most heinous tyrants in history, on par with Nebuchadnezzar and Haman. Just before the Jews reclaimed their temple Antiochus IV died. While on a campaign against the Parthians in Persia he succumbed to disease.

The temporal and geographical settings identified for the reception of the vision are significant for its content. **The third year of King Belshazzar's reign** was approximately 548 B.C. (v 1). Though a few years later than the time of the vision in ch 7, the affairs of Babylonia had not improved. The internal and external pressures that erupted when Belshazzar took control of the kingdom continued to increase, and the future of the empire was in question (see *Behind the Text* for ch 7). Under the leadership of Cyrus the Great, Persia was establishing itself as the dominant political force of the region.

The vision takes place in **Susa,** which was the main city **in the province**

of Elam (v 2). At the time of Belshazzar Elam was likely under the dominion of Babylonia, though it is possible the Medes may have taken control of this region. Ancient records are lacking at this point. What is clear, however, is that Elam had experienced days of influence prior to this time and would do so again. The height of Elamite power came around 1300-1100 B.C. At such time even Babylon fell under its domain. Following some years of obscurity, Susa once again gained prominence in the struggle against Assyrian oppression in the eighth century B.C. In the end, however, the Assyrians devastated the city in 640 B.C. during the reign of Ashurbanipal. When the power base in the Middle East shifted to Babylon, Nabopolassar and Nebuchadnezzar incorporated Elam into their empire.

When Babylon fell in 539 B.C., Elam was absorbed into the Persian Empire and Susa became one of the main royal residences for its kings. Darius II began building a magnificent palace there around 521 B.C. and used it as a main administrative center for the kingdom. It remained one of the most impressive bastions of Persian power throughout the era of that empire. Jewish readers remember Susa at this time as the setting for the book of Esther and the opening chapters of Nehemiah (Neh 1:1; Esth 1:2). When the Greeks gained dominance in the region, Susa continued to serve as a significant center of governance. The Seleucids renamed it Seleucia-on-the-Eulaios.

Another location designated in the vision is a body of water called **Ulai** (vv 2 and 16). This feature is difficult to identify precisely. It appears that several watercourses related to Susa were called Ulai over the years, later Eulaios by the Greeks. Some of these are at a distance from the city and others run near or in it. A few scholars have amended the phrase **Ulai Canal** in v 2 to read "Ulai gate," following the lead of the Old Greek, Syriac, and Vulgate versions (see Hartman and Di Lella 1978, 223-24). This would place the vision at a gate of the city that presumably led in the direction of the Ulai River. Most commentators, however, understand the Ulai to be some body of water in or near the city of Susa.

Chapter 8 is a report of a symbolic vision. This is a subgenre of the basic genre of vision report employed in the final six chapters of Daniel (see *Behind the Text* for ch 7). Since chs 7 and 8 include symbolic images, they are distinguished as symbolic vision reports, whereas the visions in chs 9—12 are called epiphany vision reports (see *Behind the Text* for 10:1—11:1). Essential features of the symbolic vision report form are evident in ch 8: (1) an indication of circumstances (vv 1-2), (2) a description of symbolic images (vv 2-12), (3) a request for understanding (v 13), (4) an interpretation (vv 19-26), and (5) a concluding statement (v 27). A special feature of ch 8 is the element of audition, what the visionary hears, in vv 13-14 and 16. This feature also occurs in the final verses of the final vision in 12:5-13.

The images of the vision are drawn from the ancient world. A **ram** and

goat appropriately represent powerful empires in conflict (vv 3-8). Both animals are aggressive and combative by nature. Biblical tradition often uses them as symbols of power and leadership (Prov 30:31; Isa 14:9; Jer 50:8; Ezek 34:17; 39:18; Zech 10:3). Their meat, skin, hair, and horns were prized commodities (Gen 31:38; 2 Kgs 3:4; Josh 6:4). They were also select animals for Hebrew sacrificial rites, particularly for the Day of Atonement (Exod 25:5; Lev 4:23; 16:7). Elements connected to the Day of Atonement may provide some background to vocabulary and concepts mentioned in the vision (Doukhan 2000, 125-32).

Some scholars have proposed that the association of these animals with Persia and Greece could have roots in astrology. A list of the signs of the zodiac from the first century A.D. connects the ram with Persia and the goat with Syria (a major portion of the Greek Empire). But these are late references and may not reflect the thinking of an earlier time (see Lucas 2002, 213). The same may be said for the military background associating Persia and the ram. In the fourth century A.D. a Persian king reportedly wore a ram's-head helmet in battle.

Daniel's interaction with heavenly beings is more pronounced in this chapter than previously. Chapter 10, however, will describe such an encounter with even greater detail (see *Behind the Text* for ch 10 for more discussion). This element in the text is common among extracanonical Jewish and Christian apocalypses. Yet several aspects are paralleled in canonical books as well. This feature accentuates the otherworldly nature of the vision and heightens its significance for the recipient.

Much like the previous chapter, ch 8 begins with an introduction referencing the time the vision came to Daniel (v 1) and ends with notice of Daniel's reaction to the experience (v 27). Between these two ends the images Daniel sees are reported (vv 2-14) and their interpretation given (vv 15-26). Conversations between heavenly beings occur at the end of the report (vv 13-14) and the beginning of the interpretation (vv 15-16). These dialogues serve to link the two main sections as well as focus attention upon the primary concern of the vision. That concern is the question of the duration of affliction for God's people.

IN THE TEXT

I. Introduction (8:1)

■ **I** The opening verse provides both thematic and temporal contexts for the vision. Reference to **Belshazzar's reign** recalls the story of ch 5 and its images of arrogance, sacrilege, divine judgment, and political upheaval. Such themes are replayed in the current vision. **The third year** of his reign, as noted above (see

Behind the Text), was a time of increasing unrest internationally as well as domestically. Such political instability is an important motif of the vision as well.

Mention of **Belshazzar** also highlights the close relationship between chs 7 and 8. The two visions occur only a few years apart. The phrase **after the one that had already appeared to me** refers to ch 7 as well and further emphasizes the connection. This assures that the reader will listen to the vision of ch 8 in light of the one in ch 7. The meaning of the former bears upon the interpretation of the latter. The vision of ch 8 illustrates in greater detail the kind of ungodly kingdoms and tyrants described in ch 7.

2. Report of the Images (8:2-14)

■ **2** Daniel's report of what he sees begins in v 2. He notes the geographical setting (v 2) before describing three scenes of conflict related to a ram (vv 3-4), a goat (vv 5-8), and a horn (vv 9-12). A final scene involves two angels speaking together (vv 13-14). The cycle of each animal on the stage of history is similar. They emerge, become great, create conflict, and then fall. It is a pattern familiar to the reader from ch 7. Description of the horn follows a comparable pattern except that its demise is not noted.

The place where the vision takes place seems significant. Reference to **the citadel of Susa** and **the province of Elam** is striking for the time of Daniel (v 2). Babylon was Belshazzar's seat of power, not Susa. As the center of ancient Elamite kingdoms, Susa represents a rival power of another era. That Daniel's vision should come in such a place subtly underscores the shift in the balance of powers that the vision portrays. For Jewish audiences after Daniel's time, Susa induces images of Persian power during the lives of Esther and Nehemiah (Neh 1:1; Esth 1:2). It became a key administrative center for the Persians within a generation of Belshazzar's reign (see *Behind the Text*).

Reference to the **Ulai Canal** invites comparisons to another prophet of exile, Ezekiel. He received visions beside a body of water in a foreign land also (Ezek 1:1). In addition, Ezekiel saw himself being transported to another place within a vision (Ezek 8:3) just as Daniel does.

Several verbal features of the text heighten the sense of mystery contained in the vision. Within the first few verses Daniel belabors the terms **saw, looked up,** and **watched,** all of which derive from the same Hebrew term (*r'h*). The root occurs seven times within vv 1-4. In addition, within the first two verses Daniel employs the first person pronoun (*'ănî*) three times to emphasize his personal involvement and surprise over the vision. An element of wonder is communicated throughout the chapter. Clearly the vision amazes Daniel, and the reader should be amazed as well. The extent of his astonishment is described more fully toward the middle (v 17) and the end (v 27) of the vision.

■ **3-4** The first character to appear in the vision is **a ram** (v 3). Daniel notices its horns, its movements, and its strength. Typical of adult male sheep, this one has **two horns.** What is unusual, however, is that the horns do not grow at the same rate nor attain the same length. One horn, which lags behind the other, eventually becomes **longer than the other.**

At first the ram is **standing beside the canal** (v 3). Then Daniel observes it charging in various directions, engaging in conflict with other animals. It rushes **toward the west and the north and the south** (v 4). Some Old Greek manuscripts and one Qumran scroll add "the east" to complete the four directions of the compass. But Theodotian, the Vulgate, and Peshitta agree with the MT at this point. Reference to only three directions is most likely original and seems to indicate that the ram came out of the east.

Verse 4 emphasizes the dominating strength of the ram. Like ancient monarchs who wielded absolute authority, the ram is one who does **as he pleased** (v 4). No victim can withstand its aggression or find anyone who can **rescue from his power.** Some form of the term **stand against** (ʿāmad lipnê) is employed repeatedly throughout the vision report to indicate conflict (vv 3, 4, 7, 15). In the interpretation of the vision, the verb "stand" without the preposition continues the idea (vv 22, 23, 25). As a result of its conquests the ram became **great,** just as the others that would follow it do (vv 8 and 11).

■ **5-8** The vision of the ram sets Daniel to **thinking** deeply (bin) about what he has seen (v 5). The appearance of another animal, however, breaks his thoughts. A combative male **goat** with unusual features appears on the horizon to engage the ram. As with the ram, Daniel notes the goat's horns, its movements, and its strength.

The goat has **a prominent horn between his eyes** (v 5). Normally male goats would have two horns, like the ram, and they are not located between the eyes. So this feature is abnormal, which perhaps explains why Daniel describes it as **prominent** or conspicuous. The goat comes **from the west,** a point of origin different from the ram. It moves onto the scene rapidly and attacks the ram with intensity. **Crossing the whole earth without touching the ground** portrays an animal charging at great speed. The goat engages the ram **in great rage** and subdues it (v 6). Verse 7 depicts a scene of intense conflict and utter conquest. The goat attacks **furiously, striking . . . and shattering** (v 7). As a result, the ram is rendered helpless. It is **knocked to the ground and trampled on.** It is **powerless to stand against** the goat. Like those it had conquered (v 4), the ram found **none could rescue** it from the power of its attacker. Just as the ram had dominated, now the goat overpowers and becomes **very great** (v 8).

At this point another unusual thing is noticed about the goat's horn. The large horn breaks off and is replaced by four. The four horns grow **toward the four winds of heaven,** which is to say they point in all directions—north, south, east, and west (v 8).

■ **9** The vision continues but does not introduce another animal. Instead it focuses upon the horns of the goat. One particular horn that grows from one of the four horns is of primary interest. As with the ram and goat, its movements and strength receive special attention.

The horn of interest is described as **small** (*sĕʿîrâ*) at first, which may refer to its insignificance (v 9). The language of the text at this point is reminiscent of the previous chapter where "another horn, a little one" is also mentioned (7:8). This invites comparisons between the two horns in these chapters. There are some similarities, but also many differences (see Lucas 2002, 214). After comparing the two, scholars are divided as to whether or not the two should be identified. The differences are significant enough to assume that the two horns are not intended to represent the same person. The horn in ch 8 is best viewed as one example of the kind of horn described in ch 7.

From an obscure beginning the horn increases **in power** (v 9). Literally, it *becomes exceedingly great* (*tigdal yeter*). The ram and goat were also described as becoming great (vv 4 and 8), but the horn seems to be even greater. The adverb *exceedingly* intensifies the description and suggests that the horn's power is even more impressive than that of the ram and goat. The greatness of the horn is further emphasized in the next few verses. Some form of the Hebrew term for "great" (*gādôl*) appears two more times in vv 10 and 11 to describe the rising influence of the horn.

The horn moves first **to the south and to the east** before coming **toward the Beautiful Land.** The last location, literally *the beauty* (*haṣṣebî*), is a reference either to Judah, Jerusalem, or the temple area in particular. Biblical writers frequently refer to these places as pleasant, fair, or beautiful because of God's special presence and blessing there (for example, Ps 50:2; Jer 3:19; Lam 2:15; Ezek 20:6; Zech 7:14). In this context, the term most likely refers specifically to Jerusalem or the temple mount since the focus of the horn's activities is against worship activities in Jerusalem. Further support for this understanding is found later in Daniel where Judah is called "the Beautiful Land" or more literally, "the land of the beauty" (11:16 and 41).

■ **10-11** The horn does not attack another animal as the ram and goat did. Rather, the horn moves against **the host of the heavens** and **the Prince of the host** (vv 10-11). Though the Hebrew text of these verses is difficult, a portrait of blasphemous behavior clearly emerges. In a climactic act of ambitious pride, the horn attempts to exert authority over religious practice in Jerusalem and thus the heavenly realm. It reflects the kind of hubris found in "the morning star" of Isa 14:12-14 who seeks to raise his "throne above the stars of God" (Isa 14:13).

The term **host** (*ṣābāʾ*) fundamentally means army. Depending on context, it can refer either to stars in the sky, heavenly beings, pagan deities, or God's people. Commentators differ on which understanding fits the current passage best. Reference to **the starry host** being cast **down to the earth** suggests a meaning of either heavenly bodies or beings (v 10). The primary offense of the horn has to do with the Jerusalem temple, however, which indicates the host constitutes earthly persons. Also, the interpretation given later in v 24 speaks of "holy people" coming under attack. Perhaps, **host** intends to evoke both heavenly and earthly referents since an assault upon worship involves both realms.

The leader of those under attack is **the Prince of the host** (v 11). Such a title seems to refer to God, but commentators have offered other possibilities as well. In v 25 this person is also called "Prince of princes." As the discussion of that verse will show, no matter how one understands this title, the heavenly realm is the object of attack.

A decisive act of sacrilege occurs when the horn takes away **the daily sacrifice** (v 11). This is the burnt offering of a one-year-old lamb, accompanied by flour, oil, and wine, offered every morning and evening in the temple (Exod 29:38-42; Num 28:2-8). The cessation of sacrifice causes **the place of his sanctuary** to be **brought low** (v 11). That is to say, without the regular sacrifices the temple no longer functions according to its intended purpose as a place where Israel's God is appropriately honored.

■ **12** Such aggressive behavior by the horn might be called **rebellion** (*pešaʿ*), that is, an act of defiance against God (v 12). The same term is used in v 13 to identify the horn's oppressive activities. The Hebrew text is ambiguous at this point, though. The rebellious action could be that of the people of God rather than the horn. If this is understood, then the sins of the people are the cause of the disruption of temple activities.

Translating Verse 12

Translating the Hebrew of the first half of v 12 is particularly problematic. Literally it reads *and the host was given with* (ʿal) *the daily offering through* (bĕ) *rebellion.* The meanings of the two prepositions and of the verb (*nātan*) are difficult to determine. Various proposals have been offered to make sense of the text (see Collins 1993, 334-35).

The most common English rendering is that of the NIV and NRSV. It takes the verb *nātan* to mean "give over," the preposition ʿal to mean "in addition to," and the preposition bĕ as causal. Thus the meaning is that the host and the sacrifice fall into the hands of the horn because of the rebellion. This is supported by the phrase "the surrender of the sanctuary and of the host" in v 13.

Another alternative understanding, however, is to take "host" as referring to armies of the horn (Goldingay 1989, 197). In this case the verb *nātan* would be translated "set over." The meaning of the sentence then would be that a foreign army oversees the affairs of the temple precincts. In the days of Antiochus IV such a thing happened (see Dan 11:31 and 1 Macc 1:34). This understanding of "host," though, requires a shift from its meaning in the surrounding verses.

The horn's power seems absolute. **It prospered in everything it did** and successfully achieves what it wants in oppressing Jewish worship (v 12). Yet the passive thrust of the verb **given over** suggests something else. Though translation of this verse is difficult, the text indicates that events unfold apart from the horn's directives. Whether one understands that an army is set over something or the people of God are given over, another hand is at work. From the context of the book and of this chapter (see v 25), readers know that this hand is that of God. Thus the horn's activities are not so overpowering as they may seem. Rather, the text suggests that God allows them to happen. The divine hand is still in control even in the midst of chaotic circumstances such as the ones described in this text.

The effect of the disruption of temple worship is that **truth** is treated like a piece of animal prey. It is **thrown to the ground** to be devoured (v 12). The law of Moses, which reveals what is true about God and a proper relationship to him, ends up as a conquered combatant. Just as the goat knocks the ram "to the ground" (v 7), so the horn suppresses God's truth.

■ **13** As the report of the images draws to a conclusion, the vision shifts away from visions of animals and horns to conversations between heavenly beings. At this point Daniel does not describe what he sees but rather what he hears. This segment in the report serves a critical function in the vision. It focuses attention upon the primary issue of the chapter, the duration of suffering. It also links the vision report to the vision interpretation (vv 15-26), which begins with another conversation between heavenly beings.

Each being involved in the conversation is called a **holy one** (v 13). This term is employed previously in the book to refer to angels as well as human beings (see 7:18). In this context, the term most naturally refers to angelic beings as it does in 4:13, 17, 23, where they are also called "watchers" or "messengers" (ʿîrîn).

When the first angel speaks, it identifies the central question of the vision, **how long** (v 13). This is a typical request expressed by distressed persons in biblical laments (Pss 6:3; 79:5; 80:4) and prophetic speeches (Isa 6:11; Jer 12:4; Zech 1:12). It emerges in this text as a result of the anguish inflicted upon God's people by the horn.

The question of the angel contains a review of the horn's offense. His misdeeds include three elements: (1) taking away **the daily sacrifice,** (2) **rebellion that causes desolation,** and (3) **the surrender of the sanctuary and of the host** (v 13). These are not necessarily three separate events but rather three aspects of the same event. The phrase **the rebellion that causes desolation** (happešaʿ šōmēm) is a summative expression of the horn's activities. It is referred to later in the book as "the abomination that causes desolation" (šiqqûṣ šōmēm) in 9:27; 11:31; and 12:11 (see also Matt 24:15; Mark 13:14). The phrase conveys the shocking nature of a trespass against God and his people. **Desolation** could also be translated as *that which is appalling or horrifying.*

The phrase seems to mock the divine title "Lord of Heaven" (*ba'al šāmaîm*), which was commonly used for pagan deities. The similar sounds of "heaven" (*šāmaîm*) and "desolation" (*šōmēm*) initially evoke the play on words. Then, replacing "Lord" (*ba'al*) with "rebellion" (*peša'*) follows naturally. The title "Lord of Heaven" is equivalent to the Greek title Olympian Zeus. This is the god for whom an altar was erected in the temple of Jerusalem at the time of Antiochus IV. The presence of this altar was a major disgrace to the Jewish people at that time and provoked widespread revolt according to 1 Macc 1 and 2 Macc 6 (see *Behind the Text*).

■ **14** A second angel answers the question posed by the first. The horn will be successful for **2,300 evenings and mornings** (v 14). This answer is both revealing and concealing. While a certain amount of time is designated, a mystery remains as to its precise meaning. Commentators have suggested three possibilities: 1,150 days, 2,300 days, and 2,300 years. Since previous verses refer to the daily sacrifices that occurred each evening and morning, one could assume that 2,300 sacrifices or 1,150 days is in mind. On the other hand, one might take "evening and morning" as an expression of one day, as in Gen 1:5, and calculate 2,300 days. Finally, assuming that days may be symbolic of years, the reference could be to 2,300 years.

Regardless of how one might interpret the amount of time indicated, the number appears to be symbolic as are most numbers in the book of Daniel. Commentators have made a number of calculations related to known historical events (see the sidebar "Calculations of '2,300 Evenings and Mornings'"). But none of these is fully convincing. One point of the phrase is clear, though. The suffering and destruction brought on by the horn will cease. An end for its activities has been divinely determined, and the temple in Jerusalem **will be reconsecrated** (*niṣdaq*), literally *be set right.* The restoration of the temple contrasts with what is described in v 12 when truth is "thrown to the ground." Things will be set right when proper worship of Israel's God is reestablished with appropriate daily sacrifices. God will once again be honored as sovereign of the universe.

Calculations of "2,300 Evenings and Mornings"

Numerous calculations have been made in order to connect "2,300 evenings and mornings" in v 14 with known historical events. Three different ways of interpreting the amount of time mentioned in this verse—1,150 days, 2,300 days, and 2,300 years—suggest different possibilities.

On a 360-day lunisolar calendar 1,150 days is about three years and two months. During the time of Seleucid rule, this is roughly the amount of time regular

Jewish sacrifice ceased and an altar to Zeus stood in the temple courts of Jerusalem. The altar was set up on Kislev 15, 167 B.C. and replaced on Kislev 25, 164 B.C. (1 Macc 1:54; 4:52). The actual time was three years and ten days or about 1,090 days. In order to bring this number up to 1,150 one could assume that daily sacrifices ceased a few months before the altar was erected (Archer 1985, 103).

If v 14 refers to 2,300 days, then a time frame of approximately six years and four months must be considered. This could correspond to the six to seven years of intense persecution of the Jews by Antiochus IV (Miller 1994, 229-30). This period begins with the murder of the high priest Onias III in 171 B.C. and concludes with the cleansing of the temple in 164 B.C. Another six-year period of time that might fit begins with the erection of the pagan altar in 167 B.C. and ends with the final defeat of the Seleucids in 160 B.C.

The suggestion that years rather than days are in mind shifts the focus of the passage to the end of human history. In this scenario reference to reconsecration of the sanctuary would have to do with the second coming of Christ. Thus, one could calculate the end of human history if one knew the beginning point of the 2,300 years. Various starting points and calendars have been used to project a date for Christ's return. The most famous of these may be that of William Miller (1782-1849), who identified 1843, then 1844, as the end of human history. Since this date has passed, other ways of understanding the 2,300 years have been presented by more modern commentators (Doukhan 2000, 152-55).

The entire discussion is complicated by alternate numbers given in Dan 12:11-12. In reference to the cessation of sacrifice and "the abomination that causes desolation," these verses announce times of both 1,290 days and 1,335 days. See commentary on these verses.

3. Interpretation of the Images (8:15-26)

■ **15-16** The interpretation section begins as the report ends, with a conversation between heavenly beings (vv 15-16). An account of Daniel's reaction to the vision follows (vv 17-18), and then the interpretation proper is given (vv 19-26). The conversation and Daniel's reaction delay interpretation and thus build suspense. The pattern of the interpretation unfolds along the same lines as the report by giving explanation first of the ram, then the goat, and finally the horn. The last of these three receives the most attention.

The heavenly conversation is between a seen and an unseen being. The unseen being is known only by the sound of its voice. Daniel describes it as **a man's voice from the Ulai** (v 16). One might assume this is the voice of God, but that is unclear from the text. As with "the voice . . . from heaven" in 4:31, one cannot be certain whether God or an angel is speaking. Later in the book, however, in a comparable scene, an angel hovering over a body of water speaks to another heavenly being (12:6-7). In any case the ultimate authority behind such a voice is God.

The voice commands the being that Daniel sees to provide an interpretation of the vision. The visible being has the appearance of **a man** (v 15) and, according to the voice, is named **Gabriel** (v 16). There is a play on words here. The Hebrew word for man is *geber*, which is the basis of the name Gabriel (*gabrî᾿ēl*). The term refers to a person of distinction who possesses exceptional strength and influence, such as a warrior or political figure. While the name Gabriel could simply be translated "man of God," it more likely means something like "God is my warrior or hero." This is the first time in the Bible that an angel is named.

The Role of Angels

Only two angels are named in the Bible, and both appear for the first time in Daniel. The two are Gabriel (8:16; 9:21) and Michael (10:13, 21; 12:1).

Throughout the Bible Gabriel performs the typical role of an angel by conveying messages from God. In the book of Daniel Gabriel provides explanation for visions the prophet has seen. In the NT he announces the births of John and Jesus (Luke 1:11, 31).

Extracanonical Jewish literature imagined Gabriel to be one of the four or seven archangels. He is identified as one of those who delivers the prayers of martyrs to God (*1 En.* 9) and is placed in charge of paradise (*1 En.* 20). He sits at the left hand of God (*2 En.* 24) and executes judgment upon the wicked (*1 En.* 54).

■ **17-19** The description of Daniel's response to his experience accentuates the contrast between the heavenly and earthly realms and reminds the reader of the solemn significance of the vision. Daniel is **terrified** and falls **prostrate** (Dan 8:17), a position of profound reverence. With his **face to the ground** he goes into a **deep sleep,** perhaps a trance since he seems aware that the angel is speaking to him (v 18). He is utterly helpless and dependent before the angel but is strengthened enough to stand when **touched** by the angel. Daniel will experience similar things again in the final vision of the book (10:8-10).

8:15-19

Gabriel further confirms Daniel's frailty by addressing him as **son of man** (v 17). This time the term for man is *᾿ādām*, which connotes the earthly origins of humans. It contrasts with the description of the angel as a *geber* in v 15. As with Ezekiel (Ezek 2:1, 3, and many other times), this designation stresses the humble position of created humans standing before their omnipotent Creator.

In a succinct phrase Gabriel identifies the main focus of the vision. It has to do with **the time of the end** (v 17). This expression is paralleled and given greater clarification by two additional phrases, **later in the time of wrath** and **the appointed time of the end** (v 19). The basic meaning of these phrases is relatively clear. The vision deals with the final consummation of a period of evil. The Hebrew word **end** (*qēṣ*) connotes the point at which something ter-

DANIEL

minates or, literally, is cut off. In prophetic literature it sometimes refers to the cutting off of a period of iniquity (Amos 8:2; Ezek 7:2-3). Later in the book of Daniel the term is used to designate the end of various periods of time (9:26; 11:6, 13, 27, 35, 40, 45; 12:4, 6, 9, 13).

According to 8:19, the **time of wrath** is the period of evil that is coming to an end. **Wrath** (*za'am*) literally means "indignation." It can refer to human ire (Hos 7:16), but most often it conveys God's anger over sin that leads to the exercise of his judgment (Isa 26:20-21; Jer 10:10). Within the vision **the time of wrath** undoubtedly refers to the period of God's judgment upon the Jews described in Dan 8:9-13 and 23-25. It is the evil inflicted upon God's people by the little horn. Verse 23 describes this as a time "in the latter part of their reign, when rebels have become completely wicked."

Scholars debate what specific historical period is meant by **the time of wrath.** Positions vary depending on how the little horn is interpreted. Some suggest that a period just before the end of human history is in mind, while others believe it only refers to the time surrounding the Syrian persecution Jews experienced in the second century B.C. Still other commentators offer additional alternatives (see Walvoord 1971, 192-96, for a summary of various positions).

As the commentary below on vv 23-25 will suggest, the specific time of evil in mind seems to be the persecution of Antiochus IV. This does not eliminate the possibility of applying the point of the prophecy to end times, however. The vision of ch 8 presents a type of kingdom described in ch 7. In principle the tribulation wrought by the little horn in ch 8 represents what will unfold under the regime of human tyrants at various junctures in human history, including the end of time. According to Matt 24 and Rev 8—19, followers of God should expect intense oppression and unrest much like that found in Dan 8 before the final consummation of history.

Throughout this discussion one should not miss the essential message relayed by Gabriel. The period of judgment brought on by the little horn does have a point of termination. There is an **appointed time of the end** (v 19). This phrase emphasizes the same message as the "2,300 evenings and mornings" in v 14. A divinely ordained moment has been established when suffering caused by evil powers ceases.

■ **20** At long last, the angel explains the primary images of the vision (vv 20-25). It identifies the ram (v 20), the goat (vv 21-22), and the small horn (vv 23-25) with progressively longer explanations. The last of these three sections displays poetic qualities and can be laid out in verse (see *BHS* and NRSV). This feature focuses additional attention upon the small horn and its particular significance. It also allows for greater expression of emotion related to the actions of the small horn and supports the depth of response Daniel exhibits in the preceding and following verses.

The **two-horned ram** symbolizes **the kings of Media and Persia** (v 20). This identifies the ram with a known political entity of history, the Persian Empire that dominated the Middle East from 550 to 331 B.C. (See *Behind the Text*.) In light of this identification, the features that describe the ram in vv 3-5 make more sense and seem to correspond to characteristics of that kingdom. The two horns of the ram could allude to the two dominant ethnic elements of the empire, the Medes and the Persians. That one horn is longer than the other highlights the fact that the more prominent of the two groups was the Persians. From its point of origin east of the Tigris, the empire conquered peoples to its west, north, and south as did the ram. It expanded westward to Babylonia, Syria, and Asia Minor, northward to Armenia, Scythia, and the Caspian Sea region, and southward to Egypt and Ethiopia. Though the Greeks ultimately withstood the aggression of the Persians, the image of the ram's extensive dominance is accurate for this empire. A comparable description of Persia's intimidating conquest is given in Isa 41:1-7.

An Issue for Interpreters

The references to Persia and Greece in 8:20-21, along with Babylon (or Nebuchadnezzar) in 2:38, are the only times in the book that known world kingdoms are specifically identified with images in visions. This lack of overt connection between images and particular historical entities raises a dilemma for interpreters. Many scholars have taken this as a cue to search for actual kingdoms that could be identified with other images in visions. Other scholars, however, have thought that the text is directing readers to do otherwise. Perhaps the text's reticence to identify specific kingdoms instructs readers to avoid making speculations unless the vision makes a connection clear. This is a question with which every interpreter of Daniel must wrestle.

■ **21-22** The second animal, **the shaggy goat,** is also specifically identified with a known world power, **the king of Greece** (v 21). This refers to the empire established around 331 B.C. by Alexander the Great. The goat's **large horn,** then, symbolizes Alexander and the **four horns** signify **four kingdoms** that eventually came from his empire (v 22). As a result of these identifications, the description of the goat in vv 5-8 takes on added meaning. Like the goat, Alexander the Great came from the west, Macedon, and rapidly subdued his rival, the Persian Empire. Following a quick and decisive conquest, Alexander met an untimely, early death and his empire broke into a number of smaller kingdoms. Four major kingdoms eventually emerged like the "four prominent horns" that grew from the "large horn" of the goat (see *Behind the Text*).

■ **23-25** One of the derivative Greek kingdoms was known as the Seleucid Empire, which dominated the affairs of the Jews from 198 till 164 B.C. It is during **the latter part of their reign** over Jerusalem that a horrific tyrant comes into power, according to the vision (v 23). This tyrant is clearly the small horn of Daniel's vision, though that identification is never made explicit in the interpretation. The text does not identify this king by name, but the vast majority of scholars are convinced that this could only be Antiochus IV who ruled the Seleucid Kingdom from 175 to 164 B.C. The descriptions of the horn in the vision and of the king in the interpretation fit well with what is known of Antiochus. He was a scheming despot who came to power by wresting control of the kingdom from its rightful heirs. With his base of power located in Syria, he undertook major military campaigns toward the south and east, like the horn in v 9. Antiochus IV displayed an odious aggression toward the inhabitants of "the Beautiful Land" (v 9), the Jews. He massacred thousands of them, seized the Jerusalem temple, and forbade practice of the faith (see *Behind the Text*).

The reign of this king is described as a time **when rebels have become completely wicked** (v 23). The phrase denotes a period of intense evil that finally evokes divine response (Gen 15:16). Along with the related phrase "in the time of wrath" in v 19 it suggests a time that is ripe for God's judgment. The term **rebels** translates the Hebrew *happōšᶜîm*, but most ancient versions and some modern translations (NRSV) read "transgressions" (*happĕšaᶜîm*) instead. The word derives from *pešaᶜ*, a frequent term for sin that emphasizes transgression or violation of one's obligation to another. In this context the transgressors might be either foreign rulers or local Jewish leaders who compromise with them. Both could be viewed as rebelling against God. Earlier in the vision the horn's actions are described as "the rebellion that causes desolation" (Dan 8:13).

This tyrant is characterized as **a stern-faced king** (v 23). The term **stern-faced** (*ᶜaz pānîm*) suggests the fierce and unyielding demeanor of an insolent person such as a prostitute (Prov 7:13). One wonders if some association with a goat is intended since *ᶜez-* (she-goat) and *ᶜaz* (stern) sound very similar. His impudence is further highlighted when he is described as one who **will consider himself superior** (Dan 8:25). Such arrogance is reminiscent of Babylonian monarchs that God humbled in Dan 4 and 5.

The king is **a master of intrigue** (v 23). Literally, he *understands riddles.* The ancient world typically admired the characteristic of cleverness in monarchs. It could be a good quality but too often was mishandled (Ezek 28:1-7). For this king it is likely the means by which he becomes **very strong,** because it is **not by his own power** (Dan 8:24). As the phrase **he will cause deceit to prosper** suggests (v 25), he achieves and maintains control of his realm through treachery. The text provides an illustration of such double-dealing. It mentions a time when the king will make people **feel secure** and then **destroy** them (v 25). Some scholars suggest that this could refer to an attack upon Jerusalem in 167 B.C. by the forces of Antiochus IV. According to 1 Macc 1:29-32, the Syrian soldiers acted as if they were coming in peace and then suddenly turned on the inhabitants of the city, slaughtering thousands. For other examples of Antiochus IV's treachery, see 2 Macc 4:7-29.

This insolent and clever king will produce havoc for those under his realm. He will (1) **cause astounding devastation,** (2) **destroy the mighty men and the holy people,** (3) **destroy many,** and (4) take his stand **against the Prince of princes** (Dan 8:24-25). These phrases are another way of describing the appalling actions of the small horn catalogued in vv 10-13. Three times the verb *šāḥat* (translated **devastation** and **destroy**) is used in these verses to describe the behavior of the king. The term connotes ruining or spoiling what is good.

Those under attack are **the mighty men and the holy people** (v 24). These are the people who identify with the holy God of Israel and faithfully worship at his temple. Some have taken **mighty men** (*ʿăṣûmîm*) to refer to political figures in conflict with Antiochus IV. While these might be included in the reference, the term is broader in meaning and generally connotes might in terms of numbers. Thus it could be translated ***numerous ones*** corresponding to the **many** (*rabbîm*) mentioned in v 25. From a grammatical standpoint, the latter phrase **the holy people** may be taken simply as a further explication of **the mighty men.** Together they describe the earthly element involved in "the host" of v 12.

Though God's people bear the direct assault of the king, his primary enemy is really **the Prince of princes** (*sar śārîm*) who, in v 11, is designated "the Prince of the host" (v 25). The most natural interpretation for these titles would be God since they reflect other divine appellatives such as "Lord of lords" (*ʾadōnê haʾadōnîm*), "the LORD of hosts" (*yhwh ṣebāʾôt*) and "Lord of heaven" (Aramaic, *marē šāmaʿin*). Such titles emphasize God's sovereignty over all other entities and rulers.

Scholars, however, suggest two other possibilities for understanding these titles. They could refer to the angel Michael or a high priest. The proposal for Michael rests upon his appearance later in Daniel as the protector of Israel as well as leader of a heavenly army (10:13, 20-21; 12:1). In those contexts he is called "prince" (*śar*). The argument in favor of a chief priest derives from his function as leader of Judah's faith community. If a high priest is in mind, scholars suggest that Onias III, who was assassinated during the reign of Antiochus IV in 171 B.C., could be the specific person designated (2 Macc 4:34).

Regardless of how **the Prince of princes** is understood, the image of blasphemy remains. God is under attack. Chief priests and angels merely stand as representatives of the divine realm. Thus this king is like Nebuchadnezzar in ch 4 and Belshazzar in ch 5 in taking **his stand against** the heavenly realms. Yet, just as no animal could "stand against" the ram (v 4) and the ram could not "stand against" the goat (v 7), so also this arrogant king will not be able to stand long against heaven.

209

In the end, the ruthless king **will be destroyed** (v 25). The text literally says, *he will be broken* (*yiššābēr*), which reflects the language of horns breaking early in the vision. Like the "large horn" that represented the first king of the Greeks (v 8), the small horn will be "broken off" and become the last king. His end will come **not by human power,** though. This suggests divine intervention like a similar expression in 2:45. God will see that the perpetrator of evil ceases. According to 1 Macc 6:1-16, Antiochus IV died of an unspecified illness, perhaps depression, rather than in battle or by natural causes.

■ **26** A concluding word from Gabriel emphasizes the vision's main focus and great value. The angel clarifies that the vision is primarily about **the evenings and mornings** (v 26), that is, the extent of time daily sacrifice will be suspended and its attendant suffering will last.

The importance of the vision is affirmed in typical fashion for apocalypses (Dan 10:1; 12:4, 9; Rev 19:9; 21:5; 22:6). The vision is first of all proclaimed **true** (Dan 8:26). Its message is certain and dependable because it originates from the source of all truth (2:20-22). That message **concerns the distant future** (8:26), events that will unfold over several centuries after Daniel's lifetime. For that reason Daniel must **seal up the vision.** It must be kept safe in order to preserve it from corruption and to ensure its availability for the time to which it applies. This implies writing it down, tying a string around the document, or placing it in a container and impressing a signet upon a clay stamp (see Jer 32:9-12).

4. Conclusion (8:27)

■ **27** Once again Daniel's reaction to the vision is described to highlight its significance (see Dan 8:17-18). As on other occasions when he saw visions, Daniel is overwhelmed by his experience and confused (4:19; 7:28; 10:2-3, 7-9). As might be expected, the vision of "the rebellion that causes desolation" has left him *desolate* (translated **appalled** in the NIV). The terms "desolation" and **appalled** derive from the same root (*šāmēm*). Even though the images were explained to some measure in the interpretation, Daniel confesses that it was still **beyond understanding.**

FROM THE TEXT

The vision of ch 8 affirms the same message that God spoke through Isaiah to Judah regarding the Assyrians, "O my people who live in Zion, do not be afraid of the Assyrians, who beat you with a rod and lift up a club against you, as Egypt did. Very soon my anger against you will end and my wrath will be directed to their destruction" (Isa 10:24-25). In the tradition of Israel's prophets over the centuries, Daniel acknowledges a world in constant conflict inflicting suffering upon God's people. The news of comfort, however, is that heaven truly empathizes with their affliction and sets a boundary upon it.

The stage of human history is filled with conflict because of the desire for self-sovereignty. It is the way of nations, according to Dan 8, to engage one another like combative animals. With the temperament of aggressive rams and goats, they attack their prey, subdue it, and become great. In turn, though, another arises, attacks, subdues, and becomes great. The top position is temporary in the animal kingdom and also among the human kingdoms. One brief portion of human history, the Persian and Greek periods, illustrates this.

The motive for such aggression is made clear in the third figure of the vision. The small horn manifests a determined drive to displace God as sovereign authority over this world. Like the people of ancient Shinar, the horn attempts to build "a city, with a tower that reaches to the heavens" (Gen 11:4). He sets himself up **to be as great as the Prince of the host** (Dan 8:11). More than that he takes his **stand against the Prince of princes** (v 25) and attacks **the host of the heavens** (v 10). Like a ferocious animal devouring prey, he throws **some of the starry host down to the earth** and tramples on them (v 10). In many ways he is the manifestation of Satan, who the NT describes as one that "prowls around like a roaring lion looking for someone to devour" (1 Pet 5:8).

This is the posture of evil empires and their kings, whether or not they acknowledge it. They are in conflict with heaven. Their goal is self-sovereignty rather than God-sovereignty, which is the fundamental expression of sin. Such misbehavior is appropriately called **rebellion** (Dan 8:13) because it breaches a covenant between creature and Creator. The earthly prince is attempting a coup in the realm of **the Prince of princes** (v 25).

Such trespass is not restricted to nations or tyrants alone, though. It is the struggle of every human. Thus the images of ch 8 reflect a conflict engaged by each person living on earth, not just that of kingdoms. James 4 puts a finger on this struggle when it asks, "What causes fights and quarrels among you? Don't they come from your desires that battle within you?" (Jas 4:1). Those desires are the longings to possess and control, James explains, rather than submit to God. This is the struggle for self-sovereignty illustrated in Dan 8.

The person locked in a struggle with God causes the people of God to suffer. The horn's grasping for self-sovereignty manifests itself in a very tangible way in the lives of those who worship God. His strategy involves subversion of anything on earth that acknowledges God's rule. Thus he takes away the daily sacrifice from God's people and disrespects the holy sanctuary (v 11). The sacrifice and sanctuary stand as essential symbols of God's sovereignty in this world. The sanctuary is the earthly palace of the heavenly king and sacrifice is an act of obeisance from his subjects. Though these are only symbols, the reality behind them is of critical importance. When they are removed, the **truth** about God and his sovereign right to rule over the lives of people is **thrown to**

the ground (v 12). Without sacrifice and sanctuary God's people lose a major means of acting out their devotion to God and witnessing to his sovereignty over this world.

If commentators are correct to interpret the actions of the horn as an allusion to the initiatives taken by Antiochus IV in the second century B.C., then the depth of the affliction is even more extensive than Dan 8 describes. First and Second Maccabees tell a harrowing story of oppression, slaughter, and sacrilege under Antiochus IV. Literally thousands of Jews died at his hand, which gives added meaning to the phrases **he will cause astounding devastation** and **he will destroy many** (vv 24-25). It was a holocaust of the Jewish faithful. In addition, the temple area was completely profaned and renamed the temple of Olympian Zeus. Second Macc 6:3-5 describes the situation: "Harsh and utterly grievous was the onslaught of evil. For the temple was filled with debauchery and reveling by the Gentiles, who dallied with prostitutes and had intercourse with women within the sacred precincts, and besides brought in things for sacrifice that were unfit. The altar was covered with abominable offerings that were forbidden by the laws."

Throughout history God's people suffer because of those who operate under the illusion of self-rule. Jesus warned that such would be the case (John 15:20), and his followers acknowledge the reality (2 Cor 1:8-9). They found comfort, though, in realizing that their suffering not only brought them closer to Christ but also provided the means by which he could be revealed to this world (1 Pet 4:13).

God's people also suffer because of their own sin. While self-seeking tyrants inflict great suffering upon God's elect, they may not be the only source of hardship. The vision of ch 8 hints that the affliction brought on by the horn is in fact God's judgment for Israel's sin. God is using the hubris of an earthly king to provide punishment for the waywardness of believers. This does not diminish the previous point, but it does provide additional perspective.

The text is not entirely explicit on this issue. The ambiguity with regard to **rebellion** in v 12, **the time of wrath** in v 19, and **rebels** in v 23 leaves room for alternative interpretations. Chapter 9 clarifies matters, however. It affirms that Israel's sin did evoke the judgment of God that begins with the exile and reaches new heights during a time when "the abomination that causes desolation" occurs (see commentary on ch 9). This is a hard word to hear, but it is consistent with the message of Israel's prophets over the centuries. God disciplines those he loves (Deut 8:5; Hos 11:1-6).

Regardless of the source of suffering, heaven shares in the afflictions of God's people. The vision of ch 8 implies that the heavenly realms are involved in the conflict created by the horn. God is not disconnected from those who suffer on earth. Once again the ambiguity of the text opens up a possibility that is made plainer in later visions. **The host** of vv 10-13 could refer to either earthly or heavenly personalities, and commentators have suggested both over the years. Chapter 10 will clarify that an attack upon God's people is an attack upon God. The battles of earth in some way parallel battles in the heavenly realm (see commentary on ch 10).

For the context of ch 8 it is a comfort to know that the people of God are not alone in their affliction. God and the heavenly realm are aware and engaged. Just as the story of Shadrach, Meshach, and Abednego in ch 3 affirms, in some manner God joins the faithful in their most desperate trials. God's promise to Joshua is fulfilled over and over again throughout Scripture, "As I was with Moses, so I will be with you; I will never leave you nor forsake you" (Josh 1:5).

God sets a time for evil to end and his kingdom to come. Though believers may find comfort in heaven's participation in their suffering, knowing that an end is in sight is even more reassuring. The key question of the vision is **How long will it take for the vision to be fulfilled?** (v 13). This is a vital question for those who suffer (Ps 35:17; Rev 6:10). People can endure better when they know the pain will cease.

Yet the concern of the vision is not only with ending the suffering of God's people; the period of affliction is also a time when God's sovereignty is mocked. The attack on sacrifice and sanctuary signify disregard for God's control over this world. This is the greater issue, as the rest of Daniel, both its stories and other visions, attest. Thus the end of evil also means the absolute rule of God is manifested on earth. As the vision puts it, **the sanctuary will be reconsecrated** (v 14). God will once again be rightfully acknowledged as sovereign in his temple. Thus, the reign of God and the end of suffering coincide. They are two sides of the same coin (Isa 25:8; 35:10; 65:19; Rev 21:4).

The vision's answer to the question of how long is similar to what Jesus said about the time evil would end and his kingdom come (Matt 24:36; Acts 1:7). It is firm that it will take place but not precise about when. The response of the angel is that **it will take 2,300 evenings and mornings** (v 14). The number is cryptic and leaves uncertainty as to the exact moment the end will come. So at the conclusion Daniel confesses that it is **beyond understanding** (v 27). What is perfectly clear, however, is that God has a plan in mind. God remains in control and determines the end of evil tyrants. Just as God overruled the ungodly reigns of Nebuchadnezzar, Belshazzar, Darius, and grotesque beasts earlier in Daniel, so also he terminates the terror generated by the stern-faced king of this vision.

Many commentators have connected the details of this vision with end-time events. The number "2,300" has been viewed as a means for calculating the end of human history and "the small horn" has been identified as the antichrist who would be a part of this era. In the view of this commentary such interpretations are questionable but do not entirely miss the mark. The historical referents to Persia and Greece appear to locate the vision's fulfillment within human history. This does not preclude, however, comparison of the message of the vision to the last days. As this commentary has affirmed, the events of ch 8 illustrate elements of the broader picture of world history outlined in ch 7. The character of the horn in ch 8 certainly reflects that of ungodly personalities like that of the little horn in ch 7 and the antichrists described in the NT. This does not mean ch 8 is specifically speaking of this person, though. It simply illustrates the kind of ungodly ruler the world will encounter over and over again and particularly just before world history draws to a close.

The same kind of understanding can be taken regarding references to "the end" in ch 8. Though what is spoken of in ch 8 refers to the end of suffering under Greek rulers, the message regarding the end of evil applies to the culmination of history as well. According to Dan 7 as well as numerous other scriptures (Isa 2; Zech 14; Rev 19—20), God will eventually pull the plug on evil empires and once again manifest his sovereignty in this world.

C. Vision of Seventy Sevens (9:1-27)

Overview

Daniel sounds like other prophets of Israel in ch 9 more than anywhere else in the book. His lengthy prayer of confession draws heavily upon the words and thoughts of the great prophetic tradition of the Hebrew Scriptures. Yet the familiar speech of this prayer gives way to a vision whose language is ambiguous. Its cryptic expressions have evoked a wide variety of interpretations. Thus one of the most debated visions in the book of Daniel is found here. The message of God's control over the affairs of his people, however, remains clear. In this chapter it is particularly evident in the demonstration of God's righteous character with regard to the covenant with Israel.

BEHIND THE TEXT

The content and form of ch 9 differs from other visions reported in the book so far. Fantastic images—such as a metal statue (ch 2), a cosmic tree (ch 4), or ferocious animals (chs 7—8)—do not occur in ch 9. The image here is simply that of the number seventy. Thus the overall genre of ch 9 can be distinguished from that of chs 2, 4, 7, and 8. Scholars identify it as an epiphany vision report as opposed to the symbolic vision report of the previous chapters. The vision report of chs 10—12 also follows the same form as ch 9 (see *Behind the Text* on 10:1—11:1 for more discussion of this genre).

A feature of the epiphany vision is an extensive description of the context in which it comes. In symbolic visions this is normally a minor detail, briefly described in a few sentences. In ch 9 the reading of scripture and a long prayer of confession lead to the heavenly vision. The divine revelation itself is actually much shorter than the description of the context in which it comes. The vision report of chs 10—12 has an even more elaborate description of the visionary's setting. In the final outcome, though, the revelation in that vision still remains much longer than the setting.

This focus upon the context of the vision suggests a strategy for reading the angel's message. The prayer provides perspective from which to interpret the vision. According to Gabriel, the vision comes as a direct response to Daniel's prayer (vv 22-23). The vision's numerous allusions to the prayer confirm this integral connection. Although some commentators have viewed the prayer as disconnected and even nonessential material, its centrality to the vision's message must not be overlooked.

The prayer of Daniel is a corporate confession of sin that reflects the language and style of such prayers throughout the Hebrew Scriptures. In the tradition of Abraham and Moses, Daniel stands as an intercessor for his people (Gen 18:23-33; Exod 32:7-14; Num 14:13-19). He employs stereotypical expressions reminiscent of prayers found in penitential psalms, postexilic books, and especially Deuteronomistic material (1 Kgs 8:46-53; Ezra 9:6-15; Neh 9:6-37; Ps 79).

The logic of the prayer rests upon Israel's understanding of its special covenantal relationship to God. According to Hebrew Scriptures, the descendents of Abraham have entered into a unique bond with their God that calls for commitment on both sides (Gen 12:1-3; 17:1-14). Daniel's prayer emphasizes this relationship by employing the language of covenant making and breaking. Such terms as "love" (ḥesed), "laws" (tôrôt and mišpaṭim), "commands" (miṣwōt), "the Law of Moses" (tôrāt mōšeh), and "covenant" (berît) occur throughout the prayer, along with reference to the exodus from Egypt. God is the one **who keeps his covenant of love** (Dan 9:4). He is known by his special covenant name, **the LORD,** which is used six times in this chapter and nowhere else in the book. Because of the covenant, God is justified in his judgment of his people. They have sinned and thus broken covenant. At the same time, mercy is expected because of the covenant. God forgives because he is committed to his people.

This covenantal thinking is at the heart of Jeremiah's prophecies, which provide important background for ch 9. Daniel references **the word of the LORD given to Jeremiah** (v 2), a message about **seventy years** found in Jer 25:11-12 and 29:10. But Daniel also alludes to many other passages in Jeremiah in support of his covenantal theology. For Jeremiah the covenant was the basis for words of doom as well as of hope. He, perhaps more clearly than any-one else of his time, recognized the inevitability of judgment for Judah because they had broken covenant with God (Jer 11:1-14). Yet he was also filled with hopeful expectations for the future of Judah because of the covenant (Jer 31:1-14). Jeremiah envisioned the day when a new covenant would be established between God and his people (Jer 31:31-34). The prayer and vision of Dan 9 captures some of that same hopeful future with God.

The meaning of **seventy years** mentioned by Jeremiah, as well as the **seventy sevens** of the vision, is crucial for understanding Dan 9. An interpreter must decide whether to take these numbers literally or symbolically. Many scholars argue that the numbers in the text are intended literally (Archer 1985, 119; Miller 1994, 257-58). Since the seventy sevens are broken down into three specific divisions—**seven sevens, sixty-two sevens,** and **one seven**—a precise accounting seems warranted. Further, references to seven literal years with regard to sabbatical years and jubilees in other parts of the Hebrew Scriptures indicate that these could be taken literally as well (Lev 25:1-12). Finally, the near accuracy of seventy years for the length of Judah's exile might support a literal reading.

A survey of the use of the numbers seven and seventy throughout the Bible, however, reveal a predominance of symbolic usage. Seven represents completion or perfection from Genesis to Revelation. The conceptual foundation for this number derives from the seven days of creation (Gen 1:1—2:4). Thus the seven-day week is a complete cycle of time. The multiplication of seven by ten intensifies the sense of wholeness and conveys a forceful image of fullness. Seventy combines seven, the symbol of perfection, with ten, the symbol of totality. Perfection is multiplied ten times, to the maximum power. Therefore seventy is used throughout Scripture to indicate a full or perfect amount of something, such as nations (Gen 10), sons (Gen 46:27; Judg 8:30; 2 Kgs 10:1), palm trees (Exod 15:27), elders (Exod 24:1), and years of life (Ps 90:10). Canaanite and Mesopotamian text reveal similar kinds of usages for seven and seventy.

Within such a milieu, it would seem likely that the **seventy years** for the desolation of Jerusalem should be understood symbolically. Rather than being a literal calculation of time, seventy years could be a reference to a full amount of time. In this case, it is the entire time needed for God's judgment upon Jerusalem to be completed. One could compare this to the seventy years Tyre lay wasted in judgment (Isa 23:15-17). Chronicles added an additional twist to this symbolism by connecting seventy years of Judah's judgment with the Sabbath rest of the land. "The land enjoyed its sabbath rests; all the time of its desolation it rested, until the seventy years were completed in fulfillment of the word of the LORD spoken by Jeremiah" (2 Chr 36:21). This text seems to refer to the period from the destruction of Jerusalem in 587 B.C. till the edict of Cyrus in 539 B.C. Thus the "seventy years" for Chronicles represents forty-nine years.

The symbolism of Jeremiah's seventy years remains even though some calculations of Judah's exile come close to this amount of time. For example, the fall of Babylon in 539 B.C. was approximately seventy years after the Babylonians took control of affairs in Judah around 605 B.C. It is also true that from the time the temple in Jerusalem was destroyed in 587 B.C. till it was rebuilt in 516 B.C. is almost seventy years. In Zechariah an angel seems to notice this connection to the temple when it speaks about "these seventy years" that God has been angry with Jerusalem (Zech 1:12). That vision came around 519 B.C., sixty-eight years after the temple was destroyed. Such calculations tend to confirm that seventy is a rounded symbolic number because the time is not exactly seventy years.

Since the meaning of Jeremiah's seventy years is likely symbolic, one might expect the **seventy sevens** of the vision to be as well. This is particularly so since the number occurs within a vision and all other numbers in the visions of Daniel appear to be symbolic (see comments on 2:44-45; 7:17; 8:14; 12:11-12). It is also true that no attempt to relate this number to specific historical events has ever been completely successful (see the sidebar "Calculations of Seventy Sevens").

The word **sevens** (*šabū'îm*) conveys seven units of things and could be translated "weeks." The combination of seventy with this plural form of seven is most often understood as "seventy weeks of years," which would be "seventy times seven" or 490 years. The number could have been written more traditionally in Hebrew as "four hundred and ninety years" (*'arba' mē'ôt wetiš'îm šānâ*). Thus the expression **seventy sevens** signals something of symbolic significance. The number may well signify an undetermined, excessive amount of time, perhaps into infinity. It is similar to the "seventy times seven" (or "seventy-seven times") in Jesus' saying to Peter about forgiveness (Matt 18:21-22). The point of this saying is not that Peter is required to forgive a specific number of times but that Peter is required to forgive as often as needed.

The connection of seventy sevens to the Israelite Jubilee concept is hard to miss. This was a time marked for restoration of the land every 49 years (see Lev 25:8-17). Ten Jubilee periods (less the fiftieth Year of Jubilee each time) add up to 490. The first division of the seventy sevens is indicated as seven sevens, the number of years before the Year of Jubilee. The exile of Judah could be viewed as a time of Sabbath rest for the land, according to 2 Chr 36:21. Thus seventy sevens could convey an extended time of sabbatical periods needed to restore the land. In effect, the Jubilee pattern has been reversed. Forty-nine years of work have been replaced with forty-nine years of rest, ten times over.

The schematization of history into periods of seven, ten, and seventy is also found in other apocalyptic works. One speaks of seventy generations from the flood till the end of time (*1 En.* 10:12). Another divides all of human history into ten "weeks" with the seventh "week" being a crucial turning point and the time of the author (*1 En.* 93:1-10 and 91:11-19). The *Sybylline Oracles*, which are technically not apocalypses, also schematize history into ten periods. Whether or not these works are dependent upon Daniel is a matter of debate. At the very least, though, they indicate a way of thinking in ancient times.

The historical setting identified for the prayer and vision of Dan 9 is significant. **The first year of Darius** refers to 539 B.C., when Babylon fell to the Persians as described in 5:31 (9:1). The historical issues related to Darius have been discussed earlier (see *In the Text* on ch 6). The fall of Babylon marked a new era for Jewish fortunes. The Persian policy of returning exiled peoples to their homelands provided the opportunity for the Jews to go back to Jerusalem and reestablish it. According to historical records, the Persian king Cyrus issued a decree in 539 B.C. authorizing this action. Biblical records affirm the impact of this edict upon the Jews in particular (2 Chr 36:23; Ezra 1:2-4). Both the prayer and vision of Dan 9 should be read in relationship to this context.

Verbal, structural, and thematic connections between ch 9 and the other visions of the book are significant and indicate that each should be read in light of the other (see *In the Text* on ch 7). The vision of ch 7 sketches a broad outline of human history, while the visions of chs 8—12 provide details of more specific eras within that portrait. A number of elements draw together the three visions of chs 8—12, particularly the focus upon a time of intense suffering for God's people when an "abomination that causes desolation" occurs (see further in *Behind the Text* on ch 8).

Chapter 9 displays a special relationship to ch 8. Aside from the reference to Gabriel in both, numerous other verbal features link these two chapters. Most of these occur in relation to activities of the little horn in ch 8. Replicated terms and concepts include: "the rebellion," "the abomination of desolation," "desolation of Jerusalem," "the end of sacrifice and offering," "seal up the vision," and "the holy place" (see more in Goldingay 1989, 259-60). This feature indicates that ch 8 provides background for reading ch 9. At the very least, ch 9 relates to a similar kind of event as in ch 8, if not the same. Whether or not one agrees that these two visions speak of the same historical venue, ch 9 provides a further explication of the life of God's people in the midst of such happenings. It gives a more detailed picture of what the end of "the 2,300 evenings and mornings" might look like along with a progression of events that could accompany it.

The vision of ch 9 is preceded by an extensive description of the context in which it comes. As noted above, the length of this introduction is unique to the book and figures significantly in the interpretation of the vision. Daniel's insight from Jeremiah (vv 1-2) leads to his prayer of confession (vv 3-19), which provokes the arrival of a heavenly messenger (vv 20-23) and finally the message (vv 24-27).

IN THE TEXT

1. Insight from Jeremiah (9:1-2)

■ **1** The chapter begins like all other vision reports in the book, with notice of a specific time. **The first year of Darius** refers to 539 B.C., when the Persians conquered Babylon (v 1). This assumes that this is the same Darius mentioned in Dan 5:31 and 6:1, which is reasonable. That person is also identified as **a Mede** and as the one **who was made ruler over the Babylonian kingdom.** The passive form of **was made ruler** might indicate a divine hand. But it could also reflect the appointment of Darius by a higher authority. The debate related to the identity of Darius the Mede in the book of Daniel has been discussed previously (see *Behind the Text* for ch 6).

This verse gives additional information about Darius's family. He is called the son of **Xerxes** (Ahasuerus in Hebrew). This is a name borne by two kings in the Persian Empire after this time period (see Ezra 4:6 and Esth 1:1), but unknown earlier. Therefore, scholars are uncertain as to whom this may refer. Some have suggested it is a throne name, while others see it as historical error.

The reference to Darius links this chapter with ch 6, where Daniel is also portrayed as a person committed to prayer. In that context he faithfully prays three times a day despite official opposition to such prayers.

■ **2** Regardless of the identities of Darius and Xerxes, the temporal notation identifies a moment of major political change when Babylon fell and Persia began ruling the Middle East. It is in this context that Daniel gains insight into some words from Jeremiah. **The first year of his reign** is repeated as if to underscore the connection with Daniel's reading Jeremiah and events surrounding this date (v 2). He identifies these words as being **from the Scriptures,** literally *in the books* (*bassĕpārîm*). This term seems to designate some authoritative texts of the community of faith since he also calls them **the word of the LORD.**

From the words of Jeremiah Daniel comes to understand that **the desolation of Jerusalem would last seventy years** (v 2). This suggests that Daniel has been reading Jer 25:11-12 and 29:10. The first passage projects the era of Babylonian dominance when "this whole country will become a desolate wasteland, and these nations will serve the king of Babylon seventy years" (25:11). It goes on to predict judgment for Babylon as well. "But when the seventy years are fulfilled, I will punish the king of Babylon and his nation" (v 12). The other passage from Jeremiah focuses upon the hope of return from Babylonian exile. It says, "When seventy years are completed for Babylon, I will come to you and fulfill my gracious promise to bring you back to this place" (29:10).

These prophecies identify two things that will take place at the end of **seventy years:** (1) Babylon's judgment and (2) Judah's restoration. At the time Daniel is reading Jeremiah's words, the first of these has taken place. His concern, then, is that the rest of Jeremiah's prophecy would find fulfillment and the **desolation of Jerusalem** end.

The most thorough **desolation** (*ḥārĕbôt*) or ruin of Jerusalem occurred in 587 B.C. when the Babylonians utterly destroyed the city and its temple. It is possible, though, that Daniel is thinking of the entire period that the city remained under the rule of Babylon, which was 605 to 539 B.C. Though this was about **seventy years,** that number is not intended to be a precise calculation, either in Jeremiah or Daniel. It is a rounded number, symbolic of a full amount of time needed for something to take place (see *Behind the Text*). Whether Daniel reckons that Jerusalem has suffered desolation for forty-nine years or sixty-eight years, he hopes that its restoration is about to happen.

2. Prayer of Confession (9:3-19)

■ **3** Daniel's response to the insight from Jeremiah is to voice a prayer of communal repentance. In this he is following the directive prescribed in Lev 26:40-45 and reflected in Jer 29. After the seventy years of Babylonian dominance, God envisions that his people "will call upon me and come and pray to me, and I will listen to you. You will seek me and find me when you seek me with all your heart" (Jer 29:12-13). Daniel appears to be seeking a fulfillment of Jeremiah's prophecy through his prayer. At the least, he is following its admonition. When the angel responds to his prayer, however, he will discover that there is more to understand about those words.

Daniel's preparations for prayer are described (vv 3-4*a*) and then the words of the prayer given (vv 4*b*-19). The prayer unfolds in a logical progression from confession of sin (vv 4*b*-6), to affirmation of God's righteousness (vv 7-14), and finally to supplication for restoration (vv 15-19). Each of these sections begins with an invocation that characterizes God. The elements of confession and affirmation are interwoven throughout the prayer. This highlights the contrast between the covenant-keeping God and the covenant-breaking people. The sin of God's people is abhorrent over against God's thoroughly justified judgment. This feature also recognizes that a prayer of confession not only confesses the awfulness of sin but also confesses the awesomeness of God.

Daniel's demeanor is that of an authentic penitent in Scripture. He comes before God **in prayer and petition** (v 3). The first term (*tĕpillâ*) is the most common word for prayer in the Hebrew Scriptures and is often used in the sense of intercession (1 Kgs 8:28). The second term (*taḥănûnîm*) designates a request for favor. Together the two terms may be taken as a hendiadys and translated *prayer of supplication.*

Literally, Daniel says, *I set my face to the Lord God to seek,* which conveys special intensity. The word *seek* (*bāqaš*) could suggest that Daniel is looking for further illumination, but it can also be about merely pursuing audience with God. The tenor of the prayer indicates that Daniel is more concerned with reestablishing genuine communion with God. Whatever the intent may have been, Daniel will receive additional insight into the meaning of "seventy" as a response to his prayer.

Fasting and putting on **sackcloth and ashes** underscore Daniel's earnestness. These are the actions and attire of those who mourn or passionately pursue God (2 Chr 20:3; Neh 9:1; Esth 4:1). Daniel also fasts before he receives the final vision recorded in the book (10:2-3).

■ **4** Daniel's prayer is directed **to the LORD my God** (v 4). This way of designating God emphasizes the covenantal understanding upon which the prayer is based. The special name of Israel's God, **the LORD,** is used five other times within this chapter (vv 2, 8, 10, 13, 14). Its usage evokes the story of Israel's deliverance from Egypt and covenant at Sinai, both of which are specifically mentioned in the prayer (vv 11, 13, 15). The term **my God** accomplishes the same purposes. Its several occurrences (vv 4, 18 [NRSV], 19, 20 [2 times in NRSV]) along with those of "our God" (vv 9, 10, 13, 14, 15, 17) highlight the covenantal bond that exists between God and his people. It is because of this covenant that Daniel prays as he does.

The prayer begins with an invocation that extols the character of God. These are the first of several lofty qualities ascribed to God throughout the prayer. Besides being a means of appropriately honoring God, such descriptions further establish the logic of the prayer. Daniel comes before God, confesses, and makes requests because of who God is. This invocation is similar to that of Nehemiah in his prayer for Jerusalem (Neh 1:5).

The opening words address God as **Lord** (*ʾădōnāy*). This appellative, which occurs seven times in the prayer (vv 4, 7, 9, 15, 16, 17, 19), appropriately identifies God as sovereign over all things. It claims a broader realm of authority than the particularized Israelite name **the LORD.** The power of such a one is to be feared, for God is **the great and awesome God.** The word **awesome** (*nôrāʾ*) could be translated "fearful" or "terrible" and conveys the kind of unquestioned might held by a sovereign monarch (Deut 7:21; Pss 47:2; 68:35).

Though absolutely powerful, God **keeps his covenant of love** (Dan 9:4). This phrase affirms God's trustworthiness and commitment to his people. It recalls similar statements ascribed to Moses and Solomon (Deut 7:9, 12; 1 Kgs 8:23). God's covenant is one founded on **love** (*ḥesed*). This term is often translated "kindness" or "steadfast love." It connotes a determination to prefer a person regardless of the response. This kind of covenant is a binding agreement based on loyal commitment, not convenience or appropriate reciprocation. It functions best with **all who love him and obey his commands.** People demonstrate their **love** (*'ahab*) or preference for God by doing what his laws prescribe. Such persons are responding appropriately to the covenant relationship and can expect the full benefits of God's loyal commitment to them.

■ **5-6** Before this powerful yet loving God Daniel confesses forthrightly on behalf of his community. He articulates the sin of his people initially with six different phrases. It is as if Daniel desires to cover any and all possible transgressions. He admits that they have (1) **sinned,** (2) **done wrong,** (3) **been wicked,** (4) **rebelled,** (5) **turned away,** and (6) **not listened** (vv 5-6). Later in the prayer Daniel confesses to "unfaithfulness" (v 7), that "all Israel has transgressed" (v 11), and that they "have not sought the favor of the LORD" (v 13).

These are all classic expressions of sin in the Hebrew Scriptures and each conveys a particular facet of it. **Sinned** (*ḥāṭā'*) is the most common term for spiritual failure and denotes the aspect of missing the goal God has designed for a person. **Done wrong** (*'āwōn*) derives from a root describing what is crooked or bent. Sin veers from the straight path of God. Such actions mark a person as **wicked** (*rāša'*), that is, they have done what is wrong and stand guilty of crime. The crime committed is treason or revolt against God's authority. In other words, they have **rebelled** (*mārad*) against God and **turned away** (*sûr*) from the directives God has given for life.

Just like the hard-hearted pharaoh before Moses (Exod 7:13), the people have **not listened** (*lō' šāma'*). The Hebrew term *šāma'* can also be translated "obey" as it is later in the vv 10 and 14. When people truly listen, they respond with action.

God had sent his spokesmen, his **servants the prophets,** to warn them, but people did not pay attention to them. They did just as the northern kingdom had done when they suffered destruction by the Assyrians (2 Kgs 17:13-14). It was a pattern throughout the history of God's people, especially in the years that led up to the exile (Jer 25:3-7; 26:5; 29:19). Prophets like Jeremiah had spoken to everyone, from the greatest to the least, from **kings** to **all the people of the land.** No portion of the population remained unwarned.

■ **7-9** While continuing to confess sin, Daniel shifts the focus of the prayer to God's righteousness. The term **righteous** (*ṣĕdāqâ*) functions as an inclusion for this portion of the prayer (vv 7-14). It occurs at the beginning as a noun and in its adjectival form (*ṣadîq*) at the end. The word is often used in legal contexts to describe one who conforms to a right standard. Such a connotation seems fitting for the prayer since it affirms that God lives up to all the covenant obligations. God is portrayed as the righteous covenant partner of Israel as well as its righteous judge.

In this section, Daniel also asserts that God is **merciful and forgiving** (v 9). Within the context of covenant these characteristics express another side of God's righteousness. God does right by the covenant, not only in his judgment, but also in his compassion. God did the right thing when he exacted judgment and **scattered** his people to Babylon, Egypt, and elsewhere (v 7). But God also does right by expressing compassion and offering pardon. It is on this basis that the prayer will turn toward a request for restoration in vv 15-19.

In contrast to the honorable behavior of God toward the covenant, his people are **covered with shame** (vv 7, 8). This is a gripping indictment for a culture that is sensitive to honor and shame, such as Israel's. The people have embarrassed themselves in the eyes of their world by breaking covenant with their God. They have become "an object of scorn" to the surrounding community (v 16), something to be hissed at and mocked. God had warned that this would happen if they failed to keep covenant (Deut 28:37; Jer 19:8; Ezek 22:4).

Their shame is a result of **unfaithfulness** (*mā'al*), a term that connotes intentional betrayal or treachery, such as marital infidelity (v 7). Since Israel is committed to covenant with God, a breach of the relationship is rightly portrayed as infidelity in marriage (see Jer 3; Hos 3). Thus their sin is personal. It is against God, not just a formalized rulebook. This personal aspect of sin is highlighted again throughout the prayer in phrases that speak of sin being **against you** and **against him** (vv 8, 9, 11).

■ **10-11a** The most consistent illustration of such effrontery is Israel's treatment of God's laws. They **have not obeyed** . . . **or kept the laws** but rather **transgressed** and **turned away** from them (vv 10-11a). This reiterates what is said in vv 5 and 6. The word **transgressed** (*'ābar*) pictures a person walking past a boundary as if it is not there. The **laws** (*tôrôt*) that have been ignored are the ones God gave **through his servants the prophets** (v 10). This refers to God's life-giving instructions that were first communicated through Moses and later confirmed by Israel's other prophets. They are also called "commandments" (*miṣwōt*) and "judgments" (*mišpāṭîm*) in v 5.

■ **11b-12** As a result of their sin, God is justified in bringing the judgment of exile. **The curses and sworn judgments** (v 11b) that have fallen upon Judah can be found in Lev 26; Deut 27—28; and elsewhere (v 11). They project **great disaster** even to the point of what was **done to Jerusalem** when it was destroyed in 587 B.C. and its people taken into exile (v 12). These specific consequences for breaking covenant were laid out ahead of time (Lev 26:27-35; Deut 28:63-68). They should, therefore, be expected.

■ **13** Yet, the judgment of exile did not accomplish the desired results. Instead of responding positively to God, Daniel admits that still **we have not sought the favor of the** LORD **our God by turning from our sins and giving attention to your truth** (v 13). The idea of one seeking **favor** (*ḥālâ pĕnê*) comes from the royal court where a person approaches a king in preparation for making a request. Daniel implies that repentance and obedient living could be the means of gaining God's favor. **Turning from** (*lāšûb*) . . . **sins** is a common way of speaking of repentance for the prophets. It evokes the picture of a person changing directions. **Giving attention to . . . truth** (*śākal ba'emet*) employs the language of Israel's sages. It describes one who is wise in handling God's instructions about life. The wise thing to do, of course, is to obey them. But Daniel's generation has not been wise and they have **not obeyed.**

Verse 13 clarifies that Daniel is confessing sins not only of the fathers but of the contemporary generation as well. The people at the end of the exile remain just as disobedient as their predecessors. Therefore, continual judgment for sin might be expected. As Leviticus points out, when people refuse to respond to judgment appropriately it will continue "seven times over" (Lev 26:18, 21, 24, 27). This is the point of the angel's message in v 24. The people of God are in for more judgment.

■ **14** God is ready to exact judgment whenever it is needed. He **did not hesitate to bring the disaster** upon the exiles (v 14). The text literally says that God "watched over" (*šāqad*), which reflects the language of Jer 1:12 and 44:27. In those texts God watches to make sure the right thing, judgment for sin, takes place. God does this because he is **righteous in everything he does** (v 14). Whether God judges sin in the past, in the present, or in the future, he is justified in doing so because he always does the right thing in this regard.

Verses 13 and 14 pave the way for hearing the message of the angel in vv 24-27. There is no indication in the text, though, that Daniel expects further judgment that is announced there. His theological assertions of God's righteousness, however, do support the possibility.

■ **15-16** At this juncture, Daniel moves to close the prayer with a supplication for restoration (vv 15-19). He has established that Israel has sinned and continues to sin and that God is right in judging that sin. Therefore, within the context of a "covenant of love" (v 4), God could do right by extending grace and forgiveness as well. While pleading for mercy, Daniel continues to confess sin as he has done throughout the prayer. This feature assures that the penitent is not presumptuous of the favor requested. Any mercy issues from sheer grace.

To begin his petition Daniel evokes the most memorable act of God in the Hebrew Scriptures, the Exodus from Egypt. God is identified as the one **who brought your people out of Egypt** and **made . . . a name** among the nations (v 15). This characterization of God highlights God's mercy, honor, and righteousness. These are the three motivations that could propel God to respond. The Exodus from Egypt was not only a profound act of grace but also an act that brought recognition. God became known through the exodus event as a deity with great power, great faithfulness, and great compassion. As such, it is called one of God's **righteous acts** (v 16). It was, in fact, the greatest act of God in OT history. In the Exodus God did what was right by the covenant with Abraham.

Before the God of the Exodus, then, Daniel makes his request to **turn away your anger and your wrath from Jerusalem** (v 16). This plea recalls the language of Jeremiah once again (see, for example, Jer 18:20). The term **turn away** (*šûb*) fundamentally means to move in another direction from the current one. This entails both turning away as well as turning toward. Thus the word frequently conveys the idea of repentance in the Hebrew Scriptures, as it does in v 13. But it also connotes restoration to a new way. Daniel calls for the **anger** and **wrath** of God, his instruments of judgment, to subside. The image is that of a storm calming. As such the plea also implies newness of life.

The fury of God's wrath had made Jerusalem and its people **an object of scorn** (v 16). Literally they had become something to be taunted or spoken about derisively. They were a shameful embarrassment to themselves and God as already noted in vv 7 and 8.

Daniel plays upon the motive of God's honor by emphasizing **Jerusalem** as **your city** and as the place of **your holy hill** and **your people** (v 16). The emphasis on the second person personal pronoun "your" highlights God's personal connection with the city. A few lines later, Daniel speaks of "your desolate sanctuary" (v 17) and "the city that bears your Name" (v 18). The prayer finally closes with reference to "your city and your people" (v 19). This is part of the strategy of the prayer. God's honor is at stake in the restoration of Jerusalem because he is personally connected to it.

■ **17-18** In a manner typical of laments in the Psalms, Daniel requests God's attention to his dilemma. He pleads for God to **hear** (two times), **look with favor, give ear,** and **open your eyes and see** (vv 17-18). The request to look with favor recalls the petition of the Aaronic blessing in Num 6:25 (see also Ps 31:16). It is a plea for God's "face to shine" favorably upon someone or something.

The objects for which God's attention is sought are **the desolate sanctuary** (v 17) and **the desolation of the city** (v 18). The words **desolate** and **desolation** derive from *šāmēm*, which connects the passage to 8:13 and 9:27 where the phrase "abomination that causes desolation" occurs (see also 11:31 and 12:11). These terms also recall "the desolation of Jerusalem" mentioned in v 2, although a different word is used there.

The motive of God's merciful character is evoked once again. The **great mercy** (*raḥamîm hārabbîm*) of God could also be translated **many mercies** (v 18). The reason God might respond to Daniel's prayer is not **because we are**

righteous. In fact, the lack of right living has been punctuated throughout the prayer. Rather the basis of hope is the ***many mercies*** God has shown time and again to his people throughout history (Neh 9:19, 27, 31).

■ **19** Daniel closes his prayer with one more series of pleas interspersed with divine vocatives. The staccato structure of this final verse communicates deep emotion. These are urgent pleas for God to act now. Daniel cries, **O Lord,** three times in appealing for God to **listen, forgive, hear and act** (v 19). Then he addresses God as **my God** to make it more personal and urges **do not delay.** The fourfold use of the second person personal pronoun accentuates one final time a primary motive for responding to this prayer. It is for the **sake** of God's honor that something must be done.

3. Arrival of a Heavenly Messenger (9:20-23)

■ **20** The prayer of confession attains one of its primary objectives. God responds. A heavenly messenger arrives (vv 20-21) and introduces God's answer to the prayer (vv 22-23).

Daniel summarizes the two primary components of his prayer. He says, **I was** . . . (1) **confessing my sin and the sin of my people Israel** and (2) **making my request to the LORD my God for his holy hill** (v 20). The use of the personal pronouns in these statements continues to emphasize the perspective of the prayer. Daniel is standing before God as a representative of his people. He might have said "your people" as he did in vv 15, 16, and 19. But this time he calls them **my people** and acknowledges that the people's sin is also his. He identifies fully with them and as such becomes a true intercessor.

The primary concern of his petition has been for God's **holy hill,** that is, the temple mount in Jerusalem. Again, the third person personal pronoun is significant. It reiterates the prayer's emphasis upon God's personal connection to Jerusalem.

■ **21** Though the prayer seems complete as recorded in the book, Daniel suggests that he is not done praying when he is interrupted. An angelic being named **Gabriel,** whom he had met **in the earlier vision** of ch 8 and perhaps ch 7, comes to him (v 21). His appearance is that of a **man,** which agrees with the description given in 8:15. The role of Gabriel in the Bible is to relay divine messages, and he does so here (see comment on 8:15-16). He is described as coming in **swift flight** like a bird, but this does not necessarily imply he has wings.

The encounter takes place at **the time of the evening sacrifice.** Since the temple was not functioning at this time, this is simply a traditional reference to an hour of day, either late afternoon or sundown. Ezra made a prayer of confession at this time as well (Ezra 9:4-5). Perhaps it was a regular time for these kinds of prayers. Psalm 4, the psalm for the evening sacrifice, encourages such prayer.

■ **22** Gabriel identifies his mission as that of providing **insight and understanding** (v 22). These two terms often stand as synonyms for wisdom, but they each convey particular nuances. **Insight** (*haśakîl*) emphasizes knowledge that is carefully considered and well reasoned, while **understanding** (*bîn*) connotes an ability to distinguish clearly between things. These are qualities that Daniel possessed in unusual measure according to stories earlier in the book (1:17). But they only come about because God entrusts them to him (2:20-23). The current passage relates the circumstances surrounding one of those times when Daniel receives the gift for which he became known.

■ **23** Gabriel confirms that God earnestly desires to respond to Daniel's prayer. He tells Daniel that an answer was on the way **as soon as you began to pray** (v 23). While this might suggest that the content of the prayer was in some way unnecessary, it most likely intends to convey eagerness on God's part. This is similar to what God says in Isa 65:24, "Before they call I will answer; while they are still speaking I will hear."

The reason God responds so readily is because Daniel is **highly esteemed** (*hămûdôt*). This description identifies him as one who is treasured, presumably by God as well as others. Daniel apparently pleases God in such a way that the reward of divine audience is given. Throughout the Hebrew Scriptures response to prayer is regularly expected (Pss 17:6; 86:7), and God promises he will answer (Isa 58:9; Jer 33:3). Yet, the response is sometimes delayed, even for the godliest persons (Job 19:7; Ps 22:2). The next vision in the book confirms that even Daniel does not always receive immediate results (see Dan 10:2, 12-14).

Gabriel instructs Daniel to **consider the message** and to **understand the vision** (v 23). This could refer to two different things: (1) **the message** (*dābār*), literally "word," of Jeremiah mentioned in v 2 and (2) **the vision** that is about to be given. One could also read these as parallel expressions referring to the same thing. The challenge, in either case, is to contemplate carefully the meaning of this entire experience. Gabriel has just told Daniel that he would provide "insight and understanding" in the previous verse. But Daniel must give effort as well in order to understand.

4. Message from Heaven (9:24-27)

■ **24** Gabriel's message responds to Daniel's prayer in a way he had not likely anticipated. Though Daniel asked for an immediate end to judgment, Gabriel announces its extension (v 24) and then reveals events that will take place during the extended period of struggle (vv 25-27).

The angel's message exchanges the familiar prosaic language of biblical prayers and narrative for cryptic poetic expressions. Previous terms such as "seventy," "your people," "your city," "sin," "righteousness," "holy," and "desolation" are reused, but with less clarity. Gabriel's use of these words, along with vague statements and new images, promotes the possibility of a variety of interpretations. The entire message is clothed with a mystery that might be expected of a heavenly vision.

Seventy sevens introduces the first enigma of the vision (v 24). In Hebrew **seventy** (*šibĕ ʿîm*) sounds very similar to **sevens** (*šābu ʿîm*), which adds to the poetry and mystery of the vision. **Sevens** is normally translated "weeks" as it is in 10:2-3. The term basically designates a group of seven things, but throughout most of the Hebrew Scriptures it is used in reference to a unit of days. The connection to days, however, is not clearly made in this passage.

The number **seventy** occurs in v 2 of this chapter to designate the number of years Jerusalem would suffer God's judgment. This reference provides a context in which to understand the combination **seventy sevens.** On the basis of this connection and other factors, most scholars understand the phrase to mean "seventy weeks of years" or "seventy times seven years" (see Miller, 1994, 257-58; Hartman and Di Lella, 1978, 244). Accordingly **sevens** is understood as a week of seven years. The total number of years designated, then, is 490.

Many scholars take this number literally, but this does not appear to be the intent of the text. Both the numbers seven and seventy are regularly employed symbolically both within and outside of the Hebrew Scriptures. The expression **seventy sevens** seems to represent an exceptionally long period of undetermined time (see *Behind the Text*). If the number is taken literally, its connections to history remain uncertain. No calculation of dates relative to it has ever satisfied all the elements of the text (see the sidebar "Calculations of Seventy Sevens").

Regardless of one's position on the meaning of the **seventy sevens,** the multiplication of seventy years by seven indicates that the words of Jeremiah are being reinterpreted. The seventy years of Jerusalem's desolation are being extended seven times longer. Instead of ten cycles of sabbatical years, the angel announces ten cycles of Jubilees. Leviticus 26 establishes the principle of extended judgment. In that passage, adversity continues "seven times over" when people do not respond to God's judgment and change their lives (Lev 26:18, 21, 24, 28). Verses 13-14 indicate that this is the posture of the people for whom Daniel prays. They are still guilty of ignoring God's instructions and thus worthy of further judgment.

This new understanding of Jeremiah's word is not merely a human interpretation. It is **decreed** from heaven. God, who is declared as "righteous in everything he does" (v 14), has expressed his will like an ancient monarch. This edict specifically affects those for whom Daniel had just prayed, his **people** and the **holy city** of Jerusalem.

The period of extended judgment allows several things to be accomplished. The six phrases that describe these outcomes can be read as either two sets of three phrases or three sets of two phrases. The first three phrases are each two words long in Hebrew and deal with the issue of sin. The last three phrases are each three words long and promise restoration. Three significant words for sin are used in the first triplet: **transgression** (*pešaʿ*), **sin** (*ḥāṭāʾ*), and **wickedness** (*ʿāwōn*). The last two terms are specifically mentioned in v 5 where **sin** conveys failure and **wickedness** conveys crookedness. The term **transgression** is similar to the word *mārad*, used in v 5. It also expresses the idea of rebellion against authority. **Transgression** has a definite article, which could suggest a specific rebellion is in mind. If so, "the rebellion that causes desolation" in ch 8 is the most immediate connection (8:13). The three words obviously focus upon spiritual deficiencies. Whether or not they describe the people of God or other persons is not made clear. The ambiguity of the vision allows for either interpretation or both.

In contrast to the first triplet, the terms in the second triplet express positive outcomes of God's redemptive work. As in Jeremiah, tearing down leads to building up (Jer 1:10). **Everlasting righteousness, vision and prophecy, and the most holy** are once again restored. God's **righteousness,** the basis of judgment as well as hope in the prayer (vv 7, 14, 16), will be fully manifested in the world. **Vision and prophecy** (literally, "prophet") is best understood as a hendiadys and translated *the prophetic vision.* This has been a primary tool of God's communication with humans according to v 6. **The most holy** (*qōdeš qādāšîm*) identifies that which is especially reserved for God. The phrase could refer to a person and is thus translated in the Vulgate. But it more naturally refers to the temple or a place within it, such as the holy of holies or the altar (see Exod 26:33-34; 29:37).

When the six phrases are read as couplets, additional insights emerge. The infinitive verbs in each of the three couplets parallel one another and thus help to define each other. **Finish** corresponds to **put an end**, **atone** to **bring,** and **seal up** to **anoint.**

The root of the word **to finish** (*lĕkallēʾ*) is debated. If it derives from *kālāh*, then it means "complete" or "accomplish." If the root is *kālāʾ*, however, it would mean "restrain" or "withhold." Its connection to the verb in the second half of the couplet **put an end** (*lĕhātēm*) suggests that the first alternative is correct. The root of this word is also questionable, but both alternatives carry a similar meaning of bringing something to an end. If the root is *tmm*, then it means "cease" or "be consumed." If the root is *htm*, then it means "seal" and would be the same word as "seal up" in the last couplet. The first couplet then describes a time when rebellion against God's authority and failure to meet his standards will come to an end.

The second couplet accentuates the justice of God, just as Daniel's prayer does. **Wickedness** is appropriately dealt with by means of atonement. **Atone** (*kāpar*) means "cover over." In the sacrificial system of Israel it refers to the act of sprinkling blood to symbolize God's dealing with sin. The blood of an animal in some way accomplishes reparation for the sinner. This opens the way **to bring in everlasting righteousness,** a moment when all things align with the purposes of God. It is the time when God, who "is righteous in everything he does," rules (v 14).

The final couplet confirms the consummation of a new order. **To seal up** a prophecy suggests validating the authenticity of the divine word. When it finally comes to fulfillment, the prophetic word is confirmed as true. **To anoint the most holy** implies a similar act of finality. Anointing (*lĕmšōah*) is a ritual of consecration in which oil is placed upon a person or object as a symbol of dedication to God (Exod 40:9, 13; 1 Kgs 1:34). Whether **the most holy** is understood here as a person or a place, the anointing indicates that that which is designated for God is appropriately committed to his service.

The poetic nature of the passage suggests that the author of these words intended both the triplet and couplet groupings to be noticed. As such the six phrases stand as a unified idea with each phrase expressing a different aspect of the same thing. What is being described is a vision of a renewed world. It is a hopeful vision of a time when sin ends and God is acknowledged as sovereign. This is the hope shared by all the prophets of Israel as they looked forward to a resolution to sin both within and at the end of human history (Isa 2:2-4; 13:9-11; Jer 31:31-34; Ezek 7:24; Zech 14:20-21).

It is for just such a world that Daniel so earnestly prays in this chapter. It is also the kind of world Daniel glimpsed in Dan 8. The vocabulary of these six phrases recalls the circumstances surrounding the activity of the little horn and his demise in ch 8 (see *Behind the Text*). Thus ch 9 provides a fuller picture of what the conclusion of "the 2,300 evenings and mornings" will look like.

■ **25** At this point, Gabriel begins to describe specific events that will take place during the period of seventy sevens. The period is divided into three parts: seven sevens, sixty-two sevens, and one seven. The last seven is divided further into half. Both personalities and events are associated with each division. Gabriel admonishes Daniel to **know and understand** (v 25) these things. Similar to the challenge in v 23, the angel wants Daniel to pay attention and wisely consider what is being said.

The ambiguity of the Hebrew text of vv 25-27 has produced a variety of interpretations and translations over the years. There are more options for interpreting these verses than any others within the book (see the sidebar "Calculations of Seventy Sevens"). In spite of such obscurity and varied opinions, a basic message from the angel can be discerned and should not be overlooked. Gabriel affirms (1) a period of restoration for Jerusalem, (2) the coming of a divinely ordained leader, (3) the emergence of an enemy of God's people, (4) an attack on the institutions of God, and (5) the final demise of the enemy. The image of a divinely ordained leader also appears in ch 7. All the other items are familiar from the visions in both chs 7 and 8 and will recur in the final vision of the book in chs 10—12. This portion of Gabriel's message begins with hope (v 25) but moves on to a note of doom (vv 26-27c) before offering one last word of encouragement (v 27d).

The first designated period starts with **the decree to restore and rebuild Jerusalem** (v 25). The exact **decree** (*dābār;* literally, "word") to which this refers is difficult to determine. For those who attempt to calculate specific dates based on 490 years, this starting point is very important. Thus interpreters have offered a number of suggestions, each of which has merit. If 490 years, however, is taken as entirely symbolic, then identifying a precise date for the decree is not so significant. The most natural assumption would be that this **decree** is the one issued shortly after the vision is dated. In 539 B.C. the Persian king Cyrus decreed that the Jews, along with other exiled peoples, could return to their homeland and rebuild their temple (2 Chr 36:23; Ezra 1:2-4). Though it does not specifically mention the rebuilding of Jerusalem, such is implied by the edict. (For other options for this decree, see the sidebar "Calculations of Seventy Sevens.")

Whether or not it is this particular decree or another, the point of the angel's message is that a time of restoration for Jerusalem is announced. In response to Daniel's prayer, the ruined city will be repaired. **Streets and a trench** suggest a well-planned city, secure and functioning. **Streets** (*rĕhôb*) are squares and plazas where people meet and exchange goods. **A trench** (*hārûṣ*) might refer to a dry moat outside the city wall or some other feature, such as a sewer ditch. A city where "the sounds of joy and gladness . . . will be heard once more" seems in view (Jer 33:11, 10). Reconstruction will be challenging, though. It will take place **in times of trouble.** Ezra 4—6 and Neh 4 describe the kinds of opposition that those who rebuilt Jerusalem encountered.

The coming of **the Anointed One . . . the ruler** (*māšiah nāgîd*) marks the end of the first division of the seventy sevens (v 25). The term for this person could also translate as "an anointed prince" (NRSV) or "an anointed leader" (Lucas 2002, 227), since the nouns do not have definite articles. The word **comes** is not in the Hebrew text but does seem implied.

The Anointed One translates the term *māšiah*, which during the intertestamental and NT periods of Judaism became a technical term for a great deliverer envisioned by Israel's prophets. Early Christians identified Jesus as this person and boldly called him "the Christ" (the Greek translation of *māšiah*). The Hebrew Scriptures, however, do not use this term to refer to the "messianic" figure of the prophets. That person is more often called "the branch," "a root," or "my servant." The prophets only use *māšîaḥ* to refer to Cyrus (Isa 45:1) and a king of Judah (Hab 3:13). Most uses of the term in the Hebrew Scriptures refer to one of Israel's kings, particularly Saul or David (for example, 1 Sam 2:10; 12:3; 2 Sam 19:21; Ps 2:2). A few times the high priest is designated "the anointed one" (Lev 4:3, 5, 16) and once prophets are called "anointed ones" (Ps 89:51; 1 Chr 16:22). If **the Anointed One** in this verse refers to the "messianic" figure of the prophets, then it is unique within the Hebrew canon.

Nevertheless, many commentators over the centuries, both Jewish and Christian, have been convinced that **the Anointed One** does refer to the "Messiah" of Judaism. This is why the NIV and NLT capitalize the word **Anointed One.** (KJV and NASB translate "Messiah the Prince.") Christianity has a long tradition of interpreting the term in relation to Jesus, based on a sense that the text is describing events related to both his first and second comings. Some interpreters, however, hold that the anointed one more likely refers to a priest or leader in Judah during the early restoration period. The high priest Joshua and the leader Zerubbabel are often suggested. Cyrus has also been proposed since he is actually called "an anointed one" in Isa 45:1. Regardless of whether Jesus, a person of the restoration, or no specific individual is in mind here, the angel's message remains. The coming of **the Anointed One** announces that a God-ordained leader will once again rise up and guide Israel. There is hope for a new agent of God's grace in this world.

The duration of the initial period between the decree and the coming of the anointed one presents a problem. Many translators understand the Hebrew text to mean it includes only seven sevens (NRSV, ESV). However, other translators, including ancient ones such as Theodotian and Jerome, understand sixty-two sevens to be included within this period. They read the text to say **there will be seven "sevens," and sixty-two "sevens."** So the entire period would be sixty-nine sevens. This would be an unusual way for Hebrew to express this number, though. The punctuation of the MT indicates that the seven sevens and sixty-nine sevens are not intended to be read together but as parts of two different thought units. How one reads these numbers affects calculations of years and events associated with them (see the sidebar "Calculations of Seventy Sevens"). If the numbers are taken symbolically, though, a decision on the reading of this text is less crucial.

■ **26-27** In any case, **after the sixty-two "sevens"**—or a total of sixty-nine sevens—the hopeful picture of a restored Jerusalem with an anointed leader fades. In its place emerges a description of doom for both the leader and the city during the last seven. The first setback comes when **the Anointed One will be cut off and will have nothing** (v 26). The phrase (he) **will have nothing** (*'ên lô*) is difficult in Hebrew. Its relationship to **cut off** (*kārat*), however, seems to suggest **the Anointed One** comes to some kind of end, either death or loss of position. Whether or not this is the same "Anointed One" in v 25 is a matter of debate. Those who identify Jesus as that person believe they are the same. As such, the verse becomes a reference to his crucifixion. Others who see Cyrus, Joshua, or Zerubbabel in v 25 hold that **the Anointed One** in v 26 is a different person. Typically scholars identify him as Onias III, who was removed from the high priesthood and eventually murdered in 171 B.C.

The next event described is the devastation of **the city** of Jerusalem and **the temple.** Its **end will come like a flood** in a time of **war** and **desolations** (v 26). There will be **an end to sacrifice and offering** in the temple and **an abomination that causes desolation** will be set up (v 27). This description recalls the havoc caused by the little horn in 8:11-13 and 23-25. In that context such happenings appeared to be connected to the activities of Antiochus Epiphanes IV in 167 B.C. (see comments on 8:23-25). This ruthless Seleucid ruler forbade sacrifice at the Jewish temple and erected an altar to his god there. The last act was called "the rebellion that causes desolation" (*happeša' šōmēm*, 8:13), a term similar to what is here called **an abomination that causes desolation** (*šiqqûṣîm mēšōmēm*). The phrase occurs again in 11:31 and 12:11 where it also seems to refer to the period of Antiochus IV. It describes an appalling act of sacrilege for the Jews.

On a wing may identify the location of the act, but the term is obscure. It could refer to a portion of the temple complex. The words **of the temple** are not actually in the Hebrew text and are simply supplied by translators. An alternative suggestion is to emend the Hebrew text to read "in their place" (*'al kannam*, instead of *'al kĕnap*) as the NRSV does. Thus the text would be saying that **the abomination** is set up in place of the **sacrifice and offering.**

If Antiochus is the one responsible for such blasphemy, then the altar to his god and the sacrifice offered there is probably in view (see 1 Macc 1:54-59; 2 Macc 6:2-5). If what is being described refers to Christ, then some other events must be associated with this description. Some think it refers to the destruction of Jerusalem by the Romans in A.D. 70. Others, however, believe these events are yet to occur toward the end of human history.

The people of the ruler who will come are responsible for this blasphemous deed. Who **the people** are depends upon who **the ruler** is. Again the text is vague. **The ruler who will come** could refer to **the Anointed One** who is also called "the ruler" in v 25 or to a new personality in the story. Most scholars believe it is the latter, since this person seems to be the subject of the destructive actions that take place in the remaining verses. By contrast, "the Anointed One" in v 25 is associated with the rebuilding of Jerusalem.

According to Gabriel, **the ruler** will do three things: (1) **confirm a covenant with many,** (2) **put an end to sacrifice and offering,** and (3) **set up**

9:26-27

an abomination that causes desolation. Confirming **a covenant** could be positive. But since the last two actions are clearly negative, the first must be as well. This could be some kind of clandestine pack that serves to undermine the stability of the city and temple. While all three actions take place throughout the final period of sevens, the covenant is made during the first half of this time. The other two attacks against the temple come **in the middle of the "seven."** Half of seven is three and a half, which recalls references to "time, times and half a time" in other visions (7:25 and 12:7).

Based on the profile of **the ruler** given in the text, many scholars have identified Antiochus IV as this person. Some have proposed Jason, the successor to Onias III as high priest, but he does not seem to fulfill all that is credited to this despot. The **covenant with many,** in this setting, could refer to deals that were struck with Jerusalem's elite during the time of Antiochus IV (see 1 Macc 1:11). If the details of this passage refer to events of NT history, however, then the ruler must be a Roman leader, perhaps an emperor or general such as Titus who destroyed Jerusalem. The covenant, in this case, could be taken positively as the new covenant that Christ instituted by his death (Matt 26:28). If the setting for these verses is the end of human history, however, "the ruler" is the antichrist of that era and "the covenant" could refer to some sort of deceptive agreement that advances the cause of evil (see Rev 13:16-17).

Accordingly, the three options for "the ruler" provide the basis for three options for **the people of the ruler** who are responsible for the devastation of Jerusalem. These could be the Syrians, the Romans, or those that follow the antichrist. It is possible to equate **the people** with **the many** who make a covenant with the ruler. Thus they would be those who work in complicity with the evil ruler's plans.

The concluding clause of the angel's message returns to the hope with which it begins. It projects finality for evil, using the same or similar root as found in v 24. There the angel proclaims a time to "finish transgression," while v 27 proclaims **the end** of the wicked ruler. Just as heaven **decreed** the completion of Israel's judgment (v 24), the restoration of Jerusalem (v 25), and its desolation (v 26), so also the ruler's demise is pronounced (v 27). Using another image of rushing water, the angel describes the ruler's end. In the same manner that he caused Jerusalem's suffering to come "like a flood" (v 26), so also judgment would be **poured out** (*nātak*) like water upon him. This is the same treatment God's people received for their sin. In v 11 God "poured out" (*nātak*) his judgments upon them.

The final three words of the angel's message literally translate *upon the desolator.* The ruler is identified as "the one who desolates" (*šōmēm*). It is an appropriate title that marks him in reference to his most heinous act, "the abomination that causes desolation." Whether this ruler is Antiochus IV of the second century B.C., the antichrist at the end of the age, or a tyrant of another era, the final words of the vision encourage the reader. Evil eventually ends.

Calculations of Seventy Sevens

Many calculations of the seventy sevens have been offered by interpreters over the years. Each theory attempts to fit all elements of the text into a chronological scheme. However, none has been entirely successful in this endeavor.

The reason so many options exist is the result of several factors. These include: (1) whether the numbers are taken literally or symbolically, (2) whether a calendar of 360 or 365 days per year is adopted, (3) whether the hope in v 24 is viewed as eschatological or historical, and (4) whether key phrases in the text are translated one way or another. Some of the key phrases in dispute are: (1) the time of "the decree to restore and rebuild Jerusalem" (v 25), (2) the identity of "the Anointed One" (vv 25 and 26), (3) the punctuation between "seven sevens and sixty-two sevens" (v 25), and (4) the identity of "the ruler" (v 26). Other minor translation problems are less significant.

Two major groups of theories have emerged: (1) those that associate the vision with the Messiah of Israel and (2) those that associate it with Antiochus IV. Within each group numerous variations exist.

The most predominant "Messiah" interpretations begin from one of three points: (1) the Cyrus decree in 539 B.C. (2 Chr 36:22-23; Ezra 1:1-4), (2) the Artaxerxes decree to Ezra in 458 B.C. (Ezra 7:12-26), or (3) the directive from Artaxerxes to Nehemiah in 445 B.C. (Neh 2:5-8).

Those who begin with the Cyrus decree believe the seventy sevens are essentially symbolic for either the 608 years leading up to the destruction of the temple in A.D. 70 or an undetermined amount of time before the second coming of Jesus (Young 1949, 202-21). The seven sevens represent the 94 years from 539 to 445 B.C. when Nehemiah rebuilt Jerusalem's walls. The sixty sevens signify the 475 years from 445 B.C. to A.D. 30 when Christ was crucified. The final seven designates the 40 years till A.D. 70 when the Romans destroyed Jerusalem or the period of time that extends until the second coming of Jesus.

Starting from the decree of Artaxerxes to Ezra allows for more literal calculations, but not entirely. In this scenario seventy sevens signifies the time from the decree in 458 B.C. till the second coming of Christ (Archer 1985, 113-19; Miller 1994, 257). The initial seven sevens are the 49 years from 458 to 409 B.C. when the rebuilding of Jerusalem under Ezra and Nehemiah was completed. The sixty-nine sevens is the exact number of years (483) from the decree in 458 B.C. to the beginning of Jesus' public ministry in A.D. 27. After the sixty-two sevens— about three and a half years later—Christ was crucified in A.D. 30. At this point a gap of undetermined duration ensues until the final seven years occur just before Christ returns. An alternative understanding of the final seven years is that they represent the period from A.D. 27 to A.D. 34, which ends with the stoning of Stephen and the conversion of Paul (Shea 2005, 160; Doukhan 2000, 142-52).

235

Beginning with the directive of Artaxerxes to Nehemiah in 445 B.C. (Neh 2:5-8) it is also possible to see both the first and second advents of Christ referenced (Walvoord 1971, 216-37). This theory uses a calendar of 360 days per year rather than 365 days. The seven sevens identifies the period of rebuilding Jerusalem that is initiated under Nehemiah. Sixty-nine sevens is the time from the Artaxerxes proclamation till either the triumphal entry or the crucifixion of Jesus. Following this an indeterminate gap transpires until the final seven years arrive, which lead up to the second coming.

The major "Antiochus" interpretations begin from various starting points as well. These include beginning with: (1) Jeremiah's word in 605 B.C. (Jer 25:12), (2) Jeremiah's word in 597 or 594 B.C. (Jer 29:10), or (3) Jeremiah's word in 587 B.C. (Jer 30:18-22; 31:38-40).

A fairly literal interpretation of years can be calculated between Jeremiah's prophecy in 605 B.C. and the rededication of the temple in 164 B.C. (Behrmann 1894, 63-66). Seven sevens or 49 years transpire from the prophecy in 605 B.C. to the accession of Cyrus in 556 B.C. Sixty-two sevens or 434 years elapse if one begins counting from 605 B.C. again and goes to the death of Onias III in 171 B.C. Thus the sixty-two sevens overlap with the seven sevens in this scenario. The final seven is the period from the death of Onias till the dedication of the temple in 164 B.C. About halfway through this final seven years, in 167 B.C., Antiochus suspended regular Jewish sacrifice and set up an altar in the Jerusalem temple courts.

Those who begin with Jeremiah's word in 597 or 594 B.C. (Jer 29:10) understand the numbers mostly as symbolic (Hartman and Di Lella, 1978, 250). As such seventy sevens approximates the 430 years from Jeremiah's prophecy till the death of Antiochus IV in 164 B.C. Seven sevens could represent the fifty plus years from either 597 or 594 B.C. until the return of the high priest Joshua in 538 B.C. Sixty-two sevens represent the 367 years from 538 B.C. to the death of Onias III in 171 B.C. The final seven is a literal seven years from 171 B.C. till the death of Antiochus in 164 B.C.

If one begins calculating from Jeremiah's prophecy in 587 B.C., then the first and last periods of the seventy sevens can be taken almost literally (Russell 1981, 187; Anderson 1984, 114-16). The first period of seven sevens is the 49 years from the fall of Jerusalem in 587 B.C. to the coming of Joshua the high priest in 538 B.C. The last period of sevens would be the seven years from the death of Onias III in 171 B.C. till the cleansing of the temple in 164 B.C. Sixty-two sevens, then, stands as a symbolic number for the intervening 367 years.

FROM THE TEXT

Interpreters of ch 9 can easily become fascinated by the calculations of seventy sevens. Some of the correspondences to historical events are quite remarkable. But the primary intent of the chapter does not seem to be to lay out a detailed blueprint for human history to the end of time, the time of Jesus, or even to the second century B.C. Such things, Jesus said, are not for humans to know (Matt 24:36; Acts 1:7). The purpose of ch 9, rather, is to reaffirm God's sovereign control over his world just as every other portion of the book of Daniel has done.

The particular aspect of God's sovereignty emphasized in this chapter has to do with the expression of God's righteous character in this world. This righteousness is demonstrated in the way God handles the covenant relationship with his people. God always does the right thing, both in extending judgment and in extending mercy. Such righteousness explains why God acts in human history as he does. The flow of human events unfolds in response to the actions of people standing before a righteous God.

God always does what is right for his people. The prayer of ch 9 establishes two foundational points: (1) God is committed to a covenant relationship with his people and (2) God always does the right thing in that relationship. Daniel's God is **the LORD,** the One who **made . . . a name** among the nations when he remembered his covenant with Abraham and rescued his people from Egypt (v 15). He is the God **who keeps his covenant of love with all who love him and obey his commands** (v 4). This is sometimes called faithfulness (Deut 7:9; 32:4; Pss 71:22; 89:14) because God is true to his commitments.

These points provide the basis for Daniel's request for forgiveness. He acknowledges that God has done right in judging his people. They have sinned and deserve **the curses and sworn judgments written in the Law of Moses** (v 11). But God could also do the right thing by extending mercy. That is part of God's commitment as well. He promised, "I will restore the fortunes of Jacob's tents and have compassion on his dwellings" (Jer 30:18). The history of God with his people has proven God to be **merciful and forgiving** (v 9; see Neh 9:17, 19, 27, 31).

Mercy is another side of God's righteousness. Judgment is one side and mercy is the other. When God judges he is doing the right thing. When he shows compassion he is right as well. Mercy is the only way the covenant bond can be restored. As the prayer affirms, restoration cannot depend upon human righteousness. Only God's **great mercy** can make it happen (v 18).

The righteousness of God, expressed both in judgment and mercy, explains the patterns of human history. They unfold consistent with God's righteous character. Gabriel proclaims that time is needed **to finish transgression,** before God will **bring in everlasting righteousness** (v 24). During that time people will see Jerusalem struggling to restore itself, anointed leaders of God's people arise and be cut off, opposition from evil persons who attack God's sovereignty, and finally judgment for God's enemy (vv 25-27). All this will take place because God responds in the right way to the actions of humans.

Thus, human history unfolds by means of interaction between God and human beings. The vision presents a scheme of history that could suggest a predetermined world. Many devout and competent interpreters have understood the text in this way. Three periods within an era of seventy sevens are outlined. Events and personalities arise in connection with each period appearing to be predestined for a moment in time. It would seem that if one could identify each person and event precisely, then key junctures in human history would be known.

But the text is ambiguous at every turn, and precision eludes even the best interpreters. A multitude of proposals offered over the centuries stand as a monument to the obscure character of the vision. Such ambiguity, however, could be a clue to understanding the text. Its vagueness may be intentional in order to steer readers away from setting dates and marking history. It may also intend to allow the reapplication of its message to a variety of settings.

Both the prayer and the vision guard against a fatalistic view of the world in which things are preprogrammed. Four particular features of the text affirm that human actions affect history:

(1) The prayer confesses that the desolation of Jerusalem resulted from human decisions. Daniel admits his people willfully breached the covenant with God. Though they had been warned by the prophets, and were thus culpable, they **rebelled** and **turned away** from God's **commands and laws** (v 5). In response God rightly **poured out** his judgments upon the people (v 11). The exile was no accident or predetermined event of history. It came about because of choices people made.

(2) The prayer also confirms that God can reverse judgment at will. The entire appeal of the prayer is based upon this belief. Daniel believes God can **turn away** his **wrath** (v 16) and **forgive** (v 19). God can extend **great mercy** (v 18) and change the course of events in Jerusalem. Such conviction is based upon solid biblical tradition of the Exodus, when God brought his people **out of Egypt with a mighty hand** (v 15). So Daniel pleads with God to act, not in vain desperation but with confident expectation.

(3) God's response to Daniel's prayer further illustrates the impact of human efforts. "The prayer of a righteous man is . . . effective" (Jas 5:16). Even before Daniel finishes his prayer, God responds. In fact, he is told, **as soon as you began to pray, an answer was given** (v 23). Daniel experiences the fulfillment of God's word through Jeremiah, "You will seek me and find me when you seek me with all your heart" (Jer 29:13).

(4) Finally, the content of the vision solidifies the significance of human action or inaction. The vision announces an adjustment to God's previous announcement of the seventy years for exile. The time is extended seven times longer in accordance with guidelines laid out in Lev 26. The contingency states, "If in spite of this you still do not listen to me but continue to be hostile toward me, then in my anger I will be hostile toward you, and I myself will punish you for your sins seven times over" (Lev 26:27-28). The prayer confess-

es that the people were indeed still hostile toward God. Therefore, in response to the people's lack of response, the period of judgment is lengthened seventy times seven. Additional time is needed **to finish transgression** and **to put an end to sin** of the people (v 24).

This presentation of God's sovereignty makes an important contribution to the book of Daniel. The visions, as well as the stories, have emphasized a dominating divine hand that overrules all earthly powers. One might conclude that there is no room for human response and that God's people are mere pawns among the powers of this world. But ch 9 asserts that human decisions do make a difference. Wicked despots are not the only reason God's people suffer. Neither **the ruler** of ch 9, Nebuchadnezzar of chs 1—4, Belshazzar of ch 5, Darius of ch 6, the little horn of ch 7, the stern-faced king of ch 8, nor the contemptible person of ch 11 is solely to blame. All of these God can overrule. Though they do wreak havoc in this world, ch 9 reminds the reader that breaking covenant with God unleashes suffering as well. Thus God's people are not allowed to think they are simply victims of evil forces. They are also responsible for the movements of human history.

Throughout the history of Christianity the vision of seventy sevens has been connected to the advent of Jesus and the end of human history. While such exegesis might be debated, the application cannot. From the perspective of this commentary, the setting of Antiochus IV's reign of terror in the second century B.C. seems most fitting for the text. Connections with chs 8 and 10—12 and the nature of other allusions in the text appear to make this the most likely focus of the vision. It seems that God is sending a message to people of that horrific era, assuring them that their afflictions are within the scope of a divine plan. The vision explains the struggles of the postexilic age and particularly of the time of Antiochus IV's persecution. They are living in a period of "extended exile." Not only an evil despot, but also sin in the community, is responsible for their suffering. Yet, the message says, this, too, shall pass. God will bridle the evil one. He will **bring in everlasting righteousness,** . . . **seal up vision and prophecy,** and **anoint the most holy** (v 24).

This focus upon the second-century B.C. crisis should not thwart reapplication of this passage to the time of Jesus and beyond, however. Though Joshua and Onias III may have been the original anointed ones of the text, Jesus fulfills that role to an even greater degree. He was "the Christ of God" (Luke 9:20). He entered the world during a time when Jerusalem and the temple were being built to new levels of grandeur and offered hope to the city. But he, too, was cut off and evil rulers rose up to challenge God's sovereignty and destroy the city. In Jesus prophecy was validated and his kingdom initiated all the glorious outcomes to be accomplished during the seventy sevens (v 24; see Duguid 2008, 171-72).

One might expect a similar pattern of events as human history draws to a close, whenever that may be. The NT predicts a time of intense conflict before Jesus returns (Matt 24:4-31; Rev 8—19). It even envisions another "abomination that causes desolation" (Matt 24:15). At this time God will **put an end to sin** for all time and once and for all set up a kingdom of **everlasting righteousness** (v 24; Rev 20—22).

Daniel 9 sketches this pattern of human conflict: restoration and destruction, anointed leaders and wicked rulers, and finally the termination of evil. It asserts that the choices people make play an important role in how these events will unfold. Nevertheless, God remains sovereign over all that happens and orchestrates his final plan as he sees fit.

D. Vision of a Great War (10:1—12:13)

Overview

The last three chapters of the book contain the final vision of the book. It focuses even more sharply upon the time of intense affliction, "a great war" (10:1), already spoken about in the previous two visions. Several features heighten its dramatic effect and make it an apt conclusion for the book. Bringing together a number of key elements in Daniel, the vision accentuates one more time the absolute rule of God over this world and underscores the significance of that sovereignty for God's faithful.

This fourth vision report is the longest by far, consisting of seventy-nine verses. It divides into three major sections: the vision setting (10:1—11:1), the vision message (11:2—12:4), and final clarifications (12:5-13). To better manage the lengthy material, we will consider each section of the vision separately. However, each portion of the vision must be interpreted in relation to the whole. Though extremely long, the vision remains one unit.

1. Vision Setting (10:1—11:1)

BEHIND THE TEXT

The final vision of Daniel functions as a fitting conclusion to the second half of Daniel as well as the book as a whole. It reconnects with other sections in a variety of ways in order to bring closure. The opening verses of ch 10 recall ch 1 to form a literary inclusion for the entire book. They speak of **the third year of Cyrus, Belteshazzar,** and **choice food** (10:1-3). **The third year of Cyrus** echoes back to "the third year of Nebuchadnezzar" (1:1) and "the first year of Cyrus" (1:21), which mark the limits of ch 1. Daniel's Babylonian name, **Belteshazzar,** along with its significance, was first given in 1:6, and **choice food** was the focal challenge of ch 1.

Reference to **the third year of Cyrus** also accentuates the unity of the four visions in chs 7—12. It completes the alternating pattern of historical notes in these visions, creating a sense of symmetry among them. The first and third visions take place in "the first year" of a king, while the second and fourth occur in "the third year." Notation of **the first year of Darius** in 11:1 highlights this cycle by reversing the order. The cycle of one-then-three becomes three-then-one in the final vision report. This notation not only brings readers back to ch 9 but also leads them to ch 7.

Other points of interrelationship between the final four visions of the book have been discussed previously (see *Behind the Text* in ch 8). Chapter 7 presents a broad sweep of history, while chs 8—12 deal with particular kingdoms within that scheme. The three visions of chs 8—12 come to focus upon a period of intense upheaval culminating in a horrific act called "the abomination that causes desolation" (8:14; 9:27; 11:31).

The content of this final vision parallels that of ch 8 in several ways. Both sketch a history of Greek kingdoms replacing Persian kingdoms. They allude to the strength of Persia, the rise of Alexander the Great, the breakup of his empire into four kingdoms, and the development of an oppressive Seleucid domain under the rule of Antiochus IV. Both visions mention Persia and Greece by name.

The form of the vision report in chs 10—12 follows more closely that of ch 9, however, than either chs 7 or 8. The genre of chs 7 and 8 may be distinguished as symbolic vision whereas that of chs 9 and 10—12 might be labeled epiphany vision. The first involves fantastic images that require angelic interpretation. The latter includes no such images but rather a direct revelation from a heavenly messenger. The epiphany vision is also characterized by extended description of the context for the vision, which includes supplication, appearance of an angel, and words of assurance. While all visions provide some notation about the setting in which the vision comes, this feature is more elaborate in this genre. (For further observations on this genre, see Lucas 2002, 31-36.)

The two specific dates mentioned in the text establish a historical setting in which to hear the vision. These dates are **the third year of Cyrus** (10:1) and **the first year of Darius** (11:1). These dates form an inclusion for the first section of the vision report (10:1—11:1) and mark it as a distinct unit. The first date identifies the year the vision was received, which was 536 B.C. The book of Ezra describes this as a time when the Jewish exiles began returning to Judah. The decree of Cyrus in 539 B.C., a date that corresponds to **the first year of Darius,** authorized those the Babylonians had displaced to return to their homelands and rebuild them. The Jewish version of this policy is found in 2 Chr 36:23 and Ezra 1:2-4 (see the heading "Original Audience" in the Introduction). The Persians apparently intended to establish loyal subjects and a more thriving economy by encouraging local development and identity.

The relevance of these dates to the content of the vision is significant. Readers acquainted with the Hebrew Scriptures recognize this time as one of great hope. Based on the words of Isa 40—66; Jer 30—33; Ezek 40—48; and others, expectations regarding the restoration of Judah and Jerusalem ran high. Isaiah and Jeremiah, in particular, envisioned this as a day of "new exodus" modeled on the pattern of the deliverance from Egypt (Isa 43:14-21; 52:1-12; Jer 31:1-14, 31-34). Perhaps this is why Daniel's vision comes just after the traditional time for celebrating the Exodus, **on the twenty-fourth day** of Nisan (10:4). The Passover and the Feast of Unleavened Bread begin on the fourteenth of Nisan and end on the twenty-first.

The books of Ezra, Haggai, and Nehemiah, however, reveal the harsh realities of restoration. Renewal envisioned by the prophets did not transpire to the measure expected. The restoration was difficult politically, economically, and spiritually. The message of Dan 10—12 confirms the arduous experience of Jews during the restoration. It describes this period as one of intense struggle with world powers still oppressing God's people. Beginning with Cyrus the vision moves through a series of monarchs toward one who causes unprecedented turmoil and hardship for the Jews. Its message of continual conflict helps explain why the hopes of returning exiles were not fully realized.

The reference to **the third year of Cyrus** might appear to conflict with 1:21, which says that Daniel served in the royal court "until the first year of King Cyrus." This could be an indication of a lack of attention to historical detail. However, the text in ch 1 could just as well be speaking of Daniel's role in the Babylonian court. It did end with the demise of the Babylonian empire and the beginning of his service in the Persian court.

Daniel's encounter with heavenly beings in this final vision builds upon previous references to angels in the book and assumes understandings current in the ancient world. Angels take on different roles throughout the book. They serve as protectors of God's faithful (3:25, 28; 6:22), messengers of judgment (4:13-17), interpreters of dreams (7:16-27; 8:13-26), and communicators of divine messages (9:21-27). In chs 10—12, their interaction with Daniel becomes even more pronounced than elsewhere in the book. Extended descriptions of angelic encounters occur both before and after the divine message in 11:2—12:4. Similar to 9:20-27, these experiences include notations of the angel's appearance, Daniel's response, and the dialogue between them. These are regular features in both Jewish and Christian apocalypses (see, for example, 2 Bar. 55 and Rev 7). Within the Hebrew canon Zechariah and Ezekiel also have comparable experiences (Ezek 37; Zech 1).

According to the Hebrew Scriptures angels are heavenly beings that do God's bidding (Ps 103:20). They surround the throne of God, along with the rest of the heavenly host, and offer praise (1 Kgs 22:19; Ps 148:2). Their roles on earth include conveying messages from God (Gen 31:11-13), executing judgment (2 Sam 24:16), protecting humans (Ps 91:11-12), and fighting for God's people (Exod 33:2). Noncanonical, rabbinic, Qumran, and NT writings all agree with this portrait and elaborate further upon it.

Angels are typically portrayed as human in appearance. At times their heavenly origins are not even recognizable at first (Judg 13:21). This distinguishes them from cherubim and seraphim that have features other than human, such as wings. Ezekiel describes the cherubim he saw as having four faces and eyes all over (Ezek 1:4-24; 10:1-22). They are said to guard the tree of life (Gen 3:24) and to transport God on his throne (2 Sam 22:11; Ezek 10:1-22). Isaiah's description of seraphim identifies them as winged creatures hovering over the throne of God, giving praise to God and conveying divine forgiveness (Isa 6:2-7).

Several references in Dan 10—12 indicate that some angels serve as heavenly counterparts to earthly kingdoms. The designation of two angels as **the prince Persia** and **the prince of Greece** suggest this (10:13, 20). Michael's role as protector of the Jewish people also underscores the idea (10:21; 12:1). The concept that angels have special attachments to earthly entities relates to the ancient concept of patron deities for nations. Marduk, for example, was Babylon's primary protector and lord. Within the Hebrew Scriptures the idea of patron angels is vaguely referenced in some passages outside of Daniel. Isaiah 24:21-23 speaks of the hosts of heaven punished alongside kings of the earth, and Ps 82 could be interpreted this way as well. Deuteronomy 32:8-9 may support the concept as well. Otherwise the Hebrew Scriptures certainly confirm heaven's involvement in earthly activities, especially battles. God is the divine warrior who commands the armies of heaven (Isa 42:13). His engagement in war, or lack of it, matters. God and his heavenly hosts can fight for or against his people (Exod 14:14, 24-25; 15:1-10; 1 Sam 4:3; 17:45-47).

The text begins with an introduction to the circumstances of Daniel (10:1-4) before describing the arrival of a heavenly being (10:5-9). A dialogue with the heavenly being follows (10:10—11:1) and prepares Daniel for the extended message to come.

IN THE TEXT

a. Circumstances of Daniel (10:1-4)

■ 1 The introduction to the setting for the vision identifies the circumstances Daniel finds himself in when the vision comes. It notes a very specific time and location as well as Daniel's spiritual condition.

Like all other visions in the book, this one begins with reference to a king's reign. **The third year of Cyrus** was 536 B.C., which marks the beginning of the restoration period in Judah (v 1). At this time Jewish exiles were returning to their homeland with grand hopes of renewal (Ezra 1). The message of the vision in Dan 11:2—12:4, however, warns that this will be a time of continual conflict rather than peace and prosperity. Reference to Daniel's Babylonian name, **Belteshazzar,** may foreshadow this disappointing outlook of continued captivity.

At this juncture in history **a revelation was given to Daniel.** This phrase can literally translate as *a word was revealed to Daniel.* The term *revealed* (*niglāh*) means "to uncover something" such as the eyes or a secret. Its passive form implies a divine hand at work. For this reason the vision may be taken as reliable, just as the vision in ch 8 was (8:26). God only utters what is **true.**

A great war seems to summarize the basic content of the vision. The angel's message given in 11:2-45 describes a long period of "great conflict" (NRSV) during the reigns of Persian and Greek kings. Particularly noted is the severe crisis of the Maccabean Revolt in 11:30-35. In this case the term **war** (*ṣābā'*) could also be a veiled allusion to Isa 40:2, where it refers to the period of exile as "hard service." Perhaps, like the vision in ch 9, the events of 11:2—12:4 are being viewed as an extended exile.

Some translators, however, suggest that **great war** could be translated "great task" and thus refer to Daniel's struggle to understand the revelation (JPS). This is an important motif of the visions in the book (7:16; 8:15, 27; 9:23) and especially in this final vision. At the end of this vision, Daniel still seems confused and continues to ask questions. He flatly confesses at one point, "I heard, but I did not understand" (12:8). This appears to contradict the next statement in 10:1 that **understanding of the message came to him in a vision.** Yet, this may provide some clarification regarding Daniel's comprehension of the vision. The statement may be interpreted to mean that Daniel gained new insight but did not fully grasp all that was said.

The opening verse is written in third person like the introduction to the vision in ch 7. This feature does not necessarily suggest a contributor other than Daniel, though it may. It can simply be a literary device employed to intensify the significance of the vision by having another voice set up the first person account of Daniel. This feature also connects this final vision with ch 7 and signals a conclusion to the vision section of the book.

■ **2-3** Daniel begins his first person testimony of events by identifying his personal circumstances **at that time,** that is, the time just prior to receiving the vision. **For three weeks** he had humbled himself before God (v 2). Three days of seeking God intensely would be normal (Exod 19:15; Esth 4:16). But Daniel multiplied that time by seven. During this period he had fasted, taking **no choice food,** and left off normal body grooming of applying fragrant **lotion.**

These actions, along with reference to mourning, indicate that Daniel was repenting as he did in ch 9 just before receiving a vision. In 10:12 the angel says, "You set your mind to gain understanding and to humble yourself before your God." The reason he had been doing this is not made explicit. One could assume a similar sense of concern for the state of his people like that expressed in ch 9. Perhaps rapidly changing events of a new empire and returning exiles provoked his actions. Some have suggested that news of opposition to the rebuilding of Jerusalem had already reached him (see Ezra 4—6).

■ **4** The vision came **on the twenty-fourth day of the first month** (v 4). This indicates that Daniel had been fasting during a time ordinarily reserved for celebration and feasting. **The first month** is Nisan, which is in March or April on modern calendars. Passover begins on the fourteenth of the month and the Feast of Unleavened Bread lasts through the twenty-first. These annual holy days celebrate Israel's deliverance from Egypt. They are some of the most significant days in the Jewish calendar. As part of the Passover meal participants pass portions of the Passover lamb and cups of wine. But neither of these touched Daniel's lips (see v 3).

Daniel identifies his location as **standing on the bank of the great river, the Tigris.** That Daniel was standing near the Tigris and not the Euphrates places him away from Babylon. The Euphrates ran beside Babylon, but the Tigris, located about forty miles east of Babylon, was more significant for the heart of the Persian Empire. One of the great cities of the Seleucid Empire, Seleucia, was located on the Tigris. The reference to a river recalls the experience of Ezekiel standing on the banks of the Kebar River, where he, too, saw a vision of God (Ezek 1). Daniel's description of the experience that follows displays many parallels in images and language to Ezekiel's.

b. Arrival of a Heavenly Being (10:5-9)

■ **5-6** Daniel's vision begins with the arrival of a spectacular heavenly being. Its appearance is that of an earthly being, **a man** (ʾîš), aflame with fire. It is well dressed in a garment of **linen,** the prized fabric of priests (Exod 28:42), and accessorized with a sash of **finest gold** around its waist. As a whole its body looks like it is made of translucent greenish mineral such as **chrysolite,** or perhaps yellowish topaz. Its **face** and **eyes** glow like **lightning** and **flaming torches.** Its **arms** and **legs** radiate **the gleam** of highly polished **bronze.** When it speaks, its **voice** sounds like the roar of a great crowd.

Nearly every phrase in the description of the heavenly being is paralleled in Ezekiel's portrayal of God and the creatures surrounding him (Ezek 1:7-28). The NT pictures the resurrected Christ in the similar terms (Rev 1:13-15). This raises the question of whether Daniel is seeing an angel or God. Most scholars believe it is an angel based on the conversation that follows. Some, however, think it must be God, even the preincarnate Christ, since its appear-

245

ance is so extraordinary (Miller 1994, 281-82). In this case the angel of v 10 and following would need to be a different being. The text, however, does not clearly indicate that another being is present.

■ **7-9** At this point the reader discovers that some **men,** perhaps his entourage, are present with Daniel. They **did not see** the vision, but whatever they experienced terrified them so much that **they fled and hid themselves.** So Daniel is **left alone,** transfixed upon **this great vision** before him.

The impression of the heavenly being is overwhelming. It exudes the very essence of majestic holiness of the divine world. Therefore, Daniel responds to this vision as he has to others (7:28; 8:17-18, 27) and like so many who encounter the divine in Scripture (Josh 5:14; Ezek 1:28). This spectacular spiritual experience has dramatic physical affects. Daniel's **strength** is drained from him and his countenance disfigured. The **deep sleep** that comes upon him recalls the experiences of Adam (Gen 2:21) and Abraham (Gen 15:12), who had similar divinely induced sleep. Falling **face to the ground** is characteristic of those expressing profound reverence for a king (2 Sam 14:4) or for God (1 Kgs 18:39). The picture is that of one who has become utterly **helpless** before an overwhelming presence.

The extensive description of Daniel's response to the heavenly being, along with the comment on the terror of those with him, serves to heighten the magnitude of the revelation. The dramatic encounter portends a significant announcement. The dialogue that follows raises more expectations. It builds further suspense by delaying the primary revelation from heaven.

c. Dialogue with the Heavenly Being (10:10—11:1)

■ **10** Through touch and words the angel prepares Daniel for the revelation. Both impart strength to Daniel and provide explanation of the angel's mission. Three cycles of touch and words structure the unit. The first explains the angel's purposes and where he has been (10:10-15). The second enables Daniel to express his feelings (vv 16-17). The third confirms the angel's mission once again, but this time projects where he is going (v 18—11:1).

A number of elements in this dialogue recall the angel's response to Daniel's prayer in 9:22-23. The notation on Daniel's character, the challenge to contemplate the vision, and God's eagerness to respond to prayer recur here.

The restoration of Daniel is gradual. A touch from **a hand** of the angel imparts a level of strength (10:10). He rises to the position of an animal on his **hands and knees.** Then words from the angel enable Daniel to stand to his feet as a man (v 11) and eventually he is able to speak (v 16). The heavenly touch that infuses strength recalls the experiences of Elijah, Isaiah, Jeremiah, and Ezekiel (1 Kgs 19:5, 7; Isa 6:7; Jer 1:9; Ezek 2:2).

■ **11** The angel's words do three things. They encourage, challenge, and instruct Daniel. The angel first reminds Daniel that he is **highly esteemed,** meaning people regard him well, as a person to be treasured (see 9:23). Presumably God makes this value judgment, but others did as well (see 1:20; 2:48; 4:9, 18; 6:3).

Next the angel admonishes Daniel to **consider carefully** the revelation that is about to be given. This is the same challenge he was given in the previous vision (9:23). It entails measured assessment of words. Finally the angel confirms that he is on a mission specifically to Daniel. He has **been sent** as an emissary from God for a particular purpose. That purpose is revealed in the following verses.

■ **12** The angel continues his speech by focusing upon further encouragement and explanation. A common admonition from angels throughout the Bible is **Do not be afraid** (2 Kgs 1:15; Matt 28:5; Luke 1:13, 30; 2:10). It is God's frequent word to his people (Gen 15:1; Deut 31:6, 8; Isa 41:14; Jer 1:8; Ezek 2:6; Matt 14:27). The angel will encourage Daniel again with these words in Dan 10:19.

Perhaps the most encouraging word for Daniel is to know that God hears his prayer. From **the first day** that Daniel undertook his fast, his **words were heard.** Daniel's prayer in ch 9 received a similar response, "As soon as you began to pray, an answer was given" (9:23). Such statements express heaven's intense interest in human affairs.

■ **13** But the angel was **detained** throughout the **twenty-one days** of Daniel's fast. Issues in heaven apparently delayed action on earth. As the angel explains, **the prince of the Persian kingdom resisted me** before **Michael . . . came to help me.** What is being described is a conflict in the heavenly realms. The angel who is speaking to Daniel joined forces with another angel named Michael to engage still another angel who is connected to Persia.

Prince (*śar*) regularly denotes various levels of earthly leaders, often military (Num 21:18; Judg 5:15; 1 Sam 22:2; Ezra 8:24; Ezek 11:1). In this chapter, however, the word is used in reference to heavenly beings, as it is in Josh 5:14. **Michael** is **one of the chief princes** in heaven and, according to 10:21 and 12:1, Israel's patron angel. Extrabiblical traditions agree with this role for Michael and speak of him as one of the top four archangels.

The opponent of Michael and the angel speaking to Daniel is **the prince of the Persian kingdom.** This angel is later simply called "the prince of Persia" in v 20. The association of this angel with Persia indicates that it is a heavenly representative of the earthly entity (see *Behind the Text*). Since Michael and the angel speaking to Daniel oppose this angel, one could assume it is an evil angel. In the NT such beings are called demons (Matt 9:34).

Michael the Archangel

Michael appears by name for the first time in the Bible in Dan 10:13 and 21. Three other times he is specifically identified. In Dan 12:1 his role is that of protector of Israel. Jude 9 calls him an archangel based upon an apocryphal story the author references. In Rev 12:7 Michael is responsible for throwing the dragon out of heaven.

Michael became a popular personality within Jewish and Christian traditions. In noncanonical Jewish literature he is identified as one of the four archangels who stands before God (*1 En.* 20:5). His roles vary from messenger of judgment (*1 En.* 10:11) to mediator of the law to Moses (*Jub.* 1:27). Rabbinic tradition identified him with various Bible passages where unnamed angels appear, such as the one who wrestled with Jacob (Gen 32:24) or the destroyer of the camp of Sennacherib (2 Kgs 19:35). Christians have made similar connections between Michael and Bible stories. They came to honor him as Saint Michael, healer of the sick and patron of warriors, with an annual feast on September 29.

■ **14** The arrival of the angel indicates that he and Michael have been successful in their battle to some degree. The angel can now deliver a divine message. The message concerns **what will happen to your people in the future** (v 14). **In the future** (*bĕ'aḥărît hayyāmîm*) is literally *in the following days.* Throughout the Hebrew Scriptures it is used to refer either to the end of time or to an undesignated time in the future (see 2:28).

Part of the angel's message announces that the Greeks will bring Persian rule to an end (11:2-4). This could be the reason for the heavenly conflict. The angel that defends the interests of the Persian kingdom would not likely want such a message spoken. In biblical thinking, once a word is uttered it is in effect.

■ **15-17** Once again Daniel describes his sense of weakness, which is followed by a strengthening touch and a word. He is bowed in reverence and unable to speak. The **one who looked like a man** (v 16) most naturally refers to the being described in vv 5-6. This seems to indicate that only one heavenly being is involved with Daniel. References to being **speechless** (v 15), touching the **lips** and opening the **mouth** (v 16) recalls experiences of others. Moses, Isaiah, Jeremiah, and Ezekiel all felt the insufficiency of human speech in the presence of the divine (Exod 3:10-12; Isa 6:5-7; Jer 1:6-9; Ezek 3:26-27). They also knew that only God could enable them to speak for him.

This time Daniel, rather than the angel, speaks the word that follows the touch. He expresses his profound sense of inadequacy with emotion-filled words. He is in **anguish, helpless** (Dan 10:16), lacking **strength,** and at a point where he **can hardly breathe.** Appropriately he identifies himself as a **servant** who is unworthy to speak with his superior and identifies the angel as his **lord** (v 17). Such a submissive spirit has been the hallmark of Daniel throughout the book (1:8-13; 2:27-28; 4:19; 6:21).

■ **18-19** One final time the touch and word of the angel strengthen Daniel. The angel admonishes Daniel once again **do not be afraid** and reminds him that he is **highly esteemed** (v 19; see vv 11-12). Then the angel pronounces **peace** upon him and challenges him with a double admonition to **be strong.** Peace is the great Hebrew word *shalom* that wishes wholeness and divine blessing when used as a greeting. The Hebrew term for **strong** (*ḥāzaq*) denotes firmness or hardness, as imaged in the tight grip of the hand. It is the same charge God gave to Joshua (Josh 1:6, 7, 9).

At this point, after three touches and two words of encouragement from the angel, Daniel is ready to hear the content of the message. This ability to hear, though, is not of his making. It only comes because the angel has **given . . . strength** to his body and mind.

■ **10:20—11:1** In response to Daniel's readiness, the angel does not immediately speak the message. He infuses one more dramatic delay by restating his purpose and the concomitant struggle in heaven. The angel's words are arranged in parallel fashion. The question about his purpose in v 20*a* is echoed with an answer in v 21*a*. Information about the struggle of heavenly princes in v 20*b* is expanded in v 21*b*—11:1. The effect of this interweaving is to highlight the connection between heavenly and earthly events.

The angel's question may seem strange since he has already explained in v 14 **why** (v 20) he has come. Yet it challenges listeners, both Daniel and later readers, to be attentive to the message. That message is based on **the Book of Truth** (v 21), which apparently contains details of future events presented in 11:2—12:4. This is the only time such as book is mentioned in the Hebrew Scriptures. It is different from the book of past deeds mentioned in 7:10 but could be comparable to the record of a person's life mentioned in Ps 139:16. In an apocalyptic section of *1 Enoch*, heavenly tablets reveal future history to Enoch (*1 En.* 93:2).

The essential content of the message, from an earthly perspective, is that Persia will end and Greece will ascend. In heavenly terms, the angel will **fight against the prince of Persia** and **the prince of Greece will come.** A cosmic battle apparently lies behind the earthly realities the angel is about to describe. The fact that Michael is designated as **your prince** underscores the angel's connection to Daniel's people (see 12:1). It also suggests that the battle is on behalf of the Jews.

In their struggle, Michael and the angel speaking to Daniel are mutually supportive. Michael's singular support may not be because he is the only one available but because he is the only one needed. The two have worked together from **the first year of Darius,** which is when Babylon fell and Persia began

(5:31). It is also the year Daniel was rescued from the lions' pit (ch 6) and the vision of seventy sevens came (ch 9). This last connection might suggest that the angel who is speaking to Daniel is the divine messenger in that vision. He is identified there as Gabriel (9:21).

FROM THE TEXT

The elaborate introduction to Daniel's final vision prepares readers for a dramatic revelation from God. Within itself, though, the introduction communicates powerful messages. It provides perspective to Daniel and those who find themselves in his circumstances. It gives direction to people whose hopes have been rearranged. A glimpse of the majestic holiness of God and of the spiritual realities behind this world encourages continual participation in the life of God.

A new vision is needed when hope meets harsh reality. In **the third year of Cyrus** (10:1) unrealistic expectations regarding restoration ran high. With the pronouncement of Cyrus authorizing the return of exiles to their homeland, the words of Israel's prophets took on new meaning. Jewish exiles were journeying to Judah in fulfillment of prophetic visions. Through Jeremiah, for example, God had said of the land, "I will bring health and healing to it; I will heal my people and will let them enjoy abundant peace and security. I will bring Judah and Israel back from captivity and will rebuild them as they were before" (Jer 33:6-7).

Reports from the land of Judah were not so glorious, however (Ezra 4—6). The realities of restoration were harsh. At first things went well. The returnees laid the foundation of the temple and began regular worship. Then opposition arose from outside as well as within the community. Resources dwindled and the economy struggled. People eventually became preoccupied with their own survival rather than the things of God (Hag 1:3-11).

When expectations are rearranged, a new vision offers new perspective. Hope must be tempered by reality. The final vision of Daniel does just that. It reveals **what will happen . . . in the future** (Dan 10:14). The battle for planet earth and the invasion of God's kingdom continues. Opposition remains. **The prince of the Persian kingdom** (v 13) stands in the way of the full manifestation of God's kingdom. When he is gone, **the prince of Greece will come** (v 20). The ultimate fulfillment of the words of the prophets is not yet. God has gathered his people and begun restoration. The Creator is once again re-creating creation, but not without struggle. The battle to redeem the world persists, and suffering is inevitable. But before the details of the future unfold, God offers an inspiring glimpse of heaven.

A new vision of the majesty of God infuses fresh perspective into the present. A heavenly being comes to Daniel with a dazzling display of power and purity.

In previous visions it has not been so dramatic. The ones who communicate with Daniel in chs 7, 8, and 9 do not overwhelm him nearly so much. In those visions he is smitten by fantastic images and ideas and by their interpretation. But this time the presence of heaven engulfs him, takes his breath away, and drains his strength. Whether this heavenly being is God or one of his celestial messengers does not matter. The startling epiphany conveys a profound measure of the absolute holy otherness of God.

In this moment Daniel has a genuine encounter with heaven. It is more than a time of learning about God. It is an experience of God. He gains new knowledge and insight into God, himself, and his people. But more than that, he participates in the life of God. Such an experience is profoundly transforming. It goes much deeper than the mind. It penetrates to the heart.

The authenticity of his experience is born out by the humbling weakness Daniel feels. Like Isaiah, Jeremiah, and Ezekiel, he is undone in the presence of God (Isa 6:5; Jer 1:6; Ezek 3:14-15). He is rendered **helpless** and **speechless** (Dan 10:8, 15). There is no pride in having audience with God. Nor is there arrogance over gaining divine knowledge, only utter humility.

The point of this heavenly demonstration is not to crush Daniel but to orient him. The dramatic epiphany poignantly reminds him who is Creator and who is creature. Heaven can handle the present and the future of God's people. God remains in control despite the circumstances of the moment. On the other hand, Daniel is human. He does not possess the power in and of himself to alter events. He is frail, unable to stand, speak, or even hear without the strengthening hand of heaven. In such weakness though, God's "power is made perfect" (2 Cor 12:9). The treasures of God are placed within vessels of clay "to show that this all-surpassing power is from God and not from us" (2 Cor 4:7).

A fresh vision of heaven can encourage those who struggle to trust in times of despair. They can know anew that "the battle is the LORD's" and not theirs alone (1 Sam 17:47). The vision of the heavenly being reconfirms, "The LORD will march out like a mighty man, like a warrior he will stir up his zeal; with a shout he will raise the battle cry and will triumph over his enemies" (Isa 42:13). God has the capacity to affect world events and is doing so even now. This they know because an encounter with God puts it not only in their minds but also within their hearts.

Spiritual realities lie behind physical realities. Daniel's heavenly visitor offers a tantalizing glimpse of another domain where angels fight on behalf of God's people. Those who represent the interests of Judah engage those representing other world powers. Resistance from the prince of Persia is so strong that communication of God's revelation is delayed. But Michael, the patron of the Jews, joins forces with the one who speaks with Daniel. Together they hold back opposing forces and the message is delivered. Thus, two stories are happening at the same time: the story on earth and the story in heaven.

Many scholars accept this picture of angelic conflict as actuality, while others view it more as symbolic of spiritual struggles. In either case, the text confirms that what is seen is not the full story. There is more to this world than the material realities. Spiritual realities impact the course of human events. The story of spiritual conflict is a much larger story than our own and one whose details are only vaguely known. It will outlast and eventually take over the story on earth.

Paul confirms the truth of Dan 10 when he declares, "Our struggle is not against flesh and blood, but against the rulers, against the authorities, against the powers of this dark world and against the spiritual forces of evil in the heavenly realms" (Eph 6:12). This struggle is of great significance, not only because it impacts earthly existence now, but also because it is eternal. As Paul elsewhere asserts, "What is seen is temporary, but what is unseen is eternal" (2 Cor 4:18).

Humans participate in spiritual battles through prayer. The image of battles raging in heaven might suggest that humans have little affect upon world events. The text, however, asserts otherwise. As in ch 9, Daniel's prayer provokes response from heaven. Far from being a bystander on the sidelines of history, Daniel participates in the fray and his engagement makes a difference.

Paul once again agrees with the text of Dan 10. He admonishes believers to "put on the full armor of God, so that when the day of evil comes, you may be able to stand your ground" (Eph 6:13). Then, once equipped, they should "pray in the Spirit on all occasions with all kinds of prayers and requests . . . and always keep on praying" (v 18). The result will be that they will become "more than conquerors through him who loved us" (Rom 8:37). Paul was "convinced that neither death nor life, neither angels nor demons, neither the present nor the future, nor any powers, neither height nor depth, nor anything else in all creation, will be able to separate us from the love of God that is in Christ Jesus our Lord" (vv 38-39). Whatever the origin of the forces that come against his people, God can overrule them. At the same time, people can join God in the battle for this world with one of the most potent weapons on earth, prayer.

2. Vision Message (11:2—12:4)

BEHIND THE TEXT

The heavenly message to Daniel comes in the form of a prophetic survey of history. The angel predicts a succession of kings who will rule Persian and Greek kingdoms and summarizes key features of each reign. Similar material occurs in 8:23-25, where the vision of a ram and goat is interpreted. The kind of detail found in these surveys, particularly in 11:2—12:4, is unique within the Hebrew Scriptures. No other prophetic passages describe a series of future events with such precision. Prophets such as Isaiah and Jeremiah did announce the imminent fortunes of Jerusalem with some exactitude (Isa 37; Jer 32). Joshua even predicted certain details regarding the rebuilding of Jericho over four hundred years before it happened (Josh 6:26; 1 Kgs 16:34). But these projections do not include the kind of particulars nor extended history laid out in Dan 11:2—12:4.

Many Jewish and Christian apocalypses contain material that reflects certain features of this overview of history in Daniel. The so-called historical apocalypses divide history into various periods and describe events associated with each (see *1 En.* 85—90, 93; *2 Bar.* 39—40, 53—76). Yet, while these apocalypses provide some comparisons, they actually bear more affinities to the visions of Dan 2, 7, and 9 than chs 8 and 11.

The closest parallel to the material in 8:23-25 and 11:2—12:4 is found in a collection of materials known as the Akkadian prophecies. Both stylistically and semantically these texts reflect the particular method of presenting history in Daniel (see Lucas 2002, 269-72). The Akkadian prophecies derive from the twelfth to the third centuries B.C. and rehearse history in the form of prophecy up to the time of the author. They identify negative characteristics of early kings in order to commend qualities of a contemporary king. These prophecies are quite accurate since they predict after the fact. Thus they are called pseudoprophecies. Some of the language of these texts can also be associated with Mesopotamia omen texts, which also predict royal events based upon various signs.

If the Akkadian prophecies provide a basic genre for comparing 11:2—12:4, then the form has clearly been given a twist in Daniel. Instead of drawing the history toward a king to admire, the material ends focused upon a vile and unworthy person. Thus the material in Daniel has a surprise ending for this genre.

Based on this literary milieu, many scholars understand the bulk of 11:3—12:4 as pseudoprophecy. In particular, 11:2-39 is viewed this way, while 11:40—12:4 is seen as an attempt at real prophecy (Goldingay 1989, 282-83). They believe 11:2-39 presents history as if it were prophecy. An author from a time toward the end of events mentioned in the material, which would be around the mid-second century B.C., is responsible for it. The genre is employed in order to enhance the message rather than to deceive, they say. The affirmation of God's control over the movements of history encourages people to be faithful.

Other scholars agree that 11:2—12:4 may employ a familiar ancient form but believe it still remains genuine prophecy from the sixth century B.C. (Duguid 2008, 194-95). These are the kinds of materials Daniel would have likely studied, they argue, and reception of a vision in a familiar genre makes sense. The message carries more impact because it takes a turn from the traditional form in the end. These scholars also note that the full effect of this genre relies upon deception. The authority of the gods is enhanced in the Akkadian prophecies because they can predict future events. Such deception seems out of character for the Bible.

The position one takes on pseudoprophecy is connected to one's view on the authorship of Daniel (see discussion in the Introduction). The issue is not necessarily related to liberal versus conservative perspectives on the authority of Scripture. In the final analysis, the effect upon interpretation is either to lessen or enlarge the role of predictive prophecy. The essential theological message of the material remains the same. Whether viewed as real or pseudo-prophecy, the text affirms that God oversees the details of human history.

The era of Persian and Greek Empires forms the primary historical background for this survey of history. It alludes to events from the time of Cyrus the Great (556-530 B.C.) to Antiochus IV (175-164 B.C.). Within this frame, the Ptolemaic and Seleucid Empires receive special attention. This history is well documented in the records of Herodotus, Polybius, Appian, Josephus, and other ancient historians, including the authors of 1 and 2 Maccabees.

The Persian Empire lasted for over two hundred years (539-331 B.C.) guided by a succession of thirteen kings. The most powerful kings among these were Cyrus, Darius I, Xerxes I, and Artaxerxes I. The first to engage the Greeks was Darius I, but his son Xerxes I is best remembered for his near conquest of the Greek mainland in 481-480 B.C.

Persian Kings

Cyrus 539-530 B.C.	Sogdianos 424-423 B.C.
Cambyses 530-522 B.C.	Darius II 423-404 B.C.
Smerdis 522 B.C.	Artaxerxes II 404-358 B.C.
Darius I 522-486 B.C.	Artaxerxes III 358-338 B.C.
Xerxes I 486-465 B.C.	Arses 338-336 B.C.
Artaxerxes I 465-424 B.C.	Darius III 336-331 B.C.
Xerxes II 424 B.C.	

Alexander the Great (331-323 B.C.) ended Persian dominance by 331 B.C. When he died a few years after his rapid conquest, his kingdom fragmented among his successors. The two most dominant kingdoms to emerge were the Ptolemaic and Seleucid Empires. Ptolemy I (323-283 B.C.) took control of the region of Egypt upon Alexander's death and founded the Ptolemaic Empire. Seleucus I (312-280 B.C.) initially laid claim to the region of Babylonia but lost it to Antigonus, the ruler over Asia Minor. With the help of Ptolemy I, he regained the upper hand in 312 B.C. and created the Seleucid Empire. He continued to expand its boundaries until it was the most extensive of the Hellenistic kingdoms.

The Ptolemies and Seleucids competed for control of the Middle East throughout the third and second centuries B.C. The history of these two empires during these centuries is filled with conflict and intrigue. They took turns ascending and descending, invading and being invaded. The vision in Daniel mentions a number of these military conflicts (11:7, 9, 10-13, 15, 18, 25, 29, 40-45). Political maneuvering was another aspect of the history of these empires. Alliances were made through marriage on at least two occasions. One took place when Antiochus II married the daughter of Ptolemy II around 250 B.C. (11:6). The other happened during the reign of Antiochus III and will be mentioned in relationship to his deeds.

The text of Dan 11 mentions all the kings of the Ptolemaic and Seleucid Empires from 323 to 164 B.C. except for one, Antiochus I (280-261 B.C.). Of these kings, the reigns of Antiochus III and Antiochus IV impacted life in Judea more than any others. Appropriately, then, Daniel's vision focuses upon them.

Ptolemaic and Seleucid Kings in Daniel 11

Ptolemy I 323-283 B.C. (v 5)	Seleucus I 312-280 B.C. (v 5)
Ptolemy II 283-246 B.C. (v 6)	Antiochus I 280-261 B.C.
	Antiochus II 261-246 B.C. (v 6)
Ptolemy III 246-221 B.C. (vv 7-9)	Seleucus II 246-226 B.C. (vv 7-9)
Ptolemy IV 221-203 B.C. (vv 10-12)	Seleucus III 226-223 B.C. (v 10)
Ptolemy V 203-181 B.C. (vv 14-17)	Antiochus III 223-187 B.C. (vv 10-19)
	Seleucus IV 187-175 B.C. (v 20)
Ptolemy VI 181-146 B.C. (vv 25-30)	Antiochus IV 175-164 B.C. (vv 21-45)

The text characterizes Antiochus III (223-187 B.C.) as an aggressive monarch engaging in several battles with Egyptians and others. According to ancient historians, he had designs on becoming a new Alexander and achieved a fair amount of success toward reaching that goal. The text of ch 11 alludes to five specific events in his life: (1) his defeat at Raphia in 217 B.C., (2) his success at Sidon in 198 B.C., (3) a marriage alliance formed in 193 B.C., (4) his encounter with the Romans in 190 B.C., and (5) his death in 187 B.C.

As 11:10-11 indicate, Antiochus III undertook an aggressive campaign to reclaim the ancient boundaries of the Seleucids from the Ptolemies. In 219 B.C. he set out on this endeavor and made considerable advances before being stopped by Ptolemy IV at Raphia in 217 B.C. Though Antiochus suffered severe losses in this battle, reportedly seventeen thousand troops, Ptolemy did not take full advantage of his victory and counterattack. It was some time, however, before Antiochus was able to return in full force against Egypt.

Antiochus's success against the Ptolemies finally came over fifteen years after Raphia. As a result the land of Judea fell under his authority. These crucial events for the Jews are portrayed in 11:13-16. Things began in 203 B.C. when Ptolemy IV died under mysterious circumstances and his infant son Ptolemy V became king. The regent Agathocles, who directed the empire on behalf of the young king, created widespread unrest with his oppressive policies. Antiochus III took advantage of these developments and began moving against the weakened Ptolemaic Empire.

By 201 B.C. Antiochus had taken Gaza and laid claim to Judea. Some among the Jews aided Antiochus's efforts to rid the region of Ptolemaic troops. A pro-Seleucid group connected with the powerful Tobiad family in Jerusalem and the high priest, Simon the Just, headed up the insurrection. However, the commander of the Ptolemaic forces took back Jerusalem and punished those who had supported the Seleucids. The tide turned back to the Seleucids at the Battle of Paneas in 199 B.C. The crack troops of the Ptolemaic commander Scopas retreated to Sidon, which finally fell to Antiochus in 198 B.C. With this victory, the region of Palestine, including Judea, was firmly under control of the Seleucid Empire for the first time.

In order to further his influence over the Ptolemaic Empire, Antiochus III offered his daughter, Cleopatra, in marriage to Ptolemy V in 193 B.C. (11:17). This political maneuver did not accomplish its end, though, for Cleopatra proved to be loyal to her husband and the interests of the Ptolemies.

Two major missteps taken by Antiochus III conclude the survey of his career in ch 11. The first was his disregard for the power of Rome. Taking advantage of the weakness of Philip V, he undertook campaigns toward the west in Asia Minor and Macedon. Encouraged by these successes, he moved on to Thrace and Greece despite warnings from Rome to stop. In Greece he met defeat first at Thermopylae in 191 B.C. and then at Magnesia in 190 B.C. As a result Antiochus III had to give up claims to lands he recently acquired in the region and become a vassal of Rome saddled with heavy tribute obligations. In addition, several from his court, including his son Antiochus IV, were retained in Rome in order to assure Seleucid loyalty.

This led to the final and fatal error of his reign (11:19). In order to pay the Roman tribute Antiochus III attempted to plunder the temple of Bel in Elymais in 187 B.C. The local populace rose up in protest and assassinated the king and his accomplices. Thus his career ended in disgrace.

Antiochus IV (175-164 B.C.) receives the most attention of any monarch in Daniel's vision. Over half the vision is dedicated to his career. The text describes his unscrupulous character and violent treatment of the Jews, which is initially conveyed in ch 8 (see *Behind the Text* on ch 8). Additional details in this vision refer to his attempted invasions of Egypt in 169 and 167 B.C. (11:25, 29) as well as political alliances with local Jewish officials (11:23, 30, 32).

The vision focuses upon four key events in the reign of Antiochus IV: (1) the death of Onias III in 171 B.C., (2) his first invasion of Egypt in 170 B.C. and foray into Judea in 169 B.C., (3) his second invasion of Egypt in 168 B.C. and subsequent devastation of Judea in 167 B.C., and (4) his death in 164 B.C.

An allusion to the death of Onias III in 171 B.C. appears to occur in 11:22. Though some scholars believe the phrase **a prince of the covenant** may be an allusion to Egyptian rulers, with good reason many others think it refers to Onias III. Throughout the rest of the vision, **covenant** is always used in reference to the Jews. Further, this is the first in a series of key events that illustrate the animosity of Antiochus IV toward Jews. In addition the visions in chs 8 and 9 may well allude to this event as well (8:11, 25; 9:26).

Background to this incident begins with understanding the position of high priest in Judea. From the time of the Persians the high priest essentially functioned as the local ruler of affairs in Judea. Persian, Ptolemaic, and Seleucid authorities respected, or at least tolerated, the ordering of Jewish life according to Torah as long as other obligations were met.

According to 2 Macc 4, soon after Antiochus IV came to the throne, Jason won the high priesthood of the Jews by bribery and a promise to hellenize Judea. His brother, Onias III, who had held the office since Antiochus III, had been opposed to the influences of Greek culture. In 172 B.C. Menelaus, who was not of the high priest family, outbid Jason and the position went to him. Under the directives of Mosaic law the office of high priest was hereditary, so this was an outrage to conservative Jews. When Onias protested some of Menelaus's clandestine activities, he was forced into hiding and eventually murdered.

The next key event in Antiochus's reign is the first invasion of Egypt in 170 B.C. It is alluded to in Dan 11:25-28. The invasion appears to have taken place as a preemptive strike against Ptolemy VI (181-146 B.C.). With the death of his mother Cleopatra, who was also a sister of Antiochus IV, pro-Seleucid sentiments in the Egyptian court waned. Two influential courtiers, Eulaeus and Lenaeus, advised Ptolemy VI to recover Palestine and southern Syria from the Seleucids. The ill-fated plan met with disaster. Egypt was devastated and Ptolemy VI taken captive. Only the capital, Alexandria, held out against the forces of Antiochus IV.

With their king captured, court officials in Alexandria acclaimed the brother of Ptolemy VI as king. As a result Antiochus IV met with Ptolemy VI to devise a plan to reclaim the throne. Antiochus IV saw opportunity to gain control over Egypt by assisting Ptolemy VI in this endeavor. He set up Ptolemy VI as king in Memphis and returned home after one more failed siege of Alexandria. Within a year Ptolemy VI negotiated a truce with his brother, Ptolemy VII, and the empire remained secure in the hands of the Ptolemies.

During his return to Egypt, Antiochus IV came to Jerusalem and plundered the temple. According to 1 Macc 1:20-28, he stripped the temple of all its gold and costly furnishings. Historians assume he was in need of resources for his kingdom, even though Dan 11:28 said he had just gained great wealth from his success in Egypt.

The third key event of Antiochus's reign is referred to in 11:29-35. This was the second invasion of Egypt in 168 B.C., which set off events that brought about the Maccabean Revolt in 167 B.C. The invasion of Egypt is a relatively short story because the Romans thwarted Antiochus's plans. Under the authority of the Roman Senate, Gaius Popillius Laenas met Antiochus outside Alexandria and ordered him to withdraw. In one of the more dramatic moments of history, he drew a circle in the sand around Antiochus and demanded an answer before he stepped from it. Wisely Antiochus acquiesced and turned his forces back.

A report of insurrection in Judea provided Antiochus opportunity to vent his anger over his humiliation by the Romans and to recover his dignity. According to 2 Macc 5, Jason had heard that Antiochus died and launched an attempt to reclaim the high priesthood from Menelaus. Antiochus arrived in Jerusalem after the revolt had already been handled, but he unleashed his troops upon the populace anyway. He massacred thousands, plundered the temple, occupied the temple precincts with troops, and suspended practice of Jewish laws. His crowning effrontery was setting up an altar to Olympian Zeus in the temple on the fifteenth of Kislev 167 B.C. and renaming it in honor of this god. Jews were forced to participate in pagan worship or pay with their lives (1 Macc 1; 2 Macc 5).

Antiochus's actions toward the Jews precipitated what historians call the Maccabean Revolt. The family of a priest named Matthias initiated the insurrection, which was primarily led by his third son, Judas Maccabeus. The rebels miraculously achieved key victories against overwhelming odds (1 Macc 3:38—4:35). Eventually they regained Jerusalem, reclaimed the temple, cleansed it, and rededicated it to the God of Israel on the twenty-fifth of Kislev 164 B.C. (1 Macc 4:36-59). The sons of Matthias, who were also known as Hasmoneans in honor of their grandfather, continued the fight to free Judea from the Seleucids for several years (see 1 Macc 5—9). By 160 B.C. they had accomplished this task when Jonathan succeeded his brother as leader of Judea. Jonathan eliminated the last major bastion of Seleucids from the area and established the independent state of Judea.

The final event of the reign of Antiochus IV alluded to in Dan 11 is his death (v 45). Precise details of this event vary among the sources (1 Macc 6:1-17; 2 Macc 1:13-17; 2 Macc 9). The essence of the story is that he was in the eastern part of his empire dealing with an invasion of Parthians when he suddenly took ill and died. Most scholars place this in November or December of 164 B.C. just before Judas Maccabeus successfully reclaimed the temple mount in Jerusalem.

The message that the angel delivers to Daniel consists of an uneven presentation of Persian and Greek kings. Four primary units can be distinguished: (1) an overview of the Persian Empire (11:2), (2) the rise and fall of a mighty king (vv 3-4), (3) conflicts between kings of the south and the north (vv 5-20), and (4) the reign of a contemptible person (v 21—12:4). Each unit becomes progressively longer than the first, with the vision coming to focus particularly upon the final king in the list.

No king is identified by name in the vision. However, the details of each allow modern readers, who now live after most of the events have taken place, to determine with fair accuracy the identity of each king. This exegesis will make those connections in order to clarify what is being said since there is very little disagreement by commentators on these identifications, at least up to v 35. From v 36 onward another interpretation is possible and will be noted.

IN THE TEXT

a. Overview of the Persian Empire (11:2)

■ **2** The angel begins the message with one more affirmation of its truthfulness. The opening verse of the report (10:1) had confirmed that it was "true" also. In addition the angel had just informed Daniel that these words came from "the Book of Truth" (v 21). This emphasis on the reliability of the vision affirms its divine origins and increases its value. According to the book of Daniel, all truth derives from God (2:20-23).

In two sweeping sentences the angel sums up the course of the Persian Empire. **Three . . . then a fourth** (11:2) is a style reminiscent of wisdom numerical proverbs (Prov 30:15-33) and also employed by prophets (Amos 1—2). Its effect is to indicate complete coverage. An entire group is wrapped up by three, and even more so by four, the number symbolic of wholeness. Therefore, the four kings mentioned are representative of the twelve that reigned over the two hundred year period from 530 to 331 B.C. following Cyrus.

The four kings in mind may be those who immediately followed Cyrus: Cambyses, Smerdis, Darius I, and Xerxes I (see *Behind the Text*). Darius I brought Persian might to its peak. His son Xerxes I could be considered **far richer than all the others** because of the **power** and **wealth** passed on to him by his father. Darius pushed the empire east toward the Greek city-states, but his son was even more aggressive. Xerxes I did **stir up everyone against the kingdom of Greece** (Dan 11:2). With a fleet of Egyptian, Phoenician, Cypriote, and Ionian ships he subdued the majority of the Grecian peninsula and sacked Athens before being turned back in the Battle of Salamis in 480 B.C.

b. Rise and Fall of a Mighty King (11:3-4)

■ **3-4** A **mighty king** (v 3) whose kingdom comes next is undoubtedly Alexander the Great. He fits the description of one whose **empire will be broken up and parceled out toward the four winds of heaven** (v 4). Through an image of a goat the vision of ch 8 provides more details on Alexander's rapid conquest of Persia, his untimely death, and the demise of his empire (8:5-8). As in ch 8, **the four winds of heaven** (11:4) refer to the four directions on the compass but also allude to the four major kingdoms that emerged from Alexander's empire.

The vast conquests of Alexander did **not go to his descendents** nor did it ever again **have the power he exercised.** Various factions fought over the kingdom, and Alexander's heirs were eventually murdered. The result was smaller and weaker kingdoms.

c. Conflicts Between Kings of the South and North (11:5-20)

■ **5** Two of the kingdoms that derived from Alexander's empire were the Ptolemaic and Seleucid kingdoms. The remainder of the vision focuses upon the kings of these two domains down to Antiochus IV. All but one of the kings from this period is mentioned (see *Behind the Text*). Various events are highlighted in vv 5-20 before Antiochus IV becomes the center of attention in the remainder of the vision.

Throughout these verses **the king of the South** (v 5) refers to a ruler of the Ptolemaic Empire in Egypt. "The king of the North" (v 6) designates a ruler of the Seleucid Empire in Syria and Mesopotamia. The kingdoms are identified as **South** and North on account of their location in reference to Judea.

The first **king of the South** (v 5) mentioned is its founder Ptolemy I (323-283 B.C.). **One of his commanders** who would eventually rule **his own kingdom** was Seleucus I (312-280 B.C.), founder of the Seleucid Empire. While serving under Ptolemy I, Seleucus I gained control of Babylonia in 312 B.C. Over the succeeding years he continued to expand his kingdom until it became the largest and most powerful of the Hellenistic kingdoms. Thus Seleucus I **became even stronger** than Ptolemy I and clashes between the two centers of power was inevitable.

■ **6** After a generation of conflict, the two empires agreed to **become allies** through marriage. In 250 B.C. Ptolemy II (283-246 B.C.) offered his **daughter** Berenice in marriage to Antiochus II (261-246 B.C.). Part of the agreement was that the son of Berenice and Antiochus II would become heir to the Seleucid throne, which effectively brought control of the empire into the family of the Ptolemies. Berenice did **not retain her power** over the Seleucid royal family by this scheme, however. The queen that Antiochus II divorced, Laodice, arranged the deaths of Berenice, her son, and her entire Egyptian entourage. The **power** of Antiochus II did **not last** either. He also died, perhaps by poisoning at the hand of Laodice.

■ **7-9** Retaliation for Laodice's intrigue came from Berenice's **family line** (v 7). Her brother Ptolemy III (246-221 B.C.) rose to **take her place** in the conflict. He mounted a successful attack upon Seleucus II (246-226 B.C.), the son of Laodice who had claimed the throne. He plundered the **fortress** of Antioch much like Nebuchadnezzar had done to Jerusalem (1:2). He carried off to Egypt **their gods, their metal images and their valuable articles of silver and gold** (11:8).

About two years later Seleucus II reciprocated and tried to **invade** Egypt (v 9). But he had to **retreat to his own country** after an unsuccessful campaign.

■ **10-13** The **sons** of Seleucus II who would **prepare for war and assemble a great army** against the Ptolemies were Seleucus III (226-223 B.C.) and Antiochus III (223-187 B.C.) (v 10). The latter of the two was one of the most aggressive and successful kings of the Seleucid Empire. Significantly for the Jews, during his reign Judea fell under his domain. Verses 10-19 are primarily about his exploits.

The armies of Antiochus III began to **sweep like an irresistible flood** into southern Syria and Palestine in 219 B.C. They had tremendous success until the Battle of Raphia in 217 B.C. when Ptolemy IV (221-203 B.C.) checked their advance and soundly **defeated** them (v 11). Ptolemy IV was **filled with pride** over his accomplishment, but he did **not remain triumphant** (v 12). Some fifteen years later, Antiochus III assembled **another army, larger than the first,** by allying himself with the king of Macedon, Philip V (v 13). Over the next several years he began reclaiming areas controlled by the Ptolemaic Empire.

■ **14** Turmoil in the court of the Ptolemies aided the schemes of Antiochus III. **Many** throughout the Ptolemaic Empire rose up **against** the child ruler Ptolemy V (203-181 B.C.). In Judea some **violent men** of the pro-Seleucid party also plotted insurrection, **but without success.** The Egyptian general Scopas punished those who showed opposition to Ptolemaic rule. **The vision** that they fulfill may be the current one or some other prophetic word, such as Ezek 7.

■ **15-16** A decisive battle at Paneas along with the capture of the **fortified city** (v 15) of Sidon brought Antiochus III ultimate victory over Palestine (v 15). Egypt's **best troops,** the special Aeolian mercenaries under the command of Scopas, did **not have the strength to stand** on behalf of Ptolemy V. Thus, by 198 B.C. Antiochus III had successfully established himself **in the Beautiful Land** of Judea with **the power to destroy it** (v 16). The land of the Jews was now fully under the domain of the Seleucids.

■ **17** Instead of invading Egypt at this point, Antiochus III decided to try diplomacy for fear of Roman intervention. He made an **alliance** with Ptolemy V by giving him **a daughter in marriage.** However, his daughter Cleopatra remained loyal to the Ptolemies and **his plans** for control did **not succeed or help him.**

■ **18** At this juncture Antiochus III turned **his attention to the coastlands** of Asia Minor, Macedon, Thrace, and Greece. This was a crucial error, because a Roman **commander** named Lucius Scipio **put an end to his insolence.** Antiochus III was soundly defeated at Magnesia in 190 B.C. and forced to become a vassal of Rome.

■ **19** In order to pay the heavy Roman tribute required of him, Antiochus III returned to plunder **the fortresses of his own country.** While trying to pillage the temple of Bel in Elymais in 187 B.C. he was assassinated and was **seen no more.**

■ **20** The immediate **successor** to Antiochus III was a son named Seleucus IV (187-175 B.C.). According to 2 Macc 3 he sent a **tax collector** name Heliodorus to pillage the temple treasury in Jerusalem in order to pay Roman tribute. This plan was thwarted and the same **tax collector** eventually poisoned the king.

d. Reign of a Contemptible Person (11:21—12:4)

■ **21** The final king mentioned in the vision is another son of Antiochus III named Antiochus IV (175-164 B.C.). Scholars differ on whether or not description of his reign continues through the rest of the vision. Many believe it does, while many others think the subject shifts to a new personage in v 36. Most identify this person as the antichrist of the end times. This commentary agrees with the first position in seeing the remainder of the vision focusing upon events related to Antiochus IV (see the sidebar "The Subject of 11:36—12:4"). This does not discount the possibility of reapplying the material to the period of the antichrist, however.

In any case, Antiochus IV receives more attention than any other king in the vision. In various ways the preceding kings have foreshadowed his character and actions and thus prepared the reader for him. Like previous kings he invades other lands (11:7, 9, 21, 24, 29, 39, 40), even "the Beautiful Land" of the Jews (vv 16, 41). He sweeps in like a flood (vv 10, 40), gains the support of the inhabitants of the land (vv 14, 30, 32), makes deceitful alliances (vv 6, 17, 23), is opposed by Rome (vv 18, 30), plunders riches (vv 8, 24), is filled with pride (vv 12, 18, 36-37), and does "as he pleases" (vv 3, 16, 36). These interconnections explain why the lengthy survey of kings prior to this one has been given. In a sense Antiochus IV is a composite of all the evil kings who have gone before him. Therefore the reader should know that just as the reign of each previous king went, so also the rule of this one will go.

Throughout this section various phrases punctuate the account in order to emphasize the point that the reign of Antiochus is limited. These include "only for a time" (v 24), "an end will still come at the appointed time" (v 27), "until the time of the end" (v 35), "until the time of wrath is completed" (v 36), and "at the time of the end" (v 40). They remind readers that suffering under the despot will not go on forever.

This section divides into six smaller units: (1) an overview of the king's character in vv 21-24, (2) the invasion of Egypt in 170-169 B.C. in vv 25-28, (3) the invasion of Egypt and Judea in 168-167 B.C. in vv 29-35, (4) another characterization of the king in vv 36-39, (5) a final summary of the king's career in vv 40-45, and (6) hope for God's people during this era in 12:1-4.

Daniel 11:21-24 provides an initial overview of the unwholesome attributes of Antiochus IV. The first characterization is piercingly derogatory. Antiochus IV is called **a contemptible person** (v 21). The term connotes a person who is looked down upon as worthless, a person from which people turn their heads (Ps 15:4; Isa 53:3). The primary reason for this is his scheming duplicity, which is illustrated in what follows.

Antiochus was not the rightful heir to the throne. He was **not . . . given the honor of royalty** by being designated successor to his brother. Two sons of Seleucus IV stood in line before him. But Antiochus IV seized the throne **through intrigue.** Initially assuming control of the empire as regent on behalf of his nephews, he eventually did away with both and claimed the title of king.

■ **22-23** Antiochus was a successful military leader. On the battlefield all kinds of armies were **swept away before him** (v 22). At one point he even destroyed **a prince of the covenant.** This might refer to Egyptian or other rulers, but the reference to **the covenant** more likely indicates one of Judea's high priests. If so, it foreshadows the climactic entanglement of Antiochus with the Jews presented in vv 30-33.

A story told in 2 Macc 3 may provide the background to this allusion. As the story goes, Antiochus initially continued the policy of his father that allowed the high priest Onias III to oversee Jewish affairs. **After coming to an agreement with him,** however, Antiochus acted **deceitfully** (v 23). He began working with **a few people** of the pro-hellenizing faction in Judea in order to gain **power.** This included the brother of Onias, Jason, who bribed Antiochus into transferring the high priest office to him. Later Menelaus, who was not even a member of the priestly family, did the same. When Onias protested he was eventually hunted down and murdered in 171 B.C.

■ **24** Some commentators believe that reference to this event continues in v 24. Others, however, see a return to a summary of events. Such treachery certainly characterized Antiochus throughout his reign. He made **the richest provinces,** such as Egypt and Bacteria, **feel secure** by means of concessions, treaties and gifts. But he then turned on them. In this way he was able to **achieve what neither his fathers nor his forefathers did** in terms of subterfuge. He was more devious than all who preceded him.

Few surpassed Antiochus as a gift-giver either (1 Macc 3:30; Josephus, *Ant.* 12.7.2 §294). He ingratiated himself to his followers by giving them gifts from **plunder, loot and wealth** obtained from **fortresses** he pillaged (Dan 11:24). Most of these **fortresses** included temples where significant national treasures were kept, such as the one in Jerusalem.

The vision concludes an initial introduction to Antiochus by affirming that his treachery will last **only for a time.** This is the first reminder that God has set a limit on the terror of Antiochus (see vv 27, 35, 40, 45).

■ **25-26** The portrayal of Antiochus now turns from general characterization to a specific incident, the beginning of the Sixth Syrian War. In 170 B.C. his **large army** (v 25) invaded Egypt, perhaps in response to an expected attack from Ptolemy VI (181-146 B.C.). Antiochus prevailed and captured all of Egypt except for Alexandria. **Plots devised against him** led to the failure of Ptolemy VI in battle and more. The poor counsel of courtiers directed him to engage in the ill-advised war with Antiochus. Some of these same courtiers, who ate **from the king's provisions** (v 26), set up his younger brother Ptolemy VII as king in Alexandria when Antiochus captured Ptolemy VI.

■ **27** In a twist of fate, **the two kings,** Antiochus IV and Ptolemy VI, sat down **at the same table** to devise a plan for reclaiming the throne. To further their own ends both were willing to **lie to each other** and carry on this pretense of mutual support. This image of deceiving while eating with another was especially offensive in ancient Middle Eastern cultures. As a result of their summit, Antiochus set up Ptolemy VI as his puppet king in Memphis. But within a year Ptolemy VI negotiated shared power with his brother and the Ptolemaic Empire remained autonomous. Thus Antiochus's scheme to control Egypt came to **no avail.**

The reason Antiochus did not succeed at this point is **because an end will still come at the appointed time.** The phrase evokes Hab 2:3, which describes a time when the prophet must wait for the events God has ordained to unfold. It is a poignant reminder that Antiochus's fate does not rest in his own hands. While he schemes and moves about, heaven has already determined an end for him.

■ **28** Antiochus returned **to his own country,** thinking his plans were working and carrying with him **great wealth** plundered from the temples of Egypt. Before leaving Egypt, though, he attempted one more siege of Alexandria, but failed. Thus he turned his energies **against the holy covenant,** that is, Jerusalem and its people. In spite of the wealth he had gathered from Egypt he took **action against** the Jews and pillage their temple (1 Macc 1:20-28). This is the second specific action Antiochus takes against the people of the covenant in this vision (see Dan 11:22). A third, more disastrous one awaits (see vv 30-32).

■ **29-34** The most dramatic and devastating attack upon Judaism is portrayed in vv 29-35. This was **the appointed time** (v 29) of which v 27 spoke. It is the climactic conflict of the vision. What happens in these verses relates in greater detail the events alluded to in the visions of chs 8 and 9 (see 8:11-13, 23-25; 9:27).

These events begin in 168 B.C. when Antiochus returned to Egypt to finish the work of his previous campaign. **The outcome** was **different from what it was before,** however. Romans arrived in their **ships** (v 30) and forced him to withdraw. The might of the Roman Empire caused him to **lose heart.** Having served as a hostage in Rome, he knew well the folly of opposing this powerful empire.

While the Romans were humiliating Antiochus, he received word of an uprising in Jerusalem. Thus he turned to **vent his fury against the holy covenant.** Antiochus unleashed his **armed forces** upon the city massacring thousands and plundering the **temple fortress** (v 31; see 1 Macc 1:29-40 and 2 Macc 5:11-16). Then he determined to suppress Judaism entirely by abolishing **the daily sacrifice** (Dan 11:31) and forbidding other practices of the faith. His crowning assault upon the Jews was setting up **the abomination that causes desolation** in the temple courts, an altar to the Olympian Zeus (see 1 Macc 1:41-62; 2 Macc 6:1-6). As the term suggests, this was the supreme act of sacrilege that horrified Jewish sensitivities (see Dan 8:25; 9:27; 12:11).

Such oppressive policies provoked a violent rebellion from the Jews known as the Maccabean Revolt. For over seven years Jewish rebels engaged Seleucid troops in pitched battles to regain their land and freedom to worship. This may be "the great war" referred to in 10:1. The revolt brought on an unparalleled time of suffering in Judea (see 12:1).

Not everyone in Jerusalem suffered at the hands of Antiochus, though. There was a party of pro-Seleucid supporters who chose to **forsake the holy covenant** (11:30) and who **violated** its guidelines (v 32). **With flattery** of special gifts and promises Antiochus won them over. These collaborators set aside some of the regulations in Mosaic law in order to participate in the Hellenistic lifestyle (see 1 Macc 1:11-14). As a result they represented the exact opposite stance of Daniel and his friends in Dan 1—6.

On the other side were **people who know their God** and **firmly resist**

11:28-34

and those **who are wise** (vv 32-33). Whether or not these two phrases describe the same group of people in Judea is debated. Scholars have noted that the Jews did take two different approaches to Antiochus's oppression. Some picked up arms to fight with the Maccabees, while others preferred a more passive approach. Those who **firmly resist** (v 32) may represent the Maccabean freedom fighters and those **who are wise** (v 33) the pacifists. The term **resist** (*ḥāzaq*), however, can connote resolution of spirit rather than armed revolt. So the two phrases may simply define one another.

Regardless of whether the text intends to distinguish two groups, wisdom in a time of crisis is surely defined as understanding that God is in control. Therefore, **the wise** (*hammaśkîlîm*) would be those who resist Antiochus because they are convinced of God's sovereignty and trust in it (v 35). Whether resistance is active or passive, wisdom resolves to trust God alone (Prov 3:5-6). This was a key point of the earlier stories in Dan 1—6. It is also one of the final challenges given in the book (see 12:3, 10).

The Wise in Daniel

The wise (*hammaśkîlîm*) play a significant role in the book of Daniel. They are mentioned four times in the final two chapters. They **instruct many** during the oppression of Antiochus and suffer because of it (11:33). But their suffering is a process of purification for them (11:35). In the end they will be victorious (12:3) and when others are confused, they **will understand** (12:10). The profile of these persons is one of steadfastness in the midst of crisis because of trust in God's sovereignty.

Clearly these are the kind of people the book is urging readers to imitate. Because of this and other themes in the book, many scholars feel that the author of Daniel comes from the circles of the wise. Whether one looks for a sixth-century or a second-century author, most scholars agree with this proposal.

Those who view the book as a second-century work suggest connections with a number of groups from that era and later. Two proposals are the Hasidim of 1 Macc 2:42 and the separatist that eventually formed the Essenes at Qumran. Other theories have been put forth as well, but none has gained universal backing (see Lucas 2002, 288-89).

Those who persisted in the battle gained additional support. Though many fell **by the sword** or were **captured** and their homes were **burned** and **plundered,** the Maccabees had remarkable success (v 33). This encouraged people to join the revolt, even though they were **not sincere** in their devotion to God (v 34). Because their hearts were not fully in the right place, they were considered only **a little help** for the cause.

■ **35** The angel notes that the suffering and loss of life among **the wise** had spiritual implications. Through this trial they were **refined, purified and made**

DANIEL

11:32-35

spotless until the time of the end (v 35). Using the imagery of metallurgy, the text suggests that a refining process takes place during this time. Just as fire removes impurities from metal ore, so the afflictions of this era purify people. This could refer to the individual as well as the community. In the midst of persecution people examine their commitments and either deepen or abandon them. The angel reconfirms this same outcome again in 12:10. This purifying of evil recalls the purposes of the period of seventy sevens in ch 9 when time is given "to finish transgression, to put an end to sin, to atone for wickedness" (9:24).

Once again **the end** of this suffering is assured. God identified **the appointed time** for it to cease. This episode in Antiochus's career begins and ends with the assurance of God's sovereign control of these events (see v 29).

■ **36** At this point the text speaks about one who is simply called **the king** (v 36). Commentators take different positions as to who is intended here and, thus, who is the subject of the rest of the angel's message. Many believe the text shifts to eschatological concerns and the subject of the antichrist. Others, however, understand that Antiochus continues to be the focus through the end of the vision. The latter interpretation follows the natural flow of the text and requires reading less into it. The position of this commentary is this last view.

The Subject of 11:36—12:4

Scholars disagree about the subject of 11:36—12:4. Since the time of Jerome, many Christian commentators have held that the vision ends with a focus upon the antichrist. They note the heightened language, reference to "the time of the end" and the problems of connecting allusions in the text to events in Antiochus's life, among other things. From this perspective, 11:36—12:4 portray events of the final days of human history and the accompanying devastation wrought by the antichrist. (See Archer 1985, 144-49; Miller 1994, 304-13; Longman 1999, 280-85.)

Other scholars recognize these same factors but deal with them differently and interpret the text in reference to Antiochus. They point out that the text provides no literary signals that a shift of subject takes place. Reference to the king in v 36 and the kings of the South and North in v 40 presuppose the same subject as before. The notation "the time of the end" can refer to the end of Antiochus's persecution as easily as the end of human history. Finally, correlations with Antiochus's career can be made at some points. This is done most easily in vv 36-39 rather than 40-45. (See Goldingay 1989, 304-5; Collins 1993, 386-90; Seow 2003, 182-86.)

These scholars deal with the problem of correlating events of vv 40-45 with Antiochus in one of two ways. Most hold that the prophecy is simply inaccurate and does not correlate. The reason for this is that prior to v 40 the vision is pseudoprophecy. That is, the author has been "predicting" after the fact. In vv 40-45, however, the author attempts real prophecy but did not quite get it right. These scholars usually go on to point out that assurance of God's power to overcome evil tyrants is more important than accuracy in details. Biblical prophecy is more about proclamation than correct prediction, they say.

Another way to view vv 40-45, however, is to understand them as a general overview of Antiochus's career. This approach relieves some of the problems of correlation, though not all issues are easily solved. This final position is the one taken in this commentary.

Verses 36-39 step away from the details of history to reflect more upon the spiritual implications of Antiochus's actions. As the introduction to the vision suggests, earthly events carry heavenly repercussions. Much like 8:10-12, the text views his deeds as an attack upon heaven. He sets himself up "to be as great as the Prince of the host" (8:11).

By his actions and words Antiochus illustrates aspirations to divinity and determination to challenge God at every turn. In the tradition of other powerful monarchs, the text says he does **as he pleases** (11:36). According to the vision, Alexander and Antiochus III, who also invaded the land of Judea, wielded the same unchallenged power (vv 3, 16). But in fact God is the only monarch who can truly do **as he pleases,** as Nebuchadnezzar found out and confessed (4:35).

Antiochus tried to **exalt and magnify himself above every god** (11:36). Ironically, however, the one he spoke against already held the position he aspired toward. The God of Israel is **the God of gods.** Earlier in Daniel, Nebuchadnezzar confirms this truth (2:47) and calls him "the Most High God" (3:26; 4:2, 17, 24, 32, 34). With this Daniel also agreed (5:18, 21). According to the psalms, only the God of Israel is truly "above all gods" (Pss 95:3; 96:4; 97:9).

Records indicate that Antiochus took his sense of divinity more seriously than most ancient monarchs. Coins struck during his reign bear an additional name "Epiphanes," which may be translated "Illustrious One" or "Shining One." The title clearly intended to communicate that he was a god manifested on earth. This may be the **unheard-of things** that Antiochus spoke of (Dan 11:36). Whether or not this is in mind, the **unheard-of things** (niplā'ôt) also belong to God and not Antiochus. Nearly everywhere else this term is used in the Hebrew Scriptures it refers to the wonders of God in this world (for example, Exod 3:20; Josh 3:5; Ps 71:7; Jer 21:2).

God does not put up with such arrogance for long, as the stories of Nebuchadnezzar and Belshazzar illustrate (Dan 4 and 5). Antiochus was permitted, however, to prosper until **the time of wrath is completed** (11:36). This refers to the period of persecution and upheaval just described in vv 31-35 (see also 8:19). God has **determined** that this time of oppression and suffering **must take place** before he deals with Antiochus (11:36).

■ **37** Antiochus is further characterized as a person who is disconnected from and offensive to his heritage. In the ancient world, disregard for ancestors was shameful behavior. In his spiritual arrogance Antiochus showed **no regard** for the traditional gods of the Seleucids and Ptolemies. **The gods of his fathers** probably refers to Apollo, the patron god of the Seleucids. **The one desired by women** likely identifies a popular goddess in Egypt named Adonis. In Mesopotamia she was known as Tammuz and particularly venerated by women (Ezek 8:14).

■ **38** **The god of fortresses** might designate Olympian Zeus, whose altar Antiochus erected beside the Jerusalem temple (see Dan 11:31). Seleucid troops stationed at the citadel overlooking the temple mount were particularly attached to this god. Antiochus himself promoted Zeus more than other gods throughout the empire. **His fathers** did know this god, but not in the way Antiochus represented him. Worship of Zeus in Jerusalem tended to be especially corrupted and sensuous (2 Macc 6:3-6).

Another way to understand **the god of fortresses** is to take it as a personification of military might. In other words, the text may be saying that Antiochus honored war and the taking of fortresses above anything else. Again this kind of god was not **unknown to his fathers,** but Antiochus took it to a new level (see v 24). He may well have poured more resources of **gold and silver, with precious stones and costly gifts** into warfare than any of his predecessors.

■ **39** As a result of this "religious" passion, Antiochus attacked **the mightiest fortresses,** including the temple of Jerusalem (11:31). Both Antiochus and his father were known for plundering temples in order to support their war efforts. **With the help of a foreign god,** the Greek god Olympian Zeus, he was successful. The irony here is that even though he set himself "above every god" (v 36), he was not opposed to gaining whatever advantage he could from religious institutions in order to aid his military pursuits. Religion for Antiochus was a tool to serve his political agenda.

Antiochus also relied on any who might **acknowledge him,** such as Menelaus and other pro-Seleucid collaborators in Jerusalem. They were handsomely rewarded with **honor,** power to rule **over many people** and **land** (see v 24).

■ **40-41** With v 40 the vision returns to listing activities of **the king of the North.** Various events are mentioned until this king finally comes to his end in v 45.

As noted before, many scholars understand vv 40-45, along with vv 36-39, in reference to the antichrist at the end of human history while others see them continuing to describe the life of Antiochus (see the sidebar "The Subject of 11:36—12:4"). The position of this commentary is the latter. Though most scholars who take this position view the prophecies as inaccurate, this commentary believes it is possible to correlate the data with Antiochus.

The events of vv 40-45 take place **at the time of the end** (v 40). The most immediate referent for this period is the persecution of Jews under Antiochus in vv 29-35. The same phrase occurs in v 35 with reference to these events. This was also the context of its usage in 8:17.

"The Time of the End" in Daniel

The book of Daniel refers a number of times to **the end** (qēṣ), which essentially means "a point of cutting off" (8:17, 19; 9:26a, 26b; 11:6, 13, 35, 40; 12:4, 6, 9, 13). The phrase **the time of the end** (ʿēt qēṣ) occurs in 8:17; 11:35; 11:40; 12:4; and 12:9 preceded by various prepositions (lĕ in 8:17; ʿad in 11:35, 12:4, and 12:9; bĕ in 11:40). The phrase "the appointed time of the end" (lĕmôʿēd qēṣ) occurs in 8:19. The phrase does not necessarily or even primarily refer to the end of human history. It identifies a period when the suffering of God's people comes to a resolution.

The preposition **at** (bĕ) introduces **the time of the end** in v 40. This preposition indicates a temporal relationship to the period called **the time of the end.** This could be understood in connection to the last few days of this period or the entire period. If the latter is understood, then what follows becomes a summary of key events in Antiochus's career. Verses 40-43 serve as a recap of incidents previously spoken about and vv 44-45 provide new details of his death. Stylistically, the summary and notation on his death bring fitting closure to the survey of Antiochus's reign. It balances the opening passage of vv 21-24, which is also a general overview of Antiochus's career.

Verses 40-43 summarize Antiochus's invasions of Egypt and Judea already outlined in vv 25-35. **The king of the South,** Ptolemy VI, engaged Antiochus **in battle** in 170 B.C. as vv 25-28 indicate. In response Antiochus brought a massive force of **chariots** and **cavalry** against Egypt both in 170 and 168 B.C. With **a great fleet of ships** he captured Cyprus and eventually subdued all of Egypt except for Alexandria.

Antiochus invaded **many countries** over the course of his career, particularly those connected with the Ptolemaic Empire. His powerful armies swept **like a flood** through these countries (for a similar image, see 9:26 and 11:10). As far as the vision is concerned, the most significant invasion took place in **the Beautiful Land** of Judea (v 41). The **many countries** that **fall** could refer to the widespread conquest of Antiochus over his career. But the **many countries** can also be translated as "tens of thousands" (NRSV) by changing one vowel (reading ribbôt instead of rabbôt). As such it could refer to the massacre that took place in Jerusalem in 167 B.C. Second Maccabees 6:14 records "eighty thousand" killed in three days.

During the invasion of Judea, **Edom, Moab and the leaders of Ammon** were spared from Seleucid attack. Judas Maccabeus later engaged these ancient Transjordan enemies of Israel as his revolt gained strength (1 Macc 5:3-6). They apparently supported Antiochus. By the time of Antiochus, Nabateans occupied the areas of **Moab** and **Edom,** though some of Edom was still known as Idumea.

■ **42-43** Antiochus's **power over many countries** was extensive, especially when he briefly controlled most of the Ptolemaic Empire in 168 B.C. (Dan 11:42). At that time he plundered the vast **treasures of gold and silver and all the riches of Egypt** in order to support his war efforts (v 43; see v 28). **Libyans and Nubians,** perhaps Ptolemaic mercenary troops from peoples to the west and south of Egypt, also fell under his domain for a time.

■ **44-45** While occupied with the Ptolemies in the west, Antiochus received **reports from the east and the north** of his empire (v 44). Eucratides of Bacteria and Mithridates of Parthia to the **east** and Artaxias of Armenia to the **north** were claiming Seleucid territories. Antiochus left his commander Lysias to handle the insurgents in Judea and set out to deal with these invasions. After a failed attempt at pillaging a temple in Persia, he contracted a disease and met **his end** (v 45; 1 Macc 6:1-17; 2 Macc 1:13-16). The mention that **no one will help** might be an allusion to the isolation he experienced because of the disease that racked his body before his death (2 Macc 9:1-29).

The reference to pitching **his royal tents between the seas at** ("and," NRSV) **the beautiful holy mountain** (Dan 11:45) creates a problem for commentators. **The seas** likely allude to the Mediterranean and Dead Seas and **the beautiful holy mountain** designates the temple mount in Jerusalem. Thus the phrase describes the encampment of Antiochus and his army within the land of Judea, near Jerusalem. On at least two occasions Antiochus did position his troops here. If the text intends to suggest he was located there at his death, however, that would be incorrect. According to ancient sources, he was in the eastern part of his empire in Persia when he died.

The text can be understood in other ways, though. It could convey a more general point. That point would be that even though Antiochus had set up camp and occupied the land of Judea during his reign, his rule did not endure. Another alternative is to take the **royal tents** in reference to Antiochus's armies and not himself particularly. Thus the meaning would be that while the tents of the Seleucid army were pitched in the land of Judea and Lysias was engaging the Maccabees in battle, Antiochus came **to his end** in another part of his empire. In either of these readings, or any other, the sentence clearly accentuates that relief for God's people comes in the midst of foreign occupation. Such a point parallels the statement of Antiochus's final demise in 8:25. It also resonates with the motif of deliverance in the midst of trial found in other stories (3:28; 6:22) and visions (2:34; 7:11) within the book.

A Date for Composition

Scholars who view 11:2-39 as pseudoprophecy and 11:40-45 as real but inaccurate prophecy believe this provides information about the date for composition of Daniel. They say the text records events accurately up to the invasion of

Judah in 167 B.C. but not about Antiochus's death in 164 B.C. Therefore, the book must have been written sometime between 167 and 164 B.C. If this theory is correct, Daniel would be the most precisely dated book in the Hebrew Scriptures.

■ **12:1** The chapter division obscures the crucial relationship between 12:1-4 and the rest of the vision. These verses contain the final portion of the angel's message to Daniel, which began in 11:2. They relate an important word of hope for those who endure the oppression of Antiochus. This final segment of the vision returns once again to a perspective from heaven and recalls the emphasis of the vision's introduction (10:1—11:1) on the vital interconnections between earthly and heavenly events.

At that time refers to "the time of the end" in 11:40, which this commentary interprets to be the period of affliction under Antiochus (12:1). Three times the term **that time** (*'ēt hahî'*) occurs in this verse in order to focus attention upon this moment. It was **a time of distress such as has not happened from the beginning of nations.** The descriptions of events in 11:31-35 and 8:23-25 convey some of the unspeakable suffering associated with those days. Accounts in 1 and 2 Maccabees and Josephus fill in additional details. While Jews have experienced ruthless persecutions over the centuries, that under Antiochus marks one of the most devastating. The direct and malicious attack upon its institutions of worship made it particularly odious.

Hope for the people of God during such a time comes from heaven. The text says, **Michael, the great prince who protects your people, will arise.** Michael is the patron angel of the Jews who fights on their behalf (see Dan 11:13 and 21). The same root (*'āmad*) is behind **arise** and **protects.** Thus, the text could literally read *Michael . . . who stands for your people will stand up.* The term can carry a judicial meaning of standing to judge, to defend, or to execute judgment in a court. In ch 8 it is used repeatedly to indicate conflict or opposition (8:3, 4, 7, 15, 22, 23, 25; see also 11:14, 16). Michael's role, then, is to defend God's people during the period of affliction under Antiochus. This could include defending them in the heavenly counsel, as some scholars have suggested. But it also surely entails fighting alongside them in earthly battles against their enemies. Such is the role of angels elsewhere in the Hebrew Scriptures (Josh 5:13-15; Pss 35:5-6; 91:11-12).

Michael's intervention will effectively bring deliverance to Daniel's **people.** However, not all will be rescued, only those **whose name is found written in the book . . . will be delivered.** This is the third time heavenly records are mentioned in Daniel (see Dan 7:10 and 10:21). The **book** here appears to be the record of those who trusted their lives to God in the midst of affliction. A similar kind of book is spoken about elsewhere is the Hebrew Scriptures (see Exod 32:32; Ps 69:28; Isa 4:3; Ezek 13:9; Mal 3:16). The character of those

whose name is found written in the book is described in 11:32-35 and further defined in 12:3.

To these people the angel promises deliverance. The term **delivered** (*mālaṭ*) basically means to escape or slip away. This could refer to escape from death (1 Sam 19:11; Jer 39:18; Ps 107:20), but the next verse clarifies that it also includes another kind of rescue, a deliverance that comes after death.

■ **2** The deliverance promised is much greater than something earthly. It includes vindication for the faithful following this life. Ultimate justice for the faithful transpires after death.

This is the first time this idea has been articulated in Daniel and one of the few times it is mentioned in the Hebrew Scriptures (see Job 19:26; Ps 17:15; Isa 26:19). Daniel 12:2 stands as the clearest statement on resurrection among these. It asserts that **multitudes who sleep in the dust of the earth will awake. Sleep** is a frequent metaphor for death in the Bible (for example, Job 14:12). Awaking, then, is the counterimage of resurrection (Jer 51:39). **Dust of the earth** might refer to Sheol, the place of the dead in Hebrew thinking (Job 17:16; Ezek 26:20; 31:14, 16, 18; 32:18, 24), or simply the condition of the body after death (Job 10:9; Ps 104:29; Eccl 3:20). Isaiah 26:19 envisions a similar thing happening when it says, "But your dead will live; their bodies will rise. You who dwell in the dust, wake up and shout for joy."

The **multitudes** who **will awake** seems to refer primarily to those who perish during the "time of distress" (Dan 12:1), since this is the focus of the preceding verses. This does not preclude the idea of a general resurrection of all peoples mentioned elsewhere in the Bible (John 5:28; 1 Cor 15:51-52). But it does not specifically support it either. Though the term for **multitudes** (*rabbîm*) can be translated "all," the immediate context restricts its meaning to the many Jews who fall during the period of affliction under Antiochus.

The angel identifies two destinies for the resurrected: **everlasting life** and **everlasting contempt.** Both destinies are **everlasting,** meaning they continue for an indefinite amount of time. This is the only place the term **everlasting life** (*ḥayyēy 'ôlām*) appears in Hebrew Scripture, though its Greek equivalent (*zoe aionios*) occurs frequently in intertestamental Jewish writings and the NT (*1 En.* 15:4; *Pss. Sol.* 3:1; John 3:16; Rom 6:23). What **everlasting life** entails is not made explicit in this context. In Ps 133:3 a similar expression, "life forevermore" (*ḥayyîm 'ad 'ôlām*), is connected with divine blessing. The same might be assumed here. Christians came to understand **everlasting life** not only as extended existence into the new age (Luke 18:30) but also as authentic relationship with God in the present (John 17:3). Daniel 12:3 provides some additional description of this state in poetic images.

In contrast to the first group, **others** will awake **to shame and everlasting contempt.** The term **shame** is plural, which indicates intensification. Therefore, **great shame** conveys the meaning more fully. This is the same fate, and more, experienced by those who failed to follow God's laws in 9:16. They were an object of ridicule among their peers. **Contempt** conveys a sense of repugnance one might feel toward a disgusting object, like a dead body full of worms (Isa 66:24). In cultures where honor is a significant value, **shame** and **contempt** identify severe punishments.

What this group did to deserve such a fate is not explained in these verses. One can assume they did not do what the other group is said to have done in Dan 12:3. They are also likely the ones who "forsake the holy covenant" and violate the guidelines laid down in it (11:30, 32).

Rhythm in 12:1-3

Some translators believe that the first three verses of ch 12 display poetic qualities (*BHS*; REB; Lucas 2002, 257). If so, it reflects a literary technique used elsewhere in Hebrew Scriptures. Literary units are sometimes closed by poetry at or near the end of the unit (Exod 15; Judg 5). This feature might be observed in Dan 6:26-27 when the stories of Daniel come to an end.

Whether or not these verses are viewed as poetry, the rhythm in them tends to accentuate the key ideas of hope within this passage: deliverance and resurrection. The first three lines of 12:1 follow a regular rhythm consisting of 3 + 3 (three words plus three words). That pattern is broken in the fourth line of the verse. At that point the rhythm shifts to 4 + 3 in order to announce deliverance for God's people. The pronouncement of resurrection in v 2 continues with a four-word line followed by 3 + 4 line. Verse 3 echoes the beat of v 2 and thus returns to a sense of regularity in rhythm. Its two lines consist of a four-word line followed by 2 + 3. The overall effect of the rhythm in these verses is to draw attention to the two central lines, which proclaim the key hope of the passage— **your people . . . will be delivered** and **will awake.**

■ **3** Verse 3 describes the state of those who awake to blessedness as well as something of their character. They **will shine like the brightness of the heavens** and **like the stars for ever and ever** (v 3). These two phrases are parallel expressions indicating the special honor given this group. Shining **brightness** recalls the dazzling appearance of the heavenly being in 10:5-6 because it reflects God's glory. Perhaps shining **like the stars** indicates witness to the world that comes when God's people are vindicated (Ezek 39:27-28). These phrases also highlight the enduring state of the blessed. It will be **for ever and ever,** as it seems to be for stars. Since these phrases are clearly poetic, they should not be taken literally to suggest that people somehow become stars or even angels.

Two descriptions of the blessed define their character. They are (1) **those who are wise** and (2) **those who lead many to righteousness.** The **wise** in Daniel are people who trust in the sovereignty of God regardless of external circumstances. They "know their God" and "firmly resist" compromise (11:32). Their model is Daniel and, like him, their steadfastness impacts their world (2:47; 6:26-27). They become instructors in faithful living and **lead many to righteousness** (see 11:35). These people recall the Suffering Servant of Isaiah who "will act wisely" (52:13) and "will justify many" (53:11).

■ **4** A word of instruction to Daniel closes the message of the angel that began in Dan 11:2. Similar to 8:26, the angel directs Daniel to **seal the words of the scroll** (12:4). The purpose of this is for preservation and not secrecy. Like a property deed, this message must be bound with a string or placed in a jar, stamped with a signet and preserved for a time when it will be most valuable (see Jer 32:14). That moment is **the time of the end,** which the message has indicated relates to the era of suffering under Antiochus (see Dan 11:40). The message of the angel is like a contract for those of that period. Its sealing assures them that things will transpire as God has revealed. Suffering will come but it will also end. The faithful will ultimately be delivered.

The last phrase, **many will go here and there to increase knowledge** (12:4) may be interpreted in two different ways. It could refer to what will happen when the scroll is finally opened or what will transpire in the interim before that. Going **here and there** refers to intense searching (Jer 5:1; Amos 8:12). The fact that **knowledge** is increased indicates that pursuit of the vision's message is in mind. The Old Greek, however, translates "wickedness" instead of **knowledge,** presumably reading *haraʿah* for *hadaʿat*. All other versions agree with the MT. Thus the sense of the phrase seems to be that when the vision is unsealed, people will search it diligently and find understanding. The word **knowledge** has a definite article in Hebrew, which suggests a particular kind of knowledge. In the context of this passage, that **knowledge** would be what is possessed by "the wise" of 11:33 and 12:3. They had insight into the sovereign hand of God over human history and the wisdom to trust it.

FROM THE TEXT

The revelation from heaven in 11:2—12:4 addresses disappointing circumstances. According to the introduction in 10:1—11:1, the message comes in response to Daniel's prayer. Though the text does not say explicitly, apparently discouraging developments for the Jews caused his concern. The foreign domination of Jewish affairs remained, and exiles returning to rebuild their homeland faced significant struggles. Hopes for a victorious end to exile had been tempered.

In response to this setting the angelic message reaffirms several themes found earlier in the book. Previous visions speak of the tiresome realities of this world: the unending conflicts between earthly powers, the astonishing arrogance of kings, and the unwarranted suffering of God's people. What is new in 11:2—12:4 is a more pronounced hope. The visions of chs 8 and 9 offer a modest hope that primarily promises an end to each turmoil and tyrant. With 11:2—12:4 the book returns to the more expanded hope projected in ch 7.

In ch 7 a vision of beasts subdued before God's throne conveys a grand hope for this world and those who are faithful. It envisions "one like a son of man coming with the clouds of heaven" (v 13) and establishing an everlasting kingdom among God's people. The message of 11:2—12:4 provides additional insights into the nature of that hope. It is a hope that resides in the hands of a sovereign God who has determined specific things about the future. God knows there will be conflicts and that his people will suffer affliction. But he also knows there will be deliverance. Those who are wise will be vindicated, not only within this present world, but also beyond it.

God knows details of the future. In 11:2-45 the angel predicts events and personalities of human history with remarkable precision. So much so, that even though names are not given, historians can match particular actions and persons with very little question. This phenomenon clearly intends to communicate that God knows the future. Regardless of whether the material is viewed as real or pseudoprophecy, the theological point and message of the text is the same. God knows what lies ahead and, because of this, people can be encouraged to trust in him.

While the idea of knowing the future is astounding from a human perspective, it is constantly asserted throughout the Bible. According to Isaiah, part of the authenticity of Israel's God is proven by his knowledge of the future. God is superior to other gods because he knows "what is yet to come" (Isa 44:7). So also, the ability to announce future events authenticates God's prophets (Deut 18:21-22). Within the Hebrew Scriptures, the prophetic corpus in particular rests upon the logic of God's words finding fulfillment in the future. God shares his plans with his prophets and they proclaim it (Amos 3:7-8). Inevitably they come to pass "in accordance with the word of the LORD proclaimed by his servants the prophets" (2 Kgs 24:2).

To say that God knows future events, however, does not mean that God predestines everything. Daniel 11 does not promote a rigid determinism. It affirms only divine foreknowledge of certain, not all, events in human history. According to the Bible, God is not bound by a predetermined world. God regularly alters plans, negotiates, and responds to human actions (Gen 6:6-8; Exod 32:11-14; 1 Sam 15:10-11; Jer 18:7-8; 26:3; Amos 7:1-6; Ps 106:45). Many passages, including the prayer of Dan 9, demonstrate that human response makes a difference in the scheme of things. Obedience or disobedience determines direction because human free will is real. Otherwise prophetic warnings and calls to repentance would be meaningless (Isa 1:18-20). So also, the admonitions to holy living would be empty words (Lev 19:2) and the model of Daniel's faithfulness without significance.

Certain events, however, apparently are predetermined and God knows what they are. Not every event is set, but the ones that are **determined must take place** (Dan 11:36). They have an **appointed time** in which they must transpire (11:27, 29, 35). The effect of such determinism is to highlight God's sovereignty. Thus ch 11 once again confirms the sovereign hand of God over human history, just as every other portion of Daniel has. Knowledge of a world in the hands of such a God offers comfort to those in affliction, because this God has also appointed other things to take place. God determines good as well as ill for people (Jer 29:10-14).

God knows his people will remain in a world at war. According to Dan 10:1, the angel's message concerns "a great war." The survey of events in 11:2—12:4 portrays just that as human history moves from one conflict to another. It is a world constantly at war. Persian authority trades out for Greek dominance (11:2-4). **King[s] of the North** invade **king[s] of the South** (vv 7, 9, 11, 13, 15, 25, 29, 40). They plot, plunder, retaliate, deceive, and destroy. The motive of such kings is outlined most clearly in vv 36-39. They want to be gods. They **exalt and magnify** themselves **above every god** and honor only what advances their political agenda (v 36).

In such a world God's people should not be surprised that they will suffer (John 15:18-25; 1 John 3:13). While kings plot and plunder, believers are caught in the middle. More than that, they are in the way. Their worship of God poses a threat to kings striving for affirmation of their deity. Institutions that honor God must be abandoned or destroyed. In their place, kings set up appalling monuments to their own glory, an **abomination that causes desolation** (Dan 11:31).

Though false prophets may proclaim peace for this world, there will be no peace for those who remain faithful to God (Jer 6:13-15; 23:16-17). Those who believe hostility among humans will cease are deluded. As Jesus said to his followers, "In this world you will have trouble" (John 16:33). Even so, believers can expect something else of their world because hope comes to a world at war. The sovereign God has determined that as well.

God knows that those who are wise will be vindicated. Wise living is eventually rewarded. In Daniel the wise are God's faithful people. They are the ones who have learned the first lesson of wisdom, "the fear of the LORD" (Prov 1:7). They imitate the hero of the book and trust in the sovereignty of God. According to Dan 11:32-33, these people **know their God,** not simply intellectually, but experientially. Because they know God, they are able to **firmly resist** the demands of an evil ruler like Antiochus and the cultural temptation to compromise with him. The testimony of such people speaks volumes to their world and becomes a means to **instruct many** in the faith.

God vindicates the wise both within and beyond this world. He delivers them from their enemies and from the grave. The message of 11:2—12:4 proclaims an **end** for the oppressor, just as previous visions had announced (7:11; 8:27; 9:27). According to 12:1, heavenly forces **arise** to fight for God's people and deliver them from suffering. It is a divine rescue similar to Daniel's in the lions' pit (6:22) and his friends in the furnace (3:25). Foes are defeated and the faithful preserved. Throughout the Hebrew Scriptures God and his angels intervene for his people in times of distress (2 Kgs 6:16-17; Pss 34:7; 35:5-6; 91:11-12). Whenever God's people suffer, God is involved, planning and working toward deliverance (Exod 3:7-10).

Many of the wise do not survive the onslaught of evil oppressors, though. Unlike Daniel in the den of lions, they fall **by the sword** and their earthly life is ended (Dan 11:33). Hope for them must lie somewhere else. According the 12:2-3, there is hope beyond this world. Those **who sleep in the dust of the earth will awake . . . to everlasting life.** Their faithfulness does not go unnoticed. It is rewarded. They receive a place of honor in the heavens where they **shine . . . like the stars.** Even though they have departed this world, the impact of their lives remains. Their faithful witness becomes a means to **lead many to righteousness.**

Such rewards vindicate the life they lived for God. Faithful living is worth the effort in the end, whether that end arrives within this world or the next.

The idea of resurrection expressed in 12:2-3 is veiled in the rest of Hebrew Scriptures. Prophets speak of new life for the community of Israel following exile (Ezek 37:1-14), and others hope to have some kind of vindication for their righteous living after death (Job 19:25-27; Isa 53:10-12). But the primary image of life after death is existence in a shadowy place of the dead called Sheol, where there is no particular reward or punishment (Pss 6:5; 30:9; 88:10-12; Eccl 9:5-6). Some psalmists, however, imagine a meaningful life with God after death, but only in vague terms (Pss 16:9-11; 49:15; 73:23-26). The closest parallel to Dan 12:2 is found in Isa 26:19, which proclaims, "Your dead will live; their bodies will rise."

Intertestamental Judaism and early Christianity gave greater clarity to what happens after death. While Jewish writers expressed hope in resurrection (*1 En.* 91:10; Wis 3:1-9; 2 Macc 7:9), Jesus confirmed for all time its reality by means of his own resurrection. For Christians this was the defining act of God in Christ, which infused power into their lives. The hope of every believer being raised to a life of blessedness was based upon it (1 Cor 15:12-19). Paul was absolutely convinced of the truth of resurrection. "Listen," he said, "I will tell you a mystery: We will not all sleep, but we will all be changed—in a flash, in the twinkling of an eye, at the last trumpet. For the trumpet will sound, the dead will be raised imperishable, and we will be changed" (vv 51-52). Because of this belief, early Christians faced intense persecution from their peers (Acts 26:6-8) but also persuaded many to trust in Christ (2:31-33).

Daniel 12:2-3 speaks of more than resurrection of the faithful to **everlasting life,** though. It also describes resurrection of others to **everlasting contempt.** The idea of judgment for sinners at the resurrection also received more definition in the NT. Jesus confirmed its reality when he said, "Do not be amazed at this, for a time is coming when all who are in their graves will hear his voice and come out—those who have done good will rise to live, and those who have done evil will rise to be condemned" (John 5:28-29). Other teachings and sayings of Jesus also confirm this sad truth (Matt 8:11-12; 13:40-43, 47-50; 22:1-14; 25:14-30, 31-46). In its final chapters, Revelation paints a dramatic scene of the judgment that accompanies resurrection. As in Daniel, **everyone whose name is found written in the book . . . will be delivered** (Dan 12:2). But those who are not receive everlasting punishment (Rev 20:12-15).

Reference to resurrection is one reason many scholars relate Dan 11:36—12:4 to the end of human history. The resurrection is an eschatological event, according to the rest of Scripture. This alone is not enough reason to assume that the entire passage speaks of this context. But this element, along with many other features in the text, does provide warrant for reapplying the message to the end times. This is what the NT writers did. They picked up on the images and concepts found in Daniel and employed them to describe end-time events.

Jesus seems to have taken the lead in this. He used several images from Daniel when describing the end of time (and possibly the devastation of Jerusalem by the Romans in A.D. 70 as well). As in Dan 11, the end will be preceded by a period of "wars and rumors of wars" when "nation will rise against nation, and kingdom against kingdom" (Matt 24:6-7). Then "the abomination that causes desolation" will be set up in the temple and a time of "great distress, unequalled from the beginning of the world until now" will follow (Matt 24:15, 21; Dan 11:31; 12:1).

Jesus finishes his description of end times with a promise to "send his angels" and "gather his elect" (Matt 24:31), which could be construed as a reference to **Michael** and the resurrection in Dan 12:1-3. In any case, those who are righteous in the end "will shine like the sun in the kingdom of their Father" (Matt 13:43) in a manner similar to those who **shine like the brightness of the heavens** in v 3.

The character of Antiochus in Dan 11 provides an apt archetype for the antichrist of the NT. Undoubtedly Paul borrowed some of his description of the person he calls "the man of lawlessness" from 11:36-39. He says, "He will oppose and will exalt himself over everything that is called God or is worshiped, so that he sets himself up in God's temple, proclaiming himself to be God" (2 Thess 2:4). John also may have had Antiochus's disregard for heaven

11:2—12:4

in mind when he notes that the antichrist "denies the Father and the Son" and "does not acknowledge Jesus" (1 John 2:22; 4:3). Revelation describes "the beast" with a similar attitude toward God. In John's vision the beast "opened his mouth to blaspheme God, and to slander his name and his dwelling place and those who live in heaven" (Rev 13:6). This passage also reflects the wording of Dan 7:8 and 11.

As noted above, when Jesus describes end times he alludes to **a time of distress such as has not happened from the beginning of nations** (12:1). Revelation significantly expands on this concept and calls it "the great tribulation" (Rev 7:14). It involves unprecedented horror on earth as well as heavenly battles (Rev 6:12-17; 12:6-14). There are those who abandon faith at this time and compromise with the beast like **those who forsake the holy covenant** in Dan 11:30. These are people "whose names have not been written in the book of life" (Rev 13:8; Dan 12:1). The conflict intensifies until a final climactic battle of history takes place near Jerusalem (Rev 19:19-20; 20:7-10). The reign of the beast is cut off during his assault on the holy city just as Antiochus meets **his end** while his troops are attacking it (Dan 11:45). Other prophets in Israel envision a similar picture of the end of human history. They also predict a time of intense conflict culminating in a battle for Jerusalem (Isa 26:20-21; Joel 3:9-15; Zech 12—14; Ezek 38—39).

The text of Dan 11, then, provides powerful images for a description of the end times. The NT application of 11:36—12:4 to the last days confirms that this is a valid use of the text. This does not mean that the angel necessarily predicted the events of those days, though some would see it that way. From the perspective of this commentary, the vision refers first to the era of Antiochus. But the reapplication of patterns and types for the end of human history is appropriate. This appears to be how NT writers made use of the text.

3. Final Clarifications (12:5-13)

BEHIND THE TEXT

The same historical context lies behind the final section as the rest of the vision. According to 10:1, the vision takes place "in the third year of Cyrus," a time when hopes of Judah's restoration were being rearranged. In 536 B.C. enthusiastic Jews returning from exile to rebuild their homeland began facing significant opposition (see *Behind the Text* for 10:1—11:1). The difficulties of restoration and the fact that the Persian Empire still remained overlords of Judah indicated that the period of suffering for God's people was not over. Apparently for this reason, Daniel mourned and fasted before God for three weeks (10:3).

In response to Daniel's prayer, a heavenly visitor appears in dramatic fashion with a message. That message reveals details of history in the Middle East from the time of Daniel down to Antiochus IV. The portrait of kings and events given pictures an era of continuous conflict for God's people culminating "in a time of distress such as has not happened from the beginning of nations" (12:1). Yet a word of hope for deliverance and ultimate vindication concludes the heavenly message.

The final scene of the vision responds to the message by asking for further clarification. In the course of dialogue with heavenly beings, Daniel and an angel each pose a question about the message. They want to know, **How long will it be before these astonishing things are fulfilled?** and **What will the outcome of all this be?** (12:6, 8). The response to these inquiries reemphasizes key themes of the divine message and serves to bring fitting closure to it.

In spite of the integral connections between 12:5-13 and the rest of the vision, some scholars suggest that these verses represent a separate vision or a later addition to the book (Hartman and Di Lella 1978, 277 and 311; Collins 1993, 371). They see evidence of glosses in two sets of numbers in 12:11-12 and discontinuity between references to sealing the book in 12:4 and 12:9. Both of these features can be understood in other ways, however.

The heavenly response to the questions in this final scene also provides opportunity to summarize key points of the entire book. Thus, 12:5-13 reconnects with the rest of the book, particularly the vision section of chs 7—12, in a number of ways. Reference to "a time, times and a half a time" and "holy people" recalls ch 7. The scene of heavenly beings in conversation echoes a similar scene in ch 8 as does the question of "how long" and mention of "the daily sacrifice" being abolished. "The abomination that causes desolation" appears again in 12:11, recalling its appearance in each of the final three visions. The emphasis on purifying and refining people also connects with the promise of atonement for sin in ch 9. Finally, the promise of ultimate vindication for those who remain faithful in a foreign environment in 12:13 reconnects with the message of the stories earlier in the book. Thus, vv 5-13 function as a meaningful conclusion for the book as a whole.

The final scene of the vision is structured by two questions. The first question is posed by one angel and addressed by another (vv 5-7). The second question comes from Daniel and receives a heavenly response as well (vv 8-10). The angel continues to speak in the last three verses, reflecting further on each of these questions and offering personal hope to Daniel himself (vv 11-13).

IN THE TEXT

a. First Question (12:5-7)

■ **5-6** This section returns to a description of the setting surrounding the vision. According to 10:1—11:1 an angel has been standing before Daniel delivering the revelation from heaven. Now the heavenly presence increases by **two others** (v 5). These are standing on either side of **the river,** which was the Tigris according to 10:4. **The man clothed in linen** (v 6), who appeared in a dazzling display in 10:5-6 and is likely the one relaying the message, remains. He is described as hovering **above the waters of the river,** apparently in a position of special authority over the other two angels.

One of the two standing along the riverbanks poses a question, **How long will it be before these astonishing things are fulfilled? How long** is a frequent and legitimate concern of those enduring affliction (Job 8:2; Ps 6:3). The question of timing is a significant motif in the final three visions of the book. In Dan 8:13 the same question is asked, and 9:2 reflects on the duration of Jerusalem's desolation. Each of these visions focuses upon the **astonishing things** surrounding "the abomination that causes desolation" (8:13; 9:27; 11:31). **Astonishing things** (*pĕlā'ôt*) recalls the "astounding" (*niplā'ôt*) actions and "unheard-of things" (*niplā'ôt*) connected with Antiochus IV in 8:24 and 11:36. Thus, the duration of Antiochus's persecution of Judaism described in 11:29-35 seems to be the concern of the angel's question.

■ **7 The man clothed in linen** gives a direct answer (v 7). He lifts both hands **toward heaven** and swears by God like a person pronouncing a solemn oath (Deut 32:40). Normally only one hand is raised, so lifting both accentuates the extreme reliability of the statement. Reference to God as **him who lives forever** underscores an important theme of the eternality of God emphasized earlier in the book (Dan 4:34; 6:26; 7:9).

As in 8:14, the angel's answer to the question of how long is direct but vague. **It will be for a time, times and half a time.** This recalls the same phrase in 7:25, which identifies the time "the saints will be handed over" to a king who emerges from the fourth beast. As in that setting, the phrase need not be taken as a literal calculation of time. Its veiled connection with the number three and a half (half of seven) signifies imperfection. The impact of the phrase is to suggest a growing intensity for a **time** and **times** before a sudden ending. The time of distress will come to a climactic moment before it is cut short.

The climactic moment that initiates the end arrives when **the power of the holy people is finally broken. The holy people** (*'am qōdeš*) is a religious term comparable to "the saints of the Most High" (*qadîšê 'elyônîn*) in 7:25 and 27 (see Deut 7:6; 14:2; Exod 19:6). It refers to followers of the covenant and not every Jew. Their **power** (Dan 12:7) might designate political or military strength, but something more seems implied. In light of the previous phrase, it may indicate their ability to resist compromise and remain faithful.

In any case, a sense of utter helplessness for God's people is in view because whatever strength they possess is **finally broken.** Literally it is **_shattered_** like a piece of pottery dashed against the ground. The text describes a moment when human resources fail and only divine ones remain. At that point **all these things will be completed.** This phrase recalls the vision of ch 9 that promises a time "to finish transgression" (9:24). **Completed** and "finish" derive from the same root *kālâ*, which means to use up or accomplish something. **All these things** that come to completion, then, may include the sins of those who bring about the time of distress as well as the suffering involved.

b. Second Question (12:8-10)

■ **8** As at other times (8:27), Daniel hears but does **not understand** entirely (12:8). Though some level of understanding undoubtedly has come to him through the vision, other things remain unclear (see 10:1). His knowledge of some things exposes ignorance of others.

His lack of understanding prompts Daniel to ask the second question of this section. **What will the outcome of all this be?** (12:8). Literally, the text reads *what after these things* (*mâ 'ahărît' ēlleh*). This might be a request for more explanation of the vision's message. But based on the answer given, the question seems to be about what comes next. Once the events revealed in the vision are over, Daniel wants to know what else is in store.

■ **9** The angel tells Daniel that no more information will be given to him. He has all he needs. The angel admonishes him to **go your way** (v 9). These words encourage Daniel to continue on with life and be satisfied with what has been revealed. The revelation that has been given and the kind of faithful living Daniel modeled early in the book are sufficient for the troubled times ahead. The source of the revelation, "the Book of truth" mentioned in 10:21, is **closed up and sealed until the time of the end.** It is preserved for the moment most needed just as the words revealed to Daniel are (12:4).

■ **10** In summary what Daniel and his audience most need to remember is a basic lesson of Proverbs. The lives of the wise and the wicked bear radically different fruit (Prov 10:16). Those who are faithful **will be purified, made spotless and refined** (Dan 12:10). This list echoes 11:35, which uses these same terms to describe what happens to **the wise** that persevere during Antiochus's persecution. Like metal in a refiner's furnace, these lose their impurities during affliction and become godlier people.

By contrast **the wicked** (12:10) do not change. Though exposed to the same fire, they **will continue to be wicked** and not alter their path. The term **wicked** (*rāša'*) connotes guilt for a crime. In reference to the vision, **the wicked** are undoubtedly those who "forsake the holy covenant" (11:30). These people ignored God's guidelines for faithful living, which makes them guilty of breaking covenant.

The path of **the wicked** leads to ignorance. **None** of them **will understand** what is really happening in the world. The truth of world events that is

12:7-10

revealed in the vision remains a mystery to them. **But those who are wise will understand** these things. **The wise** "know their God" and "firmly resist" evil tyrants in this world (11:32). They commit to the truth and "lead many to righteousness" (12:3). Such people have a perspective on the turmoil of this earth that the wicked do not.

c. Final Recap (12:11-13)

■ **11-12** The final three verses of the book reflect one more time upon the two questions just posed. The question of how long receives additional response in vv 11-12. Then v 13 responds to the second question about what next.

In response to the question of how long, the text designates two time periods: **1,290 days** and **1,335 days** (vv 11-12). The ending point for these periods is not explicitly identified. Presumably the conclusion of the conflict mentioned in the vision message is meant. The beginning point is **from the time that the daily sacrifice is abolished and the abomination that causes desolation is set up** (v 11). The two events are mentioned in 11:31 and refer to the actions of Antiochus IV in 167 B.C. At that time he forbade regular sacrifice to the God of Israel and set up an altar to Olympian Zeus in the Jerusalem temple (1 Macc 1:41-62). Both Dan 8:13 and 9:27 refer to these same events.

The meaning of these numbers is puzzling, and that may be their message. Though scholars offer a variety of proposals for interpreting them, none is satisfactory. The numbers do not correspond to other numbers in the book or to any calculation of events. Since other numbers in the book have been understood symbolically, it seems best to do the same here. Yet, **1,290** and **1,335** do not convey a particular symbolic idea like the numbers four or seven.

The symbolism of these numbers should be understood in reference to "2,300 evenings and mornings" in 8:14 and "time, times and half a time" in 12:7. These phrases also refer to the duration of a time of affliction and are just as elusive. The point of all these numbers may be to announce that an end is coming, but its precise moment is not revealed. People can note the markers along the way toward the end, "2,300 evenings and mornings," **1,290 days,** and **1,335 days.** Whether or not something significant happens at each of these junctures, the faithful know they are that much closer to the end.

A special reward comes to **the one who waits for and reaches** the milestone of **1,335 days.** They are **blessed** with true joy from God. **The one who waits** is patiently, but confidently, looking forward to something, as the term **waits** (ḥākâ) suggests. Like Habakkuk, they "wait for" God's revelation to be fulfilled even though it lingers (Hab 2:3).

Interpretation of 1,290 and 1,335 Days

The two numbers given in 12:11-12 have perplexed scholars over the years. They do not match any other numbers given in the book, such as "2,300 evenings and mornings" in 8:14 and "time, times and half a time" in 7:25 and 12:7. Thus, reconciling them with these other numbers creates a fundamental problem.

One way of corresponding these numbers is to calculate them with different calendars. Three calendars were in use during ancient times: the 354-day lunar calendar, the 360-day lunisolar calendar, and the 364-day solar calendar. Each needed periodic adjustments since the actual length of a year differs slightly from them (see Goldingay 1989, 309).

Other problems with these numbers arise according to one's view of their context. Those who take these numbers in reference to end times deal with one set of issues, while those who see them in context of Antiochus's persecution work with others.

Scholars who understand the numbers in the setting of end times associate them with the length of a final great tribulation. They understand this as approximately three and a half years, which the book seems to indicate by the phrase "time, times and half a time" in 12:7. Revelation 11:2 and 12:6 also identify this kind of time frame for a final tribulation. The forty-five day difference between the 1,290 and 1,335 can be understood as the time between the end of the final battle and the establishment of the millennial reign of Christ (Archer 1985, 156-57). There is also a theory that these numbers represent the number of years from Daniel to the end of time (Doukhan 2000, 186-89).

Scholars who connect these numbers to Antiochus's persecution must reckon with a different problem. They do not match the time period from the point Antiochus set up his altar to Zeus till the cleansing of the temple. This was just over three years or 1,090 days on a lunisolar calendar.

One way of dealing with this issue is to relate the numbers to different events between 168 and 163 B.C. Various ending points have been suggested since the text does not identify that particular event. Also, an earlier date for abolishing sacrifice in the temple has been proposed, since historians are not sure exactly when that happened (see Goldingay 1989, 310).

Another approach to understanding the numbers is to view them as successive revisions to the book's prophecy. This theory suggests that when the Maccabean Revolt did not come to satisfactory conclusion, later redactors updated the predicted end. As "2,300 evenings and mornings" or 1,150 days of 8:14 passed, 1,290 became the new prediction. Once that time expired, 1,335 days was put forth (Collins 1993, 401).

A final approach is to take the numbers symbolically. As such, their significance may be lost to us (Lucas 2002, 298). Alternatively, they may intend to signify that the precise moment of conclusion is not set, only that an end has been determined (Longman 1999, 287).

■ **13** The final verse of the book responds to Daniel's question of what comes next. As in v 9 the angel once again indicates that Daniel has all the information he needs and highlights one significant portion of it.

For a second time the angel tells Daniel **go your way** (v 13). This is a challenge to keep living a faithful life and be content with what has been revealed. Then the angel goes on to confirm the hope presented in vv 1-3. These verses describe what will transpire following the era of affliction. The angel says **you will rest** and **you will rise**. The reference is to death and resurrection. **Rest** (*nûaḥ*) means to lie down or settle in, like a bird alighting on something (2 Sam 21:10). It is used metaphorically of dying, likely referring to the body being laid in a grave (Isa 14:7; 57:2; Job 3:13, 17). **Rest** can also refer to spiritual rest, a patient trusting in God (Hab 3:16). Perhaps a double meaning is possible in this context.

In any case, the promise that Daniel **will rise** means he will be resurrected **at the end of the days** of this world. At that time he will receive his **allotted inheritance,** which is the blessings God has determined for him to have (Jer 13:25; Ps 125:3). According to Dan 12:2-3, this hope is for all "those who are wise" and it includes "everlasting life" and "shining like the brightness of the heavens." It is a hope, not only for Daniel, but for all who follow his pattern of faithful living in the midst of trying times.

FROM THE TEXT

The final segment of the final vision draws the book to a close by reflecting upon major affirmations and challenges of the book. It focuses upon crucial issues for those who have listened to its stories and visions and come to understand that believers live in a violent world. Two key questions center the thoughts of the book as a whole: how long and what is next. The heavenly response to these questions solidifies central messages of the book. To the question of how long, the angel announces that suffering lasts only for a season. To the question of what is next, heaven confirms that suffering is not the last word. Both of these answers leave some things unanswered. So in the end they indicate that suffering demands a radical trust in the sovereignty of God.

Suffering lasts for only a season. The book of Daniel makes it clear that the human experience is filled with suffering. Violent people create conflict and oppress others in order to advance their illusion of self-sovereignty. They are like beasts emerging from chaos and perpetrating destruction upon this world, in particular upon those who would follow God.

In such a world, duration of suffering is always a burning question. How long will it go on? This question has been just beneath the surface throughout the book. Nearly every chapter is introduced with a reference to time and each vision marks time in one way or another. Four kingdoms succeed each other in chs 2 and 7. Two kingdoms rise and fall in ch 8. An era of seventy sevens is divided in ch 9, and a series of kings move across the stage of history in ch 11. Thus, when 8:13 and 12:6 explicitly ask how long things will continue, they simply articulate a key concern of the book.

The answer to this question may not be what readers desire to hear, but it is the response of the sovereign God. As the history of interpretation of Daniel confirms, many would like to know precise timetables for this world. But that does not seem to be what God has in mind. Answers like "2,300 evenings and mornings," **time, times and half a time, 1,290 days,** and **1,335 days** do not offer much precision, in spite of ingenious efforts to correlate them to human history.

God's response to the question, however, does provide a definitive answer. It indicates that affliction will not last forever. An end has been determined for human suffering by the sovereign God of history. The number of days or years involved may be unclear to humans, but not to God. Whether it is **1,290 days** or **1,335 days** does not matter. God knows the right time to bring things to an end. God has an "appointed time" to deal with matters on this earth (11:35; Hab 2:3) as well as matters at the end of time (Matt 24:36; 2 Pet 3:8-10).

The divine answer also confirms that the length of affliction will be shorter than its intensity makes it seem. When suffering seems interminable, it suddenly ceases. The point of suffering's cessation comes when human resources end, **when the power of the holy people has been finally broken** (Dan 12:7). This moment is the most oppressive and yet the most freeing at the same time. Recognition of the inadequacy of human strength reveals the sufficiency of God's. The power of the tormentor ends when complete trust in God takes over.

Suffering is not the last word for the believer. Faith for the faithful is more than trusting God's control over the timing of events in this world. It also embraces the assurance that God rules beyond this world. Believers can acknowledge with the psalmist not only that God's "anger lasts only a moment, but his favor lasts a lifetime." They can testify that "weeping may remain for a night, but rejoicing comes in the morning" (Ps 30:5). There is life after affliction.

According to Dan 12, hope for believers includes vindication for faithful living after the grave. The promise to Daniel applies to all who follow his example. **You will rise to receive your allotted inheritance** from God (12:13). This inheritance "can never perish, spoil or fade" because it is "kept in heaven" (1 Pet 1:3). Such assurance encourages faithfulness in difficult times. In a world where injustice too often prevails, believers know that there is a time and place where things will be made right.

Not only does reward for the faithful come after this life though, but also within this world believers have more to look forward to than suffering. Daniel promises that they **will be purified, made spotless and refined** (12:10). Their faith, which is "of greater worth than gold," will be "refined by fire" and "proved genuine" (1 Pet 1:7).

One of the difficult truths of life is that affliction can produce positive results in those who are submitted to God. Early Christians caught on to the idea and found themselves doing more than surviving their trials. They followed Jesus' instructions to consider persecution a blessing (Matt 5:12) and encouraged one another to "rejoice in our sufferings" (Rom 5:3). They knew that "the testing of your faith develops perseverance" that leads to maturity (Jas 1:3).

There is also another reward for those who live faithfully. Daniel says they **will understand** the true meaning of life and God's designs for this world (Dan 12:10). While the wicked remain confused about such things, the wise will have insight. They will not understand all things, but they will know enough. The wise, like Daniel, know that God is ultimately in control and trust their lives to that truth. Such perspective enables faithful living.

Suffering demands a radical trust in the sovereignty of God. Neither God's elusive response to the timing nor his general sketch of hope fully answers all the questions about suffering in this world. Like Daniel, those who live in oppressive circumstances want to know more. They ask, **What will the outcome of all this be?** (12:8).

God's direct response to this question is given twice, **Go your way** (12:9 and 13). The command is simple, only two consonants in Hebrew (*lēk*), and yet profound. It challenges Daniel to be satisfied with what has been revealed, to keep living the faithful life, and to wait. In summary, Daniel is asked to provide tangible evidence of his faith in the sovereignty of God.

Perhaps the most challenging demonstration of faith is waiting. Few find it easy to wait for "the appointed time" for evil to cease, for justice to arrive, for faithfulness to be rewarded, and for the end to come. But the Scriptures regularly admonish God's people to wait for God to work (Ps 27:14; Hab 2:3). They are to wait, not passively, but confidently and expectantly.

As the faithful wait, they are asked to continue living faithful lives **till the end** (Dan 12:13). According to chs 1—6, Daniel's way of living has been to engage his culture, refuse compromise, and continue honoring God. According to chs 7—12, it includes earnestly praying for his people, humbly receiving God's revelation, and diligently seeking to understand its meaning. As the book closes, Daniel and every reader of the book is challenged to continue this lifestyle. They are asked one last time to trust that in, through, and over it all, God remains in control. This is the major challenge of the book of Daniel.